René Gnam's DIRECT MAIL WORKSHOP

René Gnam's DIRECT MAIL WORKSHOP

*1,001 Ideas, Tips, Rulebreakers and Brainstorms
for Improving Profits Fast*

René Gnam

PRENTICE HALL
Englewood Cliffs, New Jersey 07632

Prentice-Hall International (UK) Limited, *London*
Prentice-Hall of Australia Pty. Limited, *Sydney*
Prentice-Hall Canada Inc. *Toronto*
Prentice-Hall Hispanoamericana, S.A., *Mexico*
Prentice-Hall of India Private Limited, *New Delhi*
Prentice-Hall of Japan, Inc. *Tokyo*
Simon & Schuster Asia Pte. Ltd., *Singapore*
Editora Prentice-Hall do Brasil, Ltda., *Rio de Janeiro*

© 1989 by
René Gnam

10 9 8 7 6 5 4 3 2 1

Library of Congress Cataloging-in-Publication Data

Gnam, René
   [Direct mail workshop]
   René Gnam's direct mail workshop: 1,001 ideas, tips,
   rulebreakers, and brainstorms for improving profits fast
   /by René Gnam.
      p.   cm.
      Bibliography: p.
      ISBN 0-13-636622-8
   1. Advertising, Direct-mail — Handbooks, manuals,
   etc. I. Title. II. Title: Direct mail workshop.
      HF5861.G6 1989
      658.8'4 — dc20   89-32384
                                        CIP

ISBN 0-13-636622-8

PRENTICE HALL
BUSINESS & PROFESSIONAL DIVISION
A division of Simon & Schuster
Englewood Cliffs, New Jersey 07632

Printed in the United States of America

With love,

I dedicate this book

to Mom and Pop

who think and live young

at 87 and 90.

with <u>Special Thanks</u> to

Karl R. Mayer and Stan Reckler, who, at an early enough stage in my life, convinced me that I didn't know it all...and to

Ed LaBrecque, Anver Suleiman, and Somers White, who even today convince me that I still don't know it all...and to

John Caples, Tom Collins, Leo Glueckselig, Pete Hoke, Ed Ricotta, Bob Stone, Lester & Irving Wunderman, and the glorious memories of Harvey Levy and Harry Steinthal, whose patient training and kindly advisories have served me — and much of the direct marketing profession — very well...and to

Wonderful, wonderful businesspeople — men like Dave Buster, Larry Dobbs, Pete Fernandez, Larry Henrichs, Bill McVey, and Buddy Schencker, and women like Carol Enters, Charlotte Orr, Fatima Rola, Sally Saunders, Polly Stanley, and Mabel Tompkins — who came into my life and let me learn from them, thereby expanding my thresholds and my knowledge...and to

Julie Allen, Connie Arnold, Robin Bastien, Barbara Cox, Lanona Gassman, Leslie Gray, Betty Johnson, RoseMarie Montroy, Debra Mottola, Debra Sauer, Barbara Scavuzzo, MaryAnn Scelzo, Denise Taylor, and Debra Whitacre — a superior supportive ensemble without whose help it would not have been possible to gather, much less produce, one's life experience...and especially to

Joy Warech, for shouldering and succeeding with running much of my business and personal life, making decisions left and right, working into the wee hours with her husband's applause, freeing me to run as I choose...but mostly to

MOM and **POP**, who believed I could do it and said so,
and who — *thankfully!* — are here to enjoy my adult life!

FOREWORD

It might be said that there has been a plethora of direct marketing books over the past five years. Yet, there has been one void. This book by René fills the void.

René Gnam's Direct Mail Workshop provides what none of us before Gnam have provided: a single source compendium of truisms about effective direct mail techniques. This book serves as a giant checklist of combined knowledge and experience gained from in-the-mail results of mailings by the billions over time.

Without making any pre-emptive attempt to establish himself as the guru, René has reflected the combined experience of pros like himself with whom he is in constant contact. And easy access to such knowledge makes the book a source of incomparable value.

When I was honored by the request to write the foreword to this book, I accepted under two conditions: (1) that I would have the opportunity to read every single word of the manuscript, (2) that I had the right to rescind acceptance of the invitation if what had been written did not track closely with my personal experience and that of major clients of Stone & Adler. I have read every word of the manuscript: what René has written does track closely with my personal experience and that of major Stone & Adler clients.

People use reference books in different ways. Some hope to gain value by osmosis: that doesn't work. Others check their work against that definitive reference book for their endeavor: that does work. And this manual is strongly recommended for extracting golden nuggets from *René Gnam's Direct Mail Workshop*, adding them to your own and producing gems set in 14-karat gold.

Before you settle on your offer and pricing, check the 49 profit points in Chapter 3. This simple act may change your offer from run-of-the-mill to breakthrough! Before you decide what to test, review the 54 methods of testing in Chapter 4. Stuck for a powerhouse heading? Check the 23 powerhouses in Chapter 5.

And follow the same checking procedures for developing order forms, making your letters sing, using the right graphics, selecting the right premiums. Every chapter promises the opportunity to make your direct mail more effective.

I know I will continue to profit from this book: I'm sure you will too!

Bob Stone, Chairman
Stone & Adler, Inc.

INTRODUCTION

Using direct mail as a method of selling is a rapidly expanding practice today, and direct mail marketing will boom even more as many more corporations, institutions, and professional practices discover its power, its efficiency, and its remarkable return on investment.

What years ago was termed "junk" — by newspaper writers who knowingly feared the potent lead-acquisition and sales persuasion abilities of this on-target, competitive advertising force—today is respectable, growing more so, and acknowledged by the United States Postal Service as a vibrant advertising vehicle that more than pays its way.

As all of us who have competitors quickly discover, direct mail lets the user zero in on precise markets, avoiding budget waste, pin-pointing targets, educating prospects about our products and services, and turning mildly curious readers into dedicated, loyal customers who stay with us because they find value, service, and convenience in our pricing, our methods of sale and delivery, and our fulfillment and customer interest.

This moving, powerful force that we term direct response advertising —

with direct mail as its flagship — can only expand further. Costs of other lead and sales approaches are fast becoming prohibitive. The persuasive ability of other methods, while not diminished, must always compete with tons of other messages at the same time. You don't view one television commercial in a program break, for instance — you get four, six, sometimes eight messages. With magazines and newspapers, you get dozens, hundreds, even thousands of messages.

But when a properly-targeted recipient picks up a properly-written and designed direct mail package, it is the only item in his hands, the only message he perceives. Your chance for success is heightened because, without clutter, he's concentrating on your communication.

Organizations which previously relied on more traditional methods of persuasion — radio, television, newspapers, and magazines — now are devoting substantial efforts to exploiting the pulling power of direct mail at several levels of their marketing, sometimes as support for other media, sometimes as stand-alone promotions. For example, my client,

General Motors, has established a 35-person centralized direct marketing division under the leadership of John Kepshire. His mailings to dealers convince them to become "participating dealers" in various consumer promotions. Other GM mailings alert consumers about tune-ups, persuade them to switch from non-GM vehicles, invite them to new car showings, give them advance notice of new cars and trucks, and sell them insurance. GM also uses the power of direct mail to convince many companies and municipalities to use specially configured fleets of GM vehicles.

And many smaller organizations now use direct mail to acquire leads, gain new customers, get repeated and add-on sales, extend service contracts, sign up members, acquire volunteers, solicit donations, create a backdrop for public relations efforts, or to augment their media mix. An example is another client, Dr. Peter Fernandez, president of Practice Management Associates, who starts his campaigns with mailings inviting chiropractors to introductory seminars, then signs them up for continuing education, follows this with mailings promoting his consulting service, and also uses direct mail to convince the doctors to join his organization for ongoing marketing, financial, and practice management assistance.

Marketers who have given it a try, and then profited by using direct mail, are growing more and more scientific in planning, testing, writing, design, and analysis. And those who are just starting in business are now being introduced to a wonderful new technology that, I predict, will take direct mail advertising to great new heights: desktop publishing.

This entire book was produced on my desktop publishing systems, and you will find other references to this modern wonder in this volume. But let me tell you what is going to happen as exploring minds catch on to the efficiency, cost and time savings, and great convenience of desktop publishing for direct mail and sales promotion.

What once took days, often weeks, sometimes months to produce can now be accomplished overnight by a single creative person instead of a crew of outside vendors. Here's an example:

At 9:32 p.m. on May 17, 1989, the night before giving a luncheon address to a group of marketers, I had a sudden idea. Why not try to sell this book with a response handout a few months before the book comes off the presses? No promotion copy existed. No cover design. Nothing.

So I sat down at two of my three side-by-side computers, wrote the copy, designed a simulated book cover, created two offers, set all the type, did all the ruling and spacing and positioning, and printed the piece. It was done shortly after midnight. The next day, we sold 13 copies in an audience of 72 qualified prospects. That's nearly 20% response. Overnight! Two more came in later by mail. Nearly 21%. We'll get more, and the same promotion will be used for other audiences.

I'm not the only person who can do this. Today, any computer-literate man or woman who knows the essentials of direct mail and sales promotion can sit down and produce a response promotion almost instantly. He can have it ready for review quickly, insert changes easily, then finalize his piece in short order.

This means that corporations wanting a fast approach to a new market can do it. Professional practices desiring instant communications can have them. Institutions seeking funds or members or whatever can accomplish their goals. Publishers, manufacturers, seminar providers, financial organizations, entrepreneurs can create a concept and — depending on complexity — use the finished promotion in just a few days, perhaps the next day, maybe the same day.

Testing will be faster. Response will come in sooner. Analysis will be quicker. Bottom lines can be improved without previous "hurry up and wait" limitations.

To do it all effectively, with or without desktop production, the savvy marketer must comprehend and take advantage of basic and advanced concepts of direct mail. This book gives you basics *and* advanced techniques with illustrations, classified by chapters on each of 25 key categories. As you contemplate or plan a promotion, find the specific chapters you need and use the techniques as a springboard to your own creativity.

Please do not treat this volume as a bookcase Bible. Let it be a daily desktop working manual and each page will pay off for you as your direct response experience widens.

Recognize that not every technique on these pages is 100% applicable to every sales promotion or direct response marketing situation. Many of the techniques in this book may not prove feasible in each marketing endeavor you launch. Some of them are ideals. Some may not fit your budget. So view these techniques as guidelines to be *adapted* to your advertising promotions by mail.

As times change, as markets change, as your company's focus changes, and as your responsibilities change...

make notes in this book. You are a good updating service.

YES, feel free to mark up this book. Mark all over it! Jot notes in margins. Annotate it with your own personal techniques at tops of pages, your company's specific exceptions at bottoms of pages, and your own observations wherever you find a place that's appropriate. Especially mark this book for your new projects.

On that last point, I have long used two business reading and study methods that may be of help to you: (1) alphanumeric, (2) color.

Alphanumeric example:

You're an association manager using direct mail for new memberships, renewals, conventions, and seminars. As you plan campaigns, you might mark each technique like this:

N1 = New Membership Mailing #1

R5 = Renewal Mailing #5

C3 = Convention Mailing #3

S4 = Seminar Mailing #4

Similarly, you could use *B1* for Booth Mailing #1, *I2* for Insurance Mailing #2, and so on.

The same marking method applies for any field. A manufacturer might use *SS1* for Sales Support Mailing #1, *FU3*, for Follow-Up Mailing #3, *NP2* for New Product Mailing #2...and now you have the idea.

Color example:

This method is easier. *Red* = Project #1, *Blue* = Project #2, *Yellow* = Project #3. Just make sure you have a wide variety of colored pens because as you read this book you'll dream up many new projects.

But I must say that even though I have helped generate hundreds of millions of dollars in sales for my clients in almost every field of marketing endeavor, I can NOT — no one can — create a volume that encompasses every marketing situation. Thus, I'd like you to

> **Use prudent, businesslike, objective applications of the techniques in this book for your individual promotion efforts — and alter them by your specific audiences. Then your promotions should be more profitable, more productive.**

In reviewing this book, you'll find that most techniques are appropriate for business, consumer, institutional and professional markets. Where a technique is usable only for a distinct audience, it is so labeled.

These techniques are based on my extensive experience at split testing (see Chapter 4) for many wonderful clients in almost every conceivable target market arena. They allowed me freedoms with concepts, in testing, in design, in copy, and in offers. What they learned — and what I learned from them — is now transmitted to you with my best wishes.

I learned, for instance, that the most expensively produced package is not always the most profitable. The more lavishly illustrated brochure does not always pull best. The more glorious letter copy does not always convince. And as a youthful advocate of the "kiss" principle (keep it simple, Sally), I was horrified to discover that simpler reply forms almost always are not as profitable as those with some complications.

I am not promising you that your direct mail marketing will be an easy bed of roses. Thorns exist. Some of my earlier clients shook their heads as test results did not come in the way we anticipated. That sometimes still happens since marketers cannot control every aspect of the marketplace.

But today, as I visit clients in many cities or when they visit me for consulting here in Florida, we have richer references as to what works and what doesn't work — thanks to direct mail tests for hundreds of marketing situations.

Yes, I still plan, write, and design many solo mailings and complete campaigns, and I enjoy the mind-to-mind consultation meetings with clients at their offices or at my Client Guest House in Florida. All these hands-on efforts are based on the techniques you're about to explore in this book.

But I hope you do not try to use all 1,001 techniques in each mailing you produce. Pick and choose what's right for your own unique mailing situation. Every mailing situation is unique. So is every mailing. But I do not wish you good luck.

I *do* wish you GOOD STRATEGIC CREATIVITY.

Your goals with these direct mail techniques should be to emulate LuAnne Levens and George Lyman. She achieved the 114-year high in response for her *Armed Forces Journal* and he produced 40% additional sales for his machine parts — both by using many of these methods.

And now, with more than 1,000 techniques at hand, it's your turn to get

Many Happy Returns...

René Gnam,
Saturday, the 3rd of June, 1989

CONTENTS

ILLUSTRATIONS

René Gnam's
DIRECT MAIL
WORKSHOP

CHAPTER 1

PLANNING

The one vital task in direct mail marketing that most frequently does not get proper attention is planning. Far too often, marketers urgently need to get a promotion in the mail — and there they go, 1-2-3, hell bent for leather — without proper planning.

That may mean less response than you might otherwise achieve. Often, that means René Gnam gets called in on a rescue mission. That's fine by me, but before you plunge ahead with your next effort, perhaps you should consider the key points on advance planning that I'll outline for you in this introduction.

"Rescue mission," René?

Yes. An example is the client in Alabama who read an article extolling the virtues of lifetime subscriptions and promptly dispatched mailings to all his tape subscribers guaranteeing them renewals at the current year's rates, forgetting that there's a difference between present and future value of money, a change in the impact of inflation and disinflation, and an upward spiral in fulfillment costs. The rescue mission was to plan a method of ethically switching all the lifetime subscribers back to another method of payment more appropriate for the client.

More typically, a rescue mission occurs with exhibitors at a trade show who dispatch superb mailings encouraging booth attendance. Then, when the booth reps return home with pockets bulging with business cards, no one has planned for rapid follow-up mailings to switch those leads into actual sales, or book sales appointments, or dispatch promotional literature.

Thus, both newcomers to direct mail marketing and "old pros" would do well to review the 13 precise steps to take in launching a continuing program. You are usually not after initial leads or initial sales alone. So, a good preliminary step in your planning is to study two of the very best books in the field: *Successful Direct Marketing Methods* by Bob Stone, and *Profitable Direct Marketing* by Jim Kobs. Both of those volumes give you a solid direct mail marketing overview. This book, on the other hand, gives you the specific techniques you need for success.

I have adapted, updated, defined, and refined 10 points on the checklist which follows from Jim's book, and the 2nd, 4th, and 13th are points I fervently recommend if you're after long-range continued profits:

1. *DEVELOP A MASTER FINAN-CIAL PLAN.* Perhaps work with your consultant on your unique numbers before you start to create a single mailing.

2. *ESTABLISH STRICT TIME-TABLES.* Know your GO/NO-GO dates in advance. Appoint a senior management person, just one, to head all direct mail marketing efforts, working with outsiders as needed, and give that person authority in all areas except time schedules. Without clearly stated time-tables, your financial plan gets scuttled.

3. *SELECT PRODUCTS OR SERV-ICES SUITABLE TO DIRECT MAIL MARKETING.* The key here is to compute in advance which items will allow you the most back-end (see Technique No. 11) business. While just about any product or service may be successfully promoted by mail, one-shots may not be worth senior management effort.

4. *FIND A MARKET GAP.* I just said that Bob and Jim had the best overall guidebooks in di-rect mail marketing, but no one had written a techniques book. That's a market gap (see Technique No. 20). I filled it by finding the gap before writing my book. Nothing will make you more successful in direct mail marketing than finding a market gap — and filling it. Another way of looking at this, of course, is by using "market-ing warfare": determining where a competitor is weak. And, lest

you say that the cookies you sell are exactly the same as the cookies sold by your competi-tors, remember that you can create the perception of filling a non-existent market gap, and then make enormous profits by catering to that perception with revised cookies and dif-ferent marketing direction. Pepperidge Farm did just that with its "lumpy, bumpy" cook-ies.

5. *DEVISE IRRESISTIBLE OFFERS.* You formulate your offers based on what future buyers want, not on your company desires. The two frequently can be dovetailed, but your thinking should primarily be targeted to the user, not the seller.

6. *SELECT YOUR MOST POTENT LISTS.* Do not try to select tons of lists. Fringe lists, those with only a minor shot at success, can be tested after you have a successful program. Your goal at the start is to find the lists that zero in on your very best prospects. They may become your very best customers.

7. *CHOOSE FORMATS OBJEC-TIVELY.* Newcomers to direct mail marketing frequently have an idea, based on their per-sonal likes and dislikes, of which format they think will work best. Wrong. There are times, proven historically, when self-mailers are best...or enve-lope mailings...or catalogs...or newsletters. In launching a new program, use what has been proved to be efficient for oth-ers. Then you'll profit.

8. *CREATE ADVERTISING THAT SELLS.* You need two concepts here. First, workmanlike efforts

based on the success of others. Second, breakthrough efforts based on psychographics (see No. 88), or your own creativity, or the guts to develop something new with a shot at huge response. You risk little with the "workmanlike" mailing. You gamble with the "breakthrough" mailing. But it can give you greater profits, if it succeeds. Do both efforts, side by side. Tally the results. Forge ahead with the winner.

9. *PLAN TO FULFILL PROMPTLY.* You can't afford to let a lead sit still and grow stale. You can't afford to get an order and not ship rapidly. You MUST deliver what you promise and do it FAST, if you want repeat business. It is also a fact of direct mail life that fast fulfillment yields more orders from the very same campaign.

10. *ESTABLISH FUTURE TESTING BUDGETS.* You should know that direct mail marketing consists of continuing efforts to beat past successes by refining mailings, by trimming costs, by testing one mailing against another and then another. These continued tests let you keep pace with a marketplace that continually changes. The anticipated budget for them should be established at the outset, then revised as needed.

11. *ANALYZE RESULTS CAREFULLY.* Results are tricky to read because you must go below the apparent surface of your data. But a different and fatal error is made by many marketers who try to use results to prove conclusions that they want to prove. Direct mail marketing is a business endeavor. Interpret your figures in a businesslike manner: coldly.

12. *ACT FOR REPEAT SALES.* You need a structured program to get repeat business. Yes, you can establish it as you go along. But advance planning for repeat sales may alter how you go after initial business. You need this advance planning.

13. *INSIST ON ACCOUNTABILITY.* This is a René Gnam demand. Do NOT let your program progress without review. Do NOT look at the bottom line alone. Do NOT accept verbal reports alone. Since all direct mail marketing is measurable, you want to measure your progress continually, just as you want a continuing program of profits.

That's the basic thinking you need to be successful.

The balance of this book will give you the facts you need — and the techniques — to improve the knowledge you already have obtained.

> **The key point you should keep in mind is that you must analyze single *vs.* multiple goals for each mailing, looking at everything with long-range considerations. Thus, you may be well advised to work with your consultant to develop an action plan, rather than a marketing plan.**

Marketing plans tend to lock you in for months, often based on budgets which were based on hypothetical figures. Action plans give you the wonderful flexibility to change direction as results come in.

At my frequent direct mail marketing seminars, the question that is asked the most is:

René, what kind of response should I get?

My answer to that query is recommendation #1 in this hit parade of over 1,000 direct mail commentaries:

1 — TESTING YOUR CONCEPTS

Never expect anyone, no matter how experienced, to predict response or guarantee results.

It can't be done accurately.

Rough projections, based on previous history, are possible. Without history and reliable, accurate data, predictions are pure guesswork.

Asking your consultant or advertising agency to apply knowledge of results from another promoter's history and data can give you a "touchstone," but not a "measuring stick" or prognostication accuracy.

You need to test your concepts in the mail to establish your own history and data. Then you can do projections for a second mailing, but even then they are projections, not predictions — not guaranteed.

2 — EXPERIENCE PAYS OFF

I am constantly thrilled by the positively brilliant ideas expressed by bright, young, enthusiastic newcomers to the arena of direct response promotion.

Encourage those employees. But be certain to dovetail their ideas with knowledge provided by those who have "been there before" and who have had the solid experience of creating, producing, and evaluating promotions for a variety of marketing endeavors.

3 — CHEESE AND FINE WINE

Direct mail practitioners are not like athletes, whose prowess diminishes as they age.

Direct mail promoters are more like certain cheese and fine wine...improving their skills and achieving greater successes as they accumulate experience.

4 — KNOWING YOUR BUSINESS

What business are you in? You are not in the business of sales promotion, direct mail, direct marketing, direct response or mail order. The product or service you sell determines the nature of the business you are in.

EXAMPLES:
If you sell plants, seeds, and bulbs, you are in the nursery business. If you sell desks, filing cabinets, and tables, you are in the office furniture business.

It is important to remember the precise business you are in to evaluate your own position in relation to that of your competitors. Competitors are those who are in the exact same business as you, not the entire mail order or direct mail field. Sales promotion, mail order, and direct response marketing are merely methods of selling your products or services. Overall, you are concerned with the total nature of the specific business you are in, and only then should you consider refinements by media, followed then by techniques.

Expand on this concept by noting that the outside assistance you retain should be expert in fields other than your own.

Sure, it helps if your advertising agency or consultant has experience in your own business field. But, top agencies and consultants draw on the specific business experience of the client in the client's arena and bring to that client the extraordinary marketing experience and professionalism that allows client and producer to work hand-in-glove, complementing each other by merging their talents.

5 — DIRECT MARKETING IS YOUR ENDEAVOR

Direct mail is not the name of the game and neither is mail order or sales promotion. The name of the total game is direct marketing or direct response marketing, and the more creative your thinking about your markets and offers, the more successful you will be.

To achieve your greatest successes, you need to harness the power of response marketing techniques, feathered with the specifics of your markets and highly refined, tested offers.

6 — DIRECT MAIL BUSINESS

Many large corporations assume they do no direct mail business because:

1. sources of lists within the company are not recognized as direct mail properties, or

2. there is no overall direct mail manager in the company, or

3. several different divisions of a company may engage in sales promotion efforts not described as direct mail.

Think again about how involved with direct mail you really are! Then use solid direct mail marketing techniques to improve your bottom line.

The truth is you probably are doing some forms of direct marketing right now. Your organization may call it sales support, or fund raising, or retail merchandising, or lead follow-ups. Fess up! It's direct response marketing and you're probably using direct mail extensively in your direct response marketing program. But because you may not like those terms, you call your efforts "marketing" and "sales literature."

Let's look at it this way:

When you head out to a store or the theatre, you "guide" your car. Call it "guiding" and you're more relaxed, paying less attention to others on the road or upcoming obstacles and dangers. So you don't tell yourself that you're "guiding" the car. You know better than that. You say you're "driving" the car, meaning that you're truly involved in the process of getting somewhere.

Get somewhere in your marketing too, by recognizing, acknowledging and immersing yourself in your true efforts — direct response marketing, and direct mail as one of its methods. When we call something what it is, we do better at it. Just like driving!

7 — THE SAME PEOPLE

Years ago, everyone thought you had to adopt totally different techniques when mailing to businesses and institutions than when mailing to consumer audiences.

More and more today, many consumer techniques apply in mailing to the commercial world. But temper those techniques just a bit by considering the specific business functions of the specific target individuals at the specific commercial enterprises you are approaching.

Recognize that the person you mail to at a business or institutional address truly is the same person you reach at home. The environment is probably different. Relations with others are probably different. But the same motivations, addressed with a more refined tone, can be exploited for sales effectiveness.

Mail to me at home, and you tell me that I can do better with your tire inflater. Mail to me at the office, and why can't you use the same concept, that I can do better with your interface switching device? Of course you can. Just tone it down a touch.

8 — ESSENTIAL ELEMENTS

Ranked *in order of their importance* for success or failure of a direct mail program are these essential elements:

1. The right product for the right market,
2. Lists,
3. Offers,
4. Timing,
5. Copy,
6. Art,
7. Format.

Art sometimes takes a higher ranking when the product or service (like a Caribbean vacation) is highly visual and when such illustrations produce an emotional desire. Otherwise, this ranking is almost always inviolate.

Now you'll ask, "What about my budget, René?"

That's an essential element if you're doing the marketing yourself. Make it Essential Element #3 if your operation lives or dies based on the specific direct mail marketing campaign you're considering. Make it Essential Element #8 if it's "pre-ordained," or established by corporate directives, or if, as an entrepreneur, you've decided to surge forward with a "damn the torpedoes" firmness.

9 — CUSTOMER RENEWABILITY

If you're mailing a one-time offer, your acquisition-cost-per-order, product costs, and fulfillment expenses are prime factors in determining your initial direct mail profitability.

But, over the long haul, customer renewability — the ability to get increased business from the same customer(s) over a period of time — should be your major consideration in evaluating promotion effectiveness.

10 — SELECTING A LEADER

No matter how many people are involved in coordinating, producing, and masterminding your campaign, one person must be selected at the inception of the program as having overall decision-making responsibility.

That is the person on whose shoulders all final decisions shall rest, ranging from budget implementation through punctuation problems, and through approvals of lists, creative work, art, format, stock and mailing quantities.

11 — BACK-END EVALUATIONS

The only person in your organization who should be in charge of your direct mail budget is the person who understands "back-end evaluations"...no one else!

Say, René, what in the direct mail world is a back end?

The continuation of a front end, as follows:

Your front end can be a trial order, while your back end is a full-scale order.

Your front end can be a sales lead,

Illustration #1

The author's favorite example of back-end marketing, technique #11, was a two-year campaign he conducted for Practice Management Services. The larger illustration is the front of a self-mailer and the tilted piece is the front of a brochure in one of many monthly envelope mailings. Starting with a 25,000-piece test mailing, this successful campaign was eventually rolled-out (see technique #76) to 300,000 doctors and dentists per month.

These mailings invited them to a three-day resort seminar at $395 and $495 each as the front end. At the seminar, back-end sales began.

Up to 20% of attending MD's and DDS's signed up for $1,250 - $2,000 in tax consulting, and 12% bought sheltered tax investments. During the consultations, many doctors bought additional products, ongoing consultation and tax assistance.

while your back end is a conversion to an actual sale.

Your front end can be an application for a credit card, while your back end is use of the card.

Your front end can be a first-year member or subscriber, while your back end is a renewal.

In other words, the front end is the initial response. The back end is profitable sales. In direct mail marketing, your front end, or FE, is rarely as important as your back end, or BE.

EXAMPLE:

If you get 1,000 unqualified inquiries for your dynamic distress destroyer, you might get 50 people who actually buy the destroyer. Here your FE was lousy, because 5% conversion to BE sales is atrocious.

However, if you get 500 qualified inquiries for your dynamic distress destroyer and you get 150 people who actually buy the destroyer, then your FE was terrific because 15% conversion to BE sales isn't bad.

So the evaluation of your FE depends on your BE, and your future budget planner had better understand your BE if your marvelous organization plans to remain in business.

Okay, René, what should I tell my budget planner?

Fair question. Here are the seven key examinations I do in determining FE/BE Analysis:

1. Compare current sources of new names, whether they're leads or actual buyers, against previous sources to see if they match up. If you used different FE sources, your BE will vary.

2. Compare your current FE offer against past FE offers. The FE offer determines how your BE

will be. Varying FE offers produce varying back ends.

3. Compare your current FE copy against past FE copy. Back-end conversions often are positively or negatively affected by different copy approaches.

4. Consider current economic considerations, such as inflation, unemployment, rosy predictions by politicians.

5. What's happening in the news? Negative current events adversely impact direct mail.

6. Consider the speed of your follow-up mailings. The longer you wait for follow-ups, the lower your replies.

7. Consider the honesty of your FE mailing. If your mailing to get me as an inquiry or sales lead wasn't totally truthful, I'll discover that when I get your BE conversion mailing.

Is that it, René?

No. After all that, it's time to sit down with your glorious spreadsheets and review the numbers. Then, you can determine where new efforts may be needed, how to revise old efforts, or whether you should continue doing your direct response marketing exactly the way you are now.

Not going through all this may mean that you'll make less money than you otherwise might make. You have the right to make less money, but why not make more?

12 — TOUCHING BASES

No direct mail or sales promotion campaign should be printed until all department heads concerned have been consulted as to the mailing's possible effect on their daily and future operations.

This includes sales, inventory, manufacturing, fulfillment, order processing and shipment personnel.

13 — CONSUMER RESEARCH

Mistrust most of your consumer research, especially if conducted by mail.

Remember the Edsel! Consumers love to tell you what they think you want to hear.

14 — SUPPORTIVE DATA

If management insists that you use a direct mail survey or questionnaire, you may use it to compile supportive data rather than marketing data.

If your response is less than 50% of the audience surveyed, throw out the results.

15 — RELY ON TESTED BUYING HABITS

Rarely use responses from direct mail surveys or questionnaires as iron-clad directives for your marketing campaign. They are often meaningless because:

1. Those who respond are people who enjoy replying, but who may not have an inclination to purchase, or
2. Respondents are those who have time to complete surveys, but who may not be decision-makers, or
3. What respondents tell you on surveys may not be what they do when they receive your promotion, or
4. The time span between completing the survey and getting the promotion may see a

"change of heart" by the prospect, or
5. Dollars available at decision time may not be the same as at survey-time, or
6. Responses to questions may have been penned in a group situation where peers peek over shoulders and inhibit truth, or
7. A boss may have asked an assistant or a secretary to complete the form, and those people may not be the decision-makers regarding your product or service.
8. Any combination of the above...and, consider this:

For about the same cost as conducting a professional survey, you might mail a bona fide offering to the same target names, get results with dollars, and then make a decision based on tested buying habits instead of theorized wishes.

16 — USING THE RIGHT NAME

Is the name of your company too long? Could it be re-worked to be more meaningful and appropriate to your audience?

If you don't want to start a new corporation, could you rework the name by starting a new division?

17 — ABSOLUTE SPECIALIST

Do not be afraid to rename your corporation or use an alternate name for the promotion of a specific product, service, or publication.

I dramatically increased sales for a successful Long Island printing company by using a new letterhead proclaiming that the company name was Real Estate Printing Services, a division of that printing corporation. I called a second division Restaurant Printing Specialists.

Both divisions did better, financially, than the parent, in terms of promotion ROI. Why? Because the prospect's perception was that he would be dealing with an absolute specialist in his field, instead of just any old printer.

18 — DIVISION NAME

If your company name consists of initials and yours is not a true mammoth with global recognition, try your new test promotions under a division name or other fully-spelled-out name.

Initials are nondescriptive and cold.

19 — FADS MAY FAIL

Do not rush to be a copycat and market a new product which very well could be a fad.

Remember that over half the manufacturers who rushed new citizens-band radios onto the market at the height of the 1976 boom discovered that the market quickly became oversaturated, and the units couldn't be sold by normal promotion routes. They couldn't even be sold with drastic price reductions. Then came sun spots. Oh, you know that story. It's the point of the story that counts.

20 — MARKET GAP

In developing new products for direct mail or mail order sales, most of us devote too much time to studying the competition. Rather, we should search for products or services which fill a market gap. Such products and services have a greater chance of success than "knock-offs" of a competitor's product.

Market gap, René? Fill it?

Yes!

For instance, the ideal product is a Swiss Army Knife. It appeals to many

markets with multiple functions. But do not stop thinking there.

You should be looking for at least two products with at least two functions for at least two markets. Your search at this stage is to find a high-priced main product and a low-priced secondary product to be used as a gift or premium when a customer buys the main product.

EXAMPLE:
If your main product is a set of heating, cooking, and eating equipment and utensils for hikers, your premium is the Swiss Army Knife and your secondary market is R.V. owners. Your tertiary market could be affluent, traveling skin divers. Then, if successful in our country, you'd take it to Canada, then the world!

But your product or service search is for at least dual functions to dual markets with at least two products that are affinity-oriented.

Affinity-oriented, René?

Having similarity in features, benefits, purposes, or interests.

Why all this duality, René?

Because if you limit yourself to singleness, you limit your earnings.

21 — STUDYING THE COMPETITION

Think about, but don't copy, your competitors. What makes their sales efforts successful? What sales messages are they using that you are not? Why?

Now, what's your next course of action?

22 — UNIQUE PRODUCTS

Your product or service or publication is unique.

Do not believe that simply because you notice a competitor using a particular copy approach for a long time, that you can imitate his success by imitating his copy approach. You may be startled by what happens when you imitate.

EXAMPLE:

I intentionally ran unsuccessful mail order ads for more than a year, under 'til forbid contracts in off-beat media at a cost of $125,000 per 6 months, so that fledgling competitors and plagiarizers would copy them. They did and went bankrupt.

Further, because your product is unique, even though it closely parallels that of your competitor, you can come up with a winning concept that is also unique.

23 — ENDORSEMENT MEMO

An endorsement memo or letter frequently is a good technique to acquire new customers from rented lists.

In this case, the memo is on the stationery of the list owner, urging his customers to respond to your offer because he has carefully investigated it and feels that it is worthy. If he has many loyal customers and has established good fulfillment service, this rub-off effect can work wonders for you.

Some folks call this a "third party mailing." It isn't. You pay all the costs. The memo signer gets a fee or commission. But the responses all come back to you.

With a true "third party" promotion, responses come back to the third party.

24 — THIRD PARTY PROMOTIONS

To increase your revenues, do not hesitate to consider third party promotions. Frequently, your mailing piece can be syndicated by other companies to their lists simply by changing the company imprint area.

Your additional sales can be enormous. Smart negotiating reduces your promotion investment.

This is exactly what Columbia Record Club did (before it became a house) when I worked on its Eurocord Project. Eurocord was a set of records, recorded in Europe, for the popular music field. Another set was produced for classical music enthusiasts. After selling all we could to Club members, Columbia let many department stores mail the same mailings. The stores got some money from the sales. So did Columbia. And Columbia got lots of new members from the stores' charge lists.

25 — THREE-TIME MARKUP

Most products or one-time services sold by mail must have at least a three-time markup to be profitable for you.

But do not take this guideline as automatic sanctioning of a higher price than your competitors might offer, or you may wind up with disastrous results.

26 — KEEPING IN TUNE

Significant sales increases sometimes can be accomplished by restructuring or revising an existing product or service to bring it in tune with the times.

Examine your current offering and determine where you can improve the actual product or service, and then you will also have new and viable copy platforms. You can do this year after year with the same product or service.

EXAMPLE:

When promoting steel storage buildings throughout Canada and the USA for Miracle Span Buildings of Mississauga, Ontario, I sold the standard buildings the first year.

In the second year, I convinced management to "poke holes" in the sides of the buildings. "Windows," I called them. "Why," they asked, "so the cows can look out?" "Absolutely," I replied slyly, "and cover the holes with curtains." They laughed. But they tried it. It sold tons of steel.

In the third year, I said we needed holes in the floor. More laughter. "So the cows can $%&@ nicer?" "Yes," I averred, "and so the owner can flush the $%&@ away." Sold like hotcakes. Every competitor copied us.

In the fourth year, the president was ready for me at our annual meeting at the New York Hilton (always on an Easter Sunday so he had a tax-deductible excuse to hear *Parsifal* at The Met). "Where are you going to poke holes now?" "In the roof," I said. He did. We put skylights up there. The cows loved it. So did his banker.

Moral:
Sometimes you can sell less steel for more money. We did!

Fine, but René, how did curtains help?

Well, Arnie Davis, Miracle Span's president, asked me the same question a little differently. "Why curtains, René? So the cows can feel at home?"

No, I replied to Arnie. Because 70% of all orders and 80% of all checks from farms are signed by women.

I knew that from consulting for several farming magazines. Relating that to the farm marketing situation that Arnie faced, I suggested curtains, recognizing that many farm wives would see the curtains as a way of putting a nice office in the steel storage building. That, I reasoned, would be a nifty way to get the office out of the house.

Isn't that a bit silly, René?

Arnie said the same thing, but his ad manager, Bill Foster, convinced him to try this silliness. Suddenly, the branch sales managers started getting letters asking about custom-built heated offices in the steel storage buildings. Voila! Arnie had another new way to revise his existing product. What fun it is to work in direct mail marketing! Profitable, too.

Illustration #2

Pay 1978 prices on your next Quonset-style GIANT STEEL STORAGE BUILDING for livestock, grain, heavy equipment and get your $1,000.00 CASH REBATE

DELIVER ONLY TO ▽

One of several winning mailings for Miracle Span Buildings pitched discount prices and a $1,000 rebate. The photo above shows the model without holes. Models with holes, at higher prices, were shown inside. Higher sold more than lower. See technique #26.

27 — COMBINING PRODUCT FEATURES

Combining two unconnected but well recognized product features often enables you to launch a "new" product — or create a perception of additional benefits -- and it is a viable method of getting more sales for the same products from the same audience.

EXAMPLE:

A feature of a long, very long, screwdriver is its wide head. Another feature is its long shaft. Now, think creatively and suddenly you have a multipurpose tool. That long shaft can be used for prying, like a crowbar, while the screwdriver still screws and unscrews wide-slot screws.

28 — FUTURE ECONOMIC CONDITIONS

Prior to test marketing a new product or service, be certain to consider future economic conditions.

The new product that tests well during a boom period may not do well in a bust period, unless that new product is a time saver, money saver, or has other universal appeals.

29 — THE WOMEN'S MARKET

If you happen to be a male chauvinist, don't let that interfere with your marketing decisions, especially in response advertising.

Remember that over 65% of married women in the U.S. are gainfully employed and nearly 80% of single women hold responsible jobs. They are decision-makers with disposable incomes, and — whether married or single — women constitute a large market which must be approached in an inoffensive style.

Create your promotions with care.

30 — YOUR BEST MONTH FOR MAILING?

If you are doing long-range planning and want to know which is the best month in which to mail for years to come, test the same quantity (perhaps as few as 2,000 pieces) of the same list (that has already proven successful on a previous test) for each of the 12 months with no variations in the package or the offer. Tally the results and you'll be closer to determining which month is most likely to be your best month in which to mail.

Simple, isn't it? Not really...

Those results may be repeated in future years if you are promoting the same or similar product or service to a business audience. Not so with consumer marketing.

Be careful! You need to repeat key tests to verify their validity. And remember that you can sell the same product or service to consumer audiences, but they'll react differently from business audiences in different months.

31 — HOUSE ORGANS

Frequently, a newsletter or house organ that contains informative, helpful, educational articles not only spreads your company's prestige but also can be a good sales vehicle.

There are many reasons for this. Here are a few:

1. They establish a continuing contact with a prospect, showing you really care.
2. They keep your name in front of your prospects, reminding them that you exist and are able to serve.
3. They show that yours is not a fly-by-night organization because you couldn't otherwise keep publishing that newsletter.

4. Because such publications are brief, they're read. This reinforces the feeling that you know your business and can help your customers when they need you.

5. Because they give your customers information, newsletters convince them you can be very helpful, and that's what they want: helpfulness.

6. Because they're authoritative, newsletters convince people that you are authoritative, knowledgeable, reliable.

7. Because YOU as the distributor of the newsletter canNOT possibly know when customers need your services, the newsletter is an effective reminder about you when they suddenly decide that they do need you.

8. When customers become fed up with the service or lack of knowledge of your competitor, their natural inclination is to turn to a pro. Only a pro could publish a good, helpful newsletter. So, they turn to you.

9. Because newsletters DO contain newsworthy items, customers get the impression that YOU, the distributor of the newsletter, are up to date with the news in your field, with new laws, with new twists and turns, with new products and with new services. If they feel you're up to date, you're the one to call.

10. If customers regularly get a newsletter from you, it appears to me that you do a lot of careful thinking, backgrounding,

exploring, and research about your area of expertise. That makes YOU better than a competitor with no newsletter. Your customers don't know that he/she is as thorough as YOU, but YOU obviously are thorough, as witnessed by your thoughtful newsletter.

The author's newsletter, technique #31, features helpful articles on increasing response, but it is published mainly as a promotion to interest potential clients in his consulting and creative services.

32 — SUPPLEMENTING BOOK KNOWLEDGE

You are beginning to see that a techniques book like this can give you lots of useful information that you'll be able to use, and then use again, as your direct marketing activities continue.

But please don't make the common mistake of believing that everything you and your staffers need to know is contained in reference books, even if René Gnam is the author.

You need to supplement book knowledge with the experience you get from hands-on work.

In addition, you and your key staff people should be exposed to new thinking by attending seminars on direct response marketing. That's where you learn new trends and techniques that aren't in books yet. The Direct Marketing Association (New York City) sponsors many excellent courses on this subject. I present others. And, from time to time, you'll discover still more training seminars that truly can expand and improve your marketing efforts. But no matter which direct marketing seminars you select, they all allow you to ask key questions about your current projects, and that's a benefit you can't get from books.

I urge you to send your associates to some wonderful courses as a continuing education in this complex field. Send yourself, too.

33 — SEXUAL LIMITATIONS?

It is distressing to note that certain marketers feel their products can be promoted only to persons of a specific sex.

Usually, these are marketers who forget that women can buy tools and sports gear for their menfolk or for themselves, while many men frequently like to purchase personal items and cosmetic gifts for their ladies. If you are omitting the gift strategy in your mailings, you may be overlooking a vast market.

Similarly, forgetting that many services are no longer just for males, is a good way to lose out on sales to women.

34 — CONFIDENCE BUILDER

If yours is a dealer product line reaching a clearly-defined audience that frequently has use for your products, make sure you announce price increases with an advance promotion mailing that tells your dealers they are being favored by a great opportunity to stock up at the current prices.

This builds confidence in you as a merchandiser who cares about dealers and also serves notice to the dealers that future orders will be at the higher price.

35 — VARY YOUR SALES TIMING

Seasonal sales and holiday sales often are successful, but it is essential to vary those sale offerings from year to year so as not to train your customers to await the specific sale time.

Why, René?

Well, when do you buy sheets?

At "white sales," of course.

Right. That's why J. P. Stevens paid me for consultation to attempt to find ways to sell sheets at other times in the year. J.P. Stevens and all the other linen folks have convinced most of us to wait until the next white sale, even if our toes are poking out of our current (well, not so current) sheets. Guess how their sales curve looked when they summoned me?

36 — SPECIAL GIFT ORDERS

Be very careful about sending special-sale gift offers to your active customers. If used too frequently, they train your customers to wait for sales featuring gifts instead of buying at regular prices without gifts.

Reader's Digest, for instance,

cannot sell subscriptions without sweepstakes these days. Why? They trained us to wait for free homes, cars, stereos, pie in the sky. Why buy the *Digest* without such marvelous chances? Ah, you understand.

Constant sale offers, recurring sweepstakes, frequent inventory close-outs and other such direct mail gimmickry have a habit of training readers to await the next special deal instead of ordering at the regular price. While these approaches do increase one-time response, they can adversely influence the next round of mailings and trap you into using even more gimmickry in a never-ending spiral.

37 — THE AVERAGE PERSON

Now let's compliment *Reader's Digest.*

Just like Coca-Cola and Polaroid, the *Digest* built a multi-billion-dollar business by product orientation to Mr. and Ms. Average Person.

Are your products aimed at too high an audience?

38 — CHARGE CARD FEES

In budgeting and projecting response, don't forget to anticipate the fees charged by charge card companies for your use of that charge option.

What's the fee? Depending on how frequently you have credit card sales and what the billing is, it usually comes out to about 3.5 - 5%.

39 — CLASSIFIED ADS

How about using a classified ad to steer readers to your larger space ad in the same issue of that magazine? The additional cost is minimal, and it can get you a larger and slightly different audience of opportunity seekers.

Then when you follow up by mail, you may have greater conversions because you asked people to do two things before responding. The more a reader does, the more qualified for you he becomes.

40 — SUBDIVIDING YOUR AUDIENCE

If you have a large audience, see if you can divide it into separate, identifiable groups having distinctly different interests.

If so, you can tailor your promotion to those interests. Usually, that gives you dramatically increased response.

41 — COLUMBIA HOUSE

If you sell through dealers, expect them to protest your efforts to sell direct.

But consider the case of CBS when it launched its record club. Today, selling records by mail is accepted throughout the land. But all retail record dealers still stock Columbia Records, and all attest to the fact that when Columbia House mails in the multi-millions, retail sales rise.

42 — LETTER REINFORCEMENT

Merely mailing a reprint of your magazine ad with a reply card is not a potent way to use direct mail. Almost every mailer has discovered that the reprint mailing can be far more effective if a letter is added to the package. Recipients view the letter as a one-to-one, personal communication and are likely to read it.

But, René, is that a truly effective mailing?

No, so consider this:

Rewrite the ad. Redesign it into a terrific brochure. Add an order form, a letter, perhaps another insert or two. Then mail it all in an attractively-designed envelope. Guess what all that effort will bring you? More response!

43 — SPECIFIC SERVICES

If your business is young and growing, resist the temptation to try to sell "other things" to your customers if those "other things" are not related to your product or service line.

Initially, your concentration should be on selling your specific products and services. Then, expand by selling items related to the main product line.

Only after fully establishing your prime area should you consider offering unrelated products or services. You may wish to do so under the banner of a separate company or separate division.

44 — ADVANCE REVIEW PANEL

If you issue new products on a fairly regular basis, try establishing an Advance Review Panel.

Then, when you launch a new item, tell those you invite to be on the panel — even thousands of prospects and/or regular customers — that they will have an opportunity to evaluate it (perhaps on a free trial basis) prior to mass introduction.

Tally the responses carefully and you may discover that you have established an effective new marketing technique.

45 — "HOT PRODUCTS"

Products and services originally conceived merely for direct response and mail order sales eventually will die. They will lose their "fad" image.

The "hot products" of yesteryear are not with us today, and neither will today's "hot products" be with us tomorrow.

Thus, each entrepreneur, who has to merchandise an item mainly conceived for mail order or direct marketing sales, must move anew to develop new products for the same customers.

46 — BETTER BY MAIL

Products that move slowly at retail often can be sold effectively and profitably by mail.

EXAMPLE:
Sewing shops will tell you that sales of specialty scissors are slow. But, Leonard Silver's Hoffritz in New York has had more than 30 years of good profits by selling its specialty scissors, and knives, and other goodies, by mail to a variety of highly-identified buyer lists. (See also No. 41.)

47 — INTERNATIONAL FLAVOR

You can achieve an international flavor for your promotions while mailing at standard United States first class rates by purchasing United Nations stamps in the basement of the U.N. Building in New York and mailing any quantity you desire from the U.N. post office.

You must alert the U.N. post office in advance of large stamp purchases and in advance of your mail date. Such mail is dispatched by the U.N. staff, but handled by the U.S. postal people as first class.

48 — PROMOTING PRODUCTS

Let's assume you're successfully promoting one product or service by mail.

Look around your company and

see if other products or services perhaps now sold only by representatives, through dealers, or at retail could also be sold by mail.

Perhaps a separate division is required. Perhaps a separate advertising budget.

49 — QUALIFIED EXPERTS

Bring qualified experts into your company to study, review, and evaluate your current promotion efforts. At the same time, your visiting consultants should be able to give you several pin-pointed recommendations to help steer many of your future marketing endeavors.

There are two good ways of doing this on your premises or at a nearby hotel:

1. Select general subjects and inform your consultant in advance with a list of items to cover in a morning seminar that follows a short introductory period. Use the afternoon for the consultant's recommendations and specific queries from your staff.

2. Let your consultant examine all the backgrounding and samples of your mailings at his office, draw up his own listing of points to cover, and then conduct an open-ended session with your associates having an on-site opportunity for feedback, brainstorming, and general questioning.

Yes, you can accomplish these goals by visiting the experts you select, but that can be more expensive when you involve several people in your organization. And the key is to get them all involved, for education, motivation, and profitable promotions.

50 — PRO-RATING EXPENSES

Your start-up art and copy expenses should not be included in your cost-per-order analysis, but should be pro-rated over the life of the promotion. If you are content to include start-up costs for an initial testing period, you may discover your cost-per-order is too high to continue what might otherwise be a successful promotion.

If the project dies after just one mailing, then you do have to include all the start-up costs in your financial analysis.

However, if the project goes well, pro-rating those expenses will give you a truer picture of how cost-effective the mailings are.

51 — MULTI-MEDIA BLITZ

If you use lots of consumer space ads, consider using an aggressive media buying service or advertising agency to take advantage of regional splits, remnants, distress space, and the big plus: knowledge of which publications are working for which offers.

Ask your media buyer to negotiate rentals of the publication lists to coincide with publication dates. Wow...will you have an effective multi-media blitz!

52 — SETTING YOUR GOALS

Your company has long-range objectives, budgets, and performance goals for you to meet. But have you set your own goals?

How about introducing one new product every six months, or one new customer mailing format every three months, or new repeat business promotions fairly frequently?

Too often, we are content to just float with our successful promotions. Do that for a long time and floating becomes sinking.

53 — FIVE-YEAR PLANNING

Sit down and plan for the next five years when creating your overall direct response budget. This is an ideal, but the point is to not be content to look forward to the next year or maybe two.

Consider the changes in the marketplace as you create your budget and set realistic goals you can expect to achieve. Then modify your projections as you move ahead.

54 — SINGLE OBJECTIVE

It's essential that your strategy with each ad or mailing piece be singular.

You are after one objective only. However, you can employ many tactics. Let your strategy be singular and your tactics be plural.

55 — ACTUAL SAMPLES

When using components from inventory, remember to get an actual sample before you plan new mailings.

Then examine it and ask yourself: Does it fit? I'm referring, of course, to whether it physically fits the package and whether it fits the new concept.

56 — MARKETPLACE SECTION

If you are a magazine or catalog publisher, can you include a mail order marketplace section in your publication? Even if you cater to a specific audience, certain books and merchandise may be appropriate.

This section will attract additional advertisers and thereby generate revenues in addition to those you derive from the merchandise sales.

57 — ADVANCE PLANNING

René, does this mean I'm going to have to spend considerable time on advance planning?

Right!

But, once I have my plans all properly done, can I repeat them from year to year?

Yes and no. It's usually fairly easy to repeat a renewal series each year, even though you need to do some testing and upgrading with it, but it's difficult to repeat an overall marketing or action plan because your situation and market position will have changed in the next year.

You can, however, use the overall plan from this year as a guide in formulating the next year's plan. Review it with your staff executives before making changes. Encourage their input. Then, rewrite it. Finally, review the rewritten version with your consultant and your top executives before casting it in stone.

58 — SOMEONE ELSE'S CATALOG

Try selling your product, your service, or subscription by advertising in someone else's catalog. You are reaching a tried and true base of customer names. Actually, you're reaching folks who have responded more than once.

René, how so?

Well, they had to get on a list in order to get the mailing or ad that invited them to respond for the catalog in the first place.

59 — PER-INQUIRY PAYMENT

Does your product lend itself to point-of-purchase display take-ones?

Consider whether you can get added distribution for your message by offering a per-inquiry payment deal to retailers and other merchandisers who might display your take-ones.

60 — CREDIT CARDS

Many companies find it prudent to restrict use of 800 numbers for incoming orders only to those purchasers who are willing to charge their orders to a credit card.

In this manner, "crank" calls, "curiosity seekers," and "deadbeats" are turned off from responding. Just add "have your credit card handy when you call" to your copy.

USE YOUR CREDIT POWER
TO ORDER THE REFERENCES YOU NEED

Gainesville 904-378-9784   Nationwide, Call TOLL FREE 1-800-253-0541
IN FLORIDA, CALL TOLL FREE 1-800-342-7945

AMERICAN EXPRESS   DISCOVER   MasterCard   VISA®

Call Toll-Free TODAY and have your Credit Card handy

Illustration #4

While this credit box encourages purchases, the last line, technique #60, shows how the author helped a client avoid "deadbeat" toll-free orders.

61 — CROSS-TESTING

If you sell more than one product by mail, you nearly always should cross-test, attempting to sell product #2 to purchaser list #1 and vice versa.

Don't forget that your customers have established a rapport with you. That's assuming you've fulfilled properly. If so, they should recognize your company name even though the product line may be different.

62 — STOCKHOLDERS

If yours is a public corporation, remember to send your direct mail promotion to every stockholder with a covering note explaining "as a share-

holder in Gorgeous Gizmo Corporation, we know you'll be interested in seeing this direct mail offering we are making to the general public."

Frequently, you will produce orders from your own shareholders, and you also will do much to promote a good feeling about your company and about direct mail advertising.

63 — GENERATING BUSINESS

One of the best times to do direct response advertising is when business is slow.

Why? Because it generates immediate business.

Don't fall prey to the old shibboleth of believing that your advertising or your marketing budgets should be cut back during slow business periods. If no one else is promoting, you may do quite well.

64 — COUPONS AND 800 NUMBERS, ESOTERICALLY

Esoteric media, such as napkins and place mats in heavily-frequented restaurants, often can be used as supportive media for promotion campaigns. This stimulates orders, especially when coupled with the use of an 800 number or an action coupon.

Better yet, use both the coupon and the 800 number.

65 — NEWS RELEASES

Can newspapers, magazines and other media be effective, supportive exposure for your promotions? Yes, they can, but are you using them?

Often a mail marketer is so involved in pursuing his specific promotion projects that he neglects to consider news releases to media timed for placement at the time his promotion mailings would be received.

66 — THE FIRM GRIP

The chief problems with all forms of cooperative advertising and most special media buys (such as retail store inserts or matchbook advertising) are control of distribution, timing, and the long time it takes to get response.

Rarely do you have a firm grip on such matters, and this should be carefully taken into consideration when appropriating funds for these promotions.

67 — SPECIALIZED MEDIA

The cagey direct marketer will consider all available specialized media as well as normal direct mail and space advertising. Such additional promotion avenues include:

- shirt boards distributed through dry cleaners,
- inserts in egg cartons at supermarkets,
- match books distributed free in airline terminals and restaurant cigarette machines,
- direct mail packages doubling as handouts,
- pre-printed grocery store bags and shopping bags,

- college campus giveaways,
- magazine stuffers on airlines and steamships,
- tags and labels attached to garments in haberdasheries and discount stores,
- bag stuffers at checkout stands at various retail chains,
- cards attached to fake handkerchiefs at tuxedo rental facilities and tailoring shops,
- card inserts in paperback books,
- tip-in cards and multi-sponsor inserts in publications,
- special insert sections of newspapers and Sunday editions,
- side panels of milk cartons,
- grocery store package tip-ons,
- backs of subway, cable car, and railroad transfer tickets,
- take-one cards in rapid transit vehicles,
- counter cards at retail outlets,
- bulletin board take-one promotions in retail chains,
- door-to-door distributed hang-ons,
- convention throwaways,
- piggy-backs with cigarette merchandising,
- specialized airline in-flight magazines,
- ticket envelopes for flights and cruise ships,
- newsletter ride-alongs,
- and dozens of other sources of new name acquisitions.

CHAPTER 2

MAILING LISTS

One example of the thinking we might adopt when looking at lists is the simple task of selecting homeowners for a large mailing to consumers.

We know that homeowners generally constitute a viable market to approach. But, it's easy to overlook the different characteristics among homeowners such as types of homes they own, locales, marrieds vs. single homeowners, condominium vs. single-family residence owners. A savvy direct marketer, whether after a consumer or business audience, should *always look within a list to determine the key selections that can catapult results.*

Continuing with the simplified example of homeowners, there are other important considerations. The main one is this: do we want to select long-time homeowners or new homeowners? The answer frequently is new homeowners, because:

- those names are compiled daily from deed and mortgage recordings, and thus are fresh and clean,
- the names are usually heads of households, and thus are in a position to make buying decisions,

- selections can be made based on the price of the home, phone numbers, amount mortgaged, even the style house in some instances, thus enabling us to pin-point our mailings and use copy that talks to the specific experiences of our prospects,
- we can roughly determine the average annual income of the names on these lists just by dividing the purchase price of a home by 2-1/2, and thus we can target our mail to specific income levels, and
- most importantly, these people are in a buying mood, open to new suggestions, willing to change suppliers or brands, eager for new experiences and purchases.

Okay, that's a simple example of approaching just one type of list: homeowners. Now, let's complicate it.

Do you want new homeowners or newly changed addresses?

Change of address lists usually are a bit less effective than new homeowners because you have far less data and less selections with the address change names. You can't do as well in defining their incomes because that information comes from the Department of Commerce's Bureau of the Census, automatically meaning it is instantly outdated. (I know. I did some work for them.)

Moreover, you don't know whether these people moved into apartments, offices, private homes, or mobile homes, which are now called "manufactured houses." You also don't know whether they are heads of households or whether they decided to live with Aunt Audrey or Uncle Ulysses — or, whether they are part of that sizable percentage of the file composed of the 22.2 million American adults who gerontological research says share lodging simply because they can't afford to live alone.

So now you see that list selection is not a two-minute decision. It must be carefully done, sometimes with a bit of what Bill Wilson, marketing manager of Kentucky Educational Television, calls "intuitive factoral analysis." He's joking about taking an educated guess. You want few of those.

> **The serious direct marketer does his list research to find out what's available, double-checks specific lists with others who have used them, relies on his broker for counsel, and then tests his selections. It's hard work, but it pays off. So do it with care. Don't entrust this vital work to your newest staffer.**

But wait a minute, René. All I want is good names.

Wrong. You're not after a list, not after names. You're after people who can give you business today and for many, many tomorrows. Thus, you must consider the nature of the people on the lists you approach. Target your mail to the specifics that interest those people. Garner their names and add them to your own in-house database.

Database, René? Or, list?

Database! It contains your list, and much more. Buying habits. Last item purchased. Summary of prices paid. Styles or add-on items ordered. Frequency of purchase. Comments made. Cross-over selling opportunities.

Go get 'em. Carefully.

68 — PRIME TARGET AUDIENCE

Selling your products via strong promotion to the wrong market creates a weak base for repeat, renewal, or continuity sales.

Hence, selection of your prime target audience is a critical factor in your ongoing business life.

69 — FRESH NAMES

Newcomers to direct mail frequently believe the only way to reach a prime audience is to reuse their employer's house list over and over. Well, that's not necessarily so!

While there's nothing wrong (and a lot that's good) about using your own list repetitively, a good list compiler or list broker can give you many fresh names and perhaps awaken you to appropriate, available lists that can boost response, sometimes even higher than what's obtained from your house list.

Or, you might consider going to original source documents for:

- government registrations
- association rosters
- directories
- classified listings
- responder lists
- subscriber lists
- custom compilations within any given industry.

There are many ways to reach an appropriate audience, and the way it's done at "your house" may not be the best or only route.

Devote serious thought toward finding additional sources of names within the precise marketing areas you approach. If you haven't time to do this, get yourself a good list broker with experience in your field, or ask your consultant for help.

70 — NET WORTH?

When trying to promote a generalized product or service offering to the higher echelons of business enterprise, criteria such as net worth or sales volume are relatively meaningless in terms of selection of lists.

If, however, your product or service or publication is of specific interest to a given size company, then these criteria are worth using for selection purposes.

71 — NUMBER OF EMPLOYEES

When determining whether you should mail to a business list by selecting records based on net worth of company vs. number of employees vs. sales volume, always consider number of employees as your prime criterion for selection.

The more employees a company has, the more viable a prospect the company is for you, regardless of its net worth or sales volume.

72 — INDIVIDUAL APPROACH

In mailing to businesses and institutions, the greater the number of employees in the organization you are approaching, the more mailing pieces you need for that particular target company.

It is insufficient to simply send one piece of mail per target company because many different individuals, perhaps heading many different departments, can influence or make purchasing decisions after reading your mail.

A common failing is to treat each prospective company as a single target. Not wise! Try asking yourself this question:

The last time we made a major purchase, how many people in our organization were involved in the decision?

Each of those key decision-making people at a prospective company needs to receive supportive information.

Illustration #5

WHICH COMPANY IS YOUR BEST PROSPECT FOR YOUR SALES?

COMPANY A	COMPANY B
	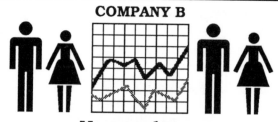
Fewer employees **Higher sales and net worth**	**More employees** **Moderate sales and net worth**

Techniques #70 - #72 indicate that Company B is your best bet because it has more people in more job functions, and thus will be more likely to have more requirements for new products, supplies, and services.

73 — RETESTING THE LIST

Do not make the mistake of thinking that just because you have used every name on a given list, it's the end of your ball game.

Retest the list a second time and then try to mail to it again. Remail to the same audience, remembering that people return from vacation, recover from illness, get promoted, earn more — become new prospects again.

74 — REPEAT LIST USAGE

When mailing to the same list more than once, you often receive a lower percentage of response each time, but this does not necessarily mean that you should stop repeat list usage in mailing.

The new responses you produce may be sufficient for you to break even and thus acquire additional customers for future profits.

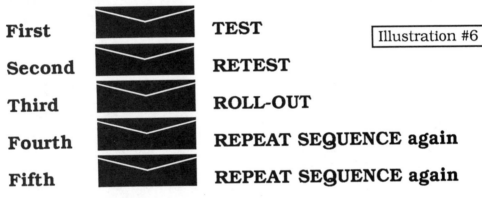

MAILING SEQUENCE TO LIMIT LOSS & HIKE PROFITABILITY

First   TEST   Illustration #6

Second   RETEST

Third   ROLL-OUT

Fourth   REPEAT SEQUENCE again

Fifth   REPEAT SEQUENCE again

WHEN MAILING TO CONSUMERS,
step four averages 65% of what you received on step three...

and, step five averages 50% of what you received on step three.

WHEN MAILING TO BUSINESSES OR INSTITUTIONS,
step four averages 50% - 200% of what you received on step three...

and, step five averages 25% - 200% of what you received on step three.

You could launch your marketing by immediately rolling out to your entire universe. But that's usually a good way to go broke in the consumer world, and it has its perils in business-to-business marketing. The better idea is to always follow techniques #73 - #76 for consumer marketing. With efforts to business audiences, there are only isolated instances when these techniques do not apply. Be safe: test, retest, then maybe roll-out.

75 — DOUBLING YOUR RESPONSE

If you mail to the same consumer list more than once, you will discover that your second use of the list should produce roughly 65% of the response you achieved the first time, while your third use should result in slightly less than 50% of the initial response.

When your mail reaches businesses, institutions, or the professions, a second use of the same mailing piece may produce as low as 25% of the first effort's response — or as high as double what you obtained the first time.

Double, René? Really?

Really! For these reasons:

1. The executive you wanted to reach may have been on vacation the first time your mailing arrived.
2. The organization may not have been ready to purchase the first time.
3. The key executives at that organization may require more than one exposure to your selling proposition.
4. Poor financial conditions may have existed the first time around.
5. Other major considerations may have preoccupied the decision-making executives the first time.
6. A substitute secretary or receptionist may have discarded your first mailing.
7. A substitute in the mail room may have misrouted your first approach.
8. Your first mailing may have been resting in a "future considerations" folder and the second mailing became an action stimulus that produced the orders you wanted.

76 — FREQUENT RETESTING

To determine how many times you can mail a given list, you must be prepared to retest it frequently, but not use entire runs when retesting.

Use the same guidelines as when initially testing a list:

1. Take a small portion of the available names.
2. If successful, take a larger portion (once or twice).
3. If still successful, roll out to the balance.

When retesting, delete the names of those who responded the first time around and follow steps 1, 2 and 3.

77 — EFFECTIVENESS OF A LIST

Deliverability of names on a mailing list has no bearing on a continuation or repeat mailing.

Your concern is whether the list works for you or doesn't work, not the number of nixies (undeliverables) that the mailing produced.

EXAMPLE:

John Farr, president of Arrow Insurance Management in Frisco, CO., asked me whether he should use a certain list that he knew was loaded with nixies.

He was trying to sell vacation condominium contents insurance to condo owners, but he recognized that most of them wouldn't be in the condos when he would send his mail.

Knowing his business, his staff procedures and his marketing aggressiveness as a result of having worked with him before, I said "sure."

A few months later, at a lovely breakfast-brunch in Denver, John reported the results. He mailed 10,000 pieces and got back 5,000 nixies, plus 1,000 sales leads. He converted

500 leads into paid policy-holders, twice the conversion rate of any previous effort.

The conclusion for you: nixies don't count — results DO!

78 — ZIP CODE ACCURACY

Never check the accuracy of zip codes on rented prospect files.

It is not worth the effort, and the percentage of accuracy most likely is not of concern to you. Results are.

79 — PINPOINTED ACCURACY

In using outside rented mailing lists, you should be prepared to accept 90 - 95% accuracy.

Pinpointed 100% accuracy does not exist on any mailing list — not even your own!

80 — OUTDATED LISTS

Any mailing list is outdated the day it is compiled, converted or otherwise put together.

People and businesses move, change, fade away.

81 — USE MOST RECENT NAMES

When testing a mailing list, try to obtain the most recent names rather than a cross-section of the entire file or multiple buyers.

The most recent names are those most likely to have a good recent experience at ordering by mail, plus a current buying or investigatory inclination. They can be an important source of immediate orders for you.

82 — AN EXCEPTION TO AN OLD RULE

If the most recent names on a mailing list you rent do not work for you, almost everyone will advise you to forget the rest of the list.

Exception:
If you discover that different promotions to attract names were used at different times in the life of the list that you are approaching, it may be worthwhile to split test the list owner's file. Use one code for names attracted by Promotion A, another code for those derived by Promotion B.

Sexy, eh?
You may discover that the older names have more value to you. Not often! Sometimes.

83 — SOURCE OF NAMES

Any time a mailing list compiler or owner says he cannot reveal the source of the names on his list, question the reputation of that list supplier.

The list may be stolen property, a duplication of an existing list you already are using, or it may come from outdated records.

84 — SOURCE VALIDATION

If a mailing list manager refuses to indicate ownership of the names on any but a donor list, it may be due to competitive reasons.

Still, attempt to learn sources used to develop the list.

85 — FUND-RAISING LISTS

If a mailing list broker refuses to give you the source of the names on a fund-raising list, accept that statement because it probably comes from a fund raiser who has promised his donors not to rent their names or does not want them to know about rentals.

In truth, the list may be rented under a name different from that of the charity to which the donors contributed.

86 — ALPHABETICAL SELECTIONS

Requesting alphabetical selections from a consumer mailing list for testing purposes is a valid technique.

It will give you an almost random sampling, except when you have large clusters of ethnic names within a given geographical region. In requesting alphabetical selections, couple that request with an Nth requirement.

87 — NAMES FROM SPACE ADS

Years ago, it was proved that direct mail sold names pulled better for new offers than names sold through space advertising.

This is no longer so. The same names are cropping up more frequently today on direct mail buyer lists.

Therefore, names acquired through space advertising, previously untapped by your promotion efforts to existing direct mail lists, may be better prospects for you.

88 — PSYCHOS AND DEMOS

In list selection, psychographics usually are more important than demographics. But, please, do use demographics in combination with psychographics to dramatically increase direct mail response.

Demographics are facts we know about names on lists.

Psychographics are lifestyle factors we read to determine how a person will react to motivating copy.

Typical qualifiers for these two selection factors are listed in the accompanying table.

You create a direct mail winner by using psychographics based on demographics. Do it!

89 — CITY SIZE

Certain offers sell well in large cities but not in small cities. The reverse is also true.

EXAMPLE:

When working for New York Mobile Telephone Company, it quickly became apparent that a car telephone filter was not needed in sparsely-populated areas. We had to seek other add-on products and services to increase our back-end revenues.

You may need to carefully consider city size as a list selection criterion for certain products and services.

90 — SOURCE DATE

When renting a compiled mailing list, always make certain to check the date of publication of the directory or source book from which the list was compiled, and remember that it took time to accumulate and publish the information in that source book.

The list is not as old as the date of actual compilation by the list compiler. It's as old as the source material used by the compiler.

Did you know that it takes more than a year to compile and publish many annual directories? Then it may take another half year (or much longer) for a compiler to convert that information to tape and make it available to you.

Ask yourself: How old are the names on that "new" compilation? They may be relatively fresh or they could be several years old.

Illustration #7		
DEMOGRAPHICS	*vs.*	**PSYCHOGRAPHICS**
Sex...Age...Education		*Lifestyle Factors*
Income...Geography		*Motivators*
Employment		*Achievement Goals*
Buying Patterns		*Personal Desires*
Job Patterns		*Job Frustrations*

91 — NAMES CAN BE WITHHELD

Will you be allowed to continue using a list that has tested successfully for you?

Maybe. Maybe not.

Usually you can, but there's no law that says a list owner has to continue providing names to you, unless you pin him down at the time that you place your initial test order.

A particular credit card company pulled this on JS&A Sales some years back. When the very famous company discovered how great its list was for the product JS&A was selling, it suddenly stopped renting to JS&A. Rumor has it that the credit card company wanted to send its own mailing on the same product to those names so it could make more than list rental income.

But, generally, the reasons why a list owner may withhold future names from you are:

1. adverse feedback that he receives from folks who didn't like your mailing,
2. you promised to mail a promotion selling Sizzling Sheep Dip, but you actually sold Galloping Goat Dip,
3. you violated your agreement on specified mailing dates,
4. you changed your copy at the last moment and added a free gift that would "cream" too many names from his list,
5. you didn't pay on time,
6. you expected him to deliver the second rental before you paid for the first,
7. you copied some or all of his names,
8. you re-rented his names to someone else.

All of those are legitimate reasons to not permit you to rent more names from the same list. Withholding names is not a frequent practice, but be alerted that it could happen to you.

When is it most likely to happen, René?

One week before you're ready to roll out.

92 — UPDATE FREQUENCY

On every list you rent, be absolutely certain to check its update frequency.

Lists that are updated frequently obviously have more value to the owners and therefore are more likely to pull well for you.

93 — HOMOGENEOUS UNIVERSE?

When a list has tested well for you, should you use the balance of that list as a homogeneous universe?

Maybe. Maybe not.

The truth is that all lists are composed of several segments or clusters that may be dissimilar.

EXAMPLE:

When I put two clients together, Science Editors in Kentucky renting from Medical Economics Company in New Jersey, Science Editors needed to reach college medical students to sell its *Roberts' Handbook of Clinical Values.* The total list tested okay, but just okay — below the breakeven point, but with sufficient results to allow for BE sales (see No. 11).

So, I suggested coding clusters within the list, and here's how they pulled:

A Medical School Freshmen	**4.0%**
B Medical School Sophomores	**3.7%**
C Medical School Juniors	**1.8%**
D Medical School Seniors	**2.2%**

There was a 205% response difference between the lowest pulling and highest pulling segments. The client needed 3.0 to break even. By testing and mailing to segments within the total market universe, Science Editors was able to reduce its risk on the overall list and do quite well with just the segments it truly needed.

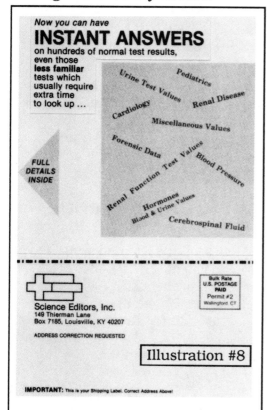

Illustration #8

This is the address side of the self-mailer used in the list test cited in technique #93. The front was a sales letter advising medical students how the handbook would help them know the standard values for blood, urine, renal, and spinal fluids. The test showed this information sold better to lower classmen than to the upper collegiate levels.

94 — AUDIENCE LEVEL

If your product, publication, or service is appropriate for a particular socio-economic level, remember that Americans tend to move into neighborhoods with remarkably similar home value assessments as their old neighborhoods.

Thus, using newly-changed address records is a viable method of continuing your communications, and therefore sales, to the same level consumer audience.

95 — SELECTIVITY FACTORS

Keep records of selectivity factors within a list. By knowing which segments of a list produce best, you can save thousands of dollars in promotional mailing expense.

Those savings can be invested in improving the creative approach in the mailing package, thus enhancing the possibility for greater dollar volume sales even though the mailing is directed to a much smaller audience.

96 — HIGH-PRICED NEWSLETTERS

Some of the strongest pulling mailing lists are those of high-priced newsletters.

Their subscribers, while relatively few in number, have exhibited a strong interest in a single business or consumer subject area and have proven their willingness to pay a good price. They are terrific targets for a variety of offers to their allied interest areas.

They've also demonstrated their fondness for direct mail advertising by responding at least twice before receiving your approach: once to get on the list the newsletter publisher used, and again to subscribe to the newsletter, perhaps again to renew the subscription, perhaps many times for many renewals and to buy books and other items promoted by the publisher.

Repeaters repeat repetitively.

97 — DATA MEMO

Consider establishing a "data bank memo" of all mailing lists that are

Grand Cayman *Flash Report*

TAX SHELTER LITIGATION REPORT

Volume 1, Number 7
August 1986

Authoritative Reviews and Analyses of Key Court Decisions

Securities Law

Supreme Court Upholds Investors' Rights to Full Recovery in Shelter Fund

As we went to press, the Supreme Court had handed down its decision in the Randall vs. Loftsgaarden case (SLR, June 1986, Page 6). The investors in a real estate shelter successfully sued the sponsor for securities fraud, but the 8th U.S. Circuit Court of Appeals ruled

Chase Econometrics Letter

Volume 1, Number 1   MARCH 1983   Route to

in brief **in brief** in brief **in brief** in brief **in brief in brief** in brief **in brief in brief in brief**

The long recession is over and the U.S. economy is now in the early stages of recovery. Even though the recovery will probably continue during the remainder of the year, careful business planning and monitoring is still essential because:

. the recovery will be moderate relative to those previously experienced.

. it will be uneven across different regions, industries and markets.

. it could be stalled by rising interest rates or other factors.

. it will be accompanied by selected cost pressures. Story on page 7.

* * *

The Federal Reserve's policy will continue to be geared toward preventing a rebound in interest rates, at least until the recovery is firmly established and international financial pressures ease. Short-term rates will edge down during the next several months -- long-term rates will remain at current levels. Story on page 6.

* * *

Consumer markets should strengthen during the remainder of the year. This will reflect:

. lower oil
are increasin
income that
nonessential

. very lar
and the next
July 1 (Cong
cancel this),
spending po

. expected
interest rate
so far have
clines in oth

. the incre
Story on p

All housing
construction
ture, applia
good gains t

Automobile
from month
clearly up,
sales will oc
Furthermore
will capture
market than

Australia:
Correspondent Office
42 Bundall Road
(B1) Gold Coast
Queensland, 4217

United States:
Membership Office
Suite 106-Box 211
4200 Wisconsin Ave. N.W.
Washington, DC 20016

Singapore:
Correspondent Office
278 Telok Kurau Road
Singapore 1542

Canada:
Correspondent Office
642 Wilson Ave.
Downsview, Ontario
M3K 1E1

Switzerland:
Membership Office
32 Rennweg
CH-8001 Zurich

The Oxford Club
Private Prosperity Tradition

England:
Editorial Office
17 Rodney Road
Cheltenam, Gloucestershire
GL50 1HX

CONFIDENTIAL

Confidential Communique, January 1989

Dear Fellow Members:

As the new year begins, questions abound and uncertainty fills the air. According to Ronald Reagan and George Bush, it is the best of times — the economy is still expanding, inflation still seems to be under control, interest rates are tolerable, employment is growing, and there will be "no new taxes."

Of course, there is that bothersome little matter of the federal budget deficit, which is out of control; the minor irritant of a banking system that, despite billion-dollar bailouts, has gone beyond the powers of the FSLIC and the FDIC; and the inconvenience of a constantly collapsing U.S. dollar. But never fear. The message from Washington is that all is for the best in this best of all possible worlds.

Some may ascribe this posture to the naivete of the new president. I, for one, do not. In fact, I believe there is an overpowering cynicism at work here that will become apparent in the months and years ahead. Even now, the policies and practices that will shape your financial future are being decided.

While the popul

Monmouth on Markets

"The party's over, it's time to call it a day.
They've burst your pretty balloon and taken the moon away.
It's time to wind up the masquerade.
Just make your mind up, the piper must be paid.
The party's over. The candles flicker and dim.
You danced and dreamed through the night,
it seemed to be right just being with him.
Now you wake up, all dreams must end.
Take off your makeup, the party's over,
it's all over my friend."

Lyrics: Comden and Green
Music: Julie Styne
Singer: Peggy Lee

Decade of Illusion

When Ronald Reagan

Agri-Business Strategist Professional Advisory Board

William A. Taggart

Richard Gilmore

Michael F. Lewis

Thomas R. Grabowski

William P. Mott III

W.D. Other

John J. O'Day

Illustration #9

Newsletters often charge high subscription fees as indicated in technique #96. Those shown are from Newsletter Management Corp., Boca Raton, FL, which also uses technique #44, an advisory panel, in mailings for subscriptions.

Using a list data memo, technique #97, is illustrated at the bottom of this page as a method of tracking which lists pull best for which offers.

The author advises combining several techniques to improve records and response.

LIST CODE	QUANTITY MAILED	PRICE A	PRICE B	TOTAL REPLIES	RESPONSE PERCENT
DMP	230176	1723	2782	4505	1.96%
FED	16802	194	202	396	2.36%
FRG	12414	101	120	221	1.78%
RGC	26228	322	325	647	2.47%
SEM	11498	84	91	175	1.52%
SEQ	13277	118	136	254	1.91%
TTY	4603	53	60	113	2.45%

appropriate to your offer. Keep a separate listing for each offer.

This reference often is valuable in defining your market when creating new promotions.

98 — MR. AND MRS.

If a study of the demographics of a consumer list you are using indicates that most of your customers or prospects from rented lists are married, and if your offer is for a product or service that could be used by either spouse, consider addressing your mailing package to "Mr. & Mrs."

99 — MANY DIFFERENT SUBSCRIPTION RATES

Magazine subscription lists pull well for a wide variety of direct mail propositions, but...

It is easy to think that a magazine's audience is just a single group of people, but that is not necessarily so. For instance, there can be 6, 10, or even 15 different types of readers who all pay different subscription prices. Carefully analyze subscription rates and the percentage of readers paying at each level prior to making your list rental or space buy.

Different prices, René?

Yes. I'm not kidding when I say that several subscription rates may exist for a single title. When I did the consulting and creative work for the 50-year anniversary campaign for *Radio-Electronics*, I had to consider 13 different rates for a 1-year subscription. This is not unusual!

100 — GETTING ATTENTION

If you use saturation mail to occupants or residents, recognize that many

people throw such mail away because it does not address them as individuals.

Get around this by slugging every computer-generated label with an attention-getting line such as: "to the taxpayer at," "to the puzzle lover at," "to the magazine reader at."

Try to be as specific as possible with reference to the main product characteristics you are selling.

101 — TELEPHONE SOLICITATIONS

Frequently, you can triple or quadruple your responses from a rented list by using telephone solicitations a few days after the promotions have been received by the prospects.

Don't be shy about this, but do observe normal courtesies and the regulations of the specific states into which you are calling. And recognize that you'll have to pay a higher list rental rate if you follow up mailings with telephone calls. Why not! It's worth it — usually.

102 — FRINGE LISTS

Don't believe that the only sources of new customers available to you by direct mail are those lists in your specific field. Those list owners do not have all the names that are appropriate to their offers and neither do you.

Consider using fringe lists.

Also consider the makeup of your typical prospective customer and search him or her out on other lists in allied or unrelated fields.

103 — PRIME SOURCES

Don't hesitate to ask your competitors whether you can rent or exchange their mailing lists so you develop additional new customers at a reasonable cost from a prime source who has acquired his names from many of the same lists you would use.

This idea is a dandy one for you.

Your natural thought is that a competitor would never allow you to use his/her list. So approach him via your professional list broker who is skilled at arranging exchanges. The goal is for both you and your competitor to increase business. And, it can be done. For example, fund-raisers and cultural event sponsors often do so. It is a major overlooked source of fresh names.

But, exercise care.

If you have 10,000 names on your file and your competitor has 100,000, you are in a dangerous position for an exchange. He will be getting your entire file — which may be more responsive because it may have more keenly-defined characteristics or buying preferences — while you receive only 10% of his file!

In that instance, let your broker negotiate an "LKQ" exchange for you. "LKQ" is a term I'm borrowing from the insurance field. It means "like kind and quality" and applies to replacing damaged equipment under your insurance policy. Similarly, in doing an exchange, you need "LKQ" names.

Let me explain further.

Your 10,000 names may be all active buyers. Perhaps the 100,000 file owned by your competitor contains buyers and prospects and former buyers. You need "LKQ," buyers for buyers, when you exchange.

104 — CREATIVE DIFFERENCES

Never assume that simply because your competitor has achieved suc-

cess with a specific mailing list you will too.

Nonsense! The slight product and marketing differences, and the ingenuity with which you attack offer-construction and creative copy, can make a significant difference in response — either plus or minus!

105 — SELECTING BY SEX

Males generally get higher pay for the same job than females. That's not fair, but it's a fact.

Therefore, if you have a minimal budget and wish to maximize your success, it may be important for you to select by sex, especially in consumer mailings to singles.

106 — REMAILING SAME LIST?

René, how many times can you remail to the exact same list?

As often as it pulls well enough to allow you profitability on the back end. Even though you may have declining front end results with each reuse of a list, factor in your back end sales and determine how low your front end response can be.

107 — RESEARCHING YOUR LISTS

The more you know about the individual clusters of names on the mailing list you use, the more successful you are likely to be with your direct sales promotion!

Spend extra time researching your lists before making list, offer, or copy decisions.

EXAMPLE:
Clusters may be 5-digit zip code selections. Certain of those may not pull well for you. Eliminate them and the

rest of your mailing life will be more profitable.

RCA Record Club did just that and increased its response to consumer audiences by 25%. I did that for my seminars to business audiences and reduced my costs by 33%.

Fascinating, eh? Advance planning counts!

108 — MERGE/PURGE

The average mail order buyer list can have a 25% duplication with other mail order buyer lists in a similar sphere.

Therefore, merge/purge — frequently, but not always — is a cost effective technique for the marketer approaching the mail order field.

109 — AN ALTERNATE APPROACH

If you suspect that there will be high duplication on the lists you are using and if you cannot afford to merge/purge, ask your list sources to give you several Nth selections of each list and mail to those separate selections on separate days.

That way, duplicate names should receive your mail on different days. And a recipient might be in a more receptive mood on the second day.

110 — ALTERNATE ATTACK

If you are worried about duplication among several outside rented lists and if you can't merge/purge, try this:

Print the carrier envelope or the cover of your catalog in two or four alternate versions and have your lettershop mail them alternately within names on the list so that chances are reduced that the same name would receive two or more identical pieces.

111 — SECOND TEST

If a particular list produces a high quantity of orders for you, try retesting the list with a small quantity second test.

Don't be afraid of alarming or offending those who just purchased from your first use of the list. Simply merge/purge, or use a duplication disclaimer (see No. 833), or both.

112 — LISTS HAVE MANY NAMES

Use the most recent, most accurate compilation that covers your market, but don't try several compilations in the same field. Ask your broker which is which.

EXAMPLE:
You want to sell disposable body boards to compete with Dixie, Inc., in Houston. Body boards are placed under dead humans. Because they're lightweight plastic, they save a mortician's back when toting an embalmed person from table to casket.

Do you mail to morticians? Or, are they funeral directors? Or, are they undertakers? Or, as their literature says, are they "pre-need counselors"?

They are known by all of those monikers. And you'll find many lists calling them undertakers, many saying they're morticians, and so on.

Don't rent all those lists! They're the same names!

Very frequently with compiled lists, one compiler says he has cosmetologists, while another says he offers you beauty salon operators, and a third says he has hair stylists. They're the same names!

Renting two or more of these compilations means you're mailing to the same names twice, or thrice, or...you get the point.

113 — SHOULD YOU MERGE/PURGE?

You certainly can use merge/purge and dupe-elimination programs on small quantity mailings. I have used it on mailings as small as 8,000 pieces.

Of course, you must weigh the cost against the specific nature of the lists you're using before determining whether to go into a merge/purge program in such small quantities.

114 — SELECT NAMES FOR LOCAL MAIL

In a localized mailing, do not make the mistake of believing your only route via mail is to every householder in your community.

Take a telephone directory listing and overlay a census tract against it so you can select those names that are most appropriate to your offer. They are selectable by income levels, education, car ownership, number of telephones, years of residency, earnings, and other factors.

115 — CENSUS-TRACT OVERLAYS

The principle of applying census-tract overlays to such large national lists as telephone names not only works well for local mailings, but also produces significant savings when used for regional or national mailings where such selection factors are desirable to reduce the volume of mail you generate and pinpoint your audience more effectively.

116 — COMBINING SELECTION FACTORS

We all know that selecting the proper lists is a vital aspect of achieving direct response success. Indeed, it is one of the key aspects. But selection of lists should not stop with major market lists! Let's precisely pinpoint our direct mail.

EXAMPLE:

Census tract information applied to zip code selection enables us to hit audiences similar in age, income, profession, managerial status, occupation, home value, religion, and even to select further by such factors as those who live in predominantly single areas, or newly-married areas, or areas having predominantly parents whose children have matured, or areas of retired citizens.

Combining certain of these selection factors, and then asking the list owner to provide only those zip code areas which meet these qualifications, often catapults direct mail from marginally successful efforts to astonishingly profitable levels.

117 — SOARING RESPONSE

When we select by census-tract overlays on zip code areas within our proven geographic markets and then merge those names with a proven list of responders to a product similar to ours, the "hit" name and address records are the viable target audiences for our new consumer prospect mail.

Now, take it a step further.

Take the "hits" and merge that new file against rented names of proven responders to a second product or service, or perhaps a publication, akin to our offering. You will have drastically reduced the quantity of names to which you'll mail. But you'll have the most logical, concise audience to attack, and your response will soar.

Do you want to do this, René?

Perhaps. A consideration to review with your consultant is whether this highly-sophisticated market definition process will give you sufficient numbers of respondents for your future marketing efforts. Yes, it will automatically give you a fabulous response rate. But that may not be enough. Think about it.

118 — SOPHISTICATED TESTING

Decades ago, when you tested mailing lists, you could be quite content to mail out just a few thousand names for each list and then make a determination as to payout and which lists would be worth continuing.

Today, that would lead you to discard many lists you could use profitably had you been smart enough to test the lists on a more sophisticated basis, such as selecting or eliminating certain sectional centers, states, five digit zips, repeat buyers, or other segments within each list.

With the increasing quantity of mail reaching your prospects today, it becomes ever more important to do these selections. It also increases your response.

119 — ZIP CODE FINAL DIGITS

In testing several different lists, it is not necessary to code each response card or code each label on your mailing piece, if each list you are selecting is designated by a different last-two-digit zip code selection.

Those two digits automatically tell you which list the respondent came from.

That's true for 5-digit coding — but not for Zip + 4.

120 — ZIP CODE SPECIFICATION

Few list owners can accurately tag each name on a mailing list to indicate that it was previously used for your test.

Therefore, pyramiding your quantities by using an additional Nth name selection on a continuation may not be valid, because if the file has been updated in any way since your original test, the Nth sequence has been destroyed, and you will likely reach a quantity of the same names you reached the first time around.

To avoid this hassle, specify last digit of zip code on your initial selection.

121 — LAST TWO DIGITS

In selecting by digits of the zip code, requesting a selection of the last two digits for a test usually will result in printing out roughly 1% of all the names on the entire file in each two-digit label selection.

This enables you to easily project future mailing quantity.

122 — THE FIFTH DIGIT

One way to random test a mailing list is to select by the fifth digit of the zip code. With the exception of the zeros, the fifth digits afford a reasonable random test, even on regional mailings.

In large cities, the exception applies to zeroes and ones.

Using only the last digit of the zip code for selection purposes will result in roughly 9% of all the names on the file being printed out, except for the zero digit which can produce as high as 15% of the file.

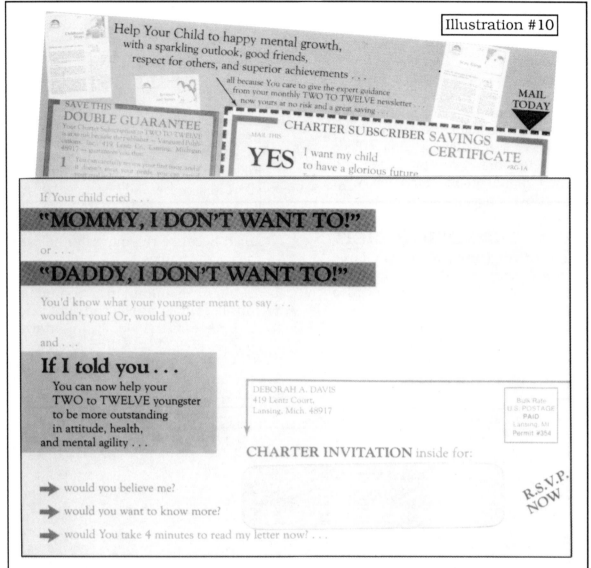

Illustration #10

Combining techniques #88 and #118 led the author to create this unusual new subscription promotion mailing for Two to Twelve newsletter. Demographic research found lists of parents of children ages 2 - 12. Psychographic study determined those parents were fed up with parenting information best called pap.

Gnam created a copy approach in the form of an involvement quiz, then followed it with a strong pitch to subscribe. Using vibrant colors, mostly purples and pinks, his design stood out from the flock of new parent mailings.

The mailing was so strikingly different from anything Vanguard Publishing had tried before that the publisher didn't want to use it. But, as the deadline approached, Vanguard tried a small test quantity, selecting within certain lists per technique #118. This mailing outpulled all others by 20 - 50%, depending on list segments. It quickly became the control mailing.

In large cities, the ones may hit 11 or 12%.

René, what's all this about zeroes and ones?

Major post offices with many post office boxes is one answer. The other answer is that those post offices are located in the highest-density areas. Post offices frequently use ending digits of zero for their main branches and ending digits of one for their next largest branches.

123 — THE FOURTH DIGIT

The fourth digit in a zip code on a large national consumer list is almost perfectly random in distribution and also presents a viable method of test selection.

The trouble with this is that many list owners do not want to bother selecting by something other than that with which they are familiar. Offer to pay a bit more. It could be worth it.

124 — THINKING IT ALL OUT

René, it seems that a lot of thought must go into mailing list selection and usage. Is it really so important?

Absolutely! There have been many instances when a miserable creative effort has succeeded because the right lists were used, and there have been instances when glorious creativity has failed because the marketer selected the wrong names.

Work carefully with your broker and your consultant to be certain that your list efforts are on the right track. And remember to do your analysis code by code, list by list, package by package -- as quickly as possible, so you can get back in the mail fast.

Illustration #11

It's one thing to know which list works well, but it's much better to know which sections of which list(s) work best.

This spreadsheet shows how lists A, B, and C performed in selected states on five packages for a client's mass mailing to professional offices (technique #124). The same concept applies to analysis by ZIP. In this instance, we have a report by quantity per package code, quantity for all five, response on all three lists, total response, and percentage of response by state.

Don't worry about the low response percentage. This client makes money at .08%. He'd do better eliminating Texas on list C and Maryland on lists B and C. Can you see why?

```
SELECT2........COMPILED BY RENE GNAM >>> 2/2/89
************************************************************
      JANUARY 1989 RESPONSE TOTALS
      /CODE   TOTAL     A     B     C   TOTAL
      -----------------------------------------------------
AL      728    3640    13     0     2     15  .41209
AK       92     460     1     0     0      1  .21739
AR      416    2080     3     0     0      3  .14423
CO      861    4305     3     0     2      5  .11614
CT     1030    5150     6     0     1      7  .13592
DE      156     780     1     0     0      1  .12821
DC      342    1710     0     4     1      5  .29240
IL     2864   14320    12     0     5     17  .11872
IN     1142    5710     6     0     4     10  .17513
KY      709    3545     4     0     7     11  .31030
LA      868    4340     6     0     4     10  .23041
ME      282    1410     2     0     0      2  .14184
MD     1194    5970     2     0     0      2  .03350
MI     2379   11895    13     0     7     20  .16814
MO     1193    5965     4     1     2      7  .11735
MS      428    2140     5     0     3      8  .37383
NC     1179    5895     7     1     2     10  .16964
ND      139     695     1     0     0      1  .14388
NE      359    1795     3     0     0      3  .16713
NH      241    1205     0     3     2      5  .41494
OH     2636   13180     9     3     7     19  .14416
OK      651    3255     2     0     1      3  .09217
PA     3237   16185    15     1     6     22  .13593
RI      274    1370     0     0     2      2  .14599
SD      128     640     1     0     0      1  .15625
TN     1004    5020     5     0     1      6  .11952
TX     3294   16470     7     3     1     11  .06679
UT      402    2010     2     0     0      2  .09950
VA     1315    6575    11     0     3     14  .21293
WI     1188    5940     5     0     3      8  .13468
WV      368    1840     7     0     3     10  .54348
WY      100     500     0     2     1      3    .6
      -----------------------------------------------------
TOTAL > 31199 155995   156    18    70    244  .15642
      -----------------------------------------------------
PERCENTAGE RESPONSE TO REPORT DATE >>>      .15642

   Jan MAILED >>>     104962 4699.8  46998
   Jan PERCENT >>       .14862 .38300 .14894
```

CHAPTER 3

OFFERS

Every time you think about creating a direct mail marketing campaign, there's a word that's highly important to you and the people to whom you mail: "offer."

An offer is a proposition you extend to the names to which you mail. Every mailing must have an offer, even if it's just the promise of learning something wonderful by reading the mailing.

Without an offer, no one reads the mail he didn't request. He needs a reason to read. The offer forces him to decide whether he wants or doesn't want your horse harness. He must read to decide.

Without an offer, you have only a bland communication that doesn't communicate, doesn't force readership, doesn't motivate, doesn't convince. You may need help in constructing proper offers and offer tests in order to get the most mileage from your postage.

This chapter gives you 50 specific points on how to construct offers for your future mailings, but in these introductory remarks I'd like you to think carefully about a point that few consultants make: the offer you mail today has an impact on the results you'll get from future mailings. Here's the basis for my remark:

Let's say you're introducing new computer software and it's a database system. You offer me the basic package with lots of razzamatazz about what it'll do for my business. You tell me it's terrific. I buy it for, say, $495.

A few months later, at $125, you sell me another disk with software letting me create longer forms with that database. Your next mailing tells me I can have an archive system, for only $225, that works with the same database. Another promotion advises me that I can give that database indexing capability for just $195. A fifth mailing gives me a chance to add automatic math functions for only $245.

All that's fine. I bought all the products. They cost me a total of $1,285. Now you tell me I can have the new, improved version for just $995. How do I feel?

Or, you change the name from Database One to Database Two and tell me that I can buy this new software for just $395. What will I think you'll do next?

In both instances, I might just sit there and tell myself there's no need to buy your improved products because the old ones work fine and you're going to change the new ones anyway. I wind up loving your products less, loving you less, and maybe wondering if I should consider someone else's software because you play all these games.

So I call in a computer consultant or, using my own cleverness, I search the ASCII contents of the five modules you sold me. I discover they're all part of one overall package. Now, what do I think of you?

Oh, c'mon, René. No one would do that?

Yes, this scenario is common with software houses. The full program is written, broken into modules, sold to you on a module-by-module basis, then offered as a total package at a big discount. How much more honest would it be to tell me that the basic package can be upgraded later? Tell me in advance that I can buy additional modules of my choice or the entire package at a saving.

> **Think of how you can adjust your initial offering so I may view your organization as caring about me and my future well-being. You can't afford to have prospects or customers thinking that you're playing games with them. They talk. Then sales decline.**

You would do well to remember that truth does NOT reduce sales. You CAN offer your product or service in a way that intrigues, enraptures, and leads to a response that will convert to long-term profits. Do it ethically. Without false bravado. By creating a solid impression for what you sell and for your organization. If you're NOT truthful, you don't create a lasting customer.

Remember these two sentences that I helped edit for the *Code of Ethics* of the Association of Direct Marketing Agencies when I was a founding director:

"We will not knowingly produce advertising which is false or misleading. We will not produce advertising we believe may be offensive to or in flagrant violation of the taste or moral standards of those to whom we direct our advertising efforts."

You can't go wrong if you follow the four basic principles of ethics in the Better Business Bureau *Code of Advertising:*

1. The primary responsibility for truthful and non-deceptive advertising rests with the advertiser who must be prepared to substantiate any claims or offers made.
2. Advertisements which are untrue, misleading, deceptive, fraudulent, untruthfully disparaging of competitors, or insincere offers to sell, shall NOT be used.
3. Advertisements should advise consumers of facts and qualities that will allow a more intelligent choice.
4. An advertisement as a whole may be misleading even though every sentence separately considered is literally true. Misrepresentation may result not only from direct statements, but by omitting or obscuring a material fact.

Spend most of your thinking time on offer construction. Construct your offers to be factual, while leading to a decision in your favor. Then, you'll have continuing business.

125 — ATTRACTIVE OFFERS

It is more important to have an attractive offer than terrific copy, so think carefully about boosting response by restructuring your offer to galvanize people into action.

126 — RESTRUCTURING YOUR OFFER

Changing or restructuring your offer can alter response by as much as 300%.

Fiddle around with the basic price, incentives, terms of sale or payment, and/or other elements of the basic offer until you have the strongest possible deal, judging which is strongest by actual results.

127 — SHIPPING, INSURANCE CHARGES

Instead of just mentioning "shipping charges," can you make that copy say "shipping and insurance charges"?

If you do, you hike interest by immediately implying that your product is so valuable that it must be insured.

128 — CUTTING DUPLICATE SHIPMENTS

If your merchandise is sufficiently valuable to include a "shipping and insurance charge," you are also saying to the recipients of your promotion that they can't claim they didn't get the product when they really did. Obviously, if they made such a claim, your insurer would check it out.

This is a dandy way to cut down on duplicate shipments to people who fall in love with the product they've received.

129 — FREE OFFERS

Whenever you want the largest number of respondents from a prospect list, consider using a free offer even if you give only additional information or a "valuable" trinket for responding.

130 — IDEA KIT

Do you sell a number of different products or services to businesses, associations or institutions?

If so, consider packaging them in an "idea kit," "press kit," or other "kit" that enhances their value to the eventual recipient and thus increases your response.

131 — CHOICE OF OPTIONS

To heighten response, give the recipient a choice of options, for example: a one-year subscription vs. a two-year subscription, or the regular model vs. the super deluxe version.

This creates a "hot potato" choice — which offer do I accept? — rather than a "yes or no" decision on whether to respond.

132 — LOWER SECOND PRICE

Consider offering a second quantity of the same product at a much lower price than your first offering in the same promotion.

This may increase dollar volume and the number of respondents.

133 — BULK-PURCHASE DISCOUNT

If the economics of your marketing are favorable, try to restructure your offer to allow for a quantity or bulk-purchase discount.

You may find respondents are

willing to purchase a greater quantity than you would normally suspect.

134 — BARGAIN PRICES

As much as possible, try to structure your offer so that it appears as a bargain.

Everyone loves bargains, even business audiences, and the opportunity to get something for less than the regular price usually is a good spur for response.

135 — DELAYED BILLING

Remember that while everyone loves a bargain, few people like to pay for anything.

Thus, you can increase your response by offering delayed billing, with terminology such as "order by June 1st and we won't bill you until Labor Day."

136 — SMALL DOWN PAYMENTS?

Bill-me-later offers frequently can be structured so the respondent sends you a small down payment and the balance on delivery.

But such offers are far more effective, often with double or triple the response, if no cash is required up front.

137 — INCENTIVE OFFER

In giving a customer a choice of responding with money or with a bill-me-later request, always offer an incentive (such as an extra issue of a magazine) for enclosing cash, check, or money order and you will achieve higher response to the paid option.

Otherwise, most respondents would naturally prefer to be billed at a later time.

138 — AFFLUENT AUDIENCE

The more educated and affluent your audience, the more you can charge for the appropriate products.

139 — SELLING AT FULL REGULAR PRICE

You are in business to sell your product or service at a profit. Thus, you should focus thoughtful consideration on methods of achieving those sales at the full regular price rather than at cut rates.

Constantly selling at cut rates eventually establishes the reduced price as the regular price.

140 — PAYING IN ADVANCE

If you ask for up-front payment, mention that paying in advance guarantees the current low price. You'd have to charge more if billing or credit orders were offered.

You are actually doing your customer a favor by permitting him to pay in advance.

141 — CUT RATES?

Do you cut rates to get new subscribers, new members, or new customers? That's okay and everyone does it.

But if your old faithful subscribers, members, or customers see those cut rates, what does that do to their feeling about you?

142 — CURRENT CUSTOMER DISCOUNTS

Unless you practice merge/purge, be certain to offer the same discounts to your current customers as you do on introductory offers or you will vex your customers.

143 — LOW-PRICED ITEMS

When selling a low-priced item, it may be better to ask for cash up front than to get involved in the expense of billing.

It also will tend to discourage trial purchasers who might return your product or not remit.

144 — THREE FOR TWO OR SIMILAR DEALS

When cutting rates, do you arbitrarily raise the stated "regular price" so you can cut? Will your prospects see through this? Might it be better to offer three for the price of two, rather than cutting the price of one?

You will have a far more believable offer and perhaps significantly increase your volume of goods moved.

145 — INSTALLMENT TERMS

When selling high-ticket items by mail to consumers, consider offering installment payment terms so your prospect will not be deterred by the high cost.

Try for a small down payment to avoid non-paying customers.

146 — CREDIT CARD PRIVILEGES

Besides offering installment payment terms to consumers, consider extending credit card charge privileges via MasterCard or Visa.

Those cards also have automatic installment payment plans.

147 — PAYMENT DELAYERS

Remember that the travel and entertainment credit cards — Diner's Club and American Express — are payment delayers rather than installment payment plans.

This works to your advantage when mailing to corporations and institutions, but not when mailing to consumers, who prefer installment payment plans.

148 — CREDIT CARD OPTION

If you sell consumer products having a sales price of $10 or more, allowing a credit card charge option can increase your orders from 16% to 25%.

Why? Because there are more than 97 million Visa cardholders in the U.S., and more than 78 million MasterCard cardholders, and more than 8.3 million American Express cardholders. Those figures are from the credit card companies. But many people have more than one card, and some have two or more of the same card.

Nevertheless, all these cardholders have a great convenience in charging their orders with you. And, anything that makes it easier to order is a good thing for you.

But, René, I've heard that asking for a credit card charge order can depress response?

Yes, it can. But only when you compare that offer with a non-payment offer. When you compare it with asking for a check, money order or cash, adding a credit card option significantly increases response.

René, can you give me an example of why credit cards would be effective in direct mail selling to both consumer and business audiences?

Certainly. On a consulting project for *Cincinnati Magazine*, which sells subscriptions to both consumers and businesspeople, I discovered that 41.2% of its subs have 9 or more credit cards, and 98.1% have at least one credit card, and 60.4% charge their subscriptions on a credit card.

And, that leads us to the next commentary:

149 — MAGAZINES AND NEWSLETTERS

Credit card options on magazine and newsletter subscription sales will usually increase paid response by 8% to 18%. Those figures are based on my work for over 270 different publications.

Generally speaking, but not always, the breakdown runs like this:

- to consumers at home ad-

Illustration #12

Offering credit card charge privileges, techniques #146 - #150, is not enough. You'll do better by making the act of charging more exciting than just normal ordering. Compare this artwork with Illustration #4 on page 20 and you'll quickly see the visual excitement. Notice that this time we've also illustrated how the customer can order, and we've said it's "easy".

Yes, the author produced all this art on a desktop computer system.

dresses, your credit card increase is 8 - 11%
- to business addresses, the
credit card boost is 9 - 13%
- when reaching entrepreneurs
or investment-oriented people,
your credit card increase is 8 -
18%.

150 — MAJOR CARDS

When offering charge privileges, it
usually is best to offer at least one of
the major travel and entertainment
cards, Diner's Club or American
Express, along with at least one of the
two major bank cards, MasterCard or
Visa.

Some folks use only one type of
card, and if the type you offer isn't the
one they carry, you can lose the order.

151 — PERCENTAGE OF
REFUNDS

Whenever you offer credit card charge
privileges, you'll find the percentages
of refunds or returns go down on
those orders acquired by credit card.

If you've ever tried to get a charge
reversed on your credit card bill, you
know how difficult this is. Diner's
Club has, in my opinion, the best
program for handling such reversals,
immediately deducting the charge
when investigating your claim with
the merchant. Contrast this with Visa
which sometimes charges you interest on the amount you dispute.

Cardholders are aware of these
difficulties, and thus tend to not make
many refund or return requests after
charging items to their card accounts.

152 — THE BUSINESS
AUDIENCE

Frequently, certain consumer products are best sold via mailings to a
business audience.

That's why a Miami direct sales organization mails only to executives at
their places of business and offers the
options of charging luggage sets to the
business or to a credit card.

153 — FREE TRIAL OFFER

The "free home demonstration" concepts frequently used with success in
space advertising can be adapted for
direct mail in terms of a "free trial
offer" when mailing to consumers.

154 — ON APPROVAL
ORDERS? YES!

The "free home demonstration" technique can be used in mailings to
businesses and institutions by calling it a "private showing" or a "free
trial" or "on approval" order.

155 — C.O.D.'s? MAYBE.

Before considering a C.O.D. offer, carefully analyze the extra effort to handle
such orders.

And speak to someone who sells a
similar product to determine your likely
"refusals" — folks who love to order,
but then refuse the package when it
arrives.

156 — FREE TRIAL OFFER

Almost any time you consider testing
merchandise on a cash-with-order
basis, also consider testing it on a free
trial basis.

Generally, the free trial offer will
pull at least half again as many responses as the cash-with-order offer.

157 — GET ACQUAINTED
OFFER

No one says you have to sell your
product or service or publication for
full term.

Try using a three-month supply, a

short-term introductory subscription, a "get acquainted" offer, or other small commitment term to entice prospects to try your deal.

158 — PULLING POWER

Offering a cash discount on mailings to consumer audiences is a good stimulus for response.

But, be careful to test it against a premium offer and determine which pulls best.

159 — ADDITIONAL REVENUES

A free gift offer often becomes more palatable by accompanying it with an offer for the same item at the regular price for a friend.

This establishes the value of your product or service and can produce additional revenues.

160 — DISCOUNT AND TRADE-IN?

Is it possible for you to offer a discount and a trade-in?

If so, you may substantially increase your response because everyone wants to get something better, at a good deal.

161 — PREVIEW CHARGE

On high-priced items, a "review" or "preview" charge, usually nominal, may succeed in getting fence-sitting recipients to respond.

In this case, clearly indicate the "preview" savings price can also be applied to a later, larger purchase, but only if this specific offer is accepted now.

162 — MEMBERSHIP DEAL

If yours is a new continuity sales program for books, records, magazines, or club memberships, try offer-ing a "charter" subscriber or membership deal. Include certain key benefits that future subscribers or members will not receive.

Charter offers are known to increase response by as much as 30% over the exact same offers not bearing the word "charter." And, frequently, you can extend charter offers for a long time and continue to receive heightened response.

How long, René?

I don't know, but for *Furniture/ Today* we ran the Charter Subscriber Offer for more than two years.

163 — TWO DIFFERENT PRICES

Using two different prices in connection with a cutoff date can significantly increase your response.

Clearly indicate that the lower price is good only if the recipient acts by a specific date and that the higher price applies to all orders received after the cutoff date.

Often this technique is referred to as an "early bird" rate. It is most effective for seminar registrations, but also works well for products and subscriptions.

Illustration #13

1990 Looseleaf NEC
#3063=Personalized, #3061=Regular

QUANTITY	Full Regular Prices Apply in 1990	1989 Discount Price Not Prepaid	Prepaid Orders Feb 15 to Apr 28, 89 6% Off	Prepaid Orders Before Feb 14, 89 12% Off	YOU SAVE per item
1 copy	32.50	27.50	25.85	**24.20**	8.30
2-4	31.85	26.95	25.33	**23.72**	8.13
5-24	31.20	26.40	24.82	**23.23**	7.97
25-99	30.55	25.85	24.30	**22.75**	7.80

Over 100 copies, call DAN toll-free today

Here's a case of taking technique #163 to the limit. Notice two early-bird deadlines and three discounts. The author created and mailed this in 1988 for a 1990 publication.

164 — EARLY-BIRD OFFER

If what you sell is normally purchased during a specific season, try structuring an early-bird offer to get prospects and existing customers to purchase earlier than normal. Or, try using a gift as an early-bird inducement. Wow, does that ever work!

I tried it at Easter, off-season for ticket sales in the Canadian National Lottery. Early respondents got the gift, up to $100,000 in free tickets. Those who responded on time, but not as early, didn't. Hot dog...our tickets sold like hot cakes. I then, very quickly, dreamed up a Labor Day early-bird gift!

My client doesn't need me any more. He now has an early-bird gift offer for every month of the year.

Illustration #14

The reasons why technique #164 is a winning concept are: (1) early cash flow for you, and (2) excitement for your reader who sees he's in on a good deal that, perhaps, is not accepted by all who get the mailing. The reader also may perceive that he is a special person who was selected to get the early-bird deal.

You can try this promotional idea on almost any product or service, and it almost always will pull beautifully.

You may not use full color as this client did, but at least give this winning method a try. It works!

165 — FREE SAMPLE

Any time you can offer a free sample of your product, you are making a very attractive offer.

Be careful, however, not to use fringe lists or convertibility will be poor.

166 — CLEARANCE SALE

Whenever you have a large inventory of products that have not moved fast enough, try offering a special inventory clearance sale, but make certain that you clearly explain that this is a one-time-only offering.

A shelving distributor in Ohio used to have an annual "Warehouse Inventory Sale" until he discovered that everyone he mailed to waited until the annual sale came along. Suddenly, his response to even the sale dropped.

How did he solve the problem? He split-tested his Warehouse Inventory Sale against a Whorehouse (I kid you not!) Inventory Sale. The brochures were alike, except for the name of the sale. You know which version won!

And it got him such favorable mail from male purchasing agents (98% of his market) that he was able to invent other zany sales. Each of them served to get the prospect's attention away from the annual Warehouse/Whorehouse Inventory Sale. Eventually, he dropped the annual sale. Later, he dropped all sales.

Sure, I could tell you his name...but he asked me not to.

167 — SMALL CHARGE

You can help eliminate "coupon clippers" who want a free sample offering, but do not wish to convert, by making a small charge for what otherwise would be a free sample.

Doing this also helps make your product appear more valuable and almost certainly assures you that more respondents will be more likely to convert because they have already demonstrated their interest in your product by paying for a sample.

168 — KIT PACKAGING?

Does your product lend itself to kit packaging?

If, for example, you sell tools and are accustomed to selling a single product at a single time, you may discover that packaging several chisels and screwdrivers together in a kit will enable you to have a greater dollar volume per sale.

Acquisition-oriented folks love kits.

This works in any field, for almost any kind of product, but my favorite story about this concept comes from Eduardo Apodaca, the marketing manager of Vocational Education Productions division of California Polytechnic State University in San Luis Obispo.

We worked on many projects together, trying to hike sales of his filmstrips. Exciting filmstrips! How to detect liver disease in rabbits. When to worm your horse. How to recognize sick chickens.

Sitting on the floor of his art department, with eager staffers and piles of papers and books and filmstrips and mechanicals all spread out, I suddenly said: "Eddie, let's sell kits."

So we put all the sheep filmstrips together, and did the same for goats, cows, horses, and pigs. Then we did likewise for all disease filmstrips, and all hoof filmstrips, and all breeding filmstrips.

Six months later, a letter from Eduardo said: "Your kits have increased our revenues by 33%."

Pretty good for such exciting products (sold to professors of veterinary medicine and similar animal lovers). Imagine what kits could do for your exciting products.

169 — DOWN-SELLING

"Down-selling" frequently can increase your overall response.

If your first promotion offers your product or service at the full price, you naturally cream the most interested customers from the prospect file. Then, your next promotion might sell a smaller quantity or be at a special price. Your third promotion might have a different, more attractive payment feature, and your fourth promotion might offer the product in combination with another.

Changing the structure of your pitch often enables you to produce additional customers from the same prospect list.

Ah, René, does that mean I can stop worrying about running out of prospect lists?

Maybe, maybe not. But now you have a potent way to go back to the same lists that proved responsive some time ago. Just don't forget to delete those who responded to the earlier, higher-priced deals.

170 — SHORT-TERM OFFER

In soliciting for new subscribers or members, test a short-term offer but maintain your "per-copy" or "per-month" price.

You may discover that you are able to reap additional income from your direct mail and pull in a substantial number of additional new subscribers or members because the cash outlay initially is lower than for a full-term subscription or membership.

171 — REPLY CARD

Spell out your entire offer — every detail — on your order form or response card, so the prospective respondent can review the entire deal as reinforcement for the sales pitch at the time he replies.

Did you think you are the only person who goes to the reply card before reading the letter or brochure? Most people with education do. I guess the others start elsewhere.

Why do folks start with the reply card, René?

Same reason as you do: to find out how much the item costs or what the commitment might be. If they don't find enough facts and persuasive copy on that reply form, they discard your mailing. You do, don't you? So why should you want to create your own reply cards on the K.I.S.S. principle? It doesn't work when you're after an order. Modifying K.I.S.S. does work when after leads.

172 — KEEPING IT SIMPLE

Always make the terms of the deal you are pitching as simple, as concise, as straightforward as you can.

Make the deal understandable. Avoid lengthy, windy descriptions of how much a customer must pay and stress the benefits of what you extend more than the payment the customer expends.

173 — LONG-TERM BASIS?

Be careful if you sell a product or service on a long-term basis.

Your costs to deliver that product or provide that service 3, 4, or 5 years from now may increase so much that you have no profit because you're serving the customer based on this year's selling price and costs.

Of course, there are two other considerations: (1) interest you might earn on the advance money you receive, and (2) the uses you'd have for that money.

Weigh your decisions carefully.

When operating and fulfillment costs are on an upward spiral, you'll be behind the eight-ball on your long-term sales. When those costs fall, you'll be ahead. Are you a forecaster?

There's still another consideration: how much do your customers need you?

EXAMPLE:

When working with *Atlanta* magazine and several trade journals owned by Joe Shore's Communications Channels (before he sold the company), we recognized that we had two distinctly different audiences. *Atlanta* had both business and consumer subscribers, but the trade journals had no consumers.

Those who subscribed to the trade journals needed to keep up with their peers in volatile industries. Thus, they wanted to renew and very little persuasion was needed. But, because of the consumers in the *Atlanta* database, we had to increase persuasive copy. Many of those subscribers really did not need the publication. They just liked it.

That gave us hints on subscriber longevity, which led to some great conclusions on how to formulate our offers.

We just didn't bother announcing price hikes in advance to the trade journal subscribers. We knew they'd re-subscribe at just about any palatable rate, so why give them a chance to renew at a lower rate and thus decrease our revenues?

But with *Atlanta,* and its blend of business and consumer subscribers, announcing the price increase in advance encouraged consumers to hurry up and re-subscribe so they'd save money.

So, I repeat the question for your careful consideration and for your future income: *how much do your customers need you?*

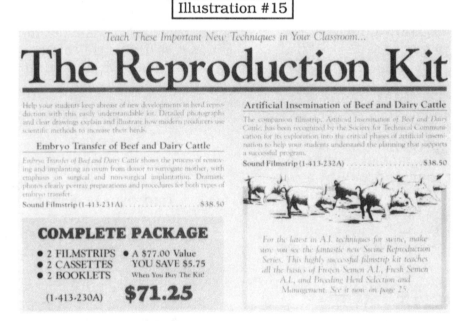

Illustration #15

This artificial insemination kit, technique #168, fits the concept of technique #173 because it can be re-priced as each new catalog is issued. The same methodology applies to products for consumer, business, and professional markets. The idea is to increase sales while holding fulfillment costs in line with the value of money.

CHAPTER 4

TESTING

Once upon a time, there was a publisher in Florida who thought how it would be lovely for Florida women to have their own magazine. She obtained a list of 40,000 women living in Florida and mailed a promotion to all of them. Because she didn't get the response she wanted, she mailed to them all a second time with a copy of the magazine. Then she went broke and abandoned her delightful publishing idea.

I was living in New Jersey when the news of her magazine's demise was published in the trade press. How unfortunate, I thought. Had she tested several different approaches, she might now be a successful publisher. Perhaps millions of women would be reading her messages. Perhaps she could have franchised her idea to other states, or published different editions for all 50 states and then expanded to the Canadian provinces.

But she didn't test.

You nearly always should test!

You can afford it. You should do it. The information you'll gain is invaluable.

Even though technique No. 217 in this chapter gives you the few instances when testing may not be wise, in just about every other instance, testing saves you money, makes you money, and gives you the information you need for your future mailings.

For this introduction, let's consider split testing. You'll split a quantity of names to determine whether the folks you mail to prefer red and white or blue and white umbrellas. The information you derive will enable you to plan your manufacturing and perhaps also your pricing and additional new products.

You can't split test unless you make certain that you code your outgoing mail. CODE each list. CODE each copy variation. CODE each offer variation. CODE each format variation and maybe you'll even need to CODE BY MAILING DATE. You must code so you'll know which responses are coming from which variation.

The simplest code method is Alphabetical — A, B, C, and so on — because it gives you 26 varieties. So, an A/B split is half the mail going with Code A and half going with Code B. An A/B/C would be one-third splits.

Codes belong on your response device, either an order form or inquiry card. They can also be used with incoming telephone numbers.

In printing, you can position codes:

1. In form number headings
2. In any corner, printed
3. As part of a return address
4. By cutting a corner
5. By drilling holes
6. On a computer label
7. As part of computer personalization

And you can also DOUBLE CODE: one code for one purpose and a second code for another purpose. For example: the first purpose might be all replies from a particular campaign, and the second might be lists or copy approaches.

On your split tests, try, as much as possible, to use the same quantity for each code. It's not necessary, but it makes your analysis so much easier. Make sure you remember that each variable gets a separate code! But, there's more.

When reviewing your results, make sure that you have counts for each day of response. That's vital to you! Do not lump a whole week's replies into one batch and then record them on a single line. Take a separate line for each day's returns. This is essential when you starting computing your half life.

What's "half life," René?

Read on...

174 — IRONIC FAILURES

The mailing piece most likely to fail is the one you fall in love with the most.

175 — OBJECTIVE RESPONSES

Your boss, your creative director, the marketing manager, the president of your organization — no one can tell you whether the promotion package you have created will work. The re-cipients of your mail tell you.

Count your responses objectively. Those responses tell you whether the package is successful.

176 — COST-PER-ORDER BASIS

One of the greatest dangers in testing is attempting to prove a result you have already concluded you want.

The marketer who says "my new package worked" simply by counting leads or orders it produced is not as prudent or as cost conscious as the marketer who determines the success of his promotion by evaluating response on a cost-per-order basis.

It's not necessarily the number of orders that the new package produces that determines its success. It's the acquisition-cost-per-new customer, back-end renewability, and customer life.

177 — STAYING WITH A WINNER

Never stop using a profitable mailing until you have one that is more profitable. Just because you and your staff are bored with looking at it is no reason to cease mailing it.

Test new packages against your winning (control) packages until you have a test package which beats the winner.

178 — STANDARD COMPARISON

Use your control package in a re-test with a new winning test package so that you have a standard against which to measure test results and reverify them.

179 — ABSORBING TEST MAIL COSTS

When testing, always use at least three (and preferably four) times the quantity of your test package for your control package.

EXAMPLE:

5,000 pieces for your test package and 15,000 or 20,000 for the control package. Then, if the test package flops, you should at least produce sufficient sales from the control package to absorb test mailing costs.

180 — NEW CODE

When testing, remember that any change in an existing mailing piece constitutes a new mailing piece, and thus requires a new code!

181 — PRIORITY RANKINGS

In testing by direct mail, your priority rankings are:

1. the lists you use,
2. the offers you construct,
3. the copy you create.

182 — PERFECTION?

There is no such thing as a perfect promotion package. All can be improved.

Testing gets you there.

183 — WEIGHING YOUR RESPONSES

Some people feel the best way to test a mailing list is to pull a sample on an Nth name basis.

Others believe the quantity of names used in a test depends on the size of the list being tested, such as 3,000 names for a list of 50,000, or 5,000 names for a list of 100,000, or 10,000 names for a list of 200,000.

A third group of marketers says the quantity of names used for each list being tested should be precisely the same regardless of the number of lists you test.

A fourth group feels that the size test you specify should be based on a percentage of the size of the list you are testing, such as 5% of the total names available on any list.

All that is nonsense.

The best way to determine test quantities is by knowing the number of responses you need to have a statistically-valid judgment and coupling that information with your likely or anticipated response.

184 — NEEDED RESULTS

The size of the sample you test depends on the results you need and has nothing to do with the size of the list you are testing.

185 — VALID RESPONSE NUMBER

A statistically valid number of respondents on which to base a judgment has been proved by a large number of mailers to be 30 responses per test code.

Therefore, if historically you produce 3% response, the minimum test sample would be 1,000 names to yield 30 responses. If you historically produce 2% response, the minimum test sample would be 1,500 names.

Hold it! Those are minimums per code!

186 — OUTSIDE OPINION

If your testing fails to give you the answers you had hoped for, seek an outside opinion and be ready to be sufficiently objective to drop the entire concept or restructure it.

Far too many would-be direct response entrepreneurs hang on to their original concept to the point of bankruptcy.

187 — ONE AT A TIME

Always test one element of a mailing at a time — list against list, or offer against offer, or copy against copy. Resist testing two elements at the same time until you have carefully refined which elements work best to which lists.

You may discover that a certain list, and it may have a huge audience for you, requires special treatment. Also, testing more than one element at a time is a good way to confuse results...as well as your incoming mailroom.

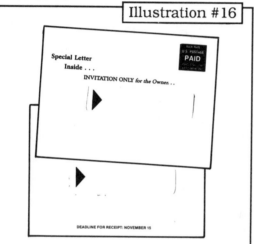

Illustration #16

A true split test by the author -- for insurance leads on behalf of The National Association for the Self-Employed -- is reproduced above to illustrate technique #187. The top envelope has one window, while the bottom envelope has two windows (the second to determine whether stressing the deadline would improve results on a cost-effective basis).

All other elements in this test were the same. And, that's how you should conduct your split tests.

188 — 4-WAY PRICE TEST

It is not wise to test more than one item in one mailing split or one A/B space advertisement split. You will delude yourself.

You can, however, do more splits. Why not A/B/C/D, for example, as a 4-way price test?

189 — COMPONENT CHANGES

When you have a winning package and you are attempting to improve its response still further, test only one component change at a time — such as revising the letter or the outgoing envelope — but not both in the same test unless you code each separately.

190 — USING GRID CHARTS

If you have historical or other extensive experience on a specific product or service to a specific audience, you can set up an inexpensive test for a number of different variables in a single campaign by establishing a grid chart, then insisting that your label source, printer, and lettershop precisely code your split designations.

Then you must tally and analyze responses by code. You'd be surprised at the number of organizations that go through all the testing machinations but forget to advise the staff to tally by code.

Then I have to come in and "divine" which code worked best.

191 — PLOTTING RESULTS

Grid testing is a reliable way to test response factors to varying copy, varying offers, and different lists all at the same time, but you must continually plot results. Otherwise, waiting until all results are in may delay your next promotion unnecessarily.

René, do you like grid testing?

Not really. It tends to delay outgoing mail. Stick to A/B or A/B/C or maybe A/B/C/D split tests, and you'll get all the information you need and get your mail out faster so your dollars come in faster.

192 — PRODUCT AS SAMPLE?

Regardless of your product or service, or the format you select, getting your reader involved with the promotion can make it dramatically more effective for you.

The best, but most costly way, to get reader involvement is to use a sample of your product or publication in the mailing.

What, René, include my product as a sample?

Heavens, yes...why not be bold? Rudy Savage, at Newstrack Executive Tape Service in Denver, is bold. He mails millions of his cassettes as product samples in his solicitation mailings. And he does quite well with those mailings. Despite the higher cost per thousand in the mail, the sample promotions beat every other concept Rudy and I have tried in cost-effectiveness — because his response is so much higher with the samples.

Gosh, René, he must be a millionaire to do that?

He is now.

193 — TEST TOKENS

Do not be afraid to test tokens, rub-off devices, tip-ons, mystery windows, stamps, and other involvement devices in mailings directed to prospects.

While the cost of using these gimmicks is high, they frequently hike response, and lower your cost per order.

194 — GOING FOR IT

When testing tokens and similar gimmicks, always go "whole-hog" in a full-blown effort at promoting and

To respond to this promotion, the reader is asked to punch out the token (magazine cover) and slide it in the slots on the reply card -- techniques #193 - #195. Another variation is a paste-on token, which is slightly less costly. This half-price mailing, created by the author in 1979, dramatically outpulled the same mailing without a token. In the other version of the test, the cover was printed as artwork, not a token.

calling attention to the value of the token, stamp, or other response device.

Don't be shy. A one-color token may not dramatize a colorful item or exciting offer. You need to dramatize it so folks know it has a value or relates to a value.

195 — USE OF TOKENS

The use of tokens on single-product offerings, like magazine subscriptions or tool kits, considerably increases the cost per thousand in mailing, but can increase response by as much as 100%.

196 — UP-FRONT MEMBERSHIP FEE

Continuity sales merchandisers frequently forget that respondents may be willing to pay an up-front membership fee in addition to purchasing on a regular basis. Test it.

EXAMPLE:

I needed cash. I had just bought *Puzzle Lovers Bulletin*, tried several consumer mailings, increased subscribers from 262 to just over 3,000, and was itching to expand it.

So I changed the name to *Puzzle Lovers Newspaper* to give it more perceived value and raised the price from $12 to $14 a year.

Then came the brainstorm.

I invented Puzzle Lovers Club, which then published the newspaper. To have the right to subscribe, you had to join the club for $5. That was an instant $15,000, minus b/w mailing costs, giving me over $12,500 to use for promotion.

Out went the mail. In a year, I had raised membership from 3,000 to 44,000. You multiply that by $5.

Suddenly having the cash I needed

Illustration #18

People like to belong. By establishing Puzzle Lovers Club and giving it a newspaper, instead of a catalog of puzzles, the author attracted thousands of members and built a million dollar direct mail business, technique #196, before moving to Florida while young enough to enjoy the sun.

for better promotions — how great it was to go from b/w to two colors! — I decided to be nice. You no longer had to pay the full $14 in advance after you paid the $5. You could elect to pay only $2 a month. What a favor, $24 instead of $14.

What happened? Well, 11,000+ decided to continue sending $14 in advance, while nearly 33,000 switched to the monthly plan. Zounds! $792,000 instead of $462,000, which really should have been $396,000. And, of course I had the extra $2 for each of the 11,000 annual people and the extra $5 for all 44,000.

All because I started a club marketing program when I was 23.

Was there a fall-off factor on the monthly plan? Sure. But with four Caribbean vacations a year, a new summer home and a 220-foot waterfall in the Berkshire Mountains of Massachusetts, a hefty stock market portfolio, and two new businesses in the Carolinas, who cared?

And for 17 years, thousands of puzzle lovers renewed their wonderful memberships. Then, I got tired of it and sold it to an employee.

But if you go driving in the Berkshires, you just might stumble across Response Road. When you see the sign, you'll know how it got its name.

But, René, don't you live on Response Road in Florida?

Yes. That's another story. And it's a legal address. Keep reading.

197 — REGULAR SHIPMENTS

If you sell on a continuity basis, consider testing an offer that calls for regular shipments until such time as the member or subscriber tells you to cancel future shipments.

You will get slightly lower initial response but greater long-term purchases.

This is called "'til forbid," similar to the space advertising term. Your buyer keeps on being obligated until he forbids you to ship any more.

Sure, it works. But it wasn't good enough to buy a second mountaintop.

198 — RISING COSTS

Increasingly intense competition means you cannot pass rising costs on to your customer. Wrong!

If your product is worth it, if your customer has been successfully wooed, if he's loyal to you because you have shown him you care, perhaps he's willing to pay for your rising costs.

Test it with a sample of your customer list.

199 — TWO OF THE SAME...

To increase your bottom line profits, test using your customer list to mail the same product or service offering at the same price to those customers who bought it originally. Very frequently, direct marketers discover that a consumer or business customer who is satisfied with a particular product or service will buy two of the same thing.

Remember my Puzzle Lovers Club? I sold lots of people two puzzle dictionaries, one for upstairs, one for downstairs. That's what my copy said. "Whenever the mood strikes you to solve a puzzle, you'll have the official dictionary at hand, whether you're upstairs or downstairs."

Does it sound crazy? Yes, but you have to be a little crazy to be successful in direct mail.

René, is this technique restricted to consumer audiences?

No, Tandy sold me more than one business computer system by using repeat mailings.

200 — ...IN SMALL QUANTITIES

If you test remailing the same offer on the same product or service at the same price to those customers who originally purchased from you, be absolutely certain to do so in small quantities.

You may discover that you have a large group of dissatisfied customers who previously did not take advantage of your refund or replacement guarantee!

201 — DETERMINING YOUR RESPONSES

To determine how many responses your mailing is going to achieve, if you use first class mail, double the number of responses you receive on the 9th or 10th or 11th day following the mail date.

You must allow a three-day variance because of weekend mail.

202 — THE WAITING PERIOD

With third class mail, you usually should receive half of your total response between the 18th and 23rd day after the first response is received.

Now, let me explain precisely why techniques No. 201 and No. 202 are so very important to you.

You are looking for your "half life" — also called "doubling day" — and I earnestly entreat you to record each day's response separately, so you can figure out your half life!

Half life occurs at the time when you have received half the responses you will receive by the end of the campaign.

For instance, when you were about two years old, you were half as tall as you are now as an adult. So, at age two, your parents could predict how tall you'd be.

The same concept works well for you with direct mail. At a given point in time, by looking at your responses day by day, you can figure out half the pull your mailing will have, and then your continuation mailings don't have to wait until all returns are in. You can mail again with the best offer, to the best lists, with the best package.

However, there are some exceptions to the doubling days I've cited:

- deadline mailings may get early pull,
- event mailings may get late pull,
- your mail might suffer from industry-wide calamities,
- weather problems could delay delivery,
- big national, international or industry news could affect the timing in your calculations, and
- competitor's mailings sometimes influence half life.

BUT, in the nearly 30 years that I have been doing direct mail campaigns for hundreds of organizations, it has been my experience that less than 15% of them know half life predictability. Most mailers sit and wait until all the replies are in before planning their next mailings. By using half-life calculations, you can get a big jump on your competition.

Your half life or doubling day will vary by the audience you approach and the nature of your offer.

For example, *Conservative Digest* found its half life by first class mail on the eighth day after drop date, and by third class on the 18th day after drop date. You must find your own half life by careful tallying on your very next mailing, and then use that information to roll-out with enthusiasm.

203 — ADAPTABLE PROMOTION

Your audience is changing constantly!

Even though you have a good winner, your promotion must change as your audience changes.

204 — SPECIAL SAVING

Traditionally, summer months are slowest in direct response.

So, test a special small quantity mailing, indicating that it is a slow period for you and that's why the customer can have a special saving.

205 — LOW-BALLING THE COMPETITION

René, here's an idea. Have you ever tried using a low-ball price in mailings only to your competitors?

No, I haven't. But it's an interesting concept.

It could easily be done in mailings that don't have the price on every enclosure. One version goes to your competitors, another to your prospects. If I'd try this, I'd mail the version to my competitors after doing the mass mailing, or perhaps simultaneously. Mailing earlier could seduce the competition into lowering its price before I received my response.

You might try this when you know your competitors are a bunch of copy cats. Let them think you've slashed your price way below breakeven. Let them copycat. Let them suffer.

206 — FIRST-CLASS RATE

Treat all your promotions as first class communications and test mail at the first class rate, either with a meter imprint or, preferably, by affixing a stamp.

The increased cost often will be outweighed by the increased response.

207 — DIRECT AND SECRET

Direct mail is an excellent medium for testing prices, offers, and markets without letting potential competition know what you are doing.

Small mailings directed to the proper audiences, although somewhat more expensive than space advertising, can elicit the information you require.

208 — TESTING IN OFF-SEASON

Direct mail testing should be mainly done in your off-season.

Testing during your prime marketing season reduces the number of pieces you can mail at the time when you should be getting the most mileage from your promotions.

Test in the off-months and roll out with full-scale promotions during your peak selling periods.

209 — CHRISTMAS IN JULY

If your product or service is mainly oriented toward a seasonal selling period, try a small test mailing in the off-season, stressing the fact that because it is the off-season, you can offer a more attractive price or additional units for those people who care to order in advance. This technique is especially useful with Christmas gift items.

The "Christmas in July" theme still works. The reason is: folks receiving it feel that they're in on a special deal before mass audiences receive it. Give it a try.

210 — RED VERSUS BLUE?

Testing superfluous items is ridiculous and expensive. Whether red outpulls blue or orange is a low priority test concern.

Concentrate first on testing lists, then an improved offer, a different term or commitment, a breakthrough copy approach, a product improvement.

211 — SECOND-TIME TEST

If you have a test mailing which has come close to the response levels of the winning control package but didn't quite make it, test it a second time, perhaps making slight improvements.

You may be astonished to discover that what was only close the first time around becomes a clear-cut winner on the second drop.

212 — PRICE TEST

A price test is simply a price test, and nothing more.

Don't clutter up test results by changing copy, colors, enclosures, or formats. Just test the price.

213 — STYLIZING DIRECT MAIL

The place to test product benefits as to their consumer appeal is in an A/B split with a space advertisement, usually not in direct mail.

Simply tally the response to Benefit A versus the response to Benefit B, and then you know how to stylize your direct mail.

214 — NECESSARY INCREASED RESPONSE

Whenever possible, attempt to determine in advance how much increased response is required to make your test effort successful.

Otherwise, you may discover that a super-creative maniac has managed to make your art and printing production costs exorbitant in his zeal to beat the previous winner.

215 — RESEARCHING THE AUDIENCE

Many direct marketers have long believed that research is unnecessary because test mailing programs constitute research.

It is true that you can research the response to your particular offer by using test mailings, but you can improve the offer significantly in advance of the test expense if you know your audience correctly through research!

216 — PRE-PUB OFFERS

Use direct response advertising to find out in advance what the prospect will buy.

Rather than rushing into print with your new 456-page book on elephant pediatrics for zookeepers, test mail to zookeepers the mailing package that you would use on a rollout but use a small quantity. If it's totally unsuccessful, you may save the investment in publication.

The same technique works effectively for mail order merchandising of new products, for testing new products before including them in catalogs, and for testing reaction to new product lines before giving them to representatives at a commission.

This is called a "pre-pub" offer, borrowed from publishers who test new concepts pre-publication. It's perfectly legal. Be prepared to make prompt refunds if you scuttle the project. Also be prepared to steam ahead if results are satisfactory.

217 — NO TESTS?

All this talk about testing, René, leads me to ask whether it ever is appropriate to not test?

Of course it is, in these instances:

1. Don't test your mailing package if you're mailing a very small quantity, say under 5,000 pieces, although there have been some instances when it has paid in very small quantities.
2. Don't test your package when you have an enormous breakthrough in a tightly-defined market which a competitor could quickly approach.
3. You may not wish to test cer-

tain mailings to your membership or subscription or customer base.

4. When seeking funds in a crisis situation, a time delay may make it unwise to go through normal testing procedures.

5. Mailings to promote exhibit booth attendance and certain regional events may not always require testing.

In these instances, you must be cautious to triple-check everything you do. Perhaps call in your consultant for a review before setting type.

218 — PINPOINTING GEOGRAPHIC AREA

When launching a new product, remember that direct mail is the only medium that allows you to effectively pinpoint your efforts to a given geographic area.

This enables you to control new product announcements so that the competition does not know what you're doing.

219 — PRODUCT IMPROVEMENT TEST

What appears to you as a product improvement may, in fact, not sell at all. Do not scrap all previous promotion pieces simply because you have developed a product improvement.

Test the product improvement with split copy against the control package. (See also No. 26.)

220 — GIMMICK OR NO GIMMICK

If you have a winning package which includes a token, stamp or other response gimmick, test the same package without the gimmick against the winning package to determine whether you can cut your costs.

Usually, however, you will find a significant fall-off in response, often as high as a 50% drop. Cost effectiveness is your goal.

221 — YES OR NO

Frequently, you can significantly increase response on a single product offering by asking all recipients to respond by saying "yes" or "no".

The "yes-no" decision option usually increases the number of "yes" orders.

222 — CO-OP ENVELOPE

Can you join with several noncompetitors in making free offers via one insert in a co-op envelope, loose deck, or bingo card promotion? Perhaps try something wilder and join with them in offering free catalogs and/or booklets via one co-op space ad in a publication reaching a generalized audience.

Test it, and you might discover that the cost-per-lead drops significantly for each of you.

223 — DOUBLE POSTCARD

The old double postcard still works!

When testing to reduce your outgoing solicitation mail expense, consider using self-mailers of every variety, and do not skip the double postcard. It enables you to slash your mail expense and still get a reply.

224 — WELL-KNOWN PRODUCT

If your product or service is very well known to the targets of your direct mail, do not hesitate to test a self-mailer directly against an envelope mailing.

You may discover that not only is the self-mailer more cost-efficient, but it sometimes produces more response per thousand pieces, most often when mailed to business audiences.

225 — THE WINNING TEST

If your winning package is the standard four- or five-piece envelope mailing, and you are attempting to test a self-mailer against it, make certain that all elements of the winning envelope mailing are included in the new self-mailer.

226 — LOADED PACKAGE

When testing by mail, nearly always start with a loaded package, going all out for success and using every technique you can incorporate, including full color rather than single or two-color promotions (that is, if full color is appropriate to your product or service).

It does no good to start with a low-cost package and have it bomb, making you wonder if you would have been successful with an all-out effort.

Test expensively and then, if you have a winner, cut the costs of your package until returns fall off. Then you can establish proper cost effectiveness for your specific marketing.

227 — AUDIENCE AND TIMING

Many organizations can not send test mailings because their deadlines are tight or new product launch timing is vital.

In those instances, adopt the techniques that have proven successful for others and call in a consultant who can pinpoint the techniques and strategies you should be using.

Illustration #19

This is the author's double postcard, technique #223, for Western Outdoors, produced in Spring 1989 with laser personalization on the address side, and with both sides in full color.

Against this card, the client used a standard envelope mailing, technique #225, to measure A/B split test results.

The envelope mailing won this time, which did not mean that the card concept was a loser. Orders from it were still coming in at press time for this book.

NOTE: *This card has a hard offer (pay or use a credit card). It would have pulled better had the client allowed a soft (pay later) option.*

CHAPTER 5

HEADLINES

Y ou can induce readership with effective headlines, but you have, of course, read that seven words in a headline is the maximum you can use to grab attention and guide the reader into your body copy. I do not know who originated that myth, but, like you, I do see it foolishly perpetuated in books, articles, and how-to manuals. And every now and then, some would-be genius repeats it from a public platform.

Let me point out that seven words can be effective — but so can four or fourteen or forty. To quote my friend John Caples, generally acknowledged as the best adwriter ever, "long headlines that say something about the reader's interest outpull short headlines that talk about the advertiser's interest."

However, because most ads and mailings have poorly-written headlines, McGraw-Hill reports that 80% of the readers of those headlines do not read any further.

Readers of my column in *"Mail Order Connection"* newsletter (now called *The Direct Response Specialist*), who formerly restricted themselves to creative constipation by slaving for seven words, were delighted when I quoted what Chilton Research

Services reports about headlines on full-page ads:

64.4% of publication recipients notice the headline and read it...but only

26.4% start to read the ad...and only

13.7% read half or more of the ad.

The Chilton research was done in March 1980 on a survey of over 2,000 trade ads in more than 100 magazines. Most of those ads used "a maximum of 7 words" in the main headline. Thus, if you adhere to foolishness, far less than half the people who read your headlines will start reading your message, and less than one-quarter of your headline readers will read half or more of your copy. The problem, clearly, is that word count restrictions drastically curb readership.

Chilton's respected researchers go on to say: "twice as many high-scoring ads use headlines longer than 12 words while headlines of 7 or fewer words did not produce ad readership as well as longer headlines." Sure, those were ads. But the same is true for mailings. I've split-tested long vs. short headlines expressing the same copy point, and usually it's the longer headline that pulls best. So...

Stop being constipated. Write headlines that will do the job for you, regardless of word count. And refer to this helpful checklist of headline techniques to hike effectiveness the next time you create an ad or mailing:

1. Use a "flash headline" in some instances: a short, telegraphic, interesting, punchy, thought-provoking message that can be used in large type to grab the eye. An example would be "End Tape Tangles." Note that in just three words, I have stated a user benefit and implied ease of operation.

2. When possible, get the name of what you're selling in your headline. It's not always possible, but when you do it you are continuing an identity for future ads and mailings. Now, our example might be "End Tape Tangles With Titan Tapes."

3. Identify or imply identification of the reader. "End Tape Tangles With Titan Tapes" implies the word "you." But if we reach a trade audience, are we selling cassette tapes, computer tapes, specific industry tapes, or what? "Plumbers: End Tape Tangles With Titan Tapes" solves the problem.

4. In all these examples, I've made a promise. Remember to always do that, and perhaps make it more inviting by recognizing that everyone loves discovery. "How Plumbers End Tape Tangles With Titan Tapes" forces the plumber to read on, to discover how he can avoid tangles. (Horrors. Eight words!)

5. Many times, you can paint a word picture with your headline and thus get your customer or prospect to agree with your statement. Agreement is half the battle in making a sale. "How Titan Helps Plumbers End the Frustration of Tangled Tapes." (Oops. Ten words!)

6. You can also pinpoint the uniqueness of your product or service by adding the word "this" or "these," implying that you sell the only solution to the reader's problem. "How Plumbers End the Frustration of Tangled Tapes With These Titan Tapes." (Hmmm. Twelve words!)

7. And you can highlight the urgency of responding instantly: "Now...Discover How Plumbers End the Frustration of Tangled Tapes With These Titan Tapes." (Gosh. Fourteen words!)

8. If your headline cites a typical problem or problems faced by your reader and then solves the problem, you've got him! The easy way to do it is: "Problem: Tangled Plumbing Tapes. Solution: Titan." Boring, isn't it. But how many headlines have you read with that lazy problem-solution presentation? Instead, involve your reader, like this: "Now...Discover How These Titan Tapes End Plumbers' Tape Tangle Frustrations at Pipe Joints." (Golly. Fourteen better words!)

9. Tell your reader he can get a bargain. "Now...Discover How These Discounted Titan Plumbing Tapes End Tangled Tape Slowdowns at Pipe Joints." (My, my. Fifteen words!)

When I write a headline, I recognize that the reader is not primarily interested in what I sell. He reads for information, knowledge, or amusement. Regardless of the title, however, he didn't open the publication to look for Titan. Regardless of the mailing format, he doesn't open his mailbox or look in his "in" box for coercements from Titan.

Thus, I must involve his mind and open it to new ideas. The longer headline allows me to do this, by getting product or service benefits in the headline. These user-oriented headlines do the job, and they tend to be longer than seven words. Simply stated: Longer Heads Grab Heads.

> **Since there is no magic number of words in a headline, I do not allow myself to be restricted. You shouldn't either.**

But, here's a tougher problem:

I gave you nine examples of plumbing tape headlines to show how to incorporate nine techniques. But suppose Titan has tapes for more than one plumbing frustration. What then?

Add more words:

"Now...Discover How These Discounted Titan Plumbing Tapes End Tangled Tape Slowdowns at Pipe and Conduit Joints." That takes care of the plumber who does air conditioning and PVC pipe as well as sinks. If the mailing reaches plumbers who don't handle PVC pipe, I'd change "conduit" to "duct."

And that's technique No. 10...

10. Be as specific as possible. Specificity allows your reader to mentally say: "I'm a ductwork man. That's for me."

I've just presented ten "do's." Here are five "don'ts":

1. Don't be cute. I look at advertising mail and publication ads only if the photos and head-lines grab me. If I don't understand your cuteness, I won't read your copy. What's cute? "Stop Carrying 15-30% in Phoney Overhead" on an ad for Sykes Datatronic phone service. It should have said: "How to Slash Telephone Overhead Costs by 15-30%."

2. Don't be too small. Gene Schwartz, who has sold zillions of products by mail order, once said a headline can be as large as one-third of the total ad. "Can be," not "must be."

3. Don't hide your pitch. "What's Penn Central Doing in Telecommunications?," a trade headline, stinks because it allows the reader to say "I don't know" and turn the page.

4. Don't use cliches. Page 35 of a recent issue of *Aloft* had this headline for Howard Johnson's: "Have you heard the one about the Traveling Salesman?" Page 36 had this headline for Zippo Lighters: "Did you hear the one about the Traveling Salesman?"

5. Don't write headlines when you're down. You must have an up attitude. Do not say, "Yuk, I must write to waste water treatment managers." Do say, "Wow, waste water people!"

That last point is vital. A poor attitude leads to poor headlines and wasted advertising dollars. Note how my headline for Pollution Control Industries, written when I was enthused about dirty water, zeros in on the waste water treatment supervisor's interest: "There's Only One Safe Way to Disinfect Water and Waste Water..." Now, he has to read on.

That's the main purpose of a headline...getting the reader sufficiently interested to read on.

228 — CREATIVE TECHNIQUES

Most people on mailing lists appear on many, many lists and therefore receive many special offers, sales pitches, and gimmick invitations by mail. They can build up resistance to direct mail.

That's why proper attention to creative techniques, especially in headlines, is vital for the success of your promotion efforts.

229 — SPACE CONSIDERATIONS

Never let space considerations lead to inadequate display of a major headline concept.

If you need longer or wider paper, buy it.

If you need to sacrifice on photo size, do it.

If you need to trim text and graphics, so be it.

Illustration #20

Here are two mailings, created by the author, that illustrate technique #230 — using headlines to make an interesting promise or offer something of value.

A business-to-business mailing, from NBI Word Processors (top), makes more than one promise — each promise coming after the word "now."

A consumer mailing, from Knape & Vogt Manufacturing (angled at the bottom), promises value with a claim of reducing heating fuel use.

Both mailings offer value. The NBI self-mailer states the price and the value of the premium, while the K&V envelope offers a free 90-day trial.

But if your main headline doesn't get read, doesn't communicate, doesn't grab the interest of your prospect, he pitches your pitch. You must take exceptional care to graphically display that major headline concept so it leads your readers right into your pitch.

230 — HEADLINE COPY

Headline copy should include an interesting promise of something exciting, or of value, or of personal interest to the target names on the specific lists to which you are mailing.

And that promise should be enticingly stated to invite the prospect to read further.

> Many people are jaded. They need your promise in order to want to read.
>
> Others are bored. Without a promise, they see little of interest to them.

Still others may think they don't need what you sell. The promise you make can intrigue them so they investigate the copy following the headline. That's what you want them to do.

231 — ORDER REQUESTS IN A HEADLINE

Some of the most successful direct response advertising asks for an order in the main headline.

That may be startling to you, since most advertising people find it difficult to boldly ask for an order in the first headline read by their prospects. But consider this remarkable response:

My client, *National Mall Monitor*, had mailed to a specific list six times before turning its problem project over to me. The problem? The list never produced over 1.4% on new subscription orders, and that was just too low for this publisher. But the list was working for his competitor, so he needed a new thrust.

I boldly proclaimed, in a main headline right on the outside envelope, that I expected recipients to send $36 after reading the contents of the envelope. This mailing pulled 2.2% in new subscribers, plus another 1% paid book orders, for a total response of 3.2% — more than double the results of any other mailing.

René, where did you get the guts to try this?

I based it on research from the Daniel Starch organization, which said (and I suggest that you memorize this) "telling someone what to do always works better than assuming he knows what to do."

So why not try it yourself! Use your opening headline to ask for the order.

232 — NO MAYBES ABOUT IT

A headline should rarely use a question that can be answered by "maybe."

That could lead to daydreaming which can lose a good percentage of your audience.

233 — ELIMINATING THE NEGATIVE

Rarely write a headline in the form of a question that can be answered by "no" or "I don't know."

If the reader answers "no" to your question, he won't read further and you won't make your sale.

234 — SO WHAT

Never write a headline statement that can be answered by the phrase "so what."

If the reader responds with "so what" to your headline statement, he is turning himself off from the rest of the mailing, and you have lost him completely.

235 — POSITIVE STATEMENTS

If you like questions in headlines, try rewording them so that they become positive statements, even exultations.

EXAMPLE:

"Do you want to enjoy good music at the beach?" can be reworded to "Now you can enjoy your favorite orchestra anywhere, even at the beach."

Many people get wrapped up posing questions in headlines. The reason is that using a question gives them the opportunity to present the answer, and the answer usually is what the writer wants to communicate. Turn it around. Answer the question you want to ask, and then you never have to ask the question and risk losing readers.

Or...

Be cagey about questions in two ways:

1. Ask a question that forces the prospect to read further to get the answer.

EXAMPLE:

My first headline for Clinic Management Associates, a St. Petersburg chiropractic advisory organization that gave chiropractors ads and mailings to solicit new patients, was "Does your daughter have scoliosis?" The reader could easily say "no" or "I don't know" and toss the mailing. So I rewrote it: "What would you say to your daughter if she has scoliosis?" That forced the reader to find the answer in the body copy. And that headline worked very well in ads and mailings for several years.

2. Ask a group of questions that enable the prospect to "keep score" on how he answers.

EXAMPLE:

"You have authorized the use of all these business machines. How many of them can you name?" That was my opening headline for Four-Star Associates, a Long Island printing and mailing service on a business-to-business mailing sent to buyers of direct mail services. It worked like a charm as readers viewed machinery, played the game of identifying it, and then had to check further to see if they were correct.

236 — SUBHEADS

Subheadlines are a direct function of the soft flow of copy.

Your subheads can tell an entire story, if read in a series. Try it.

237 — NEW POINTS

Try using subheads to mention new points coming up in the copy that follows, rather than merely using them to break up dull columns of text in a brochure.

238 — SERIOUS SUBHEADS

Resist the temptation to use humorous subheads.

Here are some samples of poor subhead use by a New Jersey photofinisher: "the envelope, please.".."pat-on-the-back department.".."the last word."

Those subheads may not appear humorous to all your readers, and humor does not serve your purpose anyway. Subheads are to be used to flag attention and convey information, making the reader want to learn more about your deal.

239 — FRONT AND BACK COVERS

Remember that a catalog, a booklet, many brochures and self-mailers, and certain other formats have front and back covers.

You cannot predict whether the

front or back will be the first page spotted by the recipient. Therefore, a strong enticing heading must be on each "face."

240 — PENSCRIPT

In consumer mailings, you may try penscript (simulated handwriting) as an effective headline technique to get away from the normal typeset appearance.

Recipients view penscript as a slightly warmer and more personal presentation. But be sure that the color you use for the penscript headline matches the signature.

241 — LUMPING THEM TOGETHER

If you have several product or service benefits, try lumping them together under a single headline using the number of such benefits as the attention getter, such as "6 ways to use our telescoping fishing rod," "16 reasons why it will pay you to read *Today's Health*, "4 advantages you get with a zinc mold."

This technique may sound corny to you. It isn't.

People just love to follow numbers. And, using numbers magnifies the total benefits you're offering. It also gives you a chance to write strong, bulleted copy that becomes exciting in its graphic presentation.

It has worked for me with *Good Housekeeping* to consumers, Trans-World Airlines to businesspeople, Sequoia Cleaning Services to institutions, and *The Practice Builder* to professionals. In fact, this headline concept is so strong that you would do well to take your current control mailing as Code A, rewrite the main headline as I've suggested under Code B, and split-run A against B.

Quickly, it can make money for you.

242 — A WIDE CHOICE

If you are offering more than one product, service or publication, do not be afraid to say in a headline that your material offers "a wide choice," or "an unusually complete offering."

Copy stressing the magnitude of your offer is impressive and tells the reader he should spend more time reviewing your literature.

243 — TWO IN ONE

Combining two unconnected but recognized facts or ideas into one totally new concept often induces people to read.

Thus, you can consider using two or more vital selling points in one main headline.

244 — TEASER HEADLINES

If you use teaser headline concepts on your outgoing envelopes, don't forget to stop the message before you give away too much of the presentation.

A teaser should not spill all the beans. That's reserved for the response command approach.

245 — TWO-WAY HEADLINES

Use different headlines that present more than one benefit on both sides of your self-mailer.

Remember that in a stack of incoming mail, you cannot tell whether your prospect sees the front or back. Both sides should have a forceful, but somewhat different, attention getter.

Since self-mailer readers scan your piece, additional benefits can lead them to read on.

246 — TERSE TEASER

When using self-mailers, if you do not have a large format, the address side should contain a brief, tersely-worded teaser headline that identifies your prospect, your product, and your offer, and tells the recipient to read on.

247 — HEADLINE REWRITING

The most appealing copy theme in your mailing should not only be presented in a headline on your letter, but also in a different headline on your outgoing envelope, and a different headline on your main insert.

But don't use the exact same words in those three positions. Rewrite that major headline making the same promises.

248 — REPEATING THE MESSAGE

The copy you use in your headlines should be restated in the body of your direct mail letter — frequently. You are using a letter, aren't you?

You've already selected the most appealing copy theme for the headline, and that's why it should be repeated in your body copy. It appeals.

Also, restating it in body copy reminds the prospect why he wants to continue reading.

249 — VARYING THE LETTERHEAD

Sometimes letterheads get in the way of more important sales messages. This can be especially true if the reader knows who you are by virtue of the outside envelope.

So try moving the letterhead to the bottom of the letter, or to the extreme upper right corner (making it small), so the sales headline is the first thing that grabs the reader's attention.

250 — NUMBERS AS NUMERALS

Try using numbers in numeric rather than alphabetic presentation in your headlines. They are easier to grasp and more familiar, especially if you are using large numbers.

Forty-two is harder to read than 42 and slows the reader from getting to the rest of the message.

CHAPTER 6

ENVELOPES

When I was a little boy, my mother always wanted to make sure that I looked my best when I left the house. As all mothers do, Mom had a reason: "People judge you by their first impression."

Your outgoing envelope is your first impression on me.

How will it look? What ideas or feelings will it evoke?

It could convey quality, or authority, or imply that a great bargain is inside, or alert your reader to information, or create a feeling of urgency...or, it could do all of those things at once.

Pick one, René?

Urgency. If my choice is limited to one impression, it will always be urgency. Without a feeling of urgency, people tend to set things aside. But you're not limited to urgency. You're not limited to anything, if you're willing to pay the cost.

Where you may frequently limit yourself is in thinking. I recall being flown to a large factory in Detroit. Several executives proudly displayed their business-to-business mailings. All the envelopes were the same. Why, I asked? "Because we order them 100,000 at a time to save money, and

besides, everyone recognizes our envelopes."

It took quite a while to convince those executives to go to the expense of designing additional envelopes. They thought sameness was appropriate. It isn't. If my feeling is "deja vu," you've lost me.

> **Design your envelopes so that each is appropriate to the message the contents deliver. Alternate envelopes in your regular series of business-to-business communications so executives don't feel they've already seen your new message.**

And please do remember that envelopes, like all other elements in direct mail marketing, should be tested. What you like may not be what your audience likes.

251 — FALL IN LOVE WITH WINDOWS

In tests conducted for several clients in dozens of fields of marketing endeavors, I have successfully proved that most of the time a window envelope significantly outpulls a closed face envelope.

Take your current borderline or successful mailing and make no change other than putting the prospect's name and address inside the package to show through a window, and then test that version against the previous version. Readership and response should increase when you use a window.

The exceptions to this guideline are:

1. Using matched addressing on the outside and inside of a mailing will outpull a window envelope, and
2. A personalized mailing with a typed outgoing envelope will outpull a window envelope. However, the reply form should also be personalized for this to work most effectively.

252 — ENGAGING ENVELOPES

Make envelopes attractive, exciting, inviting to open.

The envelope is your opening gambit, your salesman, your initial impression, your goodwill ambassador. Except for high-level CEO-to-CEO communications or those promotions which must appear to simulate stock brokerage boredom, your envelope is your outer garment. People form conclusions about new people they meet based on outer garments.

Make yours look distinctive, pleasing, enticing.

253 — ONE LINE BLURBS

If you are enclosing various vital materials in a direct mail package, try listing them with one-line blurbs on the envelope to tell the reader how important they are, and to get him to open the envelope quickly.

254 — UMBRELLA COPY

If you have a wide variety of offers, use your outgoing envelopes to focus attention on that variety, perhaps listing several of the special offers in the package, but definitely using exciting "umbrella" copy and intriguing design to stimulate interest.

Umbrella copy consists of a strong, summary lead line — like "How to save money on everything you make at home" — followed by a bulleted or indented listing of the special offers inside the envelope.

For instance:
- Save $4.62 on your next cuddly bear,
- Save $16.98 on your holiday dinner,
- Save $13.36 on your macrame supplies.

Frequently, I follow such a listing with a "total," like "Save a total of $34.96 almost instantly, just by opening this envelope now and using the money-saving coupons inside."

Reread the last headline example. You'll discover that it contains two commands: opening and using. Why not use more than one command on an envelope?

255 — EXTRA WINDOWS

If you have a full-color brochure, try using an extra window or several extra windows on your envelope so that part of the message shows through. The brochure will work twice as hard for you if it's intriguing to the recipient immediately upon arrival.

My cardinal guideline in all of direct mail is: "If one works, try two." Thus, a double-guarantee is stronger than a single guarantee, a two-para-

Illustration #22

These 6x9 envelopes are two examples of how the author uses technique #255 with double windows. Family Food Garden magazine (top) was launched with this promotion. National Investors Life Insurance (bottom) used this mailing to sell mortgage protection life insurance direct to homeowners.

How-to $4.97

NOW THERE'S HELP...
✳ expert advice
✳ timely tips and ideas
...FOR THE GARDEN YOU GROW

BULK
RATE
U.S.
POSTAGE
PAID
THE WEBB
COMPANY

It's The Family **Food Garden** and the next issue is YOURS FREE
PLUS...
your choice of valuable
28-page garden booklets...
SEE INSIDE...

FF-250

It's your home...and it's wonderful and warm...

but it's your family's home too...and one day you may not be around to pay the mortgage.

If that should happen soon, you wouldn't want your family to be forced to move from the home you struggled to provide...you wouldn't want those you love to be faced with a crisis about their home.

YOU can prevent that crisis by sending for this FREE 16 page report that shows you how you can protect those you love without investing even a penny to get facts you need...

SINCE
YOU
ARE
A
HOMEOWNER

NATIONAL INVESTORS LIFE
Second and Broadway, Little Rock, AR 72201

BULK RATE
U.S. POSTAGE
PAID
NATIONAL
INVESTORS LIFE

SPECIAL LETTER inside for:

04486965   D ADBB
MR R G DAVIS
2713 HENRY DR
IRVING TX   75062

MAIL YOUR FREE INFORMATION CARD INSIDE...
DON'T WAIT...

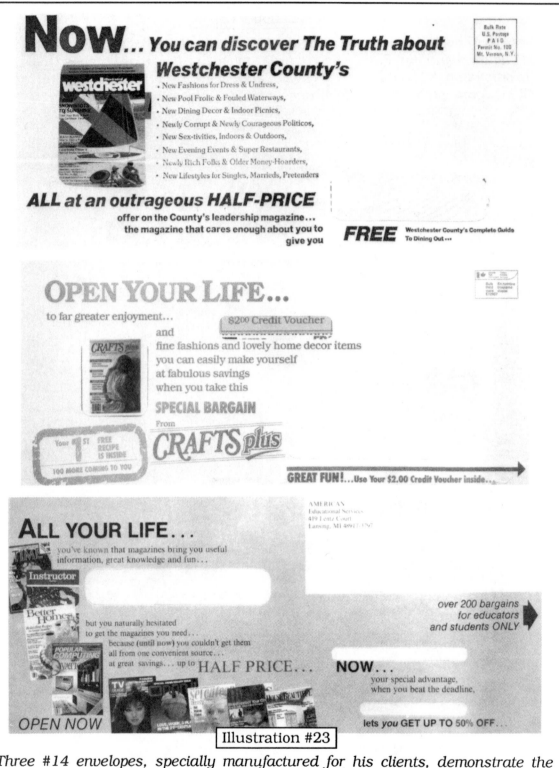

Illustration #23

Three #14 envelopes, specially manufactured for his clients, demonstrate the author's open layouts with multiple windows, technique #255.

Top: two windows were used on the launch of Westchester Illustrated *magazine.*

Middle: three windows dramatized the credit voucher for Crafts Plus *in Canada.*

Bottom: four windows emphasized savings, a certificate, and the deadline date for American Educational Services on the control mailing to students and teachers.

graph postscript gets more action than a single paragraph in that position, a mailing with two letters outpulls a mailing with a single letter.

Similarly, in creating envelopes, two windows usually get more attention and response than a single window. And, why not use windows on both sides of the envelopes. I did for the Rochester Museum of Science and Industry — in a fund raising mailing! — and it was an all-time winner.

Okay, René, how many windows can you have on an envelope?

Gee, I don't know. I used one for *School Arts Magazine*. It worked, so the next time I used two. They worked, so the third time I tried for 13. The client said that was too expensive. We settled for 4 windows, but one of them had 11 photos showing through! Yes, it paid off.

Your imagination and creativity are unlimited in direct mail. I said that somewhere else in this book, but it's worth repeating when you create envelopes.

Use that imagination. Use that creativity. Otherwise, your envelope may never be opened.

256 — ADDRESS CORRECTION REQUESTED

Placing the words "address correction requested" immediately above the recipient's address on your mailing piece calls attention to the fact that you consider the recipient's name and address important. If he thinks you feel he's important, he's more likely to read what's inside.

Sure, the Post Office recommends that those words — used to signal their sleepy people that you want a bulk mailing piece back with a correct address — be placed immediately below the return address.

But there's no regulation against

placing them above the recipient's address. And in that position, those three signal words are easier read by postal people, in addition to the new value they give to your mailing.

257 — COMPANY ANONYMITY

In mailing to prospects rather than inquirers or customers, if you absolutely must use your name, logo, and address on the outgoing envelope (and there is little reason to suspect that you absolutely must), make certain that the use of such material assists your reader in making a decision to open your envelope.

If the reader doesn't know who you are, or if he was offended by some promotion or other exposure to you in the past, emblazoning your name, logo, and address (known as a "corner card") on the envelope may serve to turn him away from your proposition.

What, René, eliminate MY company identification?

Sure! All those mailings I did for *School Arts Magazine*? None had a logo, company name, publication name, or address on the outgoing envelopes. You're not selling logos, names or addresses, are you? Why start the reader off with something he/she is not interested in?

Okay, what's the postal law?

The law, properly called a "regulation," is that the only time you have to use your identification on an outgoing envelope is if your mailing is dispatched at the special rates designated for fund raisers.

258 — PENSCRIPT CORNER CARD

In considering ways to make outgoing envelopes appear more personal, try using a penscript corner card with no other printing on the envelope face.

One more question, René. Why do you use the words "corner card"?

Many years ago, way before my dad met the lady who became my mother, most businesspeople were very cheap when it came to printing expenses. So they took their business cards and told the printer to reproduce the same material on their envelopes. Thus, it became a card in the corner, or a "corner card." It saved them a few pennies in typesetting and design cost.

The term "corner card" has since evolved to mean any use of your company name and address in the upper left corner of an envelope or shipping label.

259 — TYPEWRITER TYPE

A good technique to give more warmth to outgoing envelopes is to use typewriter type for the corner card because it has the added advantage of signaling the recipient that a letter is enclosed.

A variation of this is to use normal typesetting and logo art for your identification material, but position above it the name of the signer of the letter in typewriter type. This gives the appearance of a business communication that comes personally from an individual. Many business-to-business mailings use this technique to go beyond the impression of advertising mail.

Can you use it even if you have a headline on your envelope?

Of course. Iroquois Products does it in selling floor mats to offices. I've done it in promoting zinc dies to OEMs.

260 — POINTED VERSUS ROUNDED FLAP

Remember the difference between a pointed flap and a rounded flap on the back of your outgoing envelope. Such silliness, eh? Not so, there's an important point here:

The rounded flap is regarded by the reader as a standard "commercial" look.

The pointed flap gives your mailing the appearance of a personal communication because the pointed flap is the style used for invitations, party announcements, and greeting cards.

So if you desire a more personal look to your direct mail, consider the pointed flap. Square and rectangular flaps also resemble invitations.

261 — COLOR CHANGE

If you have just received highly favorable returns from a mailing, try sending the exact same mailing piece to a test quantity of the exact same list, changing only the color of the outgoing envelope so that the promotion appears to be something new.

Of course, you'll delete those who responded the first time. Your goal is to avoid a "deja vu" feeling. Those who didn't react favorably the first time may do so now.

262 — MAILGRAM AND TELEGRAM

It is perfectly okay to use simulated "Mailgram" and "Telegram" formats in your direct mail as long as you do not copy Western Union. Those are trademarked formats. Plagiarizing is an invitation to a lawsuit.

Instead, use a distinctive, originally-created design containing the same urgency effect. You can send your computer tapes or floppy disks to one of several suppliers of these unique formats to produce fully-personalized urgent envelopes and letters. Or, you can design your own.

And, you can vary the Western Union concept by creating the envelope to look like a simulated "gram," but let the letter look like a letter.

263 — WESTERN UNION MAILGRAM

You can use a Western Union Mailgram for incoming purposes as well as outgoing.

Test a business reply envelope or business reply card format on subscription renewal campaigns, insurance offers, retirement plans, and other promotions requiring a yes or no decision.

Again, there are other suppliers. Again, you can design your own.

264 — TAX DEDUCTIBLE

If your product or service is tax deductible, try saying so on the back flap of the outgoing envelope with copy like this:

"Important tax deduction information enclosed!"

265 — LEFTOVER BLANK ENVELOPES

For very small quantity mailings, perhaps 5,000 or under, it frequently pays to check with your envelope manufacturer to determine if he has leftover blank envelopes from another customer's order.

Frequently, these "leftovers" are of an unusual size or contain unusual window placement. A good direct mail designer can fashion your small-quantity promotion to fit the envelope manufacturer's "leftovers." The manufacturer is frequently delighted to sell you the "leftovers" at a ridiculously low price because he can't sell them elsewhere and doesn't want to pay to have them carted off for scrap.

But, René, will the mailing work if I do this?

Well, that depends on your creativity, the offer, and the lists you're using. I've done it successfully for several clients and also taken advantage of these savings for my own promotions.

266 — FIRST-CLASS MAIL

If you're mailing first class, say so on the envelope with the words "first class mail."

Why not tell your prospects that you consider your offer so valuable that it merits first-class treatment?

267 — VARIED ENVELOPES

Varying the size of envelopes you use can be particularly effective if you constantly promote to the same audience. Also consider varying ink colors, envelope layouts, and graphics.

This point is especially important when you have a series of mailings to send to the exact same universe, like subscription or insurance or membership renewals, or like an ongoing business-to-business promotion.

268 — DEADLINE DATE

If your promotion has a deadline or cutoff date, stress that urgency on your outgoing envelope with such copy as: "deadline material enclosed," or "response by January 15 is mandatory if you wish to participate."

What, René, a deadline on an envelope? How insulting?

No, not insulting. No one says you have to use 96-point Helvetica Bold Extended. This can be done tastefully. I used 10 point Century Schoolbook for *Physicians Management* magazine.

The concept is urgency (more on that in the copy chapter of this volume). Urgency always works well with consumer and professional audiences, giving people a push toward reading and responding now instead of setting your mailing aside for future reading. Future reading never gets read.

And for business audiences, René?

Of course! Here's where urgency is absolutely vital on an envelope. If you don't use a deadline, at least use copy that implies urgency. Otherwise, your communication winds up in a pile of materials on a desk and never gets read. Or, worse yet, if it doesn't look important, a secretary or assistant may use "file 13."

269 — BLANK ENVELOPES?

Don't forget to test totally blank outgoing envelopes. They arouse curiosity as to the sender and are highly likely to be opened, especially if metered or carrying a live stamp and typewriter address.

Okay, René, how about doing this with a commemorative stamp?

Yes, you can. The general guideline is that a commemorative stamp only slightly outpulls a non-commemorative stamp, but usually costs a bit more to mechanically affix.

Do you use commemoratives, René?

When they're appropriate, sometimes. Rarely.

270 — COZY CUSTOMERS

Many mailers make the mistake of thinking that an outgoing envelope without any copy will always get a lot of curiosity and thus be opened more rapidly.

Sometimes this is true (though it

must be tested for your specific offer) on prospect mailings, but not for current customer promotions. Current customers have established a rapport and a relationship with you. Use your own name and address on the envelope, at the very least as a warm greeting to them. The exception, as already stated, is when sending a series of mailings.

271 — TESTING ENVELOPE SIZES

When promoting to consumers rather than to business addresses, think about testing envelopes in several sizes.

The #10 envelope we all love is commonly recognized as a business format and is frequently viewed as "advertising mail." Many other envelope sizes are available and should be tested.

272 — ENVELOPE CONVERSION

When printing in large quantities, your envelope may be printed on a flat sheet and then converted into an envelope.

If so, you can print on the front and back of the envelope at the same time — and at no extra cost!

273 — TEST ENVELOPES

Try testing an envelope with no printing whatsoever, against an envelope with merely your corner card, against an envelope with a teaser headline, against an envelope with full-blown pitch copy.

Expensive, René?

Yes, but then you'll know which works best for your mailing.

274 — THE FLAT SIDE

Consider using the flap side of your envelope as the side for your address label or window so that the flat side of the envelope can be used for much greater promotion display.

Oh no, René, couldn't this make our company look silly?

Well, maybe, maybe not. But I've done it with super success to business audiences for Four-Star Associates on Long Island, to consumer audiences for South Central Bell Telephone in Birmingham, to institutional audiences for Don Feltner Photography in a Denver suburb, and to professional audiences for International Capital Management in an Orlando suburb.

The point, as I hinted earlier in this book, is that my thoughts and good taste, your thoughts and your good tastes, your management's thoughts and good tastes, are not quite as important as your reader's response. In short, corporate presentation is not as important as corporate profitability.

No, I don't want your organization to appear foolish or less wonderful than it is. But, this book is intended to help you get the maximum value for your advertising dollar. This particular technique opens a world of display possibilities for you. If Bob Stone can use it for Lanier Business Machines, if Jim Kobs can use it for Illinois Bell Telephone, if René Gnam can use it for a variety of clients, it may pay for you to consider it as a method of getting your reader involved with your mailing at the first moment that he holds your envelope in his hands.

275 — SPLIT GUM

Never use full gum on envelope flaps. It may make them too difficult to open and deter readership of the contents. Instead, use split gum.

What's split gum?

Small areas of gum, usually three

on a #10, that do not cover the entire sealing area of an envelope flap.

276 — UNUSUAL STANDARD DIES

Ask your envelope manufacturer which in-stock window dies are unusual and would not add to your promotion cost.

Often you can have circles, octagons, ovals, or other infrequently-used window shapes to dramatize a copy point or illustration on the inside materials.

Every envelope manufacturer has certain standard dies. And all envelope manufacturers have a variety of special dies that they've made for special envelope designs for other clients. When you can use some of these unusual shapes, you add a dimension of uniqueness to your promotion.

EXAMPLE:

I designed a tilted, rectangular window for a promotion for *Radio-Electronics Magazine*. Then, *Nurse's Drug Alert* was able to adapt the same die for its mailing.

277 — POLY WINDOW ENVELOPES

Open window envelopes and window envelopes utilizing glassine present a junky appearance.

When using window envelopes request "poly" or "cello" or "film-vu" materials which give a clearer view of the inside label or inside artwork. They also appear more classy.

278 — INCONSPICUOUS SIZES

No one says you have to use a #10 outgoing envelope simply because that's the most popular standard size available in America.

Smaller and larger sizes stand out when the mail arrives. You should strongly consider using sizes that do stand out and thereby call attention to your wonderful proposition.

279 — STANDARD ENVELOPES?

Be selective in your use of standard envelopes. Everyone knows that a 6 x 9 envelope is the usual oversized outgoing envelope when trying to be distinctive from the plethora of #10 outgoing envelopes.

But, did you know that a 6-1/2 x 9-1/2 also is a standard manufactured envelope and costs only a few pennies per thousand more, while giving you distinction in the incoming mail? Similarly, there are dozens of other "standard" size envelopes that can be used so your promotions stand out.

280 — PERSONAL INTEREST

To indicate that you take personal interest in each subscriber or customer or prospect, use the name of the signer of the letter on the reply envelope.

281 — NAME OF SIGNER

If you are using the name of the signer of the letter on the business reply envelope, consider adding the following copy to your letter: "Use the envelope I've enclosed to send your order directly to my attention. I'll be looking for it."

282 — EMPTY BUSINESS REPLY ENVELOPES

Ann Landers and Dear Abby columns, in summer 1986, told readers to send back empty business reply envelopes to direct mailers who had sent them promotions they didn't want. Besides recommending something that is totally against postal regulations (someone doing this can be fined!), those sisters apparently did not realize that all the newspapers running their columns use direct mail for frequent promotions.

But we must recognize that some columnists harbor a feeling of resentment about direct mail. Most likely, that's because our advertising mail is measurable in terms of response, but most newspaper advertising isn't. A newspaper would be totally embarrassed if it had to prove the dollar-for-dollar ROI of your ad. Direct mail is easily measured and far more cost-effective than most newspaper advertising.

However, if you've had a large influx of empty business reply envelopes, you can reduce the misuse of those envelopes. Consider imprinting the back flap with a legend that says: "It is a Federal offense to use a business reply envelope for any purpose other than intended." It is.

But, be cautious. This copy may deter response.

283 — SPECIAL OFFER

Try using the back of your reply envelopes to print a special offer contained in your promotion mailing.

EXAMPLE:

If you're selling sets of books in the mailing, try selling an individual title on the order envelope.

284 — STAMPED REPLY ENVELOPES

If you use a reply envelope, test business reply versus having the consumer affix his own stamp versus a reply envelope with a live stamp.

Which usually pulls better, René?

The stamped reply envelope nearly always pulls better because the stamp is a signal that the recipient is supposed to do something with the reply envelope. Yes, it's costlier, far more costly.

But it pulls significantly better. Test it on a small panel of names from a list you know works well. Use an A/B/C split for this technique alone.

René, to reduce the cost of affixing stamps, could I try this with a meter impression on the reply envelope?

Yes. It works fine for business audiences, but you're only saving a tiny amount of money since you must pay for the meter impressions just as though they were stamps. And, don't try this for consumer audiences! And, remember: Stamps outpull meter.

285 — BACK OF REPLY ENVELOPE

If a printed reply envelope has proven itself successful, try printing on the back of it.

The back of a reply envelope is a good place for lovely endorsements and testimonials that aver how good

Illustration #24

Two examples of unusual envelope treatment by clients in Sweden are illustrated to show how many techniques are adaptable in many markets.

Top: This is the front of a reply envelope from Svarsforsandelse, a film processor.

Bottom: Student Services A/B uses Gnam's techniques #283 and #285 with a lot of flair on the back of an outgoing envelope.

your product or service or publication is. This is a spot very close to the final decision on the order, and your reinforcement copy may go a long way toward increasing response.

286 — SEAMY IMPRESSIONS

When you print on the back of any envelope, be careful with the seams.

Seams are no problem when printing on flat sheets or web presses and then converting to envelopes. But if you print on ready-made envelopes, reproduction material going over the seams may blur, fade out, gain too heavy an ink impression, or otherwise look very sloppy.

Caution is your guideline.

287 — REPLY ENVELOPE ADVERTISING

Some department stores and other retailers will permit you to give them, at no charge, a business reply or reply envelope for their statement mailings and allow you to advertise your item(s) on the back of that envelope.

Sometimes, they won't rent their lists to you, but you can reach their customers by offering them this terrific saving that costs you far less than doing a solo mailing.

You're right, a solo mailing would outpull the inserted envelope, but if you can't get at those names in any other fashion, this could be your route.

Usually, your merchandise must be charged through the store by the purchaser. But that's okay. You've gotten new orders!

Try it with a wallet-flap for greater display area.

288 — RUSH ORDER

You can impart greater urgency to your mailings if your reply envelopes use this copy: "Rush! Order Enclosed."

That's one example. You can also invent your own copy. Just recognize that the Post Office permits you to do almost anything you want with the upper left corner of a reply envelope. So, I'd like to urge you to consider using the space that's available to you for copy that steers your respondent to reply.

Remember this: you can't control which insert I see first. It may be that reply envelope. If so, that copy could suggest that I do something.

289 — SPLIT-RUN TESTING

Some publishers — but only a few — are now discovering that they do not significantly reduce their renewal response by eliminating the business reply privilege from their in-bound envelopes.

Test it on a split run and determine if you can make this saving. Don't do it with catalog bind-ins or blow-ins.

290 — FIRST-CLASS TREATMENT

Did you know that many consumers affix first class stamps to business reply envelopes because they do not realize that business reply is first class mail? They want to speed up delivery to you.

Nice thought, isn't it? Go into your mailroom and see if this is happening with your response.

If so, try using the words "First Class Mail" in the upper left corner on your business reply envelopes (in relatively small type) and thereby remind your prospects that you provide first class treatment.

At the same time, consider making your envelope look first class!

CHAPTER 7

ORDER FORMS

René, which component should you create first when doing an envelope mailing?

The answer is this: create the reply form first, but produce the envelopes first because of their long delivery times.

When you create a mailing, the reply form frequently is the make-or-break component. It is your action device, whether it is a lead request card or an actual order form. It is true that the outgoing envelope often determines whether I will or will not open and read. But the reply form is my final decision-maker. Thus, concentrate most of your initial creative effort on the reply form.

To be successful, a good reply form may contain all the items I am about to list for you. And, since you should have an easy-to-use reply form, its copy and its design should determine the size of the outgoing envelope. If you try to cram all of these elements into a small reply form, so it fits your preconceived envelope notion, it may not be easy to use, and thus, you may not get a reply.

When you write your reply form, also called a "response device," you should consider including these elements:

1. A HEADLINE promising your reader a benefit. Your headline can be either...

    A. A commanding headline which says something like:

        "Mail this card for your Free Trial of the new Geronimo Grinding Tool that slashes your work hours and improves your efficiency."

                or

    B. An affirmative statement which says something like:

        "Yes, I accept your one-time offer to save money on Business Safety Products so we can improve our factory's OSHA rating."

2. OPTION BOXES. You must present me with at least two options (see No. 303). You may have many more than two.

3. AFFIRMATIVE WORDING in your option boxes.

EXAMPLES:

❏ Send me 67 software programs for only 19 cents.

❏ Send me 14 issues for the price of 12...so I can save $24.00 from your regular price.

4. PAYMENT TERMS, or NO PAYMENT TERMS, or BOTH. If I'm going to pay something, now or later, you must say so. Say it clearly, defining the full terms of your offer and the commitments the purchaser must make. If I don't have to pay, say so in a manner that clearly states I have no obligation. If you present a choice of "free literature" or an order, both of those situations must be fully and clearly explained.

5. PAYMENT OPTIONS, which don't apply to sales lead mailings. But, if you ask for payment, your copy must present a total picture of HOW I can pay:

● all of it up front...
● partial down payment...
● bill me later...
● credit cards...which ones...
● installment plans...
● automatic bank charge.

6. HOW TO ORDER COPY, instructions on how to use the reply form. Even on a request for an inquiry, tell me how to make my request:

"Mail this card now...and you will receive our new 43,000-page full-color catalog of upholstered seat covers for your new 747."

7. DEADLINE COPY, or copy that indicates how long you will allow me to respond to this specific offer.

8. YOUR COMPANY NAME & ADDRESS. I don't know why, but many mailers forget to put their own address information on a reply form.

9. YOUR PRODUCT PHOTO, or some other visual presentation that shows me what I get when I respond, even if it's just a free booklet, but especially if I have to pay something.

10. PREMIUM COPY, perhaps accompanied by a premium photo, telling me how valuable it will be to me, describing it, pointing out that it's only included under certain terms, perhaps telling me that I can keep it even if I cancel my order.

11. CANCELLATION PRIVILEGE, or NO OBLIGATION PRIVILEGE, or BOTH. Can I get a refund? How much ... when ... how do I get it ... can I cancel after trying... must I keep what I order ... do I have an obligation ... don't I? Your reply form copy must clarify all of this.

12. AN INVOLVEMENT DEVICE, maybe a token or a stamp...or maybe something as simple as an instruction to verify and correct my name and address.

And, of course, there must be space for my name and address, plus, perhaps:

- gift ordering information,
- a choice of regular versus deluxe models,
- a choice of long-term or short-term deals,
- a choice of premiums,
- sufficient copy and space to order more than one unit, or more than one product, or request literature on more than one item, or request a salesperson's visit.

And when you put all that together, you quickly recognize that you need space for all of it. That's why you create your reply form first. Also:

> **If you write your reply form copy first — since it's very difficult copy to write — it helps you form your COPY PLATFORM and HEADLINE TECHNIQUES for the rest of the components in your mailings.**
>
> **After you have written your reply form copy, the rest of the mailing seems to go so much easier. And you'll find that headlines and copy points spring from your reply form copy.**

Try it that way. Reply form copy first. See if I'm right. I am.

291 — PRE-ADDRESSED ORDER FORMS

Pre-addressed order forms — by typing, direct computer imprint, word processor, ink jet imaging, laser printing, plates, or label affixing — with the name and address of the recipient showing through a window in the outgoing envelope, will nearly always outpull addressing on the outside of the envelope.

Why, René?

Because you create a mystery as to "What's inside?" and "What's inside with my name on it?" That's why I often try to dramatize an address area or person's name.

292 — ORDER FORMS

Except for very rare direct mail occasions, usually the mere act of including a response card or order form, even when you do not expect a response to come back by mail, increases your readership and/or returns because the response device triggers the recipient to the fact that a decision is required.

René, when wouldn't you be asking for response?

1. When you want to disseminate information, as with catalog sheets to be placed in a loose-leaf binder.
2. When you send info sheets to "participating dealers."
3. When you advise clients or customers of new staff people.

Lots of times.

293 — ACCEPTANCE OR REJECTION

On your order form, merely indicating the items being offered and their prices is not sufficient to produce response.

Doing that creates an "acceptance or rejection" situation.

To be effective, you should communicate some benefits to stimulate action. That action might mean going back to the rest of the package to read, going back to a specific component, or it could mean responding.

294 — ACCEPTANCE STATEMENT?

You should always consider using an acceptance or affirmation statement on your order forms. It should be in fairly large type, written as though the respondent is voicing the words.

"Yes, I accept your offer," "I would like to receive your free kit," and "Please send me," are all examples of acceptance statement openings. By putting this copy in the respondent's words, you automatically start him thinking in an affirmative manner.

295 — KEY BENEFIT

Acceptance or affirmation statements on order forms become more powerful when they include a key benefit to the reader, citing to him the precise reason why he should respond.

Thus, "I accept your special offer to increase my earnings" is stronger than "I accept your special offer."

296 — ONE SIDE DOES IT

Printing order form data and offerings on both sides creates havoc for your fulfillment people.

Everything the respondent must fill in, or mark, should be on the main side of the reply form.

297 — SUPPORTIVE ITEMS

The back of an order form should be used only for supportive items, not main pitches on the proposition you

These reproductions are of the stub, technique #301, for the Furniture/Today *reply card shown on page 87.*

Notice how the montage of magazine covers in the arrow crosses the perforation, techniques #299 and #300.

The panel at the left, containing supportive date, technique #297, folds over the acceptance statement, technique #294, creating intrigue as to "what's under this thing?"

The client reported "tremendous success" with this promotion.

In reviewing the author's design for this order form, note that arrows, slanted copy, and an intriguing fold all guide the reader to places to be checked, marked, or filled in. Additional guidance points are in technique #313.

are propounding, or it should be left blank.

An easy way to remember this guideline is to keep everything pertaining to the deal on the main side.

298 — THE MAIN PITCH

Do not print on the second side of the order form if the material you are going to print will focus attention on something other than your main pitch for action.

299 — ARROWHEAD

In placing a coupon on a sheet wider than the coupon, do not neglect the very bottom next to the coupon, usually to the left of it.

Use it for a reverse with an arrow,

or a subhead with an arrow pointing to the coupon, and use copy such as "use this coupon to order."

300 — EYE FOR ACTION

When using an arrow on the stub of an order form to direct the prospect to the order form, try having the head of the arrow go over the perforation to the most important area of the actual order form.

That will cause the eye to follow the arrow right into action.

301 — ATTACHED STUB

Order forms and reply cards nearly always pull better when there is a stub attached.

The stub creates reader involve-

Technique #295, citing a key benefit, is demonstrated by the paragraph below "YES", and in the copy under the large magazine cover. Note that the author used two tag headlines, technique #302, at the bottom of this card.

ment, draws attention to a restatement of product benefits, and creates interest — often by using exciting, stimulating graphics.

302 — TAG HEADLINE

Order form stubs should always have a tag headline at the bottom to direct the recipient to return the order form.

Otherwise, it's possible for your prospect to be so intrigued by material on the stub that he forgets he's supposed to do something.

303 — EITHER OPTION

Giving a reader an option in a coupon, or on a reply form or other response device, forces him to make a choice between Option 1 and Option 2.

So, if you are selling only a single product at a single price, add another option box for purchasing multiple units. This way your prospect is not faced with a consideration of accepting or rejecting your offer. He must make a choice between offer options.

Options outpull reply forms without options.

304 — OPTIONS AND ORDERS

If you offer multiple options for ordering — such as a one-year or two-year subscription, or a regular or deluxe machine — test using more than one order form and placing each option on a separate order form.

I call this the "hot potato order form." It leaves your prospect with a choice of which order form to return, rather than a choice of ordering or not ordering.

I first invented this technique back in 1972 for *Singles World Magazine*. I put the one-year subscription offer on one card, two years on a second card, and three years on the third reply card. It worked so beautifully that now it has evolved into a "yes, no, maybe" option for many other mailers. Moreover, it can be done with separate order or reply cards, different stickers that the recipient must affix, or even different tokens that the reader is to insert.

No matter how you use it, you are dramatizing your offer and showing your prospect that he makes the decision of which option to accept. People like being in power positions.

305 — OPTION BOX

You can often sell higher priced merchandise, or longer term subscription offers, or greater quantities on your initial mailings as well as on followups to established subscribers or customers.

Therefore, include on your order form an option box for the respondent to order a higher purchase or longer term.

306 — FULL NAME

Almost always ask a respondent to print his or her full name.

Some people have a habit of signing on the line saying "name" and your fulfillment people then go into fits.

307 — ADDRESS CHECK

On any order form that you pre-address, always ask the recipient to double check his or her address for correctness.

Getting your reader involved with his name and address is a good first step in getting him to consider your offer.

And if you get him to pick up a pen to correct his name or address, you've forced his to take the first action toward filling in your order form!

308 — SEX CLARIFICATION

If you are in doubt about the sex of the recipients of your mailing piece (because many single or double initials can be either male or female), do not hesitate to use your order form to ask your recipients to check a box for Mr., another for Mrs., a third for Miss, or a fourth for Ms.

In this fashion, you not only will learn the sex of the recipient, but also the term by which a female respondent wishes herself known on your future mailings.

309 — THE HOW-TO'S

Direct mail selling, especially with products, is so complicated that we frequently forget to tell recipients of our mail precisely how to order, how to fill in the order form, how to select between product options.

While this copy may appear boring to you, it is essential in assisting the reader at the final moment of decision making.

310 — COUPON COPY

All coupon copy must be 100% clearly written, no doubt about it!

Especially concentrate on the copy that defines the terms of commitment that the purchaser must make. Be as clear and as factual as possible, but do not hesitate to include all pertinent facts.

Coupon copy frequently is the copy which makes or breaks the profitability of a direct response promotion.

311 — SIMPLICITY

Make sure your offer is clearly stated and easily understood.

Even a curiosity seeker should be able to grasp the entire essence of your mailing simply by looking at the order form and reading your offer copy. He may order from that form!

312 — NICE AND EASY

Never presume that the person to whom you are mailing wants to order your product or inquire about your services.

Therefore, do make every attempt to make it easy for the recipient of your mail to respond, and give him a reason to do so. Do not clutter his mind at the point of ordering.

313 — TAKING ME BY THE HAND

Just because you have designed a beautiful order form does not mean that I know how to complete it.

Take me by the hand visually and guide me to the essential sections of the order form that require my attention. If your proposition is very complicated, carefully enumerate the steps that I must follow so I can send you my money.

314 — PHONE NUMBERS

Don't be afraid to split test asking your customers to include their phone numbers on the order form, even though (in some instances) this technique depresses response.

Perhaps preface it with a remark concerning your attention to details and the possibility that you may have to telephone to clarify a question on the order. Customers who give you their phone numbers are less likely to cancel their orders.

315 — NON-QUALIFIED LEADS

Asking recipients of your promotions for their telephone numbers will cut down on the number of responses you receive, and that may just be dandy if you're worried about non-qualified leads.

316 — FRIENDS AND NEIGHBORS

Don't forget to suggest to recipients of your mail that they inform their friends and neighbors about the special offer they have received, thus spreading "word of mouth" advertising about your products and services.

This is another good reason for including a second order form in the same mailing.

How many order forms can you have in one mailing, René?

Who knows? Haband, selling clothes and accessories to men from its headquarters in Paterson, NJ, once did a mailing with 38 order forms. Then the Haband marketing manager came to my New York City seminar and asked me how he could get more order forms into the same envelope. He knew that more options, more choices, and more order forms all lead to more sales.

317 — INKING IT OUT

Scold the art director who uses a benday or a panel of ink behind any area on your order form that the respondent must complete.

Felt-tipped pens usually do not write well on such ink surfaces, which will:

1. cause problems for your fulfillment department, and
2. reduce the number of orders you receive, and
3. reduce the quantity of items ordered on each form.

318 — GLOSSY STOCK?

Rarely use glossy stock for your order form.

Many pens will not write on most glossy stock, and you will lose your orders!

Of course, you can varnish the gloss to make writing easier, but that costs more.

319 — DUPLICATE ILLUSTRATIONS

When selling merchandise, try repeating an illustration or photo of the product on the order form so that the customer sees it in front of him at the point of order.

This shows him what he gets when he mails the order form.

320 — LOVELY REMINDERS

Rarely design a sales promotion or direct mail piece so the respondent has to destroy the only product illustration to complete the order or inquiry form. This sometimes happens with self-mailers.

The respondent wants to retain your product illustrations and descriptions as lovely reminders of the intelligent response decision he has made. He also wants to keep them to remind him that you promised to ship.

321 — LOW-COST ITEM OFFER

Frequently, you can increase your dollar volume from a single mailing by offering a very low-cost item along with the main product.

One way to do this is to pitch the main product throughout the mailing and then add the low-priced item only on the order card.

The same concept works the other way around. You could pitch the low-priced item throughout your mailing and add the higher priced item only on the order card.

Now, that won't work, René!

Oh yes, it does! Shortly before he died, consultant Paul Bringe of Hartford, WI, pitched silver service for 6 in the entire mailing, mentioning service for 8 only in the postscript and on the order form. Service for 8 outsold service for 6...10 to 1.

322 — PROSPECT'S COMMITMENT

A good way to increase the convertibility of respondents to your free sample offer is to clearly indicate on your order form that you will ship the balance of the normal quantity if the respondent does not cancel the shipment upon receiving the sample.

Be careful, though, because this also cuts initial response.

But it does something else for you. It makes the prospect think about a commitment, and that is what you want.

323 — RESPONSE DEVICE?

There are instances when it is wrong to include only a reply card with your mailing, primarily when asking for a large pledge of money or any highly personal interaction, such as an appointment for health, religious, or sex counseling.

If you are curious as to whether your mailing should have a response device, think of how you would feel filling one out for such personalized service. Then, if you would not be likely to respond via an order card, include it anyway, but also include a telephone number, a reply envelope, or the suggestion that the reader respond by personal letter — or, all of these response stimulants.

In this instance, you include the card to act as a visual reminder to respond. But most folks then respond by phone.

Such careful consideration worked very well when I designed self-mailers and newspaper ads offering free spinal examinations by chiropractors.

Previous ads had only coupons and previous mailings had only reply cards. I added telephone numbers and the name of a female doctor's assistant to call for an appointment. Response zoomed. Folks felt it was easier to talk to a qualified lady than to mail the card or coupon. Maybe they also felt that postal workers would read the cards.

At any rate, the ads and mailings worked so well that they were syndicated to hundreds of chiropractors. So maybe it would be a good idea for you to consider this courtesy toward your prospective customers.

324 — WALLET-FLAP REPLY ENVELOPES

Wallet-flap reply envelopes reduce package costs by combining an order form with a reply envelope, but they sometimes reduce response when mailing to inquiry lists, prospect lists, and other external non-customer files.

Stay away from combination order form and reply envelope formats, except when mailing to current files of frequent customers or in soliciting donations.

325 — OPEN OPTIONS

On order forms, keep all check boxes (all the options) in one area of the order form.

Then, when the prospect uses it, he can see all available options and perhaps make additional purchases.

326 — COPY FOR QUICK ORDERS

You can increase the speed of acquiring merchandise orders from prospect mail if you use copy along these lines:

"Please give us an alternate choice in the event that the model you have specified is quickly sold out."

This does not always increase the quantity of orders, although it sometimes does. But it usually gets them in faster, and frequently gives you larger orders. When people perceive that what they want is in short supply, they like to stock up.

I fell prey to this too! Yes, me...

I bought a half-dozen khaki "cargo slacks" from Land's End when I only needed two. I have never regretted the purchase because khakis are so comfortable on airplanes. But every time I see so many hanging in my wardrobe, I remember that a smart merchandiser used my own technique on me.

327 — "NO DEALER INQUIRIES PLEASE"

If you are selling specific products by mail or in space ads, using order form copy saying "no dealer inquiries please" will impress prospective customers.

It leads them to believe your merchandise is exceptionally low-priced.

328 — SCALED-DOWN VERSION

Many sophisticated recipients of direct mail promotion go from the envelope to the order form, skipping the brochure and letter entirely.

Make sure a scaled-down but complete version of your offer appears on the order form.

329 — RESTATEMENT OF BENEFITS

Restate your product or service or publication benefits on the order form for the same reason that you restate your offer.

330 — SEPARATELY PRINTED ORDER FORMS

Separately printed order forms usually produce greater response than order forms that are printed as part of another component in the mailing.

Note that I said "usually." I have seen tests go both ways, but more often than not, it's the detached order form that wins.

331 — DISPLAYING YOUR ORDER FORM

Your coupon or order form is a command to respond. It triggers action, telling the reader that you are asking him to do something. Display it prominently and attractively. Don't hide it.

This is a major failing of many large corporations which want all paper stock in a mailing to match. I don't! I want that order form or reply card to stand out like a sore thumb. Yes, I do!

3M tested it, and non-matching paper for the reply card outpulled matching paper by 19.44% to business lists. I tested it for Litton Industries, and the increase in response for non-matching order form paper was 17.42% to consumer lists.

Now, there is a way around this Catch 22 that you find yourself in: management says all paper stock must match "because that's our corporate image," and you want to achieve the highest possible response. What do you do?

Let the paper stock match (so you keep your job). But use the most vibrant ink combinations on the reply card or order form so it still becomes a sore thumb. There is nothing wrong with a gyrating order form. You want people to find it in your mailing.

332 — EXTRA ORDER FORM

Consider printing an extra order form on your brochure as a visual reminder to order.

Why, René? Is that a sufficient reason to use up all that good display space?

Yes, it is. Orders are more important than prettiness. And, I tested this for *Cincinnati Magazine*, mailing to both consumers and business people. Repeating the order form on the brochure greatly increased response.

Why, René?

Because many folks tend to separate materials in a mailing. Often, they'll toss components they don't intend to read or look at a second time. So they retain just the brochure. If there's no order form on it, they can't order when they pick it up a second time.

333 — PASS-ALONG READER

Repeating your order coupon on a brochure gives you a chance of getting a pass-along reader to order.

Ah hah!...if that brochure sits on a desk, credenza or coffee table, someone else may look at it. Don't you have it in your heart to accept an order from someone else?

Sure you do, especially in a business-to-business mailing:

Let's say Marilyn Executive receives the mailing, orders with the order form but retains the brochure for her future reference. A few days later, Harry Executive comes to her office to discuss something. The phone rings. Harry picks up the brochure. Now you now have a chance to get Harry's order.

334 — EXTRA ORDER CARD

To measure pass-along readership of your promotions, use an extra order card or order form in half the quantity of your next mailing.

Use a different code number on both cards in this section of the split and count the orders coming back. This will tell you whether your promo-

tions are being passed on. Try this in both consumer and business mail.

335 — HIGHER PURCHASE

Often you can step up a customer to a higher purchase just by using an extra check box on the order card. In many cases, no mention need be made in the letter or brochure.

The proper wording on the order form can convince your customer to switch to the super deluxe version. Those few lines of type are a minimal expense for maximizing your direct response results.

336 — CREDIT O.K.

If you are using a rented list of mail order buyers for your promotion mailing, why not use the words "credit o.k." on your order card?

You know the credit is okay because your prospects for this mailing have purchased from another company. Telling the prospect that his credit is approved is another way of saying "you're okay and we'd like you to buy from us."

337 — FUTURE SALES POSSIBILITIES

If you want to warm up non-respondents for future sales, include reply form boxes for the non-respondent to check either or both of these choices: "I'm not interested, so take me off your list" or, "I'm not interested now, but keep me on your list."

Many will want to remain on your list, and if you mail to them a few months later and remind them of their choice, your response can be triple or quadruple the number of orders you normally would receive from non-respondents on a prospect list.

Those who want their names deleted can get another mailing asking why and pointing out the advantages of your product or service.

338 — COUPON TRANSITION

The area immediately above a coupon or reply section of an order form should be used to swing the reader from your sales message directly into the coupon.

This can be done effectively by using a small subheading saying something along these lines:

"The fastest way to get your portable computer is to mail this coupon now."

339 — FREE TRIAL CARD

Most reply forms you create should be clearly labeled as such.

You want the reader to know that this piece of paper is his heavenly route to ordering. Use terms like "members' reservation form," "special

Illustration #28

MAIL THIS **Free Seminar Information Card**

MAIL THIS CARD TODAY for free information on the next dates and topics for these René Gnam seminars that give you new ideas and effective techniques to boost your mail advertising response:

☐ FUNDAMENTALS OF DIRECT MAIL
☐ MARKETING PROFESSIONAL SERVICES
☐ SUBSCRIPTION SUMMER SCHOOL
☐ PROJECT CONSULTATION WORKSHOP
☐ NEW PATIENT ACQUISITION SEMINAR
☐ DATABASE MARKETING
☐ DESKTOP PUBLISHING IN MARKETING

Name_____
Company_____
Address_____
City/State/Zip_____
Area Code_____ Phone_____
☐ CHECK HERE for a free copy of René Gnam's Response Review newsletter.

One of the author's reply cards illustrates using technique #339 to imply that the reader wants to take the action you want him to.

discount order form," or "free trial examination card."

You will now be stimulating your reader to respond simply by telling him that he must make a decision.

340 — UNIQUE TERMINOLOGY

When promoting to a strictly professional audience, consider unique terminology such as "experts' evaluation form," "professional review certificate," "accountant's audit program" as order form headings.

Try to appeal to the professional stature of these prospects as a special group in labeling your order forms and in writing your key headlines.

341 — VALUABLE OFFER

Remember that you do not have a coupon or an order form.

You have, for example, a "money-saving order form," or a "special offer coupon," or "a handy one-time offer coupon." The intent is to make your order form and your offer valuable.

342 — MAIL WITHOUT FAIL

If you sell merchandise in different sizes or models, try using copy like this on your order form:

"Please mail today to be sure you receive the size and style you want."

Copy of this nature stresses urgency, implies limited available quantity, and galvanizes a prospect into responding.

343 — TWO-WAY COMMITMENT

Remember that an order form isn't only a commitment by the recipient.

It is also your commitment to the purchaser that you will deliver. Clearly specify delivery time and then live up to it.

CHAPTER 8

COPYWRITING

Saturdays are happy days. My doggies are loose. So am I. I sit down and relax with my morning coffee at the circular dining table in my pool or out in my gazebo. On hot Saturdays, I sometimes take a hike in my forests. On cooler Saturdays, the hike is in my fields, absorbing sunshine and the calls of peacocks and pelicans, herons and hoot owls.

Often, I try to schedule Saturdays for tough copy jobs. No phones. No people. No blueprints. No interruptions. Evenings and all-nighters work well for the same reason. I'll take a hike or a brief swim, sit under a magnolia or a palm, and daydream about that tough copy assignment.

Do you do that?

Why not?

No pool, forests or fields?

Okay, soak yourself in the tub.

But, René, I don't like baths!

Okay, fill your den with Mozart and daydream about your copy.

But, René, I don't like music!

No music in your life, in your heart? No daydreams? No fantasies? I'm sorry. Your copy will suffer.

You need to do something other than write, before you write. And it must be something that allows you to think. Try this:

Take a roast out of the freezer a few hours before you plan to write. While the roast thaws on your butcher block, sit down in an easy chair and review all the information about the project you're about to tackle. Then, take a walk. In your favorite park. Do some thinking while walking.

Come back and start trimming the roast. Think about the copy project while trimming. Slice up some carrots and onions. Think some more. Wash and clean some potatoes and mushrooms. Think again. Put it all in a crock pot or a dutch oven and start it cooking. Don't forget about a quarter-inch of water. Maybe a dash of tamarind, garlic, just a little oregano, rosemary, tarragon, cognac, a drop of bitters, and whatever wine is left over, preferably Bordeaux. You're thinking while you do this, aren't you?

Now, take a quick shower. Return to the kitchen fast. Adjust the flame down to almost off. Run to your word processor. Go to work. Now, baby! Fast, fast, furiously fast. You can. You will. You must!

Don't worry about the roast. It'll be ready when you finish. If your word processor is cooking with steam, turn the roast off on your next trip to bathroom. Not yet. Wait 'til you have to go. Keep cranking that copy out. Rough drafts only. No polish. No editing. No spelling checks. Go, go, GO!

Now, if you've only scanned the above, let me summarize what I've just edited from one of my keynote speeches:

1. Clear your head before you write.
2. Do lots of thinking before you write.
3. Have a warm, open heart as you write.
4. Be in a personally calm, relaxed mood.
5. Write only at a word processor.
6. Do not write in the office.
7. Write rough drafts. Edit later.
8. Write as fast as you possibly can.
9. Allow no interruptions.

You are creating advertising copy to sell. This means you do NOT write to please yourself or your management. You DO write to please the people on your lists. You must be in the proper frame of mind, in tip-top shape, with no worries confronting you, no appointments to interrupt your mind, no cats or kiddies crying, no specter of a big boss hanging over you, no visions of corporate letterheads staring at you in a typewriter.

You must tune yourself in to your audience. That's hard. Often, that means solitude. It means freshness and daring do.

> **When you write, you are creating income for your company. It may be your most important endeavor. You must extract from your mind the unique thoughts and concepts that will convince and persuade. All those precious creations are possible if the atmosphere, environment and mood are right.**

Create the atmosphere. Alter the environment. Encourage the mood.

Write the copy. Write it now. Write it fast.

Then, enjoy the roast with a toast!

Then, edit and polish and refine.

Do it this way just once. It'll be much easier next time.

344 — COMMON COPY FLAW

The most common copy flaw practiced by nonprofessional direct mail and sales promotion writers is to express the view of the organization for which they are writing.

Sorry. Your readers are primarily interested in themselves.

345 — STUDY OF AUDIENCE

The most frequently overlooked aspect of writing sales promotion and direct response copy is a study of the audience prior to putting the first sheet of paper into a typewriter or getting a new screen on a word processor.

Your mail cannot win for you unless you study demographic and psychographic data about the audience you're attacking. This gives you have a "feel" for the individual people on the lists to which you mail. You're after the list's broad and narrow characteristics so you can weave appropriate copy pitches into your promotion.

Only when you have truly acquired a picture of your audience should you consider turning on your writing machine.

346 — MASTER COPY

If your copy has been created by a professional, keep your hands off it!

Edit where necessary to correct errors in product benefit statements, misstated offers, and other factual references. But don't edit for the sake of editing or because you happen to like a phrase that sounds a bit different.

Your professional writer has considered all methods of concocting the phraseology for your response campaign and weighed them carefully before choosing his final presentation of wording.

347 — SOPHISTICATED AUDIENCE

Today's audience for direct response advertising is far more sophisticated than most of us would believe.

Why? Because while there are over 262 million Americans, only about 30 million receive over 75% of all direct mail.

They're wise and they have seen it before, so when you repeat important points, reword and weave in additional benefits or sales points. Make the repetition fresh and meaningful, punctuated by a request for action.

348 — EGO EXERCISE

Do not use committee-authorized or committee-written copy. It is seldom urgent, often conflicting, and frequently dilutes the sales message.

And please, pretty please, do not allow a committee to edit direct mail copy. I am reminded of the time — 13 years before publication of this book — when I wrote a series of five personalized mailings for the Bronx Zoo. Four months after delivering it, I called the curator, Eugene Walter.

"Hello, Gene, may I have some samples of the mailings?"

"Sorry, René, the committee is still editing them."

My assistant called after another four months passed. The committee was still editing.

The committee in this case con-

sisted of 33 high-flying New York corporate board chairmen who were lending their time and expertise to the Zoo. They probably were wonderful in their administrative, managerial, and financial counsel to the Zoo. But any time you give a committee a chance to edit copy, you are asking all the individual committee members to exercise their egos. To this day, I do not know whether Gene ever got those mailings out. Poor guy. He tried so hard to do a proper job. But his hands were tied by the rules of the game he played.

There's another reason to not use committees. Read the next item.

349 — ONE COPYWRITER

Whenever you start to create a mailing, sales literature, or an ad, remember that all of the copy should initially be written by one person, not by a group of collaborators.

It may be edited by several authorities in different divisions of your organization (to check factual points), but the entire initial copy draft should be prepared by a single writer so you achieve uniform copy flow, style, and proper organization leading to response.

350 — SIMPLE MESSAGE

Do not be creative for the sake of creativity, or for the sake of ego. Sparkling creativity in promotion copy does not necessarily mean effectiveness.

The simpler message, that gets to the heart of your sales appeal, may be far more effective than the creative or ego-pleasing approach.

351 — A SLOW DEATH

"No one has ever beaten this promotion letter and therefore no one ever will. I'll stick with it forever."

Sticking with it is a sure way to eventually die a slow death. *Good*

Housekeeping has run its famous "33 ways to save money" letter for over 20 years. Millions are mailed each year. But, to its credit, *Good Housekeeping* still tests several new copy concepts against that control package, and edits into the proven "33 ways" letter new language techniques that are adopted by the majority of Americans, plus proven sales points that have been discovered from the test letters.

I had the good fortune to rewrite one version of that "33 ways" letter. Some of my copy is still in the winning version today. I'm happy about that, but happier still that *Good Housekeeping* knows it should continually test updated versions.

352 — THE COMPLETE STORY

Never start your creative effort with a pre-conceived notion of how long the sales letter is going to be: one page, two pages, four pages, maybe more.

It is harder to write a short letter than a long one. Always write as much as you feel is needed to tell the complete story. Only then rewrite and edit down to shorter space.

Whenever clients ask me how long a letter I'll write for them will be, my answer is: "I won't know until it's done."

353 — ONE-ON-ONE

Never forget that each promotion you send out, even if mailed to millions of prospects on the same day, is being read by only one person at a time.

All your communication is on a one-to-one basis, not one-to-the-masses. Write to an individual and you'll get the mass.

354 — YOUR SUPERIOR PEOPLE

Be sure to use copy that indicates how much care and attention goes into the creation and production of each individual product or the delivery of each service you provide.

Perhaps mention the number of people involved in manufacturing or production, and indicate that they are skilled craftsmen. Or, cite the training of your service personnel.

Attempt to show your prospect that what he purchases, indeed, is a fine product or superior service.

Illustration #29

These are the people you can call with your questions about any order.
They have the experience and knowledge you need to be certain that everything is done right for you!

ART ANNUCCI, Plant Manager
"No order is shipped until I give the okay that it meets our standards for quality," says Annucci, who has over 25 years of binder manufacturing experience. His keen attention to quality details pleases all VIP customers.
Some of Mr. Annucci's responsibilities are: quality control, scheduling production to meet critical deadlines, warehousing, shipping and receiving.

DIANA GAFFNEY, Customer Service Manager
Diana Gaffney double-checks all orders for accuracy and logs them in our processing sequence. She often can assist you with special pricing and has the authority to "flag" your order for faster-than-usual shipment when you need it.
All orders are shipped promptly, some as fast as 24 or 48 hours, but you can always check the status of your order with a call to Mrs. Gaffney. You won't get the excuses you may have grown accustomed to elsewhere. You will get a straight, accurate answer.

TIM FLEMING, Materials Manager
Long-time employee Tim Fleming has special expertise in inspecting raw materials.
He's in charge of buying the highest-quality materials for all components in our binders, portfolios and tabs, often ordering from Europe, but mostly from the USA. His other duties include timeliness of component assemblies and supervision of your shipping dates.

Nationwide: **1-800-874-0855**   In Florida: **1-800-342-8324**

In addition to the recommendations in technique #354, it often pays to highlight specific people within your organization so the reader of your mail knows who's in charge of what aspect of his order. Here's an example created by the author for Vinyl Industrial Products, St. Augustine, FL. Note that the toll-free numbers are included so the customer can call with any questions.

355 — EVERYTHING AND THE TRUTH

When reading your direct mail offer, the recipient is faced with only one decision: to accept or reject that offer!

Therefore, don't short-change the sell copy. Be complete and tell the reader everything he must know to make a valid decision to respond.

356 — HARD-HITTING COPY

Direct mail letter writers know that proper grammar, punctuation, vocabulary, and style of writing are considerations that are automatically discarded in favor of good, hard-hitting selling copy that stresses reasons to purchase, serves a prospect's need, and backs up all claims with proof of product or service value.

To accomplish this extremely difficult task, go ahead and violate textbook idiocies.

357 — EDITORIAL-FREE

Do not editorialize in direct mail or sales promotion unless you are using a newsletter format.

Comments or opinions on the political scene, the economy, an energy crisis, or news events rarely belong in promotions. If you use those editorial comments in a newsletter, make certain they are germane to your audience and the promotional vein you are following.

358 — THE HIGHWAY ROUTE

Mountain trails twist and turn and ramble and roam. Highways go straight to designated cities.

Your promotion message should go straight to the intended prospect, aiming straight at your desired result.

Embellishments belong in tourist brochures.

359 — QUALITY OF LIFE

Consumers today have an increasingly greater and genuine concern with their quality of life.

Using copy which points out how your product, service, or publication eases the difficulties of the reader's life is a good way to get him to say:

"I like that. Maybe I'll buy it."

360 — QUALITY AND SERVICE

While we all are changing our outlooks, horizons, and desires, the good copywriter remembers that old impressions are strong, not easily erased, passed down from generation to generation.

If your copy can concentrate on the "good old impressions" like quality and service, you are appealing to well-established principles that inspire confidence.

361 — STAYING CLEAR OF FEAR

Appeals to fear, like "don't let this happen to you," work poorly if used in conjunction with a really drastic situation that could affect life or limb.

The reader concentrates on thinking about the disaster and doesn't consider your offer.

362 — EXCEPTION TO THE RULE

Appeals to fears — such as not obtaining choice theatre seats, or having to wait in line at the last day of a sale at a retail store — frequently do work well if the names on the list you're using have previously demonstrated interest in your products or services.

363 — EASE AND CONVENIENCE

Many people increasingly dislike going shopping, fighting traffic and crowds, the inconvenience of standing in line at a sales clerk's desk, the incompetence of sales clerks, the awkward embarrassment of buying certain items in a face-to-face retail confrontation.

Capitalize on these attitudes by stressing the ease and convenience of purchasing by mail, and you will improve your response.

364 — GREATER GUARANTEE

Direct response marketers often offer the prospect a greater guarantee than he can get elsewhere.

Say so. And tell him briefly how much easier it is to return or cancel your product or service by mail than by contending with an uninformed, perhaps surly retail clerk.

365 — INDIVIDUAL'S SELF-INTEREST

When you are selling intangibles, such as review courses or newsletters, some of the most potent copy appeals are those which stress the opportunity for the target to "sharpen your skills," "increase your on-the-job productivity," "strengthen your future earnings capacity."

These copy approaches should cater to the individual's self interest in becoming a more valuable employee, acquiring greater wealth, or increasing personal achievement.

366 — COMBINATION COPY BLOWS

It pays to repeat hard-hitting copy blows just as it pays the prizefighter to throw a combination of hard punches.

Remember the old commercial? It didn't say that Colgate cleans your breath "fast." Rather, Colgate cleans your breath, "fast, fast, fast...incredibly fast!"

367 — SELLING JOB

Do not write copy to win awards or impress your boss.

You have a selling job to do.

368 — FORCED COPY

Some folks create sales literature and direct mail because they "have to," not because they enjoy it.

Be careful of that attitude. It creeps into your copy. Your reader will discover it. It can turn your reader off.

369 — TIRED COPY

Do not write sales promotion or direct mail copy when you are tired, after a lover's spat or a horrid financial discussion, immediately following fine wines, or with a full belly.

You must be at your mental and physical peak to write these promotions.

370 — WORRIED COPY

Never try to write direct response copy when you are worried about something else.

Take a break, and then, when worry has diminished, approach your typewriter or word processor.

371 — PLEASANT ENVIRONMENT

Write your promotion copy in an environment that pleases you, rarely in an office that reeks of authority, deadlines, interruptive or loud people.

Having your kind of environment

is a fine way to get yourself "up" for the challenging job that confronts you.

372 — CUTOFF DATE

Urgency is vital to spur response, so always attempt to have a cutoff date, expiration date, deadline date, or other specific time limit for your offer.

373 — TIMELINESS

Timeliness is essential in direct response advertising.

If you cannot include a cutoff date, deadline date, or product fulfillment date in your sales literature, try incorporating timeliness in your copy by stressing future articles, additional products coming up in the future, additional reasons why future use of your product or service will pay off.

374 — READER PERSUASION

Give your reader a valid reason why your urgent copy is urgent, and he will consider your offer today, instead of putting it off for tomorrow and then perhaps never getting to it.

375 — URGENT COPY TIE-IN

Attempt to always have urgent copy married with a deadline, time to reply, cutoff date for merchandise shipment, product fulfillment or closing date.

376 — 30 DAYS ONLY

"This offer is good for 30 days only" is a fine way to stimulate instant reading of your mailing piece and increase response.

But that copy line would be much more effective if you could include an actual deadline date, such as "merchandise will be withdrawn following January 2, 1999."

377 — URGENCY AND BELIEVABILITY

Couple a sale or discount price offer with a cutoff date to instill urgency and believability on the part of the recipient.

This also cautions him that you don't always have reduced prices.

378 — QUICK START AND TEMPO

Airplanes, boats, and automobiles start slowly and then increase their speed as they move toward destinations.

But, direct response and sales promotion copy must start quickly, almost at a crescendo, and maintain the same tempo throughout to hold a reader's interest.

379 — STRESSING SELLING STRATEGIES

Every driving instructor admonishes you to "keep your eyes on the road."

In promotion creativity, focus your attention on selling concepts. Don't allow personal feelings or a personal preference for colors or particular wording to enter your package.

You're after sales from readers, not reader or writer enjoyment.

380 — GIVING A REASON

Always give a reason why I should take the particular action you want me to take.

Simply saying "stock up on uniquely designed pillows" is insufficient. Tell me that the pillows give me greater sleeping comfort and are available at a short-term discount. Telling me why I should do something lets me agree with your reason and thus prompts me to take the action you're after.

381 — NO SLANG

Do you use slang that is peculiar to your industry and might not be understood by your audience? Don't.

A "Norelco-type box" is the tape industry's slang for a hard plastic, hinged box for cassette tapes. Consumers and business folks may not know that Norelco pioneered that particular box. Such phrasing is confusing and unproductive for you.

382 — APPROPRIATE PHRASES

Think of phrases you use the way your audience would understand them.

To you, "a suspicious character" could be someone to stay away from. To a pedantic soul, "a suspicious character" could be a happy fellow with an investigatory mind. Make your phrases appropriate for your specific audiences.

383 — MAKING EVERY WORD COUNT

When editing, eliminate every unnecessary word.

Don't occupy your reader's time with words or phrases that don't assist your purpose.

384 — FRESH PHRASES

Find alternate wording to avoid repetitious use of words or phrases.

That's difficult, eh? Not any more! No more wrestling matches with Roget's. All you need is a few keystrokes on your valiant word processor to access your thesaurus. Marvelous!

But, a caution:

More than one thesaurus resides on my computer systems. Not once did I use them for this book. Using a

thesaurus tends to lead you to day dreams. You have to be quick with it if you expect to get your work done.

An alternate method, strictly for fast writers, is to just type a few X's for the word you can't think of at that moment. Find the word later. But continue writing as fast as you can so you don't lose vital concepts. Your mind has been working ahead of your fingers anyway, and a thesaurus search can pull your thinking in the wrong direction.

385 — SUBTLE SEMANTICS

Certain words have different meanings to different audiences, and the direct response creator must carefully consider those esoteric meanings.

What we call a "fanny" in America isn't a "fanny" in Great Britain. The average middle-class American thinks a "brim" is an edge, but the ghetto-dweller uses "brim" to refer to a hat, not the edge of a hat. Still others consider "brim" in other meanings, like bait fish. Make certain you are using the proper word in its proper context to the proper audience.

386 — NEW WORDS

This nation is gripped by an eagerness to use certain "new" words.

Dynamite! Super! Tough! Way out! Definitely! Really! Awesome!

They are examples.

Before you use the "new" words in your sales promotion or direct response advertising, remember that what you create today is to be used again and again over the course of a thousand tomorrows. How long ago was it that almost everything was "cool"? Not too many things are cool today.

Just ask yourself whether the "new" word in vogue ever makes it to *Harper's Bazaar*!

387 — NOUNS AND VERBS

In most direct mail copy, tons of adjectives and adverbs can be eliminated.

Cut your copy until it is lean and moves people to action.

388 — THE QUICK FIX

Too fancy a phrase in your direct mail copy will attract such attention that it may draw the reader away from your message, causing you to lose your chance for a sale.

I am reminded of my friend John Caples and his classic word switch. In a headline, John changed the word "repair" to "fix" and increased response by 20%.

Stick to simpler words that continue the natural flow of your powerful copy.

389 — MEANINGFUL WORDS

There are only rare instances when words like "amazing," "incredible," "fantastic," and similar adjectives are useful.

Usually they are either unbelievable or self-serving. Eliminate them from your vocabulary and search for more meaningful words to grasp the reader's attention and hold it.

390 — THE GREAT MINORITY

Never worry about the great majority of mail recipients who will never respond to your direct mail. Attempting to convince them leads to argumentative copy which turns off those who are leaning in your direction or mildly interested in your offering.

Instead, you should be concerned with those who will respond and the fence sitters who could respond if you properly present your selling proposition in terms they grasp and can get enthused about.

391 — REVERSE THINKING

Do not attempt to persuade people to reverse existing unfavorable beliefs or feelings.

You'll start unfavorable thinking by those who are likely to buy.

392 — WRITING LONG COPY

Your direct mail or sales promotion piece is the only advertising in the mind of the reader at the time he receives it. Don't be afraid to write long copy.

I knew that restaurant executives were too busy to read long copy, so I sent them a six-page letter. It was tested against many of the previous two-page letters used by *Nation's Restaurant News*. That was in 1970. The six-pager far outpulled all previous two-pagers. And it's still being used today!

393 — LONG OR SHORT COPY?

Does long copy outpull short copy? You'll never know until you test.

If there are several benefits and several noteworthy points about your offer, long copy may be more efficient. Test in small quantities and roll out in increasing cells. Of course, you'll do this on an A/B split basis so you can measure the differences in response.

394 — THE FULL PITCH

Generally speaking, long copy is better than short copy at producing actual orders because it gives you the chance to tell the complete sales pitch, just as a salesperson would in a face-to-face situation.

395 — THE EXCEPTIONS

On free applications, insurance information requests, free sales literature, catalog requests, and other free offers by direct mail, short copy often out-pulls long copy.

396 — GENERAL GUIDELINE

The choice between using short copy and long copy in direct mail frequently is keyed to the offer you are making.

Here's a general guideline:

If there is no commitment for me to pay now or pay later, short copy will probably be most effective. But if you expect me to pay now or pay later, you must tell me all I have to know about your deal, and therefore long copy most likely will be most effective for you.

397 — SERIOUS TONE

When you write long copy for a letter, make sure it is seriously presented:

- serious enough to warrant a response...
- serious enough to attract and hold attention...
- serious enough to reinforce all aspects of your deal...
- serious enough to convince the recipient that this is, in fact, a worthwhile and well-documented purchasing decision.

398 — SCIENTIFIC OMISSIONS

Do not use long copy merely for the sake of being lengthy.

Long copy must be terse, concise, and interesting. Learn to omit part of what you write. That practice becomes a science if you question every sentence, every phrase, every word as to its meaningfulness and importance to the overall message.

399 — LONG BUT TRUE

Long copy for the sake of using long copy is not successful copy.

Try overwriting, generating as much copy as you can. Put it aside and then slash it to bits, retaining all salient copy. Then rewrite. You may discover there are additional product benefits you can exploit more succinctly, more powerfully — eventually winding up with long copy that is meaningful.

400 — LETTER READERS

A letter reader will read your letter no matter how long it is, even 12 or more pages, if it interests him by:

1. telling him something new...
2. presenting a product or service he is keenly interested in...or,
3. educates him in his chosen field.

Do not hesitate to use long copy if it's concisely written.

401 — LONG AND LEAN

All copy must be lean, concise, and smooth-flowing — even if you use a 10-page letter.

Make sure long copy is tight copy — so the reader is caught up in your copy flow, rather than facing excessive, boring wordiness which turns him off.

402 — PRODUCT POSITIONING

How do you position your product or service or publication against a competitor?

How do you position your product or service or publication against a competitor's advertising?

How do you attempt to show a significant difference between your product or service or publication and a competitor's?

What can you do to strengthen your activity along these lines?

403 — MAJOR PRODUCT DIFFERENCES

If your copy gives great emphasis to trivial differences between your product and a competitor's, recognize that it is precisely that technique that makes your audience increasingly more skeptical of mail promotions.

Emphasize major product differences, stress the benefits of your product or service, give readers strong reasons to respond, and do not refer to a competitive product with respect to trivial differences.

Illustration #30

The author created this client split test to determine whether the negative positioning of Difficulties & Differences, *technique #402, would outpull the more positive, goal orientation of* Challenges & Achievements. *It didn't.*

The enumerated benefits on the front of this self-mailer show how to stress your own unique benefits, technique #403, rather than using any mention of competitive products or services.

Those benefits are presented with the serious copy tone cited in technique #397. Additional benefits are stressed, seriously, in captions and testimonials.

404 — ALL-STAR COMPANY

Don't be bashful. Come right out and say you're the best in the field, if you believe you are.

Stress the length of your operation, the honesty and integrity of your company — in short, confront the competition without knocking it.

405 — COMPARATIVE REFERENCES?

Avoid all comparative references unless you can back them up with a precise example.

Telling me that your "electric drill works faster" will not sell me. Say it will "drill 400 holes in the time other drills would only accomplish 256 holes!"

406 — GOOD VALUE

If your product or a competitor's is sold at retail at a higher price, do not hesitate to make such a comparison in your promotion copy.

Let your reader know he is getting good value with you by mail.

407 — GREATER CONVENIENCE

If your product or a competitor's is sold at retail at the same price as your promotion mailings, stress the fact that you offer greater convenience because the prospect does not have to leave his home or office to order from you.

408 — BEING DISTINCTIVE

All beer produced in the state of Michigan is the same — with only the slightest taste difference — and sells at the same price. But Stroh's Premium Beer is "fire-brewed at 2,000°."

At one time, so were all the other beers. But Stroh's said it! No matter how closely your product parallels your competitor's, you can still find a unique method to position your product as distinctive and worthy of immediate consideration.

Now that Stroh's has said it's "fire-brewed," no other beer would dare say that. It would remind beer buffs of Stroh's!

409 — WONDERFUL SERVICE

Many marketers forget to stress what would be a prime advantage in dealing with them.

Yours is that wonderful service that ships orders within the week they are received — or, better yet, on the day they are received! Be sure to say so, and then say it again.

Stressing immediate shipment on the day an order is received is a fine way to spur immediate response to your mail.

410 — CREATIVE COPY

Plagiarize concepts, not copy.

411 — STEALING COPY?

It does not pay to steal copy!

Do you remember Joe Sugarman's famous JS&A ads for CB Radios? They were creative masterpieces. He ran them everywhere. In-flights. Consumer magazines. Inserts. Co-ops.

Along came a rip-off artist. I'll be kind and not mention the company, but it called its CB radio a King&%$#. Completely copying Joe's copy, art and design, this company changed only the name of the product. It spent tons of bucks advertising the King&%$#.

It totally flopped.

There may be several reasons, but the one that strikes me as most reasonable is that Joe Sugarman had built a reputation for quality and ad readers recognized his style. I deduce they immediately saw the King&l$# people as copy cats and they probably wondered about the reliability of a King&%$#.

Just because a particular copy theme worked for another marketer or a competitor of yours does not mean it will break even when you "adapt" it to your campaign. Copy stealing usually flops! Creativity frequently succeeds.

412 — THE POSTSCRIPT

Next to the headline, the postscript is the most read item in a letter.

Possibly, as Starch once said, this is because many readers go from the headline to the signature to see who wrote it. Therefore, strengthen your postscript copy as much as possible and spend as much time on it as you would on your introductory paragraph.

413 — THE FINAL CLINCHER

Postscripts nearly always improve response to letters.

If you're not using one now, test by using it as a re-statement of your guarantee, or to mention one sales point that is a final clincher, or to stress urgency.

Are you in the mood for another story?

Connie Arnold, the first female executive at The United States Naval Academy, retained me to write a direct mail subscription solicitation for the publication that I believe had the world's longest title: *Proceedings of The United States Naval Academy at Annapolis.*

It was the only time in my life that my copy was rejected by a client. Connie called and, talking about my postscript, explained that her superior said "admirals don't have afterthoughts!"

But Connie had gumption.

I asked her if the admirals had approved all the copy above the signature. They had.

So I asked Connie if she had the courage to run all the copy I submitted, minus the postscript, as Split A, and against it run Split B. B was to have everything, minus the postscript, but move the last paragraph above the signature to the postscript position without using the letters "P.S."

She did it.

B outpulled A, 3 to 1. All the words were exactly the same. The only difference was that my closing paragraph was moved to the postscript position for Split B.

And now, will you please consider using postscripts on your direct mail letters?

Yes? Thank you!

414 — INTRIGUING POSTSCRIPT

Since many people go from a letter's headline to the postscript and might not read the letter, your P.S. must be an intriguing statement that:

1. reinforces the sales pitch expressed in the letter for those who have read it, and
2. stimulates interest in the letter for those who have not, and

3. guides the reader to the order form.

These three goals may seem difficult to achieve in a short postscript. They are. Here's just one *example* of an easy way to accomplish them:

P.S. And that's why you'll save $1,226.88 on the only office copier that prints four colors in one pass. But this big saving is yours only if you use your gold Savings Certificate before October 21.

415 — SPELLING OUT YOUR STORY

Do not assume that everyone reading your promotion will recognize all possible use or enjoyment aspects of your product or service.

Spell them all out, carefully and fully. Give examples. Show photos. Do everything you can to give your prospect all the "rationalizers" he needs.

416 — REVERSE PROMOTION

Too frequently, we tend to forget that a product or service we conceive as being strictly business-oriented can also be used by consumers at home.

The reverse is also true. When creating your promotion, be certain to stress all possible uses, and you will increase sales.

417 — EVERYONE'S ENJOYMENT

Since there are now more than 40 million single American adults — and the number is increasing daily — attempt to eliminate phrases like "your family" from mailings selling consumer products.

Phrases such as "everyone will enjoy" can serve the same purpose in a more meaningful fashion to a single or recently-divorced person who may not appreciate family references.

But if the lists you're using are of people who do have families, you may wish to reconsider this point.

418 — FEELING THE MARKET OUT

When your promotions are directed to a specific market rather than a general audience, it is a good idea to have your key copywriter study not only the interests of the audience but also meet with a few representative members of that specific market to get a "feel" for the way those people think and act.

Having this experience, the copywriter then can "relate" to a target market much better. The response to a promotion employing copy that speaks in terms understood by that specific audience should be significantly higher.

419 — PERSONAL CONTACT

Always attempt to establish some form of human or personal copy contact with me.

Tell me just how much you appreciate my business, without getting flowery, and you will make me feel more important, more likely to want to respond again.

420 — THANKS AND MORE THANKS

There is absolutely nothing wrong with thanking me for having purchased from you before.

Do so when you send me a promotion for a new product or service offering, and you are more likely to encourage me to read your entire sales message.

421 — VITALITY AND RELEVANCE

People stop reading your promotions when they become disinterested.

Make sure every sentence has vitality and meaningfulness so you don't lose your readers.

422 — DELAYED SHIPPING PROGRAM

If you have a delayed shipping program, do not hesitate to spell it out clearly so the consumer is fully informed.

But couple that copy with wording that stresses the wonderfulness your product or service will give when it finally gets to the purchaser.

423 — ANTICIPATION AND FULFILLMENT

Anyone who buys anything has a great anticipation for its arrival and ultimate use.

Make certain that your copy employs phrasing that capitalizes on this emotion of the reader by stressing the great joy, satisfaction, utility or economy that will be his when the product arrives.

424 — MYSTERIOUS LEADS

The more details you can give a prospective purchaser, the more you are likely to succeed with promotions created to get direct sales.

But that is not necessarily so with sales leads. When going after leads, you should leave a little mystery so the prospect has a reason to see your salesperson or get your follow-up mailing.

425 — SPECIAL ENCOURAGEMENT

Many people who have not responded to your previous promotion efforts require special encouragement to do so with the new campaign you are now planning.

Advise them that your product or service is fun, useful, adds to their expertise, or strengthens their knowledge. Then you may remove the disinterest of the past.

426 — KEY POINTS OF INTEREST

Many marketers plan their promotion mailings with the thought that they will mostly be reaching people who are similar to themselves in business or leisure orientation.

To avoid overlooking vast market segments, plan your creative effort to include key points of interest to youths, young adults, middle-agers, and senior citizens if you promote to the consumer world, and for neophytes, journeymen, and professionals if you attack the business world.

427 — UP-FRONT BENEFITS

"What's in it for me?" is the first question every reader has on receipt of your promotion.

Get your benefits up front and only then sell the product or service.

428 — INVOLVING THE READER

The more involved the reader gets with your mail, the more likely he is to read the entire message.

429 — SALE'S SPECIFIC REASONS

Whenever you use a sale approach, be certain to give the specific reasons for the sale to make it more believable to your audience.

Otherwise, you create an image of price-cutting as a gimmick to attract customers. Too much price-cutting, except for a discount retail establishment, leads customers to believe something's wrong in your sphere.

430 — ONE-TIME BARGAINS

If you do not accept bill-me-later orders, when asking for cash be sure to give a reason so your prospective customers won't be miffed.

EXAMPLE:

"Because of our special reduced price, we are sorry that we cannot ship orders for later payment. Please enclose your full payment to take advantage of this one-time bargain."

431 — READER IDENTIFICATION

Using active verbs is nearly always better than using passive verbs because they allow the reader to imagine himself with your product.

"Capture new knowledge to boost your wealth" is better than "Your income is increased when the facts are learned."

432 — GIVING THE READER CREDIT

"I love me. I think I'm grand. I sit in the movies and hold my hand." That's a quote from Richard Armour, and it more or less accurately describes every person's concept of herself or himself.

Capitalize on it in your direct mail advertising by always including something that lets me believe I have extra

discerning powers, super intelligence, fantastic physique, or above-average something-or-other, and you will win me to your side. However, if that presentation is too blatant, it may achieve the reverse result.

433 — FAMILIAR FRIENDS

If you have started on your way to success with a particular promotional writing style and verve, or with a writing and designing team which made you successful, stick with them.

Such efforts and style are known to your customers, making your promotions welcomed as familiar friends. Changing creative tone may change your readers' view of you.

434 — LOYAL CUSTOMER BASE?

Do you have a significantly large and loyal customer base?

If so, enhance your selling efforts by mentioning the precise number of customers. This makes recipients of your prospect promotions feel they are joining a group of like-minded people. This also tells your prospects that they're missing what others are getting.

Jealousy can work for you.

435 — NO SUPERLATIVES

Whenever possible in sales literature or direct mail copy, eliminate all faster, higher, smoother, better and similar "er" words — unless you accompany them with meaningful comparisons.

Similarly, try to eliminate "est" words, like fastest, highest, smoothest, best — unless you can document them.

Why, René, aren't those good words?

Not today. Readers are constantly deluged by those words today and tend to tune out advertising containing them. After all, how many IBM-compatible computers really can be the fastest, or the best? If you can show your prospect that those claims are, in fact, correct, do so. Otherwise, without documentation your readers will feel you're just puffing.

436 — PSYCHOLOGICAL ERRORS

Often an obvious mistake in a mailing will gain higher readership.

When the reader notices the error, he wants to know if you have additional errors. He'll read further looking for those errors and thus will pay more attention to your mailing piece.

Not too many of us want to intentionally place errors in our direct mail literature because it may adversely reflect on our expertise and professionalism. But there are times when this zany technique does work well.

The most wide-spread use of it is to say, in a memo or a even on the order form, that the price quoted in the letter is wrong due to a printing error. The correct price, much lower, is on the order form. This leads readers to feel they should act super fast to get the lower price.

437 — OBVIOUS ERRORS

If you try the adventurous technique of intentionally having an error or two in your letter, make certain that your obvious errors are few and are located very high in the letter so that someone skimming the mailing piece notices them early in the copy and keeps reading to find more errors.

I had an interesting chat about this technique with Joseph K. Weed, vice president of EBSCO Industries in Birmingham. EBSCO sells tons of

---

**TAKE ADVANTAGE OF A ONE-TIME ONLY
TAX SAVINGS...
AND SAVE 50% ON YOUR SUBSCRIPTION
OR RENEWAL TO FURNITURE/TODAY**

(Available only until midnight December 31, 1986. You must act now.)

Dear Valued Furniture/Today Subscriber:

The Income Tax Reform Act of 1986 will be in place at the end of the year so you have just enought time to take advantage of an important development regarding your personal income taxes for the next five years.

It is my obligation to keep you informed of all the information you need to make successful business decisions and increase the profitability

Illustration #31

Exercising his liberty to intentionally spell a word incorrectly, Tim McCulloch, circulation director of Furniture/Today, *correctly placed the "error" in the first paragraph of this highly-successful promotion letter, techniques #436 and #437. "Of course, I did it on purpose," McCulloch wrote the author. "A wise gnome named Gnam told me to try it, so three years later I did."*

Furniture/Today and other Gnam clients used the new tax laws as a theme to increase tax-deductible orders in advance of normal renewal dates, a concept that works well with loyal customers, technique #434.

reference manuals and magazines to librarians. Joe has tried this technique with librarians and it has increased his response in split tests. Perhaps pedantic folks like to look for errors. One thing's for sure: it gets them to read your message.

438 — HIDING LEGAL COPY

Should you put your "legal" copy in the least read position?

"Legal" copy refers to such statements as Truth In Lending, Regulation Z, likelihood of winning sweepstakes, interest rates, and other disclosures required by law. Most direct marketers like to hide that copy under a flap, and usually they want it in very small type.

Well, okay...but:

An *example* occurred in 1969 when I was promoting artificial arteries for Meadox Medicals in New Jersey. Those arteries have very positive benefits, but there's also the matter of blood seeping out. Osmosis occurs. The porosity must be stated so the cardiovascular surgeon can be knowledgeable about what he's about to place inside his patient's body. This porosity factor wasn't negative, although negativity was implied, but was a serious consideration for the surgeon, with different implications for different sized arteries in different patients.

Would hiding that copy be honorable for a manufacturer of grafts bearing the name of the famous Dr. Denton A. Cooley? The lovely logo and conservative layouts I designed would have been negated if physicians felt Meadox was trying to weasel.

Instead, I boldly stated positives and negatives side by side. My client agreed and even suggested additional

ways to be clear and honorable. The product sold very well. It may be in your body.

In 1986, I used a different technique for Elan Vital in Jacksonville. Florida law states you must define how a prospect can make money when selling a money-making kit, and you must disclose your finances and history of buying back the products that the customer makes with the kit.

Instead of hiding that legal copy, I turned it into an advantage with a headline boldly stating: "Why you have no risk in investigating this unusual opportunity."

Then, I met all the legal requirements and reinforced the advantage concept by summarizing everything with a statement of my client's bank assets and winding up with: "This disclosure is for your protection. Save it with your no-risk guarantee."

There is something to be said — a lot — for truth in advertising. Yes, I romance a bit...truthfully.

439 — SPECIFIC FEATURES

Cite what your product or service can do in specific terms your reader can understand, rather than in less meaningful generalities.

EXAMPLES:

generality	saves you money.
specificity	saves you $12 a month, each month you use it.
generality	grinds faster.
specificity	grinds at 256 revolutions a minute, 4 times faster than more costly machines which grind at only 64 revolutions a minute, sometimes with imperfections.

440 — EXCITING COPY

Have your typesetter send you separate proofs of all the body copy, without any headlines.

If the copy isn't exciting enough to make you buy the product without reading headlines, rewrite the copy.

441 — PRODUCT BENEFITS

Looking for new, wonderful things to say about your product or service?

Talk to your Plant Manager, Production Manager, Fulfillment Manager, Sales Manager, or others in your company who can reacquaint you with the benefits of your product. You may have been overlooking certain items because you are too close to the marketing scene.

442 — THE WORD "NEW"

If your product or service is new, be sure to say so and spell out what's new about it.

Newness always is intriguing, and the word "new" invites the reader to open his mind. But you must be careful to document that your "new" gizmo does work.

443 — THE WAY IT IS

If your product or service is not truly new, don't say that it is.

An educated consumer who has seen other promotions for competitive products or services will immediately tune your offer out of his mind.

444 — CONVINCING YOUR PROSPECT

Before ordering, your prospect must first be convinced that he needs what you sell.

Make sure you give him enough facts and emotional motivation to make his decision easier. He must decide that he needs what you offer more than he needs the money you ask for it.

445 — WORD PICTURES

Abstract concepts and intangibles are the hardest products or services to sell by direct mail. Make them meaningful by creating a word picture.

Instead of "a multi-faceted tax service" you really are selling "tax information that slashes your work, gives you additional leisure time, and increases your discretionary income."

Making an intangible or abstract concept understandable is the objective in increasing response.

446 — A GREAT GIFT

If your product appeals to only one sex, use promotional copy indicating that it makes a great gift.

If the recipient is of the wrong sex, he then knows that he, too, should consider ordering.

447 — SEX APPEAL

Does your product appeal to both sexes?

Say so! Don't assume your readers know it.

448 — GETTING THE PICTURE

Don't be content to merely describe your product or service in copy and just show it in pictures.

Emphasize its use and give examples of how it can enhance your prospect's life. Let him "read into" your example so that he can picture himself in the same situation.

449 — PARENTHETICAL EXPRESSIONS

Everyone suspects that wording within a set of parentheses is a disclaimer.

So why not put your most potent copy in them? I do. I use phrases like "guaranteed for an entire year" in parentheses. At the very moment when the prospect thinks you're about to issue a disclaimer, suddenly his buying inclination is reinforced.

450 — TECHNICAL ADVANTAGES

If your product has certain technical advantages, be certain to describe them fully to the reader — but in layman's terms!

Point out specifically and emphatically how your technical innovations aid the purchaser.

451 — THE CATCHALL

If the product you are selling comes with all possible accessories, instructions and guidebooks, do not hesitate to say so in your copy.

Convince your prospect that he has to make only a single purchase — conveniently by mail.

This copy approach, from Packard-Bell computers, was a strong stimulus for me to buy five new systems from P-B in 1986. Gosh, oh golly gee, you even get diagnostic disks from P-B.

When I previously bought from Tandy, I had to pay a technician for a service call to run the diagnostics and Tandy never released the disks. P-B also said they included the manuals, and didn't charge for installation because you can install it yourself instead of paying Tandy's extra installation charge. P-B also wasn't shy about citing its complete system price. IBM hid its price and then quoted much more than the others for systems that ran slower.

See what I mean? If you have an advantage, glorify it. You should see my five glorious new Packard-Bell systems. By not stressing what I would get for my money, IBM and Tandy, from whom I previously had purchased over $108,000 of hardware and software, lost those dollars. But by stressing what I would get, P-B got many new thousands of dollars. (Not that P-B has always been glorious: in 1988, I bought my first 386 from PGI because P-B fibbed about its 386 release date and refused to repair a monitor which was still under warranty.)

The point for you is to stress your advantages and, when you make a sale, support your customer.

452 — CATASTROPHIC CONNECTIONS

Unless you are a fund raising organization or have discovered terrific salvations, do not tie your copy pitch to a crisis in the economy, the shortage of food supplies, the devastating nature of the oil and energy crisis, or other catastrophies.

You will be focusing too much attention on those problems, and thus you will be telling your readers to think about the problems instead of your offer.

453 — TRIED AND TRUE

Have you been in business a long time selling the same product or service or publication?

If so, say so. It is important that your prospects know that you are not a fly-by-night.

454 — MEMBERSHIP DECISION

We are a nation of joiners. We love to belong.

If you sell memberships in a consumer or business organization, do not hesitate to use opening copy that comes right out and indicates that this is a membership decision.

"Your name has been proposed for membership" is one of the strongest opening statements you can use.

455 — PURCHASER'S RIGHT

If you have a club operation or if you are mailing to former subscribers or customers, use pinpointed copy to let them know that their previous purchasing habits "entitled them" to purchase from this promotion piece at a special discount.

Tell that they are distinguished by their previous purchase.

Copy such as "your membership entitles you to select"...or..."because you have been a long and faithful customer" immediately tells the prospect how special he is and flags his attention to your special deal.

456 — CONVINCING FENCE SITTERS

In writing letter copy to new prospects, inquiries and rented non-customer files, assiduously avoid copy that gradually builds up to making an offer.

Most of the people you're mailing to in these situations will not want your product or service anyway, and won't respond no matter how you back into or otherwise hide your offer.

Come right out and state it immediately so you have a better chance at convincing fence sitters.

457 — CURRENT CUSTOMER FILE

Never write letter copy that leads up to making an offer unless it is to your current customer file, where the people are familiar with you and know your products and services.

In that instance, especially if you mail frequently to your current customer file, you can use this copy technique if you vary your approaches and make each package distinctive and interesting to the recipient.

458 — THE BREATH TEST

Try the breath test after you have written a letter.

Hold it in your hand and, at a fast pace, continually walk around the room while reading it aloud. If you have to fight for breath in the middle of any sentence, that sentence is too long for your reader to fathom!

459 — REQUEST FOR REPLY

Repeat your request for a reply in several places:
- in the body of the letter...
- especially in the closing paragraph of the letter...
- in the P.S...
- in several locations on the brochure or accompanying sales literature...
- on the order form itself...
- on the back of the order form...and,
- perhaps on the back of the reply envelope.

460 — THE RESPONSE DEVICE

It is vital to restate a request for a response in several places in your letter and this can be done by referring to the response device in five different fashions:
1. indicating the benefits that accrue to the recipient by responding...
2. precisely stating the method of responding...
3. telling the recipient his natural inclination would be to order and therefore he should do so...

4. referring to the response device as having special value or timeliness...

5. pointing out that the response device may only be used by the recipient.

461 — IMMEDIATE SHIPMENT TIE-IN

When stressing immediate shipment, try to tie it to your guarantee and price savings or bonus items. Merging several of these response enhancers makes the reader want to buy.

EXAMPLE:

"All orders are shipped the same day they are received, at the guaranteed savings quoted in this catalog. The sooner you order, the faster you receive your bonus gifts."

462 — TAX-DEDUCTIBLE PURCHASE

Is your product or service a tax-deductible purchase? Say so!

Illustration #32

Here is an example of how the author stresses tax advantages, technique #462, of attending his seminars:

YOU MAY ACHIEVE TAX SAVINGS...
IRS Section 1.162-5 permits tax deductions of seminar registration fees/travel/lodging/meals "undertaken as educational expenses to maintain or improve skills in employment, trade or business." Check with your accountant to be certain you can deduct this legitimate business investment, and then *sign up today* to hike your productivity and your direct mail response.

Try to point out the specific section of the IRS Code as verification of this important point for business and professional people.

463 — STRESSING KEY ELEMENTS

Is there a more impressive way to couch your offer?

EXAMPLE:

Try saying "12 months' full service for $33.95" instead of "a year for $33.95."

Stress elements of your offer so they stand out and become important sales points.

464 — ORDER FORM LEAD-IN

Ideally, every component in your mailing package should refer the recipient to the order form or response device.

Letter copy especially should refer frequently to the order form. Sometimes I don't refer to an order form on the outgoing envelope, but more frequently I do if my mailing is after a direct order instead of a sales lead.

465 — APPROPRIATE APPEAL

Your main strategy in writing letter copy is to appeal to existing feelings, beliefs, and motivations held by the prospects to whom you direct your mail.

Therefore, don't attempt to persuade those who would not normally be interested. Avoid argumentative copy. Avoid answering objections which would not normally be raised by a person likely to respond.

466 — CUTE COPY?

Avoid attempts at writing "cute" or "humorous" or "intriguing" letter copy.

Such copy does make your mail more interesting, but it frequently lowers response because the reader starts day-dreaming about the interesting situation.

Start writing by acknowledging to yourself that your recipient knows you are doing a promotion mailing. Put your offer right up in the first paragraph (and headline) and you will discover that such techniques usually will pull better than almost all attempts at "clever" copy.

Use the rest of the letter to support your offer.

467 — APPROPRIATE TITLE

A signature on a letter is important to the reader, and that means:

Try inventing a meaningful title to go with the name of the signer. If the actual title is appropriate to the audience you are reaching, use it.

468 — FORMALITY AND INFORMALITY

Being formal and informal, at the same time, is sometimes possible on a signature to a letter.

Try spelling out the complete name of the signer where it appears in typewritten form and use a shortened version of the first name, a nickname, or just the first name for the actual signature.

EXAMPLE:
Gerald R. Ford could be used for the typewritten version of the signature while "Jerry" could be used for the actual signature.

469 — BRIGHT YELLOW FORM

If you have several inserts in one mailing package, your copy should not tell the reader to use "the order form," but rather specify using "the bright yellow order form."

Be as specific as possible in directing the prospect's attention to the response device.

470 — VALUE COMPARISONS

Whenever possible, give a prospective purchaser value comparisons he can understand. If you want him to part with his money, show him why your product or service is worth more than the money he will spend.

EXAMPLE:
"For less than the cost of a single steak dinner, you can use this powerful stitcher all year long."

471 — SOMEONE SPECIAL

There's nothing wrong with telling your prospect that he's special. Tell him you know he has extensive education or decent income or special interests.

You know these facts from your list research, and if you can tell your prospect that you are writing to him because you know he's special, he will view your offer more favorably.

472 — DIRECT APPROACH

Avoid "subtle" or "understated" copy.

In most consumer marketing, it doesn't pay to be afraid of offending small segments of the prospect lists you use by pitching for your product or service. You are trying to achieve response from those who would be naturally inclined to buy and from those who are fence sitters. And you must convince them quickly, so launch your letter appropriately. Never worry about those who won't buy from you.

But in most business-to-business

marketing, be less strident, less commanding, a touch less offensive. Reason? You have to maintain an image because you will be promoting to the same prospects for a very long time.

473 — GETTING TO THE POINT

Don't back into your copy by starting a letter in an overly friendly or back-grounding fashion.

Your reader considers his time precious and will not concentrate on your mailing if you take his time to tell him how great your company is.

474 — SPELL OUT PRODUCT USES

Tell prospective purchasers how to use your product or service.

Spell out the advantages purchasers will realize by its use. Copy along those lines enables them to envision themselves with the product, and that's an important step toward achieving a sale.

475 — SHORT SENTENCES

Two or three short sentences are easier to understand than one long one.

Restrict your copy to sentences which present a single thought.

476 — SEX APPROACH

You can use sex without being sexy or offensive.

EXAMPLE:

"For less than 2¢ a day, you can give the man in your life pleasure that lasts all year."

That was my successful headline used next to a photo of *Popular Mechanics* on a mailing to married women charge card customers to ask them to give gift subscriptions to their husbands. Now that was a few years ago.

Today, it's a touch too sexist, so I would probably change it to say:

"You can delight the man in your life...for an entire year...for less than 8¢ a day."

477 — IMPORTANT MESSAGE

If you feel your message is important, say so.

Copy such as "This may be one of the most important opportunities of your business life" can stimulate readership. It's far more effective than copy such as "An opportunity for businessmen."

But, René, isn't that pretty bold?

Yes, but I'm after response. In fact, I once started a letter to businesspeople with this successful headline:

"This may be the most important letter you read today."

Then I immediately followed up with the reason why that letter was so important.

478 — THE "I" APPROACH

All copy should always be written with "I want" or "what's in it for me" as the primary approach.

Only then, after provoking interest, should you establish reasons why the purchase would be a good one.

479 — YOUR OBJECTIVE

You are not out to win awards for creativity, either in copy or art.

Your objective is to attract attention, convey a message, and hold the reader until he makes a decision about your offer.

480 — CREDIT CHECK?

Do not use such terms as "credit o.k." and "credit approved" in ads, newsstand or free circulation copies of a magazine, in co-op inserts or similar promotions where the reader — having more intelligence than maybe you give him credit for — knows you had no prior opportunity to check his credit.

481 — OBVIOUS BENEFITS

Clearly state obvious benefits.

Even though you may be fully aware of all the benefits of your product or service, and even though you would reasonably expect every prospective purchaser to be equally aware of those benefits, all prospective purchasers need benefits restated.

And not all prospective purchasers view the benefits of your product or service as obvious.

482 — COMPANY CONNECTION

Is your little mail order operation a division of a much larger, well known and established company?

Say so! You will be giving more credibility to your promotions.

Have you noticed how often I've used the words "say so"? There's a reason.

Frequently, I'm asked to critique mailings. And I've noticed that most organizations are hesitant to tout themselves or their products. Maybe their copywriters are shy. Don't be. When your prospect holds your mailing in his hands, you have only that one opportunity to get his attention and his response. Make the most of it. Say so!

483 — NAMING YOUR NEIGHBOR

While mailing to neighbors of your customers is a good consumer test concept because of similarity in income and living location choice, remember that neighbors are not alike. They have different occupations, different desires.

Thus, your entire sales pitch should not be concentrated on the fact that they are neighbors. But, especially if you use a word processor or computer letter, there's nothing wrong in naming the neighbor who has bought your product or won in your sweepstakes. *Reader's Digest* has done this successfully for years. So has Publisher's Clearing House. So have I.

We all learn from each other. That's why you bought this book. May I quote you?

484 — GREAT TRADITION

When mailing to an erudite audience, especially when promoting cultural activities or educational books, don't forget the pitch to "become a part of our great tradition."

People like being identified with greatness.

485 — DUPE ELIMINATION PROGRAMS

In citing the explanation for errors occasionally occurring in dupe elimination programs, try to make the statement a positive one by suggesting that the recipient pass the mailing on to a friend.

But why mention it at all? I know, because management wants you to. Why? Because management wants to be nice. Okay, I accept that. Can you accept this:

After running your merge/purge program, ask your label supplier to give you four equal Nth name splits. Mail them on separate days. It's highly unlikely that any name would be duplicated more than four times. So no one should get duplicate mail on the same day. Bingo! You've eliminated the need to apologize.

You see, apologies of any kind tend to make readers wonder if other apologies are due.

486 — ONE-TIME PAYMENT

If you're asking for payment up front, stress the fact that it's a one-time payment so that the required advance payment becomes a benefit rather than a burden.

487 — RESEARCH AND PRODUCT TESTING?

How much research and product testing was undertaken prior to release of your product for marketing?

Can you establish a solid copy point regarding your pre-release efforts?

488 — "PLEASE"

Do not be afraid to say "please." Not when asking for the order. There you must be firm.

But "please review the enclosed" and "I sincerely believe" and "we are grateful" are phrases that show you care and weave you personally into the recipient's mind.

489 — INVITATION FORMATS

Everyone likes to be invited. Invitation formats, therefore, are quite successful in direct response.

But even if you do not use an invitation format, instead of saying "buy now," try saying "you are invited to collect," or "you are invited to acquire." It's so much warmer than "buy now."

René, do you ever use the words "buy now"?

Of course I do. When appropriate. Those words are part of an urgency thrust. But I'm still after some warmth in direct mail.

490 — SIMPLE AND CONCISE

Even if you are mailing to college professors, keep your language simple, concise, and easy to read.

Don't allow the mind to wander, examining your turn of phrase and straying from your sales message.

College professors should be able to understand what plumbers comprehend.

491 — MAIL ORDER DISTRUST

Avoid the tendency to use the words "mail order" in the name of your company or as body copy in your ad.

Despite hundreds of legitimate mail order operations and many millions of satisfactory experiences in purchasing by mail, many people still have a hesitancy in dealing with folks they don't know.

The words "mail order" can focus attention on that distrust.

492 — THE VITAL FIRST SENTENCE

The first sentence in every direct response letter must grab my attention and make me want to read on.

One way to do this is to quickly and clearly establish a bond or tone of reader communication, similar in style to the balance of the letter.

493 — UNIQUENESS AND DESIRABILITY

The more you tell the recipient of your promotion about the uniqueness and desirability of your product or service, the more likely you are to sell him.

That's especially true if you are attempting to get an order directly by mail.

494 — PROMOTIONAL LISTING

Include a promotional listing of your product, membership, service or editorial benefits — so long that virtually any recipient of your promotion will find at least a few items of interest.

495 — GENERAL THEME

If you mail into the United States from another country, you may wish to tie your promotion to a general theme, such as Swiss bankers or Italian lovers.

496 — TOLL FREE 800 NUMBER

When using an 800 number to consumers, always add the words "toll free" so the reader understands there is no cost to respond.

497 — SAYING WHAT YOU MEAN

Be explicit!

Say exactly what you mean and do not get carried away by fanciful lunges at the keyboard.

498 — RESTATING THE OBVIOUS

Find a way to restate the obvious.

A dollar off is "$1 off," but it is also "100 cents off" or "$1.00 off." Dramatize your offer so that your reader is "tickled" to respond.

499 — WHAT FOLKS BUY

When launching a new product, research often helps you decide on size, shape, number of uses, color, and a variety of other product descriptions and characteristics.

Illustration #33

In his work for General Motors, the author uses many of the recommendations in this book. Here are two in the opening paragraph of this Protection Plan letter:

Technique #492 suggests that your first sentence make the reader want to read on by establishing a bond or tone. Technique #497 indicates your copy should be explicit, leaving no confusion about your meaning.

But don't focus your main selling message on the results of such research studies.

People don't buy characteristics. They buy usefulness, service, attractive price, and what they imagine are the benefits of the product to them.

500 — YOU, RATHER THAN WE

"We at the Jones Company" is an over-used, archaic hangover from the old days of pedantic pluralists.

Drop the "we at" and just make it "we," or better yet, rewrite such copy so it appears you-oriented rather than we-oriented.

501 — GOOD AND BAD DAYS

Telling me to "have a good day" at the end of a direct mail letter is a very good way to get me to forget the message you have been propounding!

502 — GOOD MORNING?

Using "good morning" as the salutation on a promotion is totally inappropriate unless you are positive that your recipients will all receive the piece on a "good" morning.

If it's a bad day, your readers may not view your mail in a favorable light.

If you say "good morning" and your reader receives your mail at home after a work day, what does that make him think you think of him? What does he think of you?

503 — INCLUDING LETTERS

There is almost no occasion on which the inclusion of a letter in your promotion package will fail to increase response. Always use letters.

Notice that I said "almost." I did

have one experience, only one out of many thousands, when including a letter did not draw higher response. It was for the United Nations Association in New York. Apparently, ardent supporters of the U.N. didn't need the letter since the A/B split pulled equally.

But remember that that instance was the only time in 30 years of direct response experience that a letter didn't pay in an envelope mailing.

504 — ADDRESSING IT RIGHT

Never address a letter to "Dear Customer" if he is not a customer, or to "Dear Inquirer" if he is not an inquirer.

Not only do you destroy believability, but you insult the intelligence of your audience.

505 — SINGULAR SALUTATIONS

Eliminate "dear sirs," "gentlemen," and "dear sir or madam" from your direct mail vocabulary.

You are writing to only one individual and you should know who he or she is. Identify that person's interest in your salutation and you will have gone a long way toward improving response.

506 — DEAR MADAM?

Never use "dear madam" unless all recipients of your direct mail piece are located at 8th Avenue and 42nd Street in New York City.

507 — THE BOTTOM LINE

Art and design can attract attention, impress, and communicate effectively, but art and design do not get the inquiry or accomplish the final sale.

In direct mail, copy is king.

CHAPTER 9

GRAPHICS

Because many personal decisions and tastes often must be subdued or altered in our direct mail graphics, I've decided to introduce this chapter by citing just one frequent mailing component — certificates — as a single illustration of the great variety of complexities faced by graphic people you employ.

To do a proper job, your artist, like your marketing manager and copywriter, must be aware of the key reasons to use each component.

Certificates:

1. Convey a sense of value to your entire mailing, inviting a decision, and calling for action by the reader.
2. Produce instant reading of the mailing.
3. Spur additional sales from the same mailing.
4. Dramatize the offer or the premium.
5. Overcome secretarial or mail room resistance to uninvited direct mail.
6. Stimulate re-order sales from same mailing or future mail.
7. Upgrade dollar volume from same mailing.
8. Show solidity of the mailer, and thereby a desirability in dealing with you!
9. Increase dollar volume.
10. Stimulate more orders.
11. Increase frequency of sales calls.
12. Build higher unit sales.
13. Acquire new customers from prospect lists.
14. Secure new prospects.
15. Build off-season business.
16. Push slow items.
17. Introduce new products.
18. Stimulate dealer tie-ins.
19. Stimulate the sales force when the certificate is used as an incentive.
20. Revive dead accounts.
21. Switch your competitor's customers to become your customers by encouraging initial trial of your product or service.

Then, having mastered the reasons for using any given component, a certificate in this instance, the graphics person must know how to design it for maximum effectiveness:

1. Stock appropriate to the mailing offer:
   A. Inexpensive stock if used for discount promotion.
   B. Quality stock if used to enhance high-ticket sales or to promote high quality products or services.
2. Certificates must be presented with a border:
   A. Large and almost garish for discount offers.
   B. Conservative and official for high-ticket sales or high quality products or services.
3. Background must be instantly recognizable:
   A. Safety paper...has design in it already.
   B. Tints or screens...to make it look official.
   C. Paper color...indicating value.
4. Immediately, the reader should identify it as a certificate:
   A. Graphically, because it looks appropriate.
   B. With copy, because it should be named.
5. There should be short copy only:
   A. Stress value and importance.
   B. In business-like fashion, spell out the certificate's deal.
   C. Ask for action.
   D. Cite cutoff or deadline date.
   E. Identify target audience, where possible.
   F. Tell how to use the certificate.
6. Acceptable art usage includes:
   A. Product or premium photo or illustration, small as a reminder.

B. Up-front logo placement.
   C. Use tints, borders, or graphic devices to stress importance.
7. Type usage:
   A. Bold or formal style for copy headline, according to your audience and the nature of the deal.
   B. Small type for terms of the deal. It's expected on official documents!
   C. Clear, readable...no condensed type faces unless big and bold, perhaps for discount dollar amounts.
   D. General type guidelines for certificates:
      i. roman or script for headlines.
      ii. roman for terms and body copy.
      iii. roman, condensed & bold for displaying value...big display.
      iv. italics for action copy.
      v. italics for how-to-use-this-certificate copy.

Okay, now that you and your graphics expert are expert at all this, here are the certificate formats that work:

1. Tear-off top of a letter — never at the bottom.
   A. Says *read the letter*.
   B. Says *this is valuable*.
   C. Says *be immediate*...cut-off date on certificate.
   D. Flags attention to your deal immediately.
2. As an order form.
   A. with address label on it to spur easy response.
   B. to save costs of printing a separate piece on tight budgets.
3. Most effective...as a separate insert.
   A. Creates a "hot potato"

feeling...*what do I do with this valuable thing?*

    B. Makes recipient refer back to letter and brochure for details.

    C. Lets you change deadline without changing other components.

    D. Whenever you can afford it, a separate insert pays off...Test!

And, you have color considerations:

1. No white stock unless you use ample bendays and borders and ink to give an official look.
2. Certificate inks can be one or two or full color.
3. If you can only use one ink color, use green and tints.
4. If you can only use two colors, use red and black on green stock.

And there are more considerations, but why did I go through all this on just one typical component? To give you just a brief idea of the thought that's necessary when an artist sits down at his drawing board, that's why.

But, René, are certificates really that important?

Certainly! I recommended using them as order forms to The Institute for Econometrics at a 1974 conference in Los Angeles. They hiked response. And the same winning certificates were still being used at press time for this book.

That's why your artist labors to give you a proper graphic treatment. It may not, and should not, be too beautiful. But it is meant to be used for dozens of mailings beyond your initial test.

And there's another important point here:

For some reason known only to the initiators, copywriters and artists are expected to produce dramatic, compelling, result-pulling creativity overnight. Examine again, if you have the patience, all the considerations that must be taken into account on certificates alone. Quite something, eh? Similar decisions confront creators on all components. Okay, then please give your creative people adequate time to do a better than adequate job. Thank you.

But if the time just isn't available, explain that you're sorry. Point out that you know a one-month job can't be done in a weekend. Your creative people will respect you for understanding what they must go through. Besides thinking about certificates, they have to think about everything else in this chapter.

> **Sometimes a direct mail artist may have to lower his personal standards of taste and fine design in an attempt to achieve maximum response for you. Applaud this. It isn't easy to be a direct mail creator.**

One more point before we begin the chapter:

Now and then your graphics people may have to tone down the recommendations that follow in order to suit your audience and image. Not often. Just now and then.

508 — TARGET MARKET

Please don't forget to acquaint your direct mail designer with the nature of your audience.

For instance, most poor people usually have less education than folks who are better off financially. Therefore, poor people will read less and get most of their information from visual communications.

If your designer does not know the nature of your target market — whatever that market may be — he or she can not do a proper visual job for your direct response promotions.

509 — TEAM WORK

Never complete your copy and simply turn it over to an art director or production person to handle and produce.

Sit down with that vital cog in your creative team and explain your points of emphasis and reasons for them. You will have a better appearing and more productive promotion.

510 — WORKING TOGETHER

An artist and a writer involved with sales promotion and direct mail campaigns should work together, not in separate vacuums!

511 — UP-TO-DATE LOGO

Reconsider your logo.

If it is outdated, old fashioned, and does not suit the product line you now merchandise, could you redesign it to reflect the old image recognized by your faithful customers and also incorporate the proper image of your current product line?

Or, could you use a totally new logo for a new division of your company? Or, a new logo as a theme for a special mailing?

512 — THE COMPLETE COPY

Always write the complete copy for a sales promotion or direct mail package before considering design elements, color, or illustrations.

Once you have well-knit copy that flows strongly and concisely, you can consider illustrations and lots of other graphics.

513 — ARTIST LAYOUTS

Even if you have six zillion full-time staff artists, the layouts for your promotion campaign should be produced by only one artist working with the creative director or copywriter.

The layouts may be modified by others after completion, but the creative inspiration and organization of the art should be produced by a single artist so the package has a unified thrust toward its goal.

514 — GRAPHICS

Graphics set the tone and mood for a direct mail promotion.

Be aware that large screaming headlines presented in multiple decks create the tone of a carnival huckster, which may or may not be appropriate for your particular offering.

515 — DIFFERENT TONE

The graphic tone for each direct mail package — with the possible exception of mailing in a series — should be slightly different from all others you have created.

That's true because, as a good direct mail practitioner, you will want graphics to be appropriate to the offer you are making. A humorous, frivolous, or stick figure cartoon illustration on an offering such as a tax advisory service would be totally inappropriate because that service is a serious proposition. Charts or graphs would be appropriate.

Search for the art techniques and tone that your audience would identify with your proposition.

516 — READER INVOLVEMENT

Graphics should be used to get the reader involved with the product or the offer, or both.

Merely dressing up a promotion

with interesting graphics is a wasteful expense. And it detracts from the overall impact of your sales pitch.

517 — CREATIVE IMAGES?

All readers of promotion pieces are human and, therefore, likely to day-dream when you strike an image that lets their minds wander.

That may be fine to grab initial attention, but it frequently can divert concentration from your product pitch. Be wary of creative images. You are presenting information, raising funds, getting traffic, producing qualified leads...selling!

518 — FOCAL POINT

Your proposition, and then your product or service, should always be the focal point of interest in graphic lay-out — not your cleverness at graphic design!

519 — BROAD APPEAL

Style your direct mail piece to appeal to all segments of your audience whenever possible, perhaps by using several photos or illustrations that strike a chord with specific groups.

520 — SUPERIOR FOLKS

In showing a photograph of people, it is better to show folks the reader can say he is superior to than folks who are superior to the reader, unless you are selling motivation seminars!

Let me feel that "if Joe can do it, certainly I can do even better."

521 — REGULAR PEOPLE

If you use models in your photographs, make sure that they are "regular" people.

The prettier, wealthier, more at-tractive, more obviously successful your models are, the less likely it is for your readers to identify with them. Those models belong in promotions for modeling agencies, but should be rejected by most direct mail and sales promotion marketers.

522 — LARGE ILLUSTRATIONS

If your budget permits use of illustra-tions, try showing your product as close as possible to its actual size.

If that is not feasible — because, for example, on a insert you may be selling an industrial boiler that en-compasses an entire room — show as large an illustration as possible. This is what you are selling. Be proud to show it to me.

523 — QUALITY BACKDROP

If your product is dull, ordinary, and commonplace, try photographing it in a backdrop setting that indicates quality.

Your reader will automatically associate your product with the qual-ity impression of the backdrop.

524 — A PICTURE'S PRICE

It is almost always important to show me a picture of what I get when I order from you.

This makes your price more ac-ceptable and also creates desire.

525 — A SELLING MESSAGE

If you are fortunate enough to use photos in your advertising, make sure you caption each one with a selling message.

Don't assume the reader knows he can use your radio at the beach sim-ply because you show an illustration of a radio at the beach. Tell him in a caption how marvelous it is to have his kind of music at the beach.

This technique of captioning even obvious photo content works extremely well, and here's an *example:*

My problem was to sell short-term ADDM insurance for Green Shield Life Insurance of Boulder, CO. ADDM means Accidental Death and Dismemberment. Something you shudder about. So first, I changed the name of the policy to Sudden Accident Insurance. Every citizen can identify with that.

Then I searched for a photo that implied a sudden accident. I found one of a priest holding his beads, leaning over a man lying in a gutter with a car bumper over his head. There was a mailbox on the street corner.

No, the photo was not posed. I bought reproduction rights from a stock photo service. It originally was a news photo.

Even though that photograph was totally self-explanatory, I added a caption which said:

"You never know when a sudden accident may happen, so mail your Green Shield application today."

Green Shield doesn't exist today. It was bought out by a large insurance conglomerate. MacArthur Enterprises. Why? Because normal response for short-term ADDM coverage is .25%. That mailing pulled over 1.0%.

526 — PHOTOGRAPH OVER DRAWING

If you have to select between using a photograph or a drawing and if there are no other selection criteria, choose the photograph because the recipient of your promotion feels a photograph is documented reality.

He can view a drawing as a figment of an artist's imagination, therefore contrived and perhaps less realistic. And, if you believe in research, remember that UCLA says photos outpull illustrations by 22.2%.

527 — HEIGHTENING PHOTOGRAPHIC INTEREST

Photographic interest can be heightened by using silhouettes, slices of photos, cropping in circular form, even cropping to form words.

528 — THE READER'S IMAGE

Try positioning your product or service in the reader's image of how he would use it.

This can be done most effectively with an illustration showing the product in actual use: on a kitchen counter, on an executive's desk, on a yacht.

529 — STOCK PHOTOGRAPHS

Photos, illustrations, and line drawings cost more than straight type. Therefore, exercise caution in selecting them, but do not overlook their strong selling possibilities.

Frequently, a stock photograph may do the trick at moderate cost.

530 — A VISUAL IMPRESSION

If you sell large merchandise, rental space, apartments, or homes, think of using line drawings, charts, and other graphic illustrations of space and/or size rather than merely using the words in copy.

Your reader will then get a visual impression.

531 — COVER BLURBS

If your catalog, book or magazine cover, or product package contains cover blurbs, be sure to make those copy lines large enough so that your customer can read them and become further intrigued by the prospect of acquiring your super-duper, extra-virility pepper-upper!

Remember, too, that those cover blurbs must be readable when the entire cover is reduced all the way down to one inch high. Why? Because you'll want to reproduce it that small on future promotions.

This means you must select the type faces and sizes for initial reproduction of cover blurbs with extreme care.

532 — DRAMATIC TECHNIQUES

Can your product or service or publication be enhanced in its presentation by your use of fragrances, printing on cloth, printing on plastic, or enclosing a toy or token?

These are but a few of the many attention-getting techniques that often increase direct mail and sales literature response.

533 — VALUABLE DESIGN DEVICES

When your direct mail uses stamps or tokens, every attempt should be made to have those design devices appear as valuable as possible.

You can do that by:

- imprinting a price or value on them,
- drawing attention to them with copy and design,
- reminding the prospect to use them,
- highlighting their discounts on your order forms.

534 — DISCOUNT OFFERINGS

Certificates and simulated checks emphasize discount offerings and are effective in communicating the value of your offer.

535 — PRODUCT FEATURES

Make a list of all your product features and then make a concerted effort to show and tell them.

Not only should you use selling copy about product features, but if it is possible to illustrate such a showing — such as an open centerfold of your magazine, or a brochure spread of various components in your kit — do so.

Use the same technique to highlight features on a product like a radio, by pointing out graphically what all the dials and controls do.

536 — VISUAL IMPACT

If you aim at a fairly youthful audience of teens through 45, remember that they were primarily educated by visual techniques in school and by TV visuals at home — not as much by the printed word as were people over 45.

So create your promotions to have more visual impact and graphics when going after younger audiences, and use more text to an older audience.

537 — SECURING FASTER READING

If your promotions ask me to make a decision of any kind, and do so in fairly large and prominently-displayed type, you are more likely to secure faster reading on my part than if you merely have a lovely graphic presentation of your product or service.

538 — DRESSING THEM UP?

There are times when your promotions should not look too professional, too arty, too well done.

This is especially so when selling distress merchandise, closeouts or unusual sales bargains. If the mailing piece is too pretty, too slick, or too "Madison Avenue," you'll fail to convey a sense of urgency and the importance of immediate response to the bargain offer.

539 — BIG AND BOLD 800

If you are using an 800 number for orders, make certain that you play it up big and bold so it can't be missed by anyone reading your promotion.

Many people do not like to order by mail and feel that a telephone ordering system is more personal. They may be more responsive to your offer if you stress telephone ordering.

Illustration #34

THE FASTEST WAY

TO SIGN ON

Don't Wait . . . Go Online Today Call 800-345-1301!

Call between 9am-8pm EST. In Pennsylvania, call 215-527-8030.

When NewsNet retained the author to critique its mailings, Gnam recommended even stronger use of the 800 number than shown above (technique #539).

The same suggestive graphics can be used with local numbers (technique #540).

Many companies receive 40% or more of their orders by phone, and some get as high as 90%.

540 — TELEPHONE NUMBERS

Displaying your regular telephone number and your 800 number on your direct mail piece is vital because orders received by telephone usually produce a minimum of 20% higher gross dollars than orders received by mail.

541 — OFFSETTING COLORS

Try using your letter postscript in a color different from the body color, perhaps the same color as the signature so it stands out even more and commands attention — but only when mailing to consumers at home.

542 — PENSCRIPT USAGE

Penscript use for postscripts is extremely effective in mailing to consumer audiences because it makes the P.S. look like an afterthought.

Make sure that the P.S. contains some of your most potent selling copy.

And don't forget that you can use penscript as marginal notes, and for other items, too.

543 — IMPORTANT BODY COPY

Penscript marginal notes accompanied by an arrow in the same "hand" effectively pinpoint certain paragraphs of body copy as being primarily important to the recipient.

They also serve to attract the eye and get the reader following those marginal notations. Such notations usually are reading instructions or, preferably, highlights of the deal.

544 — COLOR IMPRESSION

If you want to maintain a color impression on several different pieces within the same promotion, or over

The author's favorite example of penscript, technique #542, is above. He advised Lynn Rogers, then circulation director of Teen Magazine, to do the entire letter in her daughter's handwriting and insert a photo of Julie. The mailing was so persuasive and powerful that Julie received sacks and sacks of personal letters from teens.

the course of several mailings, always specify Pantone (PMS) inks because they provide all printers with a standard, matched system — provided that you use the same paper stock.

545 — ALL-COPY PRESENTATION

There is nothing wrong with using an all-copy presentation in direct mail, sales promotion, or in advertisements in publications.

It is not mandatory that you use illustrations or art of any kind.

546 — POINTERS

Arrows, hands, and other ornaments that point are important in your promotions because they guide the reader to the action you want him to take.

547 — GRAPHIC EMBELLISHMENTS

Don't forget to use graphic embellishments — sun bursts, arrows, bullets, stars, asterisks, check marks — to direct the eye to important sales points.

Herman Zapf, the famous type designer, uses the term "ding bats" to refer to graphic embellishments.

I like to call them "doo dads." I call

the big ones "doo daddies." But, I really don't care what you call them so long as you use them — frequently.

But, René, I have a highly erudite, sophisticated audience.

Right! And they're busier than unerudite, unsophisticated, unemployed, uneducated people to whom no one mails anyway. The busier or more affluent or more sophisticated your target is, the more likely it is that he skim reads. He hasn't got the time to read every word in the sequence in which you wrote it or presented it. So you do him a favor by using doo-dads to guide his eye and point out major considerations.

Oh, c'mon, René?

Okay, let me give you an example:

When Andrew Jackson (yes, that's his real name) retained me to sell subscriptions for *OnComputing*, which later became *Popular Computing*, and then was merged by McGraw-Hill into *Byte*, he once asked me: "René, how many arrows will I get."

Smart man. He tested my promotions against much more conservatively-styled mailings. I won. Millions of my pieces were mailed by the publisher, McGraw-Hill, a rather conser-

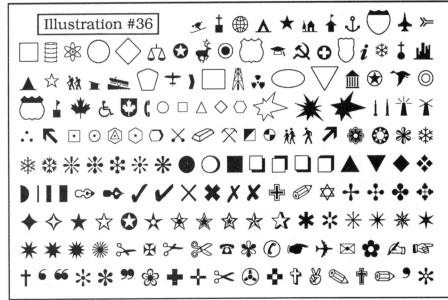

Illustration #36

Illustrated at the left are a few of the doodads, technique #547, that René Gnam uses on his twin 386 desktop computer systems when designing direct mail pieces.

Any of these graphic embellishments can be inserted anywhere in text or used as pure graphics.

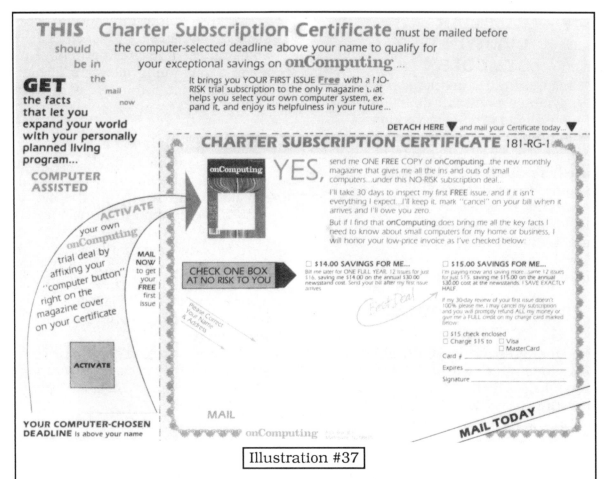

Illustration #37

René Gnam's original winning order card for OnComputing *was tested against several other pieces and rolled-out to millions of names when the magazine became* Popular Computing. *Andy Jackson got eight arrows on this piece, techniques #546 and #547, with all of them directing the eye to respond.*

The comment from Andy's superior, Greg Spitzfaden:"You whipped the challenger and soundly defeated the control. Your piece has become the new control."

This order form establishes eye direction toward the offer extended to readers, technique #518, an essential design concept when seeking response.

vative organization. Conservative, but dollar-oriented.

Andy then tested several other mailings by other consultants against my control mailing. Those arrows and asterisks and stars still won. Millions more were mailed. And please recognize that both businesspeople and consumers were prospects.

That winning mailing was so successful that *Direct Marketing Magazine* featured a write-up on it, twice. I should have charged Andy much more than I did. He used that mailing again and again, and then again.

But, René, I'm mailing to doctors?

Okay, I used the same techniques in the fall of 1986 for *Educational Reviews* and Great Medical Getaways, both mailing from Birmingham to physicians all across the country. The techniques worked. And the University of Alabama had to approve what we printed.

All I can say is this: give it a try. You, and your banker, may be very pleasantly surprised by the heightened response you'll receive.

548 — FAMILIAR EVERYDAY SYMBOLS

Do not be afraid to use familiar everyday symbols as graphic directions for the recipients of your promotions.

For instance: the color and shape of a stop sign is universally recognized as a caution or, at the very least, a point for eye direction.

Do not be gross in the presentation of such symbols, but do not hesitate to use them, especially when flagging a complicated message that must be explained carefully.

549 — DOUBLE DUTY ARROWS

Frequently, arrows can be lengthened to include sales copy in the design.

This does double duty by not only directing the eye where to go, but also telling the reader what to do.

550 — BRAINSTORMING DESIGN CONCEPTS

Long-revered virtues such as economy, frugality, sturdy construction, durability, and other long-life features often can be best communicated by using an old-fashioned layout, serif type faces, and expository copy.

Try this tastefully. Perhaps your artist can use a sepiatone to convey longevity.

There are dozens of wonderful ways to visually communicate the worthwhile nature of your proposition, and it will pay you to brainstorm your design concepts with an open-minded artist.

551 — CURRENT VOGUE?

No one says your art director must swing with the current vogue in typography and graphic design on all occasions.

There are many appropriate occasions to have an old-fashioned graphic appearance, a news bulletin appearance, a screaming telegram format, and layouts other than crisp, modern or "fashiony" graphics.

552 — TIRED EYES

Did you know that for body copy, also known as text copy (not headlines), the maximum width for the eye to absorb everything on a single line is 16.4 picas of 10-point type?

Use body copy that is wider than that, and you run the risk of the eye getting tired as it moves from the end of one line to the beginning of the next. Tired eyes contribute to falloff in readership.

Yes, you can go wider if your point size increases.

René, where did you come up with this guideline?

From Edmund C. Arnold, America's foremost expert on typography, who now teaches at Virginia Commonwealth University.

553 — BEAUTY OR MESSAGE

While backslants and other modern graphic treatments of headline type may please your eye and tickle your art director, they may not gain readership or understanding.

They may focus the reader's eye on the beauty of what you have created and not the message! Restrict selection of typefaces to those which are most readable and most appropriate for your message.

554 — REVERSE LOGIC

Avoid printing large blocks of body copy in reverse.

One of the nation's largest mailers, a catalog sales plan, prints its entire order form stub copy in reverse and no one can read it. You want your messages read.

555 — LITTLE REVERSE TYPE

Use as little reverse type as possible.

Use no reverse type if it is in a small size and has serifs. Serif type fills in when reversed, tending to increase reading difficulty.

556 — EYESIGHT CONCERN

Many people have eyesight problems. Don't reduce, cram, or jam!

Use type that is large enough and easy enough to be read by someone with bifocals or trifocals...without moving his head!

557 — UPPER CASE EMPHASIS

Upper-case type is harder to read than lower-case type. But upper case can be used for emphasis within an otherwise all lower case headline.

Here's a headline as an example:

"Vacations that TURN YOU ON to new adventure, new excitement!"

That headline is more readable because it is in lower case, but the emphasis is placed exactly where you want it, on the key point of reader excitement.

558 — THE RIGHT TYPE

Although there is nothing wrong with using type set by a typesetter for the body of a letter as long as you use serif type, typewriter type is warmer in its appeal, looks like a letter should look, and pulls better...a lot better.

559 — TWO FAMILIES

Who says you can't mix serif and sans-serif typefaces in the same di-

rect mail promotion piece! You certainly can.

But don't use so many typefaces that the reader's eye flow is disrupted or annoyed. Generally, I stick to two type families for a single mailing.

Oh, all right, you've seen some of my mailings with three type families. The third is used for titles, like the title of a book or seminar or manual. Only for titles or logos will I allow a third type family to creep into my mailings.

560 — A SECOND COLOR

One of the best ways to use a second color in headlines is to run the entire headline in one color and highlight a few key words such as "free trial offer" with the second color so that phrase has extra emphasis.

561 — THE HONEST COLOR

Did you know that red meant honesty and fair dealings to almost all North American Indian tribes? That's why the Royal Canadian Mounted Police chose scarlet as the color for their tunics over 100 years ago.

Many people still believe that red is a color of honor and prestige, and it's the least expensive color your printer offers (other than black) because it's used often. So don't be too quick to jump into other colors before you consider good old standard red and black.

Oh yes, red and black usually is the highest-pulling two-color ink combination.

562 — DARING COLORS

I am always amused by people who believe promotions to executives must be presented with black ink on gray stock, or brown ink on buff, or "non-offensive blue" on white.

Be a bit daring to attract attention and see what your results will be. Purple and orange look great on beige. So do magenta and peacock, even though those color combinations sound horrendous. Be inventive!

563 — "ROUTE TO" ENDORSEMENT

To achieve high pass-along readership within companies, of course your mailing piece will carry a "route to" endorsement.

564 — ROUTING INSTRUCTIONS

You can strengthen the effectiveness of routing instructions by including a deadline for response.

565 — A SECOND LETTER

If you use a second letter in the same package, try illustrating it with a pho-

Illustration #38

ATTENTION...
MAIL ROOM or
SECRETARY or
RECEPTIONIST
Several persons in your organization can benefit from this timely notice.
PLEASE ROUTE TO:
☐ President
☐ VP-Sales
☐ Marketing Director
☐ Sales Manager
☐ Catalog Director
☐ Advertising Manager
☐ Promotion Director
☐ Direct Mail Manager
☐ Ad Copywriter
☐ Promotion Designer
☐ _____
☐ _____
Thank You.

Typical routing box, technique #563, from a Gnam seminar mailing, gets mail passed to proper executives.

tograph of the writer of the second letter to reinforce its authenticity.

566 — BULK-RATE POSTAGE

If you are using bulk rate postage, do not try to give the appearance of a first class mailing by dropping a tint into the indicia box, stippling the type in the indicia and using a tint to give the effect of a stamp. It's legal, but...

All you're doing is attracting the eye to the indicia instead of to your selling message. You are then telling people that you consider them worth third class postage!

567 — IMPACT NUMBERS

Remember to employ numbers by the impact you wish to achieve. Here are some examples:

One tenth	appears to be smaller than 10%.
200 cents	may seem larger than two dollars.
$40 million	doesn't impress as much as $40,000,000.00.

568 — COLORFUL EFFECT

If you can only afford two colors, try duotones, other tint combinations, and colored stock to give a more colorful effect to your promotion.

569 — "RED-LETTER" TECHNIQUE

Decades ago, when there wasn't much mail, the "red letter" technique (printing the body copy of a letter in red and calling attention to it on the outgoing envelope) frequently served well as a method of attracting attention to the importance of the message.

Today there's far too much mail competition, as well as attention-getting competition from other media, to use that technique successfully. Remember, too, that printing body copy in red makes it difficult for the eye to read. The recipient's attention span can fade.

Use red, but use it for highlights and emphasis points.

570 — COMPANY NAME

If you must refer to your company frequently in the body of your letter copy, do not put your company name in all caps.

Otherwise, all the reader will see is your name and not what he can do with your products or services.

571 — POINTS OF EMPHASIS

A good letter is not all flush left and right, nor is it all flush left with ragged right edges.

It is flush left, ragged right, with indented paragraphs to intentionally guide the reader to points of emphasis or explanation.

572 — SMOOTH VISUAL FLOW

A good letter should give the reader a smooth visual flow.

While it is helpful to use attention-getting graphic devices, they should not be so disruptive that the reader — who may be accustomed to going from beginning to end — finds his eye path too disjointed.

573 — UNDERSCORING LINES

Rarely underscore more than two complete consecutive lines in a letter.

If you do, everything in the letter seems to scream that it's urgent and your reader may turn off completely or miss the true emphasis points.

Similarly, do not alternate a color paragraph with a black paragraph repetitively. The eye will go from color to color, and the balance will be unread.

Gulf Oil and Mobil Oil do this constantly. Maybe they copy each other. But no reasonable person would reasonably want to read all those red paragraphs alternating with black. And for people who have cataracts, can you imagine the problem of reading?

574 — EASY AND BREEZY

Try to set up a letter or brochure so it isn't jam packed.

A crowded page with column after column on a brochure or overly-wide reading material in a letter scares people off.

575 — READABILITY

Too many of us are solely concerned with the copy and graphic image of the promotion we create. We spend far too little time considering the readability of that mail.

Some of my seminars include 103 specific techniques for improving direct mail readability, so do not assume that the most well-intentioned graphic designer knows it all. Neither do I!

But this is a vital concern for the success of your promotion. If, at any time, any of your readers find it difficult to read and understand your promotion material easily, you run the risk of losing interest, losing a response.

576 — COPY, COPY, COPY!

Never depend on graphics or color to carry the selling load. Your copy must tell the whole story and motivate a response.

Art attracts attention, guides the eye, explains selling points, enhances the proposition, makes the product or service desirable. Copy sells.

CHAPTER 10

PRODUCTION

When you sell toothpaste for dinosaurs, and your copy says that a tyrannosaurus has 55 teeth, your readers know that you don't know your business. A tyrannosaurus has 65 teeth. It's the brontosaurus that has 55 teeth.

This is a most important point to consider: copy reading, defined as that stage at which you check all facts in your presentation.

We all know we should proofread 17,000 times. We don't want to appear as silly as Marriott Hotels misspelling its own name in the headline of an ad in *Eastern Review* magazine. And we don't want the awkwardness of *Sports Illustrated* doing a price hike mailing and citing the wrong new price. So we tend to over emphasize proofreading, and that's a correct stance. But proofreading is not copy reading. It's important that you also do copy reading (see No. 941).

Present one fact erroneously, or have a conflicting claim somewhere in your presentation, and the mother of that tyrannosaurus won't buy your toothpaste for her offspring!

Our readers judge us by the accuracy of our presentations, hoping to find that we're solid, reliable, okay to deal with. And that's a good reason to devote considerable attention to both copy reading and proofreading. But there's another stage of proofing, beyond that which we do with our copy and our printer's proofs. It's order proofing.

For instance:

A seemingly minor typing error led to a catastrophe in a direct mail campaign for Pete Delaney at *Westchester Illustrated* some years ago.

Pete was going to use a #14 outgoing envelope with an oversized order card perforated so that the recipient would return a section of it. The package also was to include a letter, a brochure, and a business reply envelope.

The order form section to be returned to *Westchester Illustrated* measured 4-1/4 inches by 4-1/2 inches. The business reply envelope was to be a #5-1/2 baronial which would accommodate that order form with ease and which would still fit in the outgoing #14 envelope.

Unfortunately, the production person who ordered the business reply envelopes sent the order to the envelope manufacturer calling for a #5 baronial business reply envelope. The difference is 1/4 inch in one direction and 1/2 inch in another direction. The #5-1/2 baronial is larger than the #5. One hundred thousand #5 business reply envelopes arrived at the lettershop. Only at that time did Pete discover that the order form would not fit the smaller business reply envelopes.

The error was traced to a secretarial typing error on the production person's order form. The production man was a very fastidious, careful individual, and his secretary was a very efficient, capable and longtime employee. It was just a small typing error that led to ordering #5 baronials instead of #5-1/2, but it cost Pete a severe delay on the mailing deadline and several thousand dollars to redo the order forms so they'd fit in the reply envelopes which already had arrived at the lettershop. (Redoing the order forms was less expensive than re-ordering the reply envelopes.)

No matter how much you trust those around you, and no matter how good they are, or how good you are, do proofread everything in direct mail, especially in direct mail production. The small amount of time you spend, even with a rapidly approaching deadline, is well worth preventing production goofs that can cost thousands, delay your mailing, and thus reduce the response you might otherwise anticipate.

The mailing I've described was scheduled to be mailed on December 26, 1978. The typing error delayed the mailing until January 16, 1979, throwing Pete's entire year's market-ing plan out of whack, affecting all follow-ups to people responding to this mailing, delaying all other promotions to those people, changing the course of his company's cash flow and thereby affecting his banking relationship on his line of credit as well as changing the number of efforts that his sales people could make based on the results of this mailing. It was a nightmare.

Based on this experience, I have a suggestion for you. Yes, have your loyal staff proofread everything, again and again. Then, after everything has been sent to those who must receive it, you take extra photocopies home and check them over again in the evening or on a weekend.

Lynda Rosenthal, Vice President of Marketing at InfoMart in Dallas before she became a top executive at Unisys, did exactly that. Susan, Lynda's secretary, prepared a set of folders in Lynda's "homework" bag. She had two of them. One went home Monday with copies of everything the 26 people in her department processed on Monday. It came back with her Tuesday morning, annotated with instructions to Susan on what should be filed and what needed further action or double-checking or correcting. As things progressed on Tuesday, Susan loaded the other bag for Lynda to take home Tuesday evening. On Wednesday, the first homework bag was ready to go again.

No one told Lynda to set up this system. She invented it. I pass it on to you with her blessing.

Does it require too much evening work? Maybe. But maybe it's among the reasons why Ms. Rosenthal was the only female Vice President at a mammoth organization that's loaded with males. It may also be among the reasons why she has a new Mercedes and earns a six-figure salary.

577 — SINGLE TOTAL IMPRESSION

Somerset Maugham once said "in anything you write, it is the single total impression that counts!"

I am always willing to spend just a touch more on production to achieve that single total impression.

578 — REVERSE DEADLINES

Always try to set up your sales promotion or direct mail production schedule on a reverse deadline, starting with the day on which you would like to mail and working backward through all stages of lettershop, printing, mechanical assembly, creative, lists, concepts — in that sequence — instead of doing it the other way around.

Then you can determine which aspects of production must be speeded up to meet the mail date.

Use a standard form (see next page), but be certain to be flexible in allowing for changes and unforeseen events like illnesses and paper shortages. The time periods on the author's form are for major projects by major corporations. Less involved projects by entrepreneurial executives usually require less time.

579 — EASY INSERT

The most basic thing to remember is that your order form should fit inside your reply envelope, preferably without folding.

It should be easy to insert, so a potential respondent has no problems. Make it easy to put a check in that envelope, too.

580 — MACHINABLE DESIGN

Make sure every direct mail piece you design is machinable, even if it is for a small test that will be hand inserted.

Carefully review folding, thicknesses, weight, and inserting tolerances.

If the test is successful, you will go to larger quantities on mechanical inserting equipment to reduce costs at your lettershop.

581 — METER IMPRESSIONS

Many newcomers to direct mail and sales promotion feel that a postage stamp gives a more personal appearance.

That's true, but meter impressions are widely accepted by recipients in both consumer and business worlds today and should not be overlooked. Meter impressions usually outpull indicia imprints, although slightly.

582 — PROHIBITIVE COST

Rarely use the endorsement "address correction requested" on mailing pieces directed to outside lists.

The cost of those nixies coming back to you is prohibitive. It's the bottom line on your mailing that counts, not the percentage of deliverability.

583 — BASIC GUIDELINE

Your company name, address, and zip code are to appear on every printed piece in an envelope mailing with the single possible exception of the outgoing envelope.

Frequently, direct mailers forget this very basic guideline and then when inserting machines skip certain inserts, recipients get less than the complete package, sometimes without an address to which to respond.

My favorite story on this point comes from New Zealand:

My client sent me a 23-piece sales lead follow-up mailing and asked me to file it so I'd be familiar with it when working on our next project. Instead, I called him instantly because seven-

Illustration #39 | *"Prodsked" is the author's standard Production Schedule form for establishing reverse deadlines, technique #578.*

Job Number_____ Job Name_____ **LOG** Start Date_____

Goal or Description of this Job_____

Client Company_____ Client Contact Person_____

Client Phone Numbers: Work_____ Home_____ Emergency_____

PRODSKED *WARNING: ALL TIMES INDICATED ARE "WORKING DAYS"*

Schedule Revised_____ Revised_____ Revised_____ Revised_____ Revised_____

NOTE: *To plan a new* Production Schedule, start with desired mail date or completion date and fill in this form from bottom up as you consult your calendar *and* the client. Mark dates *only* for items which pertain to this job and adjust required workdays according to current knowledge of what is on hand and what may require shorter or longer time. Consult with the client at every stage of work progress and *always give the client a revised schedule!*

EXAMPLES: If no photography is required, you save 10 working days. If photos are in a file, you may need just one day to assemble them. But if a specialized photographer is required, you may need more than 10 working days. If photography can be done simultaneously with other job items, you may save working time. *CAUTION: Do not be optimistic in setting any schedules!* Remember to allow delivery times.

WARNINGS: [ ] envos, [ ] extra bindery, [ ] perfs, [ ] die-cuts, [ ] new dies, [ ] windows, [ ] seps, [ ] cello, [ ] pix, [ ] split runs, [ ] tokens

START DATE	JOB STAGES	WORK DAYS	PROBLEMS/COMMENTS	ACTUAL FINISH
_____	1 Materials from Client	__1-15__	_____	_____
_____	2 Consultation Work	__1-3__	__MAKE SURE_____	_____
_____	3 Creative Work: Copy & Rough Layouts	_20-40__	__YOU THINK_____	_____
_____	4 Client Approval/Changes on Creative Work	__1-10__	__ABOUT HOLIDAYS_____	_____
_____	5 Creative Revisions per Client Comments	__1-15__	__AND UNFORESEEN_____	_____
_____	6 List/Media Selection	__1-10__	__DELAYS_____	_____
_____	7 Final Creative Approvals by Client	__1-3__	_____	_____
_____	8 Photography/Illustrations	__1-20__	_____	_____
_____	9 List/Media Ordering	__1-3__	_____	_____
_____	10 Consultation/Review Meeting with Client	____1__	_____	_____
_____	11 Typesetting, Stats, PMTs	__1-10__	__Remember:_____	_____
_____	12 Art Assembly (Mechanicals, Ruling, Etc.)	__1-10__	__SOMEONE_____	_____
_____	13 Client Approval/Changes to ArtBoard Proofs	__1-3__	__WILL TELL_____	_____
_____	14 Make Client Changes (AA's at extra charge)	__1-5__	__US THAT_____	_____
_____	15 Client Approval of 1st Client AA Revisions	__1-2__	__THE JOB_____	_____
_____	16 Make Client Changes (AA's at extra charge)	__1-5__	__IS ON_____	_____
_____	17 Client Approval of 2nd Client AA Revisions	__1-2__	__THE TRUCK_____	_____
_____	18 Final Material to Printers (MakeReady)	_2-20__	__AND THE TRUCK_____	_____
_____	19 List/Media Arrivals/Insertion Materials	____1__	__USUALLY IS LOST !_____	_____
_____	20 Client Approval of Printer/Media Proofs	__1-5__	_____	_____
_____	21 Make Client Changes (AA's at extra charge)	__1-10__	_____	_____
_____	22 Printing TimeTable (includes delivery)	_5-30__	__WE WILL TRY OUR BEST____	_____
_____	23 Lettershop TimeTable (includes mailing)	_2-10__	__TO BEAT THE DEADLINE____	_____
_____	24 Samples to Client, Final Bills, Job File Close	__1-2__	_____	_____

ALLOW 48-223 "WORKING DAYS" (9-45 weeks) TO YOUR MAIL DATE

René Gnam, Leslie Gray
René Gnam Consultation Corp.
US MAIL: Box 3877, Holiday, FL 34690
COURIER: 1 Response Road, Tarpon Springs, FL 34689
813-938-1555

Joy Warech, Sue Polan
Response Mailing Lists
Send both US MAIL and Couriers to:
20200 NE 10th Place, Miami, FL 33179
305-652-4610

teen of the nineteen pieces loosely inserted in his beautiful folder did not have his company name, address, or phone number.

584 — FILM NEGATIVES

It nearly always pays to keep a spare set of film negatives of your ad or direct mail piece in your office when you ship the finished artwork to a publication or printer.

Publications and printers are notorious for losing artwork, damaging it, or taking inordinate delays in returning it to you so that you miss your next deadline.

Does this mean, René, that I should ship negs instead of art?

Yes, for magazine ads. No, for direct mail. But, for direct mail, shoot a set of negs before shipping the art. Don't bother with opaque. All you want is insurance.

585 — HELPFUL HINTS

You will be amazed by the helpful hints you can get on preparation of space ads, direct mail, and sales literature by reading appropriate trade publications.

Check with a professional in the field for a recommended list of current favorites.

586 — WEB PRESSES

If your printing quantity is 20,000 pieces or more, investigate web presses.

Often you can achieve sizable economies.

587 — VALUABLE ALLY

Many small web presses often achieve 30 to 50% savings compared with sheet-fed presses, and in larger quantities — 50,000 or more — larger web presses do likewise.

Yes, you do lose some quality with web printing. Not much. And for most direct mail efforts, a good web printer is a very valuable ally.

588 — PERFORATED TOKENS

If you use die-cut tokens and are hunting for a method of reducing your in-the-mail cost, experiment with using perforated tokens with strip gum on the back.

589 — FULL COLOR ADVANTAGE

A general guideline used by many mass consumer mailers is that two colors of ink will slightly outpull one color, while full color will increase the response over two-color jobs by about 25%. No such figures are available for business-to-business mailings.

590 — LIMITED SPACE

Part of our problem in handling creative work and production aspects of large mailings is having insufficient working space. Because we have limited space, we can't view everything as it is or in perspective.

Here's how I handle that problem:

First, I use NO desks. Out of sight does mean out of mind. If you place projects in drawers, you tend to forget deadlines, notes that should be placed in those files, and — most importantly — names of those projects are out of mind, leaving scant chance for sudden thought development that could occur if you spotted the folders.

Instead, use tables, lots of them. A table forces you to clear clutter on many occasions, just so you can have a clean spot to write phone notes, if nothing else.

TABLE #1:

Usually semi-clear. This is your "desk" for the phone, for pressing projects, meeting staff, taking notes, checking schedules.

TABLE #2:

Cleared daily. This table is your "in box," allowing your secretary to make plenty of different piles for items that would get lost under other things in a single pile.

TABLE #3:

Cleared as projects are completed and passed to others for processing. This table is for actual working, daydreaming, sorting your current projects, developing project concepts.

TABLE #4:

Always messy. It's your constant file cabinet of "someday I'll get to it" project folders.

TABLE #5:

Usually messy, but not forever as this table is for large projects and bulky items requiring their own separate areas.

Sure, you'll develop your own table system. Try it and see how much more productive you are. It made me more productive and more alert to deadlines and projects, so much so that now I rarely use less than eight tables -- in one room -- for everyday work.

591 — SIMULATED PARCHMENT

Do you have a promotion that attempts to sell a quality item like expensive jewelry, or a plan that has obvious value like life insurance?

Try using simulated parchment paper for your letter, guarantee form or other such item. Yes, it's much more expensive. But it also gives the recipient the immediate impression that what you have to say is worth reading simply because you chose such expensive stock.

592 — METERED IMPRINT

If you use third class mail in your promotional effort, you can avoid the "third class" look of an indicia by using a third class metered imprint in washed-out or tinted black ink so it isn't closely noticed.

593 — CHECKING YOUR SOURCES

If you cannot deliver coded labels to your lettershop, ask yourself this question:

Are you better off coding your order forms on an imprinting machine at the lettershop, or having your order forms coded while on press and being perforated by your printer?

Check with both sources before making your decision.

594 — WORKING OFF LOCATION

When doing a large mailing at a location of a captive list which cannot be released to you, it may pay you to print and mail in the same city as the list owner rather than printing with your regular supplier and shipping to the list owner's lettershop.

595 — BUSINESSLIKE COMMUNICATION

When doing a two-page letter, have you considered using two pages and printing only on one side of each?

Sometimes it gives more of an executive feeling, a businesslike communication. However, this technique usually is not as cost-effective for consumer mailing unless you are selling a high-priced item or collectibles. (Collectibles are usually high priced.)

Two sides of a single sheet do not pull as well as two single sheets printed on one side only. But, the reason why you see so many two-sided letters is that there's only slight additional pull with two sheets. You should split test this for cost effectiveness.

596 — ORDER OF INSERTS

Be certain to specify the order in which inserts should be enclosed in your outgoing envelope.

Pay particular attention to the piece which faces the back of the envelope as it is most likely to be read first, but pay attention also to the piece which faces the front of the envelope since different people remove inserts from envelopes differently.

597 — SPECIFYING FOLDS FOR INSERTS

Be careful on specifying folds for inserts in your mailing package.

On a letter, for example, you may want the letterhead facing out, or if it appears at the bottom, you may not. The top may have an important headline which could face out.

What, René, print my letterhead at the bottom?

Of course, unless you're selling letterheads. Now, don't do this on every letter you print. But remember that there is no rule saying that letterheads must always be at the top of letters!

598 — IN-LINE PRINTING

If your promotion piece must be folded or perforated or consecutively numbered after printing, investigate in-line printing which frequently can reduce your costs by 25% on such services.

599 — LARGE QUANTITY PRINTING

In large quantity printing, you frequently can save as much as 35 to 40% on paper costs by purchasing a lower grade sheet for your brochures and then having the printer varnish the sheet to give a high-toned effect.

600 — ORDER CARD LOOK

Want to see how your letter or order card will look on a variety of paper stocks?

Easy! Ask your art department to order a proof of the mechanical on acetate. Then hold the acetate print over the paper stocks you're considering.

601 — PAPER STOCK COLOR

Often it pays to keep all paper stock in a mailing white or buff, or a similarly light color.

But print your order form or response device on colored stock so it stands out and attracts the eye to the point of ordering.

602 — CONTRASTING COLOR

Reply envelopes or order forms usually should be of a contrasting color rather than the same color as the rest of the components in your mailing — so they stand out and galvanize prospects into responding.

If you are stuck with using the same color stock, try printing with large benday areas in an alternate color of ink to make your order forms and reply envelopes stand out.

603 — LETTER SIZES

Do not fall into the trap of thinking that you have to use 8-1/2 x 11 letters because 8-1/2 x 11 is standard size paper in the United States.

Shorter, longer, and wider sizes attract attention by their uniqueness and can do a selling job for you.

604 — STANDARD SIZES

Several standard sizes of letter stock are available at little or no extra cost.

Some examples are: 7 x 10, 8-1/2 x 14, 4-1/4 x 5-1/2, 5-1/2 x 8-1/2. "Odd" size letters attract more attention in business environments. Small sizes appear to symbolize personal correspondence, getting rapid readership in consumer households.

A favorite letter of mine was for The Bud Company in Timonium, MD, promoting attendance at a trade show exhibit booth. I designed the letter to be 8-1/2 x 22, printed one side only. Now, how did I do that inexpensively? I just divided a 17 x 22 sheet a bit differently from most folks who turn it into two 11 x 17 sheets.

605 — CODING COPY APPROACH

If you use more than one offer or more than one list or more than one copy approach, always make absolutely certain that you code which is which, either on the address label or on the response device.

That way you can determine which response came from which effort.

606 — CATALOG OR BOOK

If you publish a catalog or book, be certain your fulfillment package includes a bookmark with a promotion for your next offer.

It will be one of the highest read promotion pieces you ever create.

607 — FOLD, POP, CUT

Do not be afraid to use odd folds or shapes, pop-ups and cut-outs.

These techniques often attract greater attention to specified copy themes and make your message better read.

608 — LOOSE, NOT STAPLED

Rarely staple two pieces together in a mailing.

People look at a lot of things falling out of an envelope. Leave everything loose, and your components will attract your prospect's eye.

609 — USING STOCK INK COLORS

For most promotion efforts that are not printed in full color, it is not necessary to pay the extra expense for PMS (Pantone Matching System) inks.

Use whatever ink colors are stocked by your regular printing suppliers, and you will save a little money.

610 — SPECIFIC COLOR EFFECT

When you want to achieve a specific color effect, use Pantone inks because they give you a selection of more than 870 different colors. Pantone system books give you swatches showing how each color looks on coated and uncoated stock.

Pantone is fairly common in North America, being used by almost every decent printer. But Japan has a new competitor, Toyo Ink Manufacturing Company.

Toyo, which hit the USA scene in the fall of 1986, offers over 700 colors and is marketing primarily to designers and artists. However, this is the wrong marketing route because if the printer doesn't have the Toyo colors that the artist specifies, delivery delays may occur.

Still, Toyo is expected to expand its marketing, so one day you may have a choice of color matching systems.

611 — AD COLOR TONES

On very expensive printing jobs where the highest possible quality is desired, specify AD (art director) color tones and insist that your printer match them.

But this is a very expensive way to go, since Pantone mixing will usually give you fine quality if you have a fine printer.

612 — GIVING LIST SEVERAL CODES

If you are using a very large list and anticipate that your lettershop may not be able to mail all of that list on one day, give the list several codes by splitting it into even quantities and insisting that the lettershop mail at least two complete codes from other lists on that day.

Then you can compare your list performance.

613 — MAILING SPLIT QUANTITIES

Never permit a lettershop to mail split quantities of the same list on different days unless they bear different codes.

All names in a given code (and preferably all codes, too) ideally should be mailed on the same day so you can accurately gauge your response.

614 — QUICK FOLLOW-UP MAILING

If you intend to do a follow-up mailing rather quickly, make sure your lettershop understands that all tests must be mailed on the same day so you can evaluate response properly (see No. 202).

Then get back into the mail with a fast continuation.

615 — THE FINAL CHECK

No promotion campaign should ever go to the printer prior to a final check by the person in supreme command of the project.

Attention to every detail is absolutely paramount at this stage. Do not allow a junior production or paste-up person to give a final okay.

Illustration #40

This looks like an easy piece to produce, but it has more details than a person might expect. Besides the two different tickets and six dates, the author created splits on alternate copy approaches and different photos, cities, gifts, singers and ministers.

That's why technique #615 is so vital to your mailing success. Triple-check all details before releasing art to be printed.

CHAPTER 11

PREMIUMS

How often we probe our minds mightily in the search for a good premium, not realizing that we may already have a proper premium, or even more than one, right in our own establishment.

May I suggest that you read the techniques in this chapter and then return to this introduction for some startling revelations as to the premiums you already have.

First...

Did you know that a checklist is a good premium? Sure is. And it's easy to develop.

For Bob Spidell's *California Tax Report*, I suggested a checklist of 79 important filing dates for accountants. The publisher already had the list, on a month-by-month basis, as part of his newsletter coverage. It was easy to put it together and give it away free.

For Dave Buster's School of Construction, I suggested a checklist of sample questions that would be asked on a contractor's state exam. The questions were already part of the school's curriculum.

For Rich Perelman's *U.S. Athletics Report*, I suggested statistics of major

track and field events to be reproduced on 3x5 cards, one for each major event. The stats were already on the computer for use in the publication.

> **You probably have at least one checklist already in your stable. Open the door to new ideas, and you'll have another one or two or ten or twenty checklists. Most people like to receive checklists to be certain they have all major points on a subject of interest and haven't overlooked anything.**
>
> **That's why checklists are well received as premiums.**

Here are some ideas on a variety of checklists, to start your thinking:

"How to know when you can discard those files of old, outdated tax forms."

"How to make maximum use of your office copier without increasing costs."

"36 Ways you can use your garlic squeezer to create tangier recipes."

"The pros and cons of owning your

own corporate plane, plus how to know when to make this investment."

"How to host an office Christmas party without running any risks."

"The 77 easiest ways to train new employees on handling daily computer database input."

Second...
You are now giving something away anyway. Why not make it a premium?

EXAMPLE:
Software is purchased or leased on a disk, but the manual often is free. Divide the manual in sections. Part One is what the customer needs to know to survive with the disk software. Part Two has extra models or advanced applications. The prospect now sees a greater perception of value when buying from you.

I proposed exactly this sort of thing to Profitable People Skills, Inc., in sales of *The People Factor*, a videotape for in-house dental staff training. Divide the tape in two, I said to John David. Let the dentists buy one tape for their staffs and get a free tape for themselves as managers. Also, do a small series of checklists as additional premiums. This enabled us to make the tape price much higher because suddenly John was selling a kit, not just a videotape.

Third...
With a little planning, you can use salesmen's literature as a premium. Of course, you can!

Imagine taking some of that literature and expanding it into a guidebook, a manual, a looseleaf binder. It can, and has, been done successfully. Miracle Span Buildings even provides a chart on which you can draw your own new building. So does Aztec, the Miracle Span competitor. Others create paperbound books.

The point is:

Search your mind and those of your associates, agencies, or consultants to determine what can be done with existing materials and knowledge.

Maybe it's a cassette, recorded by your engineers, research managers, and product managers, telling me all the wonders of your electronic ice tongs. Of course, that cassette also gives me the do's and don'ts of electronic ice tongs. Now, I've had free, valuable information from you, plus an introduction into the exciting world of tonging ice electronically.

You can do it! Give it a try!

616 — MYSTERY GIFT

In using premiums, can you offer a "mystery gift"?

Even if it's an inexpensive booklet, the "mystery" factor often entices borderline prospects to become customers.

617 — CITE DOLLAR VALUE

Never offer a "mystery" gift unless you cite its dollar or use-value so your reader can make a logical decision on whether to respond because of the attractiveness of the premium.

The exception to this guideline is when promoting party or convention attendance. Then the obvious value of the premium could be fun-related or business-related.

618 — CONTINUITY SELLING

One of the most difficult direct mail goals to achieve is continuity selling to an established or targeted base of customers.

Frequently, the way to reach your goal is to offer continuing discounts in a series (such as a coupon book) or premiums for continuing orders (such as an extra hunk of cheese if you buy from our cheese club every month).

619 — A STRONGER LETTER

If you continually use premiums to attract new customers and you're considering another test mailing, try using strong copy without a premium, or perhaps a stronger letter.

Customers who are attracted by premiums are less likely to renew or purchase again than customers who bought because they were intrigued solely by your product. And wouldn't you like to save the premium expense?

EXAMPLE:

When *The Saturday Evening Post* retained me to create a new subscriber mailing, it was giving away a set of 12 Norman Rockwell prints as its premium. That was very expensive for fulfillment.

My mailing eliminated the premium but used much more selling copy than the previous control. Not only did this new package pull more than the control, but it saved all the cost of the premiums. And, from 1972 to 1979, no mailing did better.

If you can create a seven-year winning package and reduce your premium costs, it may well be worth a test investment.

620 — EARLY-BIRD OFFERS

"Early-bird" offers are best promoted if you use a discount or premium in your promotion.

621 — PRODUCT-RELATED PREMIUMS

Using a premium can increase response by as much as 40% over the same copy without a premium.

But be certain that your prospect isn't buying your product because of the premium. To avoid this, be sure to use product-related premiums.

622 — SUCCESSFUL PREMIUM

If your test mailing shows that a premium or free gift offer has been successful, retest it with a split test of two premiums (although possibly at a lower value each) for the same offer.

You are likely to discover that multiple premiums will dramatically increase your direct mail response by appealing to "the greed factor."

623 — EDUCATIONAL MARKET

Premium offers are especially viable when reaching the educational market because educators have long been accustomed to offers containing premiums.

How so, René?

Manufacturers of audio-visual equipment and textbook publishers continually offer "review" or "preview" deals so teachers and professors can recommend certain equipment and/ or titles for "adoption." Those deals have trained educators to expect special "gifts."

Thus, if educators don't see a premium offer from you and do from your competitor, they're less likely to order from you.

624 — APPROPRIATE PREMIUM

Try to make your premium appropriate to the nature of your basic offer.

In this manner, you are relatively certain that your purchaser is interested in your product and related items and is not purchasing merely to obtain the premium.

625 — FREE TRIAL

When offering a free trial of your product or service, consider inducing higher response by an attractive free gift as a premium.

If you do this, make certain that the free gift can be retained by the respondent, even if he cancels the order or returns the product.

626 — RELATED ACCESSORY

The best free gift you usually can offer with a product or service is a related accessory or service, such as a booster antenna for a radio. This produces only respondents who genuinely want the product or service being promoted.

Examine your product to determine whether certain accessories or features can be offered as premiums.

627 — PREMIUM HUNTERS

Never use a free gift as a premium if the value of the gift is greater than the value of the merchandise being sold, because you will suddenly have a list of premium seekers rather than product purchasers. Renewability or repeat sales will be exceptionally difficult, and you will attract bad credit risks.

Oh, René, who would even consider a premium of greater value than the main item?

Lots of folks. When they want to cream names from a rented file. Or, when they have an urgent need to increase their customer base so they can sell other items.

628 — RENEWABILITY GAMBLE

Premiums do hike response, but nearly always are a gamble on renewability or repeat (back-end) purchases.

As much as possible, tie your premiums in logically with the products, services, or publications you are marketing. A purchaser motivated by a "come-on" is less likely to become a renewing or repeat customer than one who initially purchases as a result of a logically tied-in, affinity premium.

629 — UNRELATED VALUABLE PREMIUMS

Be cautious about offering premiums of great value that are not related to your product.

You will create a purchaser who sees your offer as accompanied by a bribe, and he thus will be less likely to purchase your product at the regular price on a future promotion.

630 — FREE INFO PREMIUM

One of the best methods of increasing response on a product offering is to accompany that offer with a premium of free information on a subject allied in interest to the product being sold.

631 — EDUCATIONAL BOOKLETS

Companies having small staffs and lacking publication divisions frequently find it difficult and time-consuming to create "educational" or "informative" booklets to use as incentives accompanying their offerings. They also find it hard to take an outside look at the situation.

There are several ways to handle this problem:

1. Both *Reader's Digest* and *Changing Times* offer reprint booklets at quantity discounts for use in mailings by others, and the title listings are so extensive that frequently a mail merchandiser can find a re-

print that's appropriate to his product.

2. Your ad agency may be able to create the booklets.

3. Your marketing consultant should be able to do it.

4. Check with a nearby college to find a marketing professor or a graduate student to do the rough drafts. Then, have your agency or consultant revise them.

5. Call the editor of a newsletter in your field. Perhaps he or she will moonlight for you. If not, chances are good that you'll get a referral to a writer with some experience in your arena.

Illustration #41

When John Benton, publisher of Formula Magazine, was searching for a free information premium, technique #630, the author recommended reprinting old race statistics from the magazine and producing this 54-page gift booklet.

632 — ESTABLISH EXPERIENCE

In addition to achieving high response from prospect lists, the offer of a free booklet or free information helps establish your company's specialized experience in a given field and gives you a posture of being ready to help the consumer or businessperson with valuable information.

This posture often gives you the rub-off effect of increasing later sales.

633 — MINIMUM PURCHASE

When offering premiums with purchases, consider structuring your offer toward a minimum purchase quantity or minimum purchase term.

That can step up the dollar volume from your mail.

634 — INCENTIVE PREMIUMS

Premiums used as incentives for purchasing can be cited as having actual dollar value, even though you have allocated the cost of the premium as a self-liquidator in your product and fulfillment analysis.

635 — BUSINESS GIFTS

In mailing to businesses and institutions, offering a choice of a free gift is a frequently overlooked, dramatic way to boost response.

636 — PREMIUM SELECTION

When offering a choice of a free gift in a promotion, test this selection of four distinctly different gifts:

1. a male-oriented premium,
2. a female-oriented premium,
3. an office or product-oriented premium, and

4. a premium that can be used at home or in the office.

The third choice enables the purchaser to rationalize away any objections to the "bribe" aspects of the premium. The other choices allow him to satisfy his "acquisition" orientation (otherwise called "greed").

637 — MISDIRECTING ATTENTION

Rarely consider offering a choice of premiums on mailings to consumers as you will focus their attention on the choice rather than on the basic proposition you are attempting to sell.

This misdirection of attention can result in lower response.

638 — VARIED VALUE

Certain direct mail marketers offer premiums that vary in value depending on the size of the order, term of subscription, or length of service contracted for.

Such offerings do not always increase the number of responses but usually do increase the dollar volume per response.

639 — FREE GIFT EXPECTATIONS

One of the pitfalls in offering premiums or other incentives for ordering is that you can train your customers to await the next free gift rather than purchasing your product, service, or subscription on its own merits.

That's the main reason why product-oriented premiums are best.

640 — OVER-PROMOTING THE PREMIUM

Do not fall into the trap of stressing what comes free (your premiums or accessories) to such an extent that you detract from the selling message you are trying to communicate.

You may over-promote the premium and produce less valuable customers who want only the premium.

641 — NEW AVENUE

Can your product be sold or given away by someone else?

This may open a whole new avenue to you if you consider the possibilities of offering your product as a premium or self-liquidator through other organizations.

You can even sell your own premiums. Lots of companies do. Just add an extra option to your reply form, perhaps saying:

"No, I don't want your $500 electronic juke box, but here's my $50 for the song book."

Doing this does get you a few song book orders. But its main purpose is to strengthen the perceived value of the premium right on the reply form.

Illustration #42

RG 3

PICK YOUR GIFT

FREE from South Central Bell

when you order Custom Calling Service(s)...

SPORTS CAP
One size fits all.
Print C in GIFT BOX on Certificate.

SUN VISOR
One size fits all.
Print V in GIFT BOX on Certificate.

T-SHIRT
Select Small, Medium, Large, Xtra Large. Print S or M or L or XL in GIFT BOX on Certificate.

All gift items are dark blue and white with the famous Bell symbol and the words "Ring My Bell." Allow 4 weeks for receipt as gifts are printed on receipt of your Custom Calling Service(s) order. One gift per residence. Request your gift today. Offer on the gift expires November 30, 1985.

PICK YOUR GIFT NOW

To request your gift and order SCB Custom Calling Services by mail:

1 Mark the YES boxes on your Certificate with the Service(s) you desire and then

2 Print the code letter of the gift you want in the Gift Box on your Certificate. Cap=C, Visor=V. For free T-Shirt, print the size you want in the Gift Box. Small=S, Medium=M, Large=L, Xtra Large=XL.

3 All gifts will be mailed to street address only. Please correct your address on your Certificate.

For fastest FREE Connection and FREE Gift:
"Ring My Bell" right now, by calling
1-800-233-1776 (extension 16) **TODAY!**

Technique #636 cites premium choices for business audiences. Here's the author's premium choice insert for South Central Bell Telephone's consumer lists.

CHAPTER 12

GUARANTEES

Have you noticed that these chapter introductions give you extra techniques, adding up to far beyond the promised 1,001 methods? Yes, there are 1,001 enumerated techniques. But the introductions give you about 20% more.

Why not try this yourself? It's a super way to reinforce your own guarantee. You see, if your customer gets more than he expects, he has less reason to request a refund. And...

Offering a refund if the customer is unhappy does these five wonderful things for you:

1. reinforces the feeling that yours is a good company to deal with,
2. eliminates my risk in purchasing,
3. allows me to see that I am "trying" your product or service, almost like a "home demonstration,"
4. boosts your response rate, and
5. leads me to become a steady, repeat customer.

These points are so important in today's backlash to what often is perceived, however rightly or wrongly, as a rip-off society, that the organization which does not offer a guarantee often is viewed as a less appropriate source than a competitive firm which does.

Thus, we need to offer guarantees even when our proposition is totally free. In that instance, you should use a guarantee to reassure your customer that when he responds he is under no obligation, not now, not ever.

Because we want our propositions to be seen as viable to the reader, our guarantees:

1. SHOULD be strongly worded.
2. SHOULD be clearly worded.
3. MUST leave no question that we mean what we guarantee.
4. MUST state the time period for which they apply.
5. SHOULD be positioned on a part of the mailing that is retained by the recipient.
6. SHOULD be referred to in the sales pitch in the letter.
7. SHOULD be referred to in the brochure if you use one.
8. SHOULD be referred to in the postscript of the letter unless you use the P.S. for strong urgency (deadline) copy. Even then, you can refer to the guarantee.

9. SHOULD offer an alternative, such as "if you don't like our dish towels, you can send them all back at our expense, get a full refund, and still keep the free pot scrubber."

However, do remember that if you promote a business or money-making opportunity and promise or imply a guaranteed income return, the Securities and Exchange Commission can charge you with offering unregistered securities. See your attorney on this, and also on the question of guarantee and warranty wording.

The legalities, briefly stated, are that a guarantee is on the buyer's satisfaction while a warranty is on a product's performance.

There are two types of warranties: *expressed* & *implied*.

An *expressed* warranty is an affirmation or a promise made by the seller to the purchaser. If you promise me something concerning your product, you are automatically giving me a warranty.

EXAMPLE from Boeing Aircraft:

"The 727-Series 200 has six exit doors." That expresses that the six doors must work.

An *implied* warranty is one imposed by law, for instance: fitness for the purpose for which I buy. If I buy for a given purpose and if your promotion implies that your product fits that purpose, you have automatically given me a warranty.

EXAMPLE from Eastern Airlines:

"Fly our Whisperjet." That implies that if you're in row 33 and if your ears hurt abnormally, you have a right to sue. People have!

It's tricky, so be careful about your warranty and guarantee wording to make sure the copy is how you want it to be, is cleared by your counsel, and that you're prepared to back it up fully. If there's a difference between what your attorney says and what you feel you need, call someone like me.

And now, for doubting Thomases who still are not as much in love with guarantees as I am, here's a response story for you, reported to me by my client, Larry Henrichs, publisher of *Sunshine Magazine* in Litchfield, IL:

After a consultation day, Larry left my office determined to try my recommendation of split-testing the use of a guarantee against a premium. He had limited space available and previously had always used a premium.

On some lists, the guarantee outpulled the premium by 16%...on others by 23%...and by as much as 36% on other lists. He wound up greatly reducing his costs while increasing his response. And that's why I strongly recommend that you, too, test a guarantee. It can work wonders for you.

And, why not turn a standard guarantee around? Offer 115% credit instead of a refund? Paul Richard at International Male in San Diego does that. He sells men's clothing by mail.

If you don't like an item, ship it back and get 115% credit toward your next purchase, instead of a refund or credit on your credit card. Paul says 45% of his customers have accepted this policy, and it has cut his refunds by over $100,000 per year. That means he has a greatly improved cash flow.

Or, how about this from Homer Perkins at Stanley Home Products? His agents are guaranteed a refund at 100% retail when they buy for their customers at 55% retail. Here's a quote from Homer:

"Our retail U.S. sales volume was $150,000,000. On that we wrote checks for $3,341.48 for returns. I didn't even figure out the percentage.

It's nothing! In fact, it's a plus for us! It gives a great feeling to our dealers, makes a good selling point about our quality and our customer satisfaction."

> **The technique of offering a strong guarantee works to both consumer and business audiences. Thus, try your very best to offer the very best guarantee you can.**

642 — STUBS AND GUARANTEES

Try to use a stub attached to the order form and employ that stub as a means of stressing the guarantee.

On the same stub, give the prospect a chance to complete a record of the purchase for himself. This tells him you are honorable and reputable as well as guaranteeing satisfaction.

643 — A LEGITIMATE OFFER

If you can use a guarantee, and you nearly always can and nearly always should, try putting a signature at the bottom of it.

Make the signature that of the highest ranking person in the company. This reinforces the feeling that yours is a legitimate offer, a legitimate guarantee, and a well-meaning firm.

Save this unique, Triple GUARANTEE

When you order from Construction Bookstore, you do so at our risk, not yours, because we absolutely insist that you be fully satisfied. That's why we ask that you save this guarantee.

1—Every book is exactly as described. If you find it is not what you expected, return it within 10 days at OUR COST for return shipping, and you will get a 100% refund.

2—Take 30 full days to review the book(s) you've received. Be sure they are right for you. If any book fails to be useful to you, just call "Customer Returns" at our toll-free number for instructions. Upon receipt of your return, we'll immediately send you a full refund check, or give a full credit to your credit card account, for the TOTAL amount you paid, including the shipping charges to get it to you. No questions asked. You're the only judge.

3—All our prices are guaranteed until December 29, 1989. Even if prices go up, we guarantee these prices until this date.

Our signatures below are our guarantee that we mean what we say. You do order at our risk, because you must be totally pleased or we get stung for the shipping costs!

F. Rola, President   Dave Buster, Vice-President

| Illustration #43 |

Reproduced here in actual size, this guarantee (created by René Gnam in 1986 and used in over 50 promotions since then), uses concepts expressed in techniques 643 - 647, 651 and 655.

644 — REFUND REQUESTS

In using a guarantee, can you make reference to a customer service department, ombudsman, or other party to whom refund requests should be directed?

If you tell me that I have a guarantee of a refund, and also tell me at the same time who will grant that refund, you have told me that you really intend to live up to your word.

Similarly, if I buy your product, or subscribe to your magazine, or donate to your charity, or sign a contract to use your service, to whom can I complain if I have a legitimate complaint? In your solicitation letter, your first mailing, your first space ad, tell me the name of a specific individual to whom I can direct my complaints. That gives me greater confidence in your organization and its people.

645 — CASH-WITH-ORDER RESPONSES

Almost always when asking for cash-with-order responses from rented files, offer a full money-back guarantee.

It will significantly increase your response because the new customer recognizes that you will stand behind your product.

646 — MONEY-BACK GUARANTEES

Please do not be afraid to offer money-back guarantees when asking for cash-with-order responses from house files.

Most active customers are unlikely to take the time and effort to return a product unless they are really dissatisfied with it. Active customers make fewer returns than new customers.

647 — FREE-TRIAL PERIOD

In offering a product on free trial, make sure that the length of the trial period is appropriate for the type of product you are offering.

Most people can read a book from cover to cover in a week or two, so a free trial guarantee for a period longer than that would be unneeded unless it is a research or reference volume.

But software usually takes longer to evaluate and try on a buyer's specific applications, so use a longer guarantee period. (See also No. 661).

648 — RESTATING A GUARANTEE

Try restating your guarantee in a way that makes it much more palatable and stimulating to your prospect.

One example is to switch your normal "full-price refunded if not happy" guarantee to say "we'll buy it back for the same price you pay."

649 — DEMONSTRATE CUSTOMER INTEREST

Be leery of using guarantees that offer more money back than the price of your product or service.

Such guarantees sometimes are difficult to believe.

Whoa, René, you implied in your intro to this chapter that refunds greater than the purchase price could be viable?

Yes, but then they must be very carefully and strongly worded, instilling a total feeling of honesty and customer interest, incorporating few sales pitches and sounding most authoritative and official.

650 — FULFILLING THE GUARANTEE

Any time you make a guarantee of any kind in direct mail, be absolutely certain that your entire staff knows you will live up to that guarantee.

And don't you forget it either.

651 — OFFICIAL BORDER

Try putting a border around a guarantee, calling attention to it and stressing the fact that it is, in fact, official.

652 — HOLDING CUSTOMER CHECK

Some mailers have discovered an offer that is better than a money-back guarantee.

It is telling the prospect that you won't cash his remittance check for 30 days and that if he decides to ask for a refund, he gets his own check back. Consider this version of a guarantee, but remember that you won't have use of the customer's money for the guarantee period.

653 — SEND MONEY

"If you are not fully satisfied, we will return your own check to you."

This guarantee copy also tells the customer to send you a check!

654 — A SEPARATE SLIP

Your guarantee is such an important element in a mailing that you should consider using it as a separate slip so it can be saved by the recipient. And your copy ought to tell him to save it!

So, consider making your guarantee into a valuable, perhaps separate document, using a fancy border, several ink colors, and perhaps a pretty simulated check background.

If your guarantee appears to be a valuable document, your offer must be worthwhile.

655 — ORDERING SUGGESTIONS

Guarantees can include short copy suggesting that the prospect place an order.

This concept has been scoffed at by certain "go-by-the-book" marketers at a few of my seminars. Well, here's a book that allows them to exercise their dormant creativity.

Think of it this way:

If you have a long-copy guarantee to convince me that I have no risk, why not add another line of copy suggesting that I go ahead and order?

EXAMPLE:

"That's why, since you have no risk, you'll save $48.62 by mailing your gold Discount Certificate today."

There's nothing offensive about this concept. It reinforces your own guarantee statement and guides the reader from the guarantee to your reply form.

656 — USING SMALL TYPE

Small type certainly can be used effectively in guarantees.

Many people feel that small type always contains a hidden gimmick or disclaimer. Prey on this belief by putting a dramatic statement (such as an unusual guarantee) in small type where the reader least expects it.

657 — PURCHASING CONVENIENCE

If your products or services are marketed at prices roughly equal to those of retail establishments, stress purchasing convenience and try offering a longer term guarantee to set your firm apart from retail competition.

658 — GIVE A RECORD

Guarantee copy can be strengthened by adding two lines at the bottom:

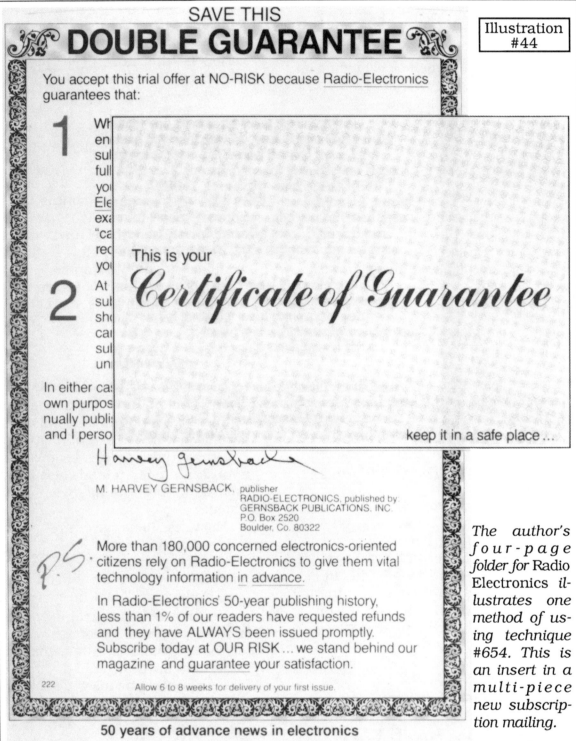

SAVE THIS

DOUBLE GUARANTEE

Illustration #44

You accept this trial offer at NO-RISK because Radio-Electronics guarantees that:

1 Wh
en
sul
full
yo
Ele
exa
"ca
rec
yo

2 At
sul
sho
ca
sul
un

In either ca:
own purpos
nually publi:
and I perso

This is your

Certificate of Guarantee

keep it in a safe place ...

Harvey Gernsback

M. HARVEY GERNSBACK, publisher
RADIO-ELECTRONICS, published by
GERNSBACK PUBLICATIONS, INC.
P.O. Box 2520
Boulder, Co. 80322

P.S.

More than 180,000 concerned electronics-oriented citizens rely on Radio-Electronics to give them vital technology information in advance.

In Radio-Electronics' 50-year publishing history, less than 1% of our readers have requested refunds and they have ALWAYS been issued promptly. Subscribe today at OUR RISK ... we stand behind our magazine and guarantee your satisfaction.

222   Allow 6 to 8 weeks for delivery of your first issue.

50 years of advance news in electronics

The author's four-page folder for Radio Electronics illustrates one method of using technique #654. This is an insert in a multi-piece new subscription mailing.

Note that this is a two-way guarantee. A cardinal "Gnamism" is: "if one works, try two." Guarantees have been effective since Ben Franklin invented the first one, so you know to use one. But if one works, double it. If two are more effective, use a triple or quadruple guarantee, and so on. Gnam has used a 13-way guarantee on insurance, a 22-way guarantee on extruded plastic, a 7-way guarantee on auto repairs, a 4-way guarantee on seminars, a 10-way guarantee on portable potties for recreational vehicles, and...well, by now you have the point!

1. Date ordered _____,
2. Amount paid _____.

The reader sees this both as a guarantee and as a method of holding you to it, because he now has a record of his transaction with you

And it works nicely for you because it implies that he should order.

659 — STRONG GUARANTEE

If you have been in business for a very long time and have had a strong guarantee, say so.

For one client, I say: "This guarantee policy has been strictly followed for 17 years."

660 — EXTENDING TRIAL PERIOD

You can never spend enough time in improving and strengthening your guarantee.

Try such tactics as extending the "on approval" or "trial" period. If you're offering a 30-day trial, what's wrong with 60 days?

I once used a two-year guarantee for *RN Magazine*, the professional journal for nurses, saying that the subscriber could keep all issues received in a two-year period and still request, and get, a full refund for the entire subscription. According to Howard Hurley, the circulation manager, refund requests did not increase. Response did.

Why is that so, René?

Read the next technique.

661 — ILLUSTRATE FAITH

The longer you make your guarantee period, the more your prospective customer will have faith that *you have faith* in your product or service.

And, the longer your guarantee period is, the more likely the customer is to order, since he knows he can give what you sell a thorough trial and evaluation.

Also, the longer your guarantee period is, the more likely the customer is to forget that he has a guarantee.

If you give me just 10 days to decide whether I'll keep your radial saw, I'll try every possible cut with it in a hurry to make sure that I've tested it within the guarantee period. But if you give me 12 months, I may not play with your saw for a few weeks or months. Then when I turn it on and start using it, I'll probably have little recall about your guarantee.

Cross Pen guarantees you can return its pens anytime. It's a lifetime guarantee. Can you do that? Try it.

662 — UNUSUAL DECLARATIONS

If you sell clothing or accessories and will not give a refund after the items have been worn, say so emphatically.

But, you will get greater response if you guarantee a refund or exchange even if the product has been "wear tested."

Heavens, René, give a refund on worn clothing?

Sure. Accept the worn item. Give a refund. Give the garment to charity as a tax deduction. Keep the customer.

You may be giving a refund on one or two sets of undershorts and turning that customer into someone who eventually buys an entire wardrobe from you, recommends you to others, and continues giving you business.

663 — REFUND PROJECTIONS

René, how many refund requests should I expect?

A rule of thumb is that more than 2% refund requests indicates:

1. A product or service problem,

2. An overzealous salesperson,
3. Inaccurately stated promotion pieces, or
4. The wrong lists.

The 2% guideline, and that's a high figure, does not apply to orders sent by C.O.D. service in response to broadcast commercials. There, you can expect up to 40% returns if your TV ads are not properly handled.

But, for most direct mail situations, when you start getting over 1.5% refund requests, you need to start investigating quickly and take steps to correct the return factor immediately.

Clairol did just that. An abornormally high percentage of buyers of *Frost 'n Tip* returned the product demanding refunds. And there I was, a male who had never used hair goo, confronted with solving a problem that went beyond *Frost 'n Tip*. Unhappy buyers might cease purchasing all Clairol products and tell their friends to similarly resist Clairol's advertising.

I couldn't find anything wrong with the advertising or packaging. So I left Clairol's conference room and returned to my office with a dozen packages. I gave 11 to my staff (we were much bigger back in my empire-building days in the Empire State), and tried to use the twelfth myself!

Bingo! Only one lady could follow the instructions. I certainly couldn't.

With Clairol's approval (certainly — they were tired of sending refund checks), I redesigned and rewrote the instruction flyer, using line drawings to illustrate the text.

Second bingo! Refund requests trickled down to a dribble.

If you're faced with an unusual return or refund situation, do what Clairol did: face up to it and issue the refunds while investigating precisely why the problem exists.

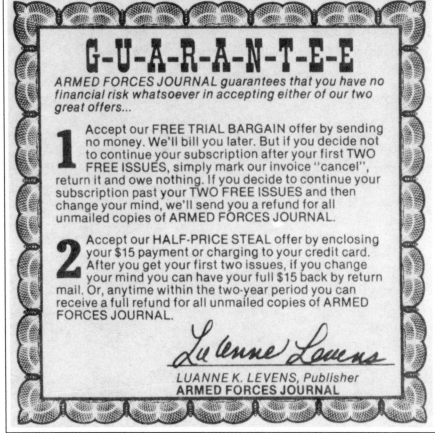

Illustration #45

As techniques #660 and #661 indicate, it is important to give a prospective buyer great confidence in your product or service, and in your company.

When you read this Gnam guarantee for Armed Forces Journal, you'll discover that the new customer can change his mind anytime within two years, and still get some money back. That inspires confidence!

CHAPTER 13

INSERTS

Never forget that each direct mail effort you dispatch, even if mailed to millions on the same day, is being read by only one person at a time. Your communication is on a one-to-one basis...always — NOT to the masses.

Therefore, concentrate on maximizing response from that one prospect, testing everything to get him/her to respond. And one excellent, low-budget test you can do to increase mail profitability is an advanced concept: a second letter as an insert in the same envelope.

While this chapter is about special inserts, both co-op and in solo mailings, I receive so many seminar questions about the popularity of second letters that I thought I'd devote this chapter introduction to a discourse on that subject. Who knows, the introduction may turn out to be longer than the chapter!

But that's not bad. If everything I'm planning for these introductions gets printed, you'll have lots of "bonus" techniques in this book.

Most marketers refer to a second letter as a second letter. Publishers call it a publisher's letter, because it's usually signed by the publisher. Savvy direct marketers refer to the second letter as a "lift letter," because its purpose is to lift your response when compared with using just one main pitch letter.

Above all, the second or lift letter must be signed by a person other than the signer of the main pitch letter. Otherwise, you look silly signing two letters. And there is another reason for the recommendation, but we'll get there momentarily, I promise.

In a *bank mailing*, the customer representative signs the main letter, while the bank president signs the lift letter.

In an *ad agency mailing*, the account executive signs the main letter, while the agency president signs the lift letter.

In a *magazine mailing*, the subscription manager signs the main pitch letter, while the publisher or editor signs the lift letter.

For a *museum mailing*, the membership director signs the main letter, but the museum's executive director signs the lift letter.

A *manufacturer* or *business company's mailing*, would have the service or sales manager sign the main letter and the president sign the lift letter.

In an *insurance mailing*, a sales representative can sign the main letter, while a famous personality signs the lift, saying that he has visited the premises and discovered that this company really is brave, clean, reverent and trustworthy.

Now you have the second reason for a second person signing the second letter: a person in top authority signs the lift letter to verify everything said in the main letter.

EXAMPLE:

"Everything our design consultant has said in his letter is true, and as president of the corporation, I stand behind his unique offer to you."

Another technique is to use the lift letter to stress the painstaking, marvelous fortitude of our staff in coming up with this new product or service. In this instance, the lift letter enables you to get a lot of essential backgrounding out of the main pitch letter so it can sell for you without being encumbered by a lot of excess detail.

Rarely are second letters effective going after sales leads. That's because short copy usually outpulls long copy for inquiry mailings. A second letter can be "just too much."

But, still, a second letter should be tested with sales lead or inquiry mailings because you don't need many more extra names as respondents to pay for that second letter. A memo, rather than a second letter, might do the trick for you.

Now, René, why is a second letter called a lift letter?

There are varying reasons for this beyond just "lifting" the total number of respondents to a mailing:

In the case of a *publication* or an *association*, the second letter lifts response to the two-year offer.

For *insurance*, the second letter lifts response to the higher coverage.

With *manufactured items*, the second letter lifts response to the deluxe or higher-priced version.

In the case of a *product mailer*, the second letter lifts response to include accessories along with the main product being sold.

For *fund raisers*, second letters lift the amount of the contribution.

For *supply firms*, they lift the amount I'll order for my inventory.

For *banks* and *S & L's*, second letters enable you to pitch one type of transaction in the main pitch letter and another transaction in the second letter.

Book publishers often use second letters to promote a subsidiary title, a second title in a series, a second line, or a back list.

Parts distributors use second letters to push their total inventories, while the main pitch letter concentrates on selling the specific "product of the month."

Your lift letter should concentrate on convincing fence-sitters to respond and that effort should lift your total response. Here's a quote from Bill Berry at the time when he was circulation manager of *Pro Football Weekly*: "use of the publisher's memo adds 15% - 20% increase in total response."

Usually, your lift letter should be a smaller size than the main pitch letter. This makes it appear quick to read and generates curiosity so it does get read and thus lifts your response.

Second letters can be enhanced by using a photo of the top honcho. "Our president stands behind everything we say" is the impression this conveys. It's convincing because it says that another person attests to product worthiness.

Second letters are valuable to you because they:

- lift the quantity on an individual order,
- lift the value of an individual order,
- lift your repeat purchase likelihood, and
- lift the executive level of the response for sales leads.

Try testing a second letter, and even a third letter, in your initial mailing to acquire new customers, new members, new subscribers, or new donors.

What? Now I know you're daffy, René. A third letter in the same envelope?

Yes, of course.

Remember the cardinal Gnamism:

If one works, try two...and if two work, try three or four.

If three or four work, go full steam ahead to even more!

So, why not try three different letters in one direct mail envelope?

This, I predict, is a coming trend, even though it is not applicable in every direct mail instance.

And, guess what, you've received lots of mail with as many as six or more letters in a single envelope.

Oh no, René, I haven't!

Oh yes, you have! From several companies!

Okay, René, name one?

Publishers Clearing House. American Family Publishers. *Reader's Digest.* Want more?

No, René, because all those little letters may be fine for a consumer audience, but how about professional people?

I made it pay for *Writer's Digest.*

I tested three complete letters in one envelope vs. two complete letters in one envelope. The third letter produced a slight difference in response, approximately 1-1/2 more orders per thousand pieces with the third letter. This slight increase in pull is significant to you if you have a product or service marketed at a price significantly higher than the one year unit of *Writer's Digest.*

Here's why:

At a $6 unit price, few marketers can afford to go to the effort and expense to put a third letter in the same package. For *Writer's Digest*, it paid off only due to back-end renewals. But, if you were selling a product or service that costs the buyer $30, $40, $50...$100 or more...that slight increase in response would mean that all you would need would be one additional order per 1,000 pieces mailed to pay for the cost of the third letter.

And now you know why you should possibly test a third letter in the same package. But, how do you use three letters in one envelope?

Let's take a museum as an *example:*

Letter #1 is the main pitch letter which talks all about the wonders of the museum and how it needs money.

Letter #2 says all the money will be for designated purposes.

Letter #3 talks about your honor, your privilege in joining the group of benefactors, and about how you will receive a plaque for your office and a plaque in the museum, both honoring you beyond your lifetime for your generous gift.

That's just one example which can

be adapted to other fields. Here are others:

A manufacturer with a new product can use...
Letter #1 to announce the item.
Letter #2 to indicate all its uses and its availability.
Letter #3 to talk about product dependability.

A publisher going after a new subscription can use...
Letter #1 to pitch why you should take a subscription.
Letter #2 to authenticate the great deal or restate a super guarantee.
Letter #3 to talk about the marvelous editorial research staff, or the meat and potatoes in the editorial gravy.

A distributor can use...
Letter #1 to pitch his entire product line.
Letter #2 to indicate fast delivery on specific products.
Letter #3 to stress fast service.

An advisory service can use...
Letter #1 to talk about the range of services provided.
Letter #2 to pitch a specific get-started service.
Letter #3 to refer to current, satisfied users.

When you test three or more letters in one package, be sure to design them to look totally different in size, in color, in shape...with folds, without folds...with photos, without photos. And remember: code your reply forms so you can accurately determine the increased response, and track your replies all the way through your conversions to sales and repeat sales.

Putting three, or four, or maybe even more letters in one direct mail piece is NOT offensive, if those enclosures produce added profits. Think

about it. Test it. It's a painless way to improve your bottom line quickly.

664 — MULTIPLE INSERTS

Some promotion managers feel you shouldn't have three, four or five inserts in an outgoing envelope because you confuse the recipient.

Wrong!

One New York department store successfully uses 27 inserts in one envelope. Many book publishers, clothing merchandisers, and supply outlets use nine or more inserts. It can work. Don't be afraid to test additional inserts. They frequently stimulate additional response.

665 — LEGAL COPY

In this era of increasing government influence and intrusion on advertising, many marketers are faced with "legal" copy that must appear in their promotions.

When possible, put the "legal" copy on a separate enclosure in a direct mail or sales promotion package. That way, it does not adversely influence the reader's flow through the selling message.

666 — SOURCE OF
REINFORCEMENT

"Legal" copy can be a source of reinforcement of your sales message.

If, for example, the "legal" copy tells how fast you will ship, this is a good sales message. Therefore, word your "legal" copy carefully to conform with the law and use some creativity in typeface selection such as italics or bold face for those portions of the "legal" copy that can contribute to your sales appeal.

If this is on a separate insert, with a strong reinforcement headline, it can increase, rather than decrease, response.

It's even stronger on an insert if that insert also contains your guarantee. Then the "legal" copy becomes supportive of the guarantee.

667 — PACKAGE INSERTS

Do not overlook package inserts as an important source of customer acquisition.

The charges are relatively low — usually between $25 and $55 per thousand pieces — plus printing and shipping. And even though package inserts produce over a long period of time which is difficult for you to assess, package inserts frequently do result in cost-effective orders that you might not otherwise have garnered.

668 — TESTING PACKAGE INSERTS

Never be afraid to test package inserts, co-ops and other alternate media.

Often, while the percentage of response will be smaller than using solo promotions aimed at your prime prospects, the acquisition cost per customer or inquiry derived from such efforts can be more attractive to you and more cost efficient for your overall budget.

669 — REPUTABLE INSERT

Any time you use a package insert, there is an implied endorsement from the mailer of the package that what you offer is reputable and worth considering!

Okay, why not take this further and also use an endorsement letter from the package mailer? Hmmm. A bright idea!

670 — MAILER'S VULNERABILITY

Even though package inserts work for a large number of mailers, each of those mailers is at the mercy of the inserter, who can vary the types of packages in which the inserts are inserted.

The only ways to guard against this factor are to clearly specify the types of packages for your insertions and to place several seeded buyer names of your own on that inserter's file, each seeded name placed at a different time period.

671 — NO CONTROL

With package inserts and co-op inserts, you have no control over the total quantity of names actually used.

Therefore, do not use a single code for a given co-op or package insert.

If your quantity is 25,000 pieces, use five different codes on 5,000 quantity lots, so you can tell when you are getting responses from the entire 25,000 universe.

672 — SPLIT CODING

By split coding the total number of names used on a given package insert or co-op insert, and by packaging the codes consecutively within a single carton in your shipment (but without blending the codes), orders coming back to you may let you know whether the mailer has dropped all the pieces within the time period you originally specified.

673 — ABSOLUTE LAW

It is almost an absolute law that your package inserts not run with competitive inserts in the same promotion.

That holds true for most co-op mailings too!

674 — TESTING REDUCED SIZE

Whenever you have a successful co-op envelope insert or package insert, test a reduced size or scaled down version of the same insert against the control piece to determine whether your cost effectiveness will improve.

Sometimes there is no fall-off in response.

675 — GROUPED WITH AFFINITY INSERTS

Your package insert will pull best for you if it is with a group of affinity inserts, so identified, and mailed to a logical prospect list for your product or service.

676 — COLLEGE CO-OP MARKETER

If you are a retailer or a co-op marketer to college audiences, the youth field and/or collectors, you can use as many package inserts in your program as you can get, and there will not be a significant fall-off in response.

677 — SPECIFYING SEX, ET CETERA

When buying package inserts, remember that frequently you can specify sex, recency, and other factors just as you can on a direct mail list.

678 — OUTSIDE INSERTS

If you sponsor your own package insert program, remember that the general rule of thumb is to have no more than four, five, or six outside inserts with your piece — and put them in a separate envelope, please!

More outside inserts could dilute attention to each piece, greatly reducing response to your own promotion.

679 — BOUNCE-BACK PROMOTION PIECES

Never overlook an opportunity to sell.

This includes using a bounce-back or additional promotion pieces and order forms in product shipments.

At the moment when your customer receives your product, he is usually entranced about opening the package, and therefore you have an opportunity to sell him again.

680 — FACT SHEET

Be exceptionally careful not to enclose complete newsletters, study lessons, education courses, or tape transcripts when attempting to sell such products.

The recipient may read that enclosure and conclude that he has learned everything he can from it or, worse yet, be completely detracted from your offer and thus not respond. It is better to illustrate, in a readable size, such items on a brochure or fact sheet. Yes, that's a separate insert.

681 — MULTIPLE PRODUCTS

Offering more than one product for sale in the same mailing, unless you use a booklet or catalog format, is risky.

But there is a way to do it.

Test by pitching a single product throughout the mailing and having a separate insert for the second item.

682 — SPECIAL ENCLOSURES

Special enclosures — like plastic records, tokens, cassettes, or imprinted napkins — get the recipient of your mail involved with your pitch.

Be careful to test them for cost efficiency and be certain that they are not so attractive that they divert attention from your sales pitch.

683 — FREE-STANDING STUFFERS

Free-standing stuffers are increasing in costs as their popularity and responsiveness increase.

So it may pay for you to investigate other co-op opportunities such as joining with two or three non-related advertisers and creating a joint free-standing stuffer for a newspaper, or your own co-op insert in a magazine.

684 — VALUABLE COMMODITY CERTIFICATE

If by responding to your promotion, a reader can win a prize or get some other valuable item (not a subscription or membership), document it by creating a certificate or a stylized check or something else that looks valuable and print that "valuable" commodity in your promotion.

René, why not on a subscription or membership?

Because in those instances, the certificate could very well be the order form itself, not a separate insert in a package with an order form.

685 — HISTORICAL SCRIPT

If your product has an interesting history, consider creating a script describing that history and including music.

Weave in a promotional pitch and suddenly you have a promotional sound sheet which can be produced on vinyl as a "phonograph record" for an insertion in your mailings.

René, do those things really increase response?

Yes. They're costly. But they certainly do work.

686 — CATALOG STYLE PROMOTION

If you don't have enough products or services for a mini-catalog or broadside, consider whether one, two, or three such additional offerings can be promoted in catalog style (photo, caption, description and price) on a separate order form in a promotion you're planning now.

Test it before you roll out.

It can be referred to on the outside envelope, if you don't detract from the main proposition. Or, you can just shove that special insert right into the package with no special explanation other than a heading which says something like: "More great bargains from Marvelous Marvin."

But, René, why should I test it before I roll out?

Because it may depress response for the main item being promoted. No one can predict this. So, split test. Then, when you tally response, your question becomes:

Did the product insert version produce fewer sales on the main item, or were we able to generate enough added product dollars to cover any decrease in main item sales?

687 — POP-UPS AND FOLD-OUTS

Remember that sales promotion and direct mail offer you the added feature of dimensional enclosures such as pop-ups and fold-outs.

Even though the postal service has launched a drive to eliminate these die-cut pieces bound in copies of publications, you can still produce a direct mail job with attention-getting pop-up devices.

They're so unusual that people start to play with them. That is called "involvement." And that's what you want.

But, I mail to business audiences, René?

Fine. Pop-ups and other dimensional items in a direct mail piece start people talking in an office environment. It goes like this:

"Hey, Joe. Look at this cute little cardboard train I got in the mail."

"Yeah, isn't that nice? Who sent it to you?"

Ah, René, now I see the technique. You want several people in an office to talk about my mail.

Right!

688 — INSERTING A SECOND ORDER FORM

Do not hesitate to insert a second order form clearly labeled "use this form for a friend."

That's for consumer mail. To business, institutional and professional audiences, substitute "colleague" or "associate" for the word "friend."

Use this technique and you may receive not only additional dollar volume but additional names you can use for future promotions.

Okay, René, give me just one example of a well-known organization

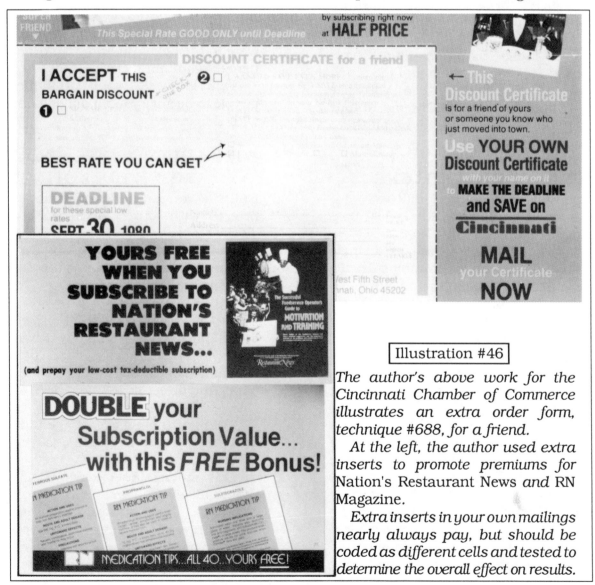

Illustration #46

The author's above work for the Cincinnati Chamber of Commerce illustrates an extra order form, technique #688, for a friend.

At the left, the author used extra inserts to promote premiums for Nation's Restaurant News *and* RN Magazine.

Extra inserts in your own mailings nearly always pay, but should be coded as different cells and tested to determine the overall effect on results.

that has succeeded with this in business mail?

Well, it worked when I did it for *Chain Store Age* in mailings to pharmacists at their pharmacies.

689 — DISCOUNT COUPON

René, in your original direct mail offer to prospects, can you try to get repeat sales by enclosing a discount coupon "good on your second purchase"?

Of course you can. It's a good idea, too. Not always. Sometimes.

Why is it good, René?

Because it alerts prospects to future savings, showing you care about them, and because you are creating a buying atmosphere.

Why not always do it?

Because many mailings have enough going for them and too much might confuse the prospect. You have to think about the total impact of your package before deciding on all these extra inserts.

690 — BOUNCEBACKS

Bouncebacks can significantly increase your sales at the lowest possible cost.

A bounceback usually is a single sheet promotion combining sales literature with an order form. It's enclosed with product shipments, statement envelopes, and other customer communications.

Yes, René, I've seen them. Do they work?

Uh huh. Very well. If you're not using them, spank your consultant for not recommending them. Here's why:

Many times a customer orders one teapot while thinking he can always order another if he likes the first when it arrives. If he loves your teapot, he can order more with a bounceback. But if you don't give him that opportunity, he may have misplaced your address or toll-free number. So, in comes your teapot. He uses it and loves it. But he's stuck with no chance to send you more money.

René, might he give the bounceback to a friend?

Certainly. Often. Especially in business and consumer markets.

I guess we should use them, eh?

As often as you can. And if you run out of bounceback ideas, call me.

Bob Senninger did. He runs Brown Deer Chemicals in Wisconsin. I made that recommendation to him in 1986. He found that it paid off handsomely. But when I received the four teak champagne glasses I ordered from him in June 1988, I was surprised to note that no bounceback materials were in the box. You know what happened: a shipping clerk forgot.

Double-check your fulfillment people to be sure you do make money with this concept.

691 — BULLETINS...AND MORE BULLETINS?

Bulletins are not bulletins if they are printed with four-color artwork on glossy stock.

Bulletins should always be separate inserts, unless you use the word "bulletin" at the top of a typewritten letter.

But what we consider a bulletin insert should be inexpensively printed, convey a sense of last-second inclusion in a mailing, be printed on cheap paper and preferably should be in one color: black!

Think of them as "garbage bulletins," my term to keep me designing them properly.

Now, wait a minute, René. Wouldn't that sully our image?

No. Go ahead and print your gorgeous full-color brochure that presents the product or service, its benefits and all the wonderful comments

Two of the author's most garish garbage bulletins, technique #691, used for his Scandinavian seminars, are: black on green (angled) and black on salmon (horizontal), both with intentionally poor photography.

Illustration #47

Seminar attendee G. Todd Hunt adapted this technique for the Evanston Light Opera Works, using a pretty, full-color brochure (angled) with a sloppily-printed, black on goldenrod garbage bulletin, mostly in penscript. Yes, that ugly black blotch is a simulation of a printer's inky thumb.

Photos from last year's production of Rose-Marie.

In 1987 almost every LIGHT OPERA WORKS performance sold out (some as early as six weeks in advance). As a subscriber you won't have to worry about that in 1988 because you'll have all your tickets safely in hand before the season begins.

on how stupendous your item is. Insert the garbage bulletin with it and you've indicated to a prospect that there's a last-minute urgency about your offer.

So we maintain our image with the prettier piece, René, and then show folks we're down to earth with the garbage bulletin?

Right.

692 — PRICE AND OFFER?

If you are in the experimental stages of direct mail development, you may be best advised to leave all mention of the price and specific offer out of your brochures or your accompanying literature.

Include it in the letter and on the order card.

This allows you to price test without going to undue expense in changing or correcting plates on the brochure, which is usually your most expensive insert.

693 — PAPER STOCK UNIFORMITY

René, should multiple-insert mailings have some uniformity in paper stock?

Yes. Some.

If there are several product brochures, they could all be on the same

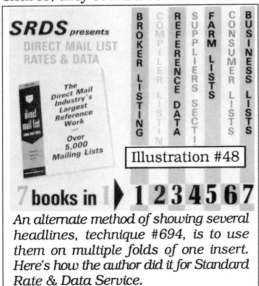

Illustration #48

An alternate method of showing several headlines, technique #694, is to use them on multiple folds of one insert. Here's how the author did it for Standard Rate & Data Service.

high-quality glossy stock. But the order form and the letter should not be on similar stock. They shouldn't be on the same stock used for the brochures either.

The letter needs to look and feel somewhat like a letter, and that does not mean gloss. The order form or reply card, or whatever you're calling your response device, should be on a matte finish to make it easy to fill in and easy for your fulfillment people to decipher. And, if you put that order form on glossy paper, are you communicating a big expense for the items you're promoting? Think about that.

694 — UNIQUE PROMOTION

Often we tend to have blinders on.

We look at mailings from our competitors and think that if they use three pieces in a #10, so should we. If they have six pieces in a 6x9, so should we.

Nonsense! Our products or services are unique. They require unique promotion treatment.

Look at some of the mailings you receive and start to critique them yourself. Could eight paragraphs have been cut from a letter and put on a separate insert to dramatize the points expressed in those paragraphs? Could a brochure have been reduced in size by taking certain accessory items off that brochure and featuring them on a separate insert?

That's the power of using many inserts in a mailing. The reader who is the slightest bit intrigued has to look at all your inserts. You'll have many more headlines to attract him to study your proposition. You'll have much more impact. You'll also be convincing him that if he orders, he gets a lot from you, because wasn't there a lot of paper in that mailing?

Ah!

CHAPTER 14

PERSONALIZATION

Many people think of mainframe computer technology as a very expensive undertaking in direct mail. But if you mail regularly to the same audiences, or to similar audiences on which you can get computer input tapes, here's an *example* of how you can lower your costs by using a service bureau's mainframe computer:

Manually typing envelopes will cost you $35 - $50 per M if you're lucky.

Printing labels and affixing them costs $9 - $18 per M.

Computer direct addressing on envelopes costs $3 - $4 per M.

But, using an IBM 3800 Laser Beam Printer, you can address envelopes for 25 - 30 per M, at 15M - 20M per hour. They'll look like they were typed and the savings are enormous.

And that same IBM 3800 can produce 20,000 different, fully personalized letters an hour, with a typewritten appearance, at costs as low as $10/M. So if you have large quantity envelope mailings, think about mainframe computer economies for highly personalized direct marketing.

Laser printing is not dangerous. It will not cut or burn paper. Currently, you can only use laser for black impressions. (IBM swears it's not working on color development for mainframe lasers, which means it probably is.) Laser printing is an outgrowth of data processing printing, and therefore the characters used for letters, until recently, were basic data processing characters. Today, you can emulate several different printing typefaces as well as standard IBM Courier on a desktop laser printer. I do it right in my office with Apple lasers that are smaller than 19" TV sets.

But one of the beauties of mainframe laser printing is that you can design any type characters you want by programming work in conjunction with a type designer. And since you also can mix two or more styles of characters with several sizes, you create instant attraction for your letter.

Thus, you can design an attractive certificate and personalize it with your recipient's name in a typeface of your choice.

In fact, with the new desktop publishing software, it is conceivable that many direct mail marketers will do most of their creative typesetting and design work in house, using the laser for fully-formed pages, visible on the screen, and then printed on a repro-quality paper stock, or perhaps on colored rag paper. That's one of the exciting concepts I'm playing with these days. It's one you should investigate too.

> **Some of the nation's biggest mail order houses, like Spencer Gifts and Foster & Gallagher, and other large mailers like *Newsweek* and National Liberty Life, report that switching to laser personalization increases response as much as 40%.**
>
> **Anytime you can call a prospect's attention to his/her name, you are creating an impression that says "they thought of me." Your prospect wants to feel that this mailing piece "is really for me!"**

Imagine taking a small, but highly-profitable database, and creating a personalized self-mailer, as follows:

It would contain type and art, fully scanned at your desk. After you've checked it carefully, you merge it with your pre-selected database fields. Load your laser with something like Kimberly-Clark Neenah Classic Laid Continental Blue. Power up and print Side One. Then do Side Two on a second pass until someone invents a laser that'll do two sides at once.

Suddenly, a one-man band is producing a high-tech mailing that appears as though it could only have been done by an organization with megabucks! And since the body type is, perhaps, Times Roman, and the display lines are, let's say, Helvetica, and the personalization is in IBM Courier, the piece has an urgency to it because it looks like you printed it

and then typed in my name and address!

Beautiful! I'll have it solved one day. Maybe by the time you read this.

695 — COMPUTERIZED COLLECTION LETTERS

Direct mail tests for a variety of my clients have shown that computerized collection letters pull better than offset versions.

We believe this is so because people feel computers store information about them. Presumably, they do not wish to have negative credit information recorded on computers and "available to the entire world."

These collection efforts should look like a computer generated them, rather than beautiful word processor letters. If you want to, you can use your word processor, but come as close to an old-fashioned computer look as possible: thin paper, upper case type, letterhead in black ink only.

You know what I'm talking about: make it look as though it was produced in the days before wide-hammer courier!

696 — MEASURING THE RESULTS

If you have always believed that personalization is necessary in direct mail, and therefore you have always used typed envelopes or directly-addressed envelopes, keep doing it! But try a small test of envelopes addressed with a computer-generated label and key your order cards differently so you can measure the results.

Perhaps there will be only a slight difference between direct addressing and label addressing. You must measure the cost effectiveness of these addressing methods. Usually, the personalized approach pulls best, but it is an important test to try to lower costs.

Your controller or accountant will appreciate this test.

697 — DIRECT MAIL PERSONALIZATION

Do everything you can to give your reader the feeling that you are interested in him and care about his well-being.

This may include personalization of your direct mail pieces so the reader feels he is an individual, not part of a mass.

And that may mean personalizing more than one element in the mailing.

Oh, René, isn't that very, very expensive?

Not if you print several items on one large sheet and then burst it! I personalized two pages of a two-page letter, a reply form, and a certificate for a Motors Insurance Corporation mailing — all on the same sheet, bursted, then collated and inserted with personalization showing through two windows of the carrier envelope.

698 — COMPLETE FIRST NAMES

If you feel it is possible that the list you have rented for label affixing to an order form contains only the first initial of the first name, do not hesitate to ask recipients of your mailing piece to supply their complete first names so you can use computer applications later on.

699 — UNIFORM FEMALE TITLES?

If a female on your mailing list has indicated the title Mrs., Miss, or Ms. as the designation she prefers, resist the temptation to program your computer letters to uniformly address all females under any one title. Sometimes a lady prefers to be Ms. or Miss in her office environment, but Mrs. at home. And some women prefer Ms., both at the workplace and at home, even though they're married.

Your job is to make certain that the titles designated by your customers are used, or, in some instances, you will turn them off.

700 — COMPUTER FILL-IN LETTERS?

Using personalization only on the prospect's name for computer or auto-typed letters is not sufficient justification for the added expense. Personalized letters should include other references that truly tailor the approach to the recipient.

But what about computer fill-in letters, René?

Yes, I know that they work better than straight offset letters, especially when you include the full name and address and salutation, but more fully personalized letters will outpull the fill-in variety.

And, let's get back to the main technique of inserting only the prospect's name in a personalized letter:

If your name is Suzanne Slivowitz, aren't you offended by seeing Suzanne Slivowitz, Suzanne Slivowitz, Suzanne Slivowitz repeated several times in a letter? And the offenses continue...

To the Suzanne Slivowitz family in Holiday, FL.

Something new for Suzanne Slivowitz.

This special offer is for Suzanne Slivowitz, and Suzanne Slivowitz only.

Dear Suzanne Slivowitz.

Suzanne Slivowitz, you and everyone in the Suzanne Slivowitz family can enjoy a Suzanne Slivowitz weekend in the Poconos where Suzanne Slivowitz can buy a Suzanne Slivowitz summer home.

Or, how about this copy, used in a magazine sweepstakes mailing that I received:

"Dear René Gnam,
"The next time you and the René Gnam family drive away from your home at Post Office Box 3877."

Well, as I write this, I'm divorced. 89 kids, but none of them have ever been children. And I live on a ranch, not in a post office box.

Almost all personalized copy of this nature is turn-offish (if there is such a word). Repeating the prospect's name forever is good way to tell him/her that you are a gimmick lover and thus your product or service must be a gimmick.

Sure, I use a lot of personalization in many mailings. But with modern database technology you are not limited to using the prospect's name.

Hold it, René, I've heard that repeating the name really works?

It does if you use it on several different pieces in a single mailing: the outgoing envelope, the letter, the order form, perhaps also on a certificate insert. But not for excruciating repetition in the same piece.

Any exceptions, René?

Yes, sweepstakes mailings to home addresses, but even then I modify the personalization, sometimes using only the last name, sometimes the city, sometimes the state, sometimes — and this is best — other data from the database.

Other data? Like what, René?

Here's an *example* of a direct mail letter opening that I sent to people on one of my databases, using an old-fashioned TRS-80 Model 12 microcomputer and a daisy-wheel printer:

"Dear Mike,
"The next time you come to our ranch seminar, you can sit in the no-smoking section, enjoy a Greek salad for lunch, and stay at the Ramada Inn.
"LeBlanc Photo Studios will really benefit from this opportunity for you to gain new direct marketing knowledge in a comfortable setting, just the way you like it. Bring Ruby too."

René, how in the world did you get all that personalization information in your database?

Mike LeBlanc attended before. He's a customer. He likes Greek salads. He does not smoke. He prefers hotels in the Ramada price range.

You should always get as much information on your customers as you possibly can. Then, when you re-use that information in personalized communications, you turn a customer into a repeat customer.

Did that letter work, René?

Yes, Mike attended again. So have others. The point is that you should tailor your mail to your prospect's habits, desires, and preferences — not take the easiest route. And, I'm sorry to say that most users of modern personalization techniques take the easiest route. As a result, they make less money than they might otherwise make.

But, René, could you go too far in personalization?

Yes, definitely. I had a personal relationship with every person on the small database I used for the above example. They were all previous seminar attendees, so I could send a letter that even referred to Mike's wife. But if you've had only minor contact with the people on your list, personalizing with references to food and smoke might be a bit too much.

Just don't lose sight of the major point I'm making:

Use the power of personalization to hike your response, but do it in a way that appears as a personalized communication, instead of a regurgitation from a robot.

Oh, René, what about robo-typed letters?

No one uses them any more.

Why not?

They look like regurgitations from a robot.

701 — SUCCESS FOR YOU

If you mail in large quantities, perhaps 50,000 at a time to consumers, investigate ink jet imaging and laser printing techniques.

Any data stored on your computer — and you do have at least one computer, don't you? — can be used to personalize the body of your promotion piece with alternating type sizes and boldness to stress how your product or service applies to me.

Gee, René, that sounds as though you're only talking about those large lasers that service bureaus use?

Right. I wrote the first two paragraphs of Technique No. 701 before

---

Every Professional Speaker wants to upgrade promotions

to get more bookings and make more sales.

It's much easier...for YOU...now...

Mr. David Alan Yoho
THE PROFESSIONAL EDUCATORS GROUP
5272 River Road, Suite 420
Bethesda, MD 20816

Dear Mr. Yoho,

You want more bookings, perhaps at higher fees, and you want to create and sell books, tapes and other profitable products.

   Fine! Retain René Gnam, the marketing consultant who has worked with many top speakers including: John V. Lindsay, Jim & Naomi Rhode, Joyce Clydesdale, Debra Jones, Don Dible, Dottie Walters, Stu Crump, Anver Suleiman, the late Hubert H. Humphrey, and many others from Australia to Denmark.

   "I'm overbooked now," Jerry Wilson says, "thanks to your help!"

Just pack your attaché case with samples of your previous promotions, new ideas, fee schedules, and every note you've ever marked "someday".

Bring your materials to René Gnam's Response Ranch for a one-day, no-holds-barred private consultation session. René will review, critique, advise, recommend, and -- if there's time -- write and design just what you need. <u>You'll have new directions and the instant answers you need to vital questions about your marketing efforts.</u>

You'll stay in our Client Guest House, use the Client Guest Car, and enjoy your SunCoast visit while profiting from René's unique counsel. Fun. Easy. Let's do it!

   You don't need much new business to make back the $3,000 fee.
   You may get that business -- <u>and</u> <u>much</u> more -- extremely fast!

   Let's work together, so you can profit more...
   RENE GNAM CONSULTATION CORPORATION

Leslie Gray, May 5, 1989

P.S. A listing of some of the seminar/workshop clients René has aided is enclosed.
     Questions about his background? I'll send you plenty of material.

         The most important thing now? Call me at **813-938-1555**.

 René Gnam Consultation Corporation
1 Response Road, Box 3877, Holiday, FLorida 33590 . . . **813-938-1555**

Illustration #49

Business-to-business lead follow-up letters now can be automatically processed using relatively-inexpensive, modern desktop equipment, technique #701.

Illustrated at the left is one of the author's 1989 promotions, produced by merging his database information on a computer word processor, then using a laser printer.

Note the headlines, indented paragraphs, and emphasis points within the text. This letter, typeset automatically in Century Schoolbook, presents a clean, uncluttered appearance. Imagine the clutter had Gnam put the date in its usual position.

The letterhead is at the bottom to eliminate a conflict with the main headline.

Only 350 of these letters were mailed, producing a profit in one week.

the advent of desk-top laser printers. Technology changed in the middle of writing this book!

Life is marvelous today. Among a zillion wonders, we can now use lasers that are no bigger than a desktop copier. They're really fancy office copiers, but they do a jim dandy job.

I bought an ITT Qume desktop laser. Less than $3,500. Prints 10 times faster than my daisy-wheels. On one draft of this book, I printed 164 jam-packed, single-spaced pages in just under 16 minutes. It works just as fast with mail merge (word processor copy merged with database information). And that has led to a new utility for direct mail marketers.

We can now afford to use fully personalized letters on very small quantity mailings. Maybe only 130 pieces.

That small, René?

Yes, I've done it with the laser. I wouldn't bother if I were selling a 5¢ O-ring to an auto mechanic. But it's perfectly fine for items offering you a decent margin, or several thousand O-rings to an automobile aftermarket distributor. And the cost is super low. You just revise your previous letter, hand it to your superior secretary, say "merge this with database selection 14," and bingo...it's done and dusted!

In fact, our experience with the ITT Qume convinced us that lasers were here to stay and perfect for our business. So, we traded it for an Apple LaserWriter Plus and then also bought an Apple LaserWriter II NTX with four megs of additional ram and a hard drive. Now we blend graphics and typeset copy with our letters.

Okay, okay, René, does it increase response?

Yes. Personalization pays.

702 — CLUSTER ANALYSIS

An individual neighborhood frequently constitutes an audience of similar characteristics, including income levels, educational levels, housing, and other preferences.

Thus, when you select by homogeneous zip code neighborhoods down to the 5th digit you are reaching a similarly-constituted audience. But homogeneous marketing truly means reaching "parts all of the same kind," and I would like to caution you about using this sometimes-touted marketing approach.

It usually is referred to as "cluster analysis," defined as a study of a community to determine in advance — using computer selectivity based on census tract information — known and desired information aspects of each specific neighborhood. Then, we can mail only to those zip code areas which are most likely to be highly populated by our target audiences.

Such highly sophisticated selectivity sometimes boosts response to startling levels. But do not assume that psychographic evaluations of neighbors will match. The demographics, maybe. Psychographics, most likely not.

That's why Ed Burnett, one of the nation's most respected innovators in mailing list usage, disdains mailing to neighbors for most, but not all, propositions. Me too.

Consider that the neighbor of your present consumer customer may have similar community interests and voting habits as your present customer. Thus, you could use personalized mail to target the neighbor for political or fund raising campaigns.

Similarly, you can obtain lists of neighbors by name and mail to them with computer personalizations, such as, "Your neighbor, John Jones, just won a prize in our sweepstakes." The feeling that my neighbor has made a positive decision may influence me to consider your proposition. And this works better than merely renting a list of neighbors and affixing a label.

RCA Record Club has done very well with cluster analysis, but remember that it offers a variety of music.

And, unless you have a wide variety in your offerings, you could be making a big mistake by going after the similarities of neighbors. The likelihood of neighbors having similar vacation desires, reading habits, food selection, or movie enjoyment is low. So it would not be wise to mail offers on lifestyle or personal-decision products.

A lot of misinformation has been published and delivered from public platforms about the great similarity of neighbors. Don't believe it. Here's a neighbor comparison as an *example*:

I have only five neighbors, all within long walking distance: Bob, Frank, Keith, Taylor, and Walter. If you approached us as similar, you'd find many dissimilarities, among them:

Land...Bob has 1.9 acres. Walter has 2.1. The rest of us have much more.

Retirement...Frank and Taylor are retired. The rest of us aren't.

Marriage...Bob, Frank, Taylor, and Walter are married. Keith never has been married. I am divorced.

Occupations...Bob is a construction worker. Frank used to be a field hand. Keith is a real estate broker. René is a marketing consultant. Taylor operates a chain of restaurants. Walter runs about 20 corporations.

Reading...Bob and Frank read only the daily newspaper, by skimming. Taylor seldom reads. Keith, René, and Walter read business publications.

Cooking and Dining...Bob and Frank can't cook, but almost never eat out. Keith can't fry an egg, and always eats out. René cooks gourmet style and eats out frequently. Taylor can cook, but nearly always eats at his restaurants. Walter barbecues and eats out.

Clothing...Bob has a good suit for weddings and funerals. Frank has a couple of suits. The rest of us have several suits.

Church...Taylor goes fairly regularly. Frank goes sometimes. The rest of us don't.

Entertaining...Bob, Frank, and Taylor don't entertain. Keith entertains only at restaurants. René and Walter entertain frequently at home and at restaurants.

Air Travel...Frank and Taylor never travel. Bob takes one trip a year. Keith travels occasionally. René travels frequently. Walter flies almost weekly.

Home styles...Bob has a small, expanded shack he rebuilt into a nice home himself. Frank has a mid-size farmhouse. Keith has a large, typical Florida home. René has a modern ranch house and a guest house. Taylor has a big colonial. Walter has a spacious, high-ceiling dutch with a tennis court, a condo in Toronto, and a hotel suite in London.

Non-employment enjoyments... Taylor has none. Bob works in his yard. Frank watches television. Keith parties. René swims. Walter squires his daughters to equestrian events.

Music...Bob likes country. Frank and Taylor like easy listening. Keith likes disco and rock. René prefers classical and jazz. Walter enjoys only classical.

Theatre...Bob and Frank never go. Keith rarely. Taylor, Walter, and René go as often as possible, and René is a supporter of a local repertory theatre.

Animals...Keith has none. Frank has cows and dogs. Taylor has only dogs. Walter has horses, a pony, two dogs, and a 1988 Christmas goat from René. Bob and René have a great variety of animals.

Visiting...René and Walter visit and bring guests to each other's homes. The others don't visit or talk with neighbors.

Ages...Keith is in his late 30s. Bob is in his early 40s. René will be 52 when this book goes on sale. Walter is in his 60s. Taylor is in his early 70s. Frank is about 80 (no one asks).

Now, how similar are we? Not very much. If you personalize your mail with a "neighbor" approach to the six of us, you won't get very far. Just look around your neighborhood and see how "similar" your neighbors really are.

Be very careful with this technique. It can work for sweepstakes, local political campaigns, and sometimes mass appeal products. But it is highly unlikely to work, no matter how much you personalize, for almost everything else. Take the advice of Ed Burnett and René Gnam: exercise extreme caution about using cluster analysis based on supposedly homogeneous neighborhoods.

But, René, what about people living in mobile homes?

Speak to Dyeann Dummer at *Mobile Home News* and she'll tell you how dissimilar those folks are. You may imagine that they're all retirees, but you're dead wrong. A goodly percentage are employed. Many rent a portion of their mobile home to other people, then share the kitchen and bath.

Okay, René, what about people living in apartments or condos?

You can't be serious with that question. There are more dissimilarities with apartment dwellers than home owners.

But, René, what about government housing projects?

Okay, you win. Folks living in those abodes are very similar in their lack of income. Do you want to mail to them? Perhaps...to give them assistance.

703 — PRESSURE SENSITIVE LABELS

If your list is maintained on computer, consider printing pressure-sensitive labels.

Then, have your lettershop guillotine those labels and affix the backing sheet with the label to the promotion piece so the reader has all the fun and involvement of transferring his own personalized peel-off label to the order form. This also gets him involved with his ego, concentrating on his own name.

Once he toys around with his name, he's more likely to order.

704 — PURCHASING AUTHORITY?

Personalized direct mail sometimes does not pay for product mailings to middle and low levels of businesses and institutions, but may pay if you seek the top echelons in those target markets.

You'll have to split test to find out.

But why might it not pay, René?

For the same reason that those names may not be appropriate for an offset mailing: they may not have purchasing authority.

705 — ACTUAL NAMES

Personalized title addressing to corporations is fine, but any time you can get the actual names of the individuals performing certain job functions, use the names with the titles.

No, I didn't say "use the names" instead of the titles. I did say "use the names WITH the titles." There is a big difference.

Here are general guidelines on mailing to names versus titles at business addresses:

If you mail to owners or chief executive officers, address by name. Owners and CEOs rarely change positions.

If you mail to middle management, address by title in offset mailings, by name and title in personalized mailings. Middle managers often get promoted — upwards and sideways — and change employment. The title, or job function, usually remains. It's filled by someone else. Using the title enables you to reach the new job performer. Using the name alone may result in your mail being unceremoniously dumped. If you have a choice between name or title in mailing to middle management, address by title.

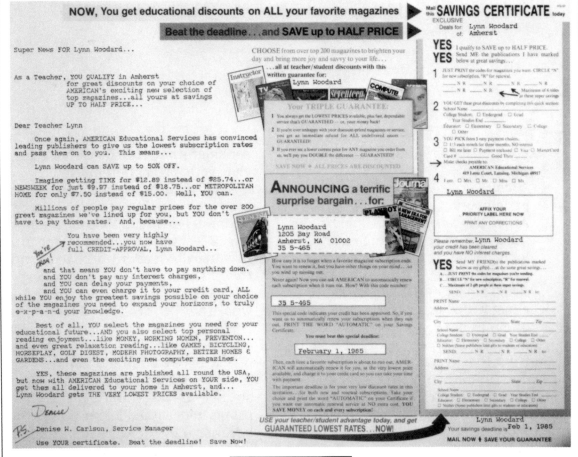

Illustration #50

The author selected his full-color winning creation for American Educational Services (reduced from 11 x 14-1/4) to illustrate three key techniques in this chapter:

#697 — personalizing in several places on one sheet, yet gaining more than one piece — *in this instance a letter, brochure display, and a perforated order form,*

#700 — using complete personalization and database information — *in this example students are identified as students and teachers as teachers, and*

#705 — inserting actual names — *in this mailing teachers getting the piece at home are approached as consumers, but when they receive it at their school addresses each teacher's name, position, and school name are used.*

CHAPTER 15

POSTCARDS & SELF-MAILERS

There are three basic formats in direct mail marketing and sales promotion:

1. A *catalog* — usually a multi-page bound book.
2. An *envelope mailing* — meaning a carrier or outgoing envelope containing a variety of inserts, or just one insert.
3. A *self-mailer* — either a single-sheet folded or a booklet, but, in either case, mailed without being in an envelope.

And it's that third category, the self-mailer, that often gets scoffed at by some corporate executives who are loath to mail anything without making sure that it's in a pretty wrapper. But, the lowly self-mailer — and its kissing cousin, the postcard — have many advantages in selected instances. Just ask me, sometime, how successful Norelco was in selling its lighting to thousands of companies across America, expanding its business-to-business operations from one office with one salesman to 33 offices with many salespeople.

Just like Norelco, after you've reviewed this chapter, you may feel that self-mailers merit some stature in your format evaluation.

Reader viewpoint is your first consideration. How does the recipient view your promotion piece?

Self-mailers are regarded by both consumer and business audiences as announcements, bulletins, or annoyances. They are immediately scanned because the reader wants to get rid of them. That means he/she will look at a self-mailer long enough to find out what the "big deal" is all about.

Reader actions are your second consideration. What will the recipient do with your promotion piece?

Self-mailers are seldom read instantly unless they're postcards or properly designed larger pieces, but, because they're regarded as bulletins and announcements, they're often passed to others in business environments.

Reader copy tolerance is your third consideration. How much wording can you use?

Because self-mailers are viewed as announcements, people don't expect a lot of copy in them. So, if you do have a lot of wording, design the self-mailer with a lot of little headings to attract the eye.

Your next consideration on format is your product or service. What is it?

There are three types of products or services:

1. SHOPPING ITEMS: those items that take careful thought before buying or signing up. This would include a new car, a condominium, an industrial boiler, a printing press, a loan, a long-term service contract, a big insurance policy.
2. RE-ORDER ITEMS: those items that we really need on a regular basis, such as food, paper for a copier, shoelaces, ink for a printing press, a contract renewal, any kind of supply or inventory items.
3. IMPULSE ITEMS: those we don't need, but spend money on anyway. These include chewing gum at a checkout counter, trinkets for a desk, your 42nd calculator, theatre tickets, a charitable donation.

Identify the nature of the item you're promoting and then learn this:

1. SHOPPING ITEMS are best promoted in envelope mailings so you can make an extensive presentation.
2. RE-ORDER ITEMS are best promoted in self-mailers so your reader can scan the piece and quickly say "that's something I need."
3. IMPULSE ITEMS are promoted well in self-mailers and also are successful with envelope mailings, except for fund-raising efforts which nearly always are more successful in envelopes than with self-mailers.

Catalogs should contain all three types of items:

SHOPPING ITEMS to make me study the CATALOG,

RE-ORDER ITEMS to make me save it, and

IMPULSE ITEMS to get me to read it now.

You can quickly see that the self-mailer isn't a low-brow format. It especially does have its place with supplies and add-ons.

In fact, complicated deals or complicated decision-making can be promoted with self-mailers to get leads or inquiries, and then envelope mailings to convert them to sales.

> **Generally speaking, self-mailers should have simple messages galvanizing the recipient to take just one action. There are some exceptions to that, such as a mini-catalog booklet mailing or a sales promotion piece that communicates several different services or talks about a full product line.**
>
> **But, usually, you'll be more successful with self-mailers by limiting them to simple messages to clearly-defined targets.**

And if you want more than one person to see your promotion, self-mailers are best in business offices. They get high pass-along readership.

Concerning the copy thrusts you'll be making:

While catalogs can be used for both serving and creating interest, and while envelope mailings can be used to create interest or demand, self-mailers are primarily a format to serve existing needs, interests and demands.

Now that you know the basic considerations in selecting self-mailers, here's an *example* of how an industrial client uses both self-mailers and envelope mailings:

The Frank D. Riggio Company in Rutherford, N.J., uses a series of self-mailers — postcards, and booklets — to prospect lists, stressing its company name, reliability, and fast delivery in an effort to get exposure and firmly implant Riggio's name in the minds of those prospects.

Then, when the prospects have become qualified leads, another self-mailer books an appointment for a salesperson to follow up. Next, envelope mailings go to active customers to announce additional services from Riggio.

Riggio sells industrial boilers, safety relief valves, and resetting services. Glorious items! If Vince Riggio, son of Frank, can use these formats profitably from a small highway office, what could your company do?

Well, for starters, you might emulate Minolta, which established a strong presence for its new office copiers by acquiring highly qualified sales leads for distributors through-

out our country. With self-mailers. Of course!

706 — GOVERNMENT-SIZE POSTCARDS

Some of the most profitable direct response promotions are on single government-size postcards.

Don't overlook this opportunity to get a potent message in a low-cost printing format.

It is a self-mailer (promotion mailed by itself, not in an envelope), and you are not limited to the size that the post office uses. If you're willing to pay the extra postage, you can mail jumbo-size cards. My longest was 14" x 3" high. My biggest was 8-1/2" x 11".

707 — "PENNY" POSTCARD

In 25 years, from 1962 to 1987, the "penny" postcard increased in cost by 466% from 3¢ each to 14¢ each, and it's up again — 15¢ at this writing,

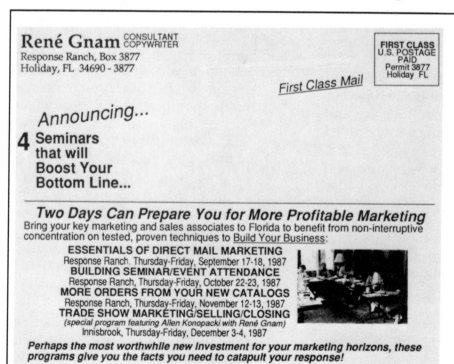

René Gnam CONSULTANT COPYWRITER
Response Ranch, Box 3877
Holiday, FL 34690 - 3877

FIRST CLASS
U.S. POSTAGE
PAID
Permit 3877
Holiday FL

First Class Mail

Announcing...

4 Seminars that will Boost Your Bottom Line...

___

Two Days Can Prepare You for More Profitable Marketing
Bring your key marketing and sales associates to Florida to benefit from non-interruptive concentration on tested, proven techniques to <u>Build Your Business</u>:
ESSENTIALS OF DIRECT MAIL MARKETING
Response Ranch. Thursday-Friday, September 17-18, 1987
BUILDING SEMINAR/EVENT ATTENDANCE
Response Ranch, Thursday-Friday, October 22-23, 1987
MORE ORDERS FROM YOUR NEW CATALOGS
Response Ranch, Thursday-Friday, November 12-13, 1987
TRADE SHOW MARKETING/SELLING/CLOSING
(special program featuring Allen Konopacki with René Gnam)
Innisbrook, Thursday-Friday, December 3-4, 1987

Perhaps the most worthwhile new investment for your marketing horizons, these programs give you the facts you need to catapult your response!

Illustration #51

Want to get the most for your money?

Try this little gem — a postcard measuring 6" x 4-1/2", the largest size Uncle Sam will permit at first class card rates.

It's the perfect way to implement technique #709.

sure to go even higher. But...

Don't let that deter you from using the postcard for special sales notices, store traffic builders, and gift announcements. This little promotion piece still pulls well!

708 — COST PER ORDER

With postcard mailers and with every other form of lead-getting mail, you can only evaluate the success or failure of the promotion based on the eventual cost per order, not the cost per lead or inquiry.

But you must lump together the cost of acquiring the leads and getting the conversions to compute the cost per order.

709 — SELF-MAILER POSTCARDS?

How many of your effective space ads could be turned into self-mailer postcards?

Think about it! The ad goes on one side of the postcard, and all you need is a good teaser line for the other side.

710 — INVENTORY CLEARANCE

For almost immediate response to an inventory clearance, try using a small memo printed in black ink on one side only and insert it in a monarch or baronial envelope with no other enclosures. Stress your phone number as the response vehicle.

You can also have success using this as a postcard self-mailer.

711 — REPLY CARDS

If you are marketing products with space advertising in publications which do not normally accept reply cards, convince them to try.

You will heighten your response, perhaps lower your acquisition cost per customer, and perhaps establish a new sales tool for the publication.

I did this with a medical journal. It never took bind-in cards until I was able to show the publisher all the money he'd get. In that fashion, my client was able to get favorable positioning as the very first card forever.

Illustration #52

Here's the back of the card on the previous page.

No one says you have to jam this much data on one card. The author wanted to give you an example of how much will fit on a single card and still be readable.

THIS POSTCARD IS A CONDENSED LISTING OF TOPICS TO HELP YOU PLAN YOUR FALL SEMINAR SCHEDULE...

SELECT the session(s) you want...CALL Debra for full topic listing...
ATTEND these informative workshops...ENJOY a Florida holiday...
LEARN which tested techniques will work best for your objectives...
RETURN to your desk invigorated with powerful new ideas...

ESSENTIALS of DIRECT MAIL MARKETING
Thursday-Friday, September 17-18, 1987...$595
542 recommendations, plus consultation in response to your important strategy questions. Lists, management goals, offers, copy and design, testing concepts, maximizing your budgets.
BUILDING SEMINAR/EVENT ATTENDANCE
Thursday-Friday, October 22-23, 1987...$595
Improve strategies for seminars, conferences, road shows, spin-offs, goals, offers, pricing, brochure copy and design, testing concepts, shrewd database use, boosting pull, more.
MORE ORDERS from YOUR NEW CATALOGS
Thursday-Friday, November 12-13, 1987...$595
Learn exciting ways to design higher-pulling catalogs, let covers guide readers and start selling, improve response to order forms, galvanize readers toward higher, multiple orders.
TRADE SHOW Marketing/Selling/Closing
Thursday-Friday, December 3-4, 1987...$695
Dr. Allen Konopacki joins René Gnam in an Innisbrook event that makes your exhibit budget yield a healthy R.O.I. Learn new pre-show, post-show marketing methods, exhibitor sales strategies, building payoff company and product recognition.
See your sales and marketing prowess go up,
instantly, on the bottom line!

Why you'll learn from René Gnam...
A wizard at creating campaigns and strategies, this top direct response consultant has also set marketing plans, written copy, designed mailings.
Gnam has consulted for giants like General Motors, DuPont, and McGraw-Hill, plus smaller firms that get new marketing clout for growth.
Uniquely, Gnam guarantees your full fee back if you haven't learned a new idea at his seminars! Now, use the impetus of these learning adventures on your career and your company's advancement.
and from Dr. Allen Konopacki...
America's leading industrial psychologist has counselled many Fortune 500 companies to use extraordinarily effective face-to-face methods on the convention floor. His practical guidance gives you new profits. (Limited seating at Innisbrook Golf & Tennis Resort. Please register early.)
HOW TO REGISTER now...
1... Call 813-938-1555 to register now.
2... Fly to Tampa International Airport where you'll be met and escorted to and from your hotel, gratis.
3... Enjoy your Florida visit and profit by the extensive facts and useful information you'll obtain.
4... Breakfasts, luncheons, refreshments included.

For more info, call Debra Sauer right now...Call **813-938-1555**

712 — BIND-IN CARD

Including a bind-in card with your space ad in almost any publication almost always will more than pay for itself in additional response regardless of whether you are selling a product, a service, or a publication!

It may not pay in terms of back-end conversions.

Calculate. Then, re-calculate.

713 — WHITE MAIL

If you have a series of space ads or small co-op inserts or postcards that are complete sales messages in and of themselves, try reprinting them in the form of a folder or booklet and inserting it with every product shipment and every response to white mail. ("White mail" is a term applied to correspondence but not orders.)

Frequently, you will receive pass-along readership and additional sales.

714 — POSTCARD BOOKLET

If postcards have been successful for you, why not take several of them and print a small postcard booklet with each card having a business reply card on one side and your promotion message and order form on the other side?

You now have a mini-catalog that can be easily used by the recipient. All he has to do is tear out and mail the card describing the product he's interested in.

715 — A BLOW-IN

The least expensive route to new added business for a publisher or a catalog mailer is the use of a blow-in, a loose card blown in the publication or the catalog at the bindery.

While the percentage of response will be extremely low, the cost to acquire orders or inquiries is dramatically lower than any other promotion.

716 — USING TWO CARDS

If you are a publisher or a catalog marketer using a bind-in card, try using two cards in different spots, or two or three cards on a single sheet with a perforation between them.

This takes advantage of pass-along readership, gets more exposures with readers, and makes your organization appear to be a popular leader in its field.

717 — TIP-ONS AND BIND-INS

Tip-ons and bind-ins in catalogs and magazines are great, but blow-ins are less expensive and may be cost effective for you.

Blow-ins also increase the response to tip-ons and bind-ins.

New postal regulations in the late 1980s permit a magazine advertiser to use a card, change his address to that of the publisher, and have replies go to the publisher. In that instance, you pay the publisher on a P.I. (per inquiry) basis.

With catalogs mailed at bulk rate, replies can go to you.

718 — CHECKING THE LISTS

In postcard mailings such as loose decks or bingo card booklets, be certain to check the lists used by the mailer before paying for your advertising space.

Responder lists work better with this format than compiled lists — in almost every instance.

719 — BARGAINS

When investigating postcard mailers, apply the same rules as when purchasing publication space ads.

Be sure to check for frequency discounts, regional splits, combination discounts, and other "bargains."

720 — BINGO CARD BOOKLETS

If your audience is primarily in the business community, don't forget to ask the publishers of appropriate trade magazines whether they sponsor bingo card booklets or loose decks to their subscription lists.

Often you will pull greater response from such postcard participation than with your paid space ads.

The most productive inquiry postcard mailers you can use, generally speaking, are those sponsored by publications to their subscription lists. Their audiences have a strong identification with the publication, and thus are more likely to read and heed the advertising messages.

721 — INTERSPERSED MAILINGS

René, can I intersperse my own postcard mailings with envelope mailings to create an interesting series of communications?

Ah, you're catching on! Of course you can. And you should.

722 — PROMOTIONAL POSTCARD

When designing your promotional postcard to be used as an insert in a co-op envelope mailing, use as many attention-getting devices as you can to avoid having your insert sorted "out" by the recipient facing a plethora of options.

723 — CO-OP POSTCARD MAILING

What? You say it's too expensive for you to do direct mail? How about investigating participation in a co-op postcard mailing?

Costs in 1988 were as low as $15 per thousand pieces for participation, including printing if you use just a standard card, plus your printing costs if you use a multi-card format or mini-catalog or other preprinted insert.

With some judicious thinking, you can pick your audience.

724 — OUT-OF-POCKET COSTS

In testing postcard mailers, rarely be willing to pay more than $25 per 1,000 for an initial run.

In 1986, the rule of thumb was to attempt to get your out-of-pocket costs between $10 and $20 per 1,000 in order to adequately test your market and evaluate the response you get on an eventual cost-per-order basis, remembering that you may have to do a conversion mailing to respondents.

725 — UP-FRONT MESSAGE

When advertising in loose deck postcard mailers, there are often as many as 100 cards in a deck, and it is vital that your message be in the first small handful.

If the recipient is turned off by the first cards he sees, he may never get to the bottom of the stack to see your message. Pay extra for this position.

726 — BINGO CARD INQUIRIES

Well over 90% of all inquiries arriving as a result of bingo cards, reader service cards, and other inquiry-getting promotions definitely are interested, if only mildly, in your product or service and deserve to be treated better than a cold prospect name.

These respondents are selective, responding only to those offers which truly fit their interest areas, because they don't have time to complete all such cards and because they don't want to risk sales visits for products or services they don't need.

727 — LOOSE CARD DECKS

Bingo card booklets and loose card decks are most effectively used to obtain inquiries, rather than sales, unless your product is a book or re-order supply item.

Why, René?

Because it's difficult to use such small space to completely describe complex, unfamiliar products, show the product, and also have room for all the pricing information and customer options. And, if it's a new product that isn't easy to understand or relate to, you need a lot of selling copy.

Instead, focus your attention on getting a lead from the booklet or deck. Then, mail to the lead to either convert it to a sale by mail or book a salesman's appointment. You can also couple this with telemarketing for a much higher closure ratio.

728 — COMPELLING HEADLINE

If you are using inserts in co-op mailings, remember that since there usually is a plethora of such promotions, the recipient tends to sort them very quickly by interest value.

He considers only those promotions which really strike him. All others are discarded. Catch his interest quickly with a compelling headline.

729 — TWO SIDES OF CARD

When using a bingo card booklet or a loose deck for your postcard promotion, you are paying for both sides of the card.

It may prove profitable to test one product on Side One and another on Side Two, rather than using one side of the postcard for business reply.

730 — LOOSE DECK MAILINGS

Loose deck postcard mailings pull slightly better than bingo card booklets.

C'mon, René, you haven't defined a "bingo card booklet"?

Sorry. It's a booklet in one of two versions:

1. A number of cards you don't mail, but you check a box on the booklet publisher's card. This is similar to a reader interest card in a magazine.
2. A number of perforated cards you can zip out and mail individually.

In both versions, there usually are three cards on a page and the booklet is usually staple-stitched at the almost non-existent spine.

Back to the main technique...

Unless you have a premium position in a bingo card booklet, you generally will discover that a loose deck will pull better for you.

Why? Because the loose cards spill all over the place, are easily shuffled and sorted, and are easily noticed. The bound bingo booklet appears more like a magazine that should be set aside and read later.

731 — ONE-SECOND MESSAGE

The more inserts you expect in a co-op envelope mailing or the more postcards you expect in a loose deck or bingo card booklet, the more your message must be simple, clean, uncluttered, and easy to grasp in a second or two.

732 — BUSINESS COMMUNITY LEADS

Postcard inserts and loose decks are excellent sources of leads in the business community, but are less effective in mailing to consumer groups because they result in a large number of nonqualified coupon clipper leads.

733 — CHARGING A PREMIUM

Some publishers of bingo card booklets or loose decks who are also magazine publishers may charge a premium for inclusion in the co-op mailing, or may ask you to purchase a minimum amount of space advertising in the regular publication in order to qualify for participation in the co-op.

This is especially true in the business field, and it may or may not be worth it depending upon the economics of the particular two-step promotion you are undertaking.

734 — POSTCARD DECK STUB

Just as in space advertising, if you use a postcard deck or a bingo card booklet that utilizes a stub, make certain that you have details of your offer along with your address on the stub so that a second user of the booklet can respond to you.

735 — MASS POSTCARD CO-OPS

Mass postcard co-ops by general merchandisers frequently are not 100% sold out.

You may be able to purchase decent remnants at attractive rates for certain geographic areas.

736 — MOST DESIRABLE POSITION

In a bound book of postcard mailers, the most desirable position is the top card on the first page.

The next most desirable position is the top card on the second page — not the second or third card on the first page!

737 — SELF-MAILER DESIGN TECHNIQUES

René, enough of postcards. What about self-mailers that are larger than postcards?

Okay, are you ready? Here are 19 potent self-mailer design techniques that can increase your direct mail response:

1. Use your NAME or your company name fairly prominently because many people want to recognize the sender before deciding whether to read on. If your company name or personal name has high recognition, consider using it within a headline, in addition to using it in address material.

2. Both the front and back of a self-mailer should use a VERY LARGE HEADLINE to clearly state the deal and/or to attract attention.

3. Use a short fold, also called a LIP, to invite the reader "in." Folding should not yield even edges. After folding, one edge should be longer or wider, yielding a LIP.

4. Use GRAPHICS or copy ON THE LIP to excite curiosity and to make the reader wonder what's inside.

5. Use a LONG HEADLINE to involve the reader so he can't stop reading once he starts. On the back of a recent self-mailer, my headline is 37 words. On the front, it's 109 words — all of them in ONE never-ending sentence until you reach the arrow which directs you inside. My longest self-mailer headline was 127 words, and it made money too. Forget about those books that tell you direct mail headlines should be limited to 7, 10, or 12 words. The people who wrote those books wanted to sell books. For whatever product or service you sell, your headline can be as long as you'd like it to be, if it's lean!

6. Use SPLASHES, not oceans, of color to guide the eye.

7. Use ROUTING INSTRUCTIONS at least once, maybe twice, to get your message to the right person within a company.

8. Stress your GUARANTEE and refer to it often. In my seminar self-mailers, I mention it in the "group registration" copy, and in the postscript of the letter, and on the coupon, and in the registration instructions.

Wait a minute, René! A letter in a self-mailer?

Yes, by all means. A large or expository self-mailer should have all the elements of a direct mail package.

Expository?

Much larger than a postcard, usually 11x17 or thereabouts.

René, does that mean I need a letter in every self-mailer that's larger than a postcard?

No, not always. Just consider when it would be appropriate. And it usually is.

9. Stress URGENCY, all over the piece, to get response. Elimi-nate urgency and I have a chance to toss the piece. I have used URGENCY copy in as many as 23 places on a single, successful self-mailer.

10. Use TAG LINES, or mini-headlines, at the end of a message. They keep the reader from tossing the piece because they get him back into it at the moment when he wants to quit. You can use as many of these as you'd like. Art directors call them "nightmares." They create design havoc. But, they stimulate re-readership. I've used 9, 10, even more tag lines on a single side of a single self-mailer. I'm interested in response, not design beauty. You decide how much havoc you want, for the goals you are after. But with self-mailers, recognize that the reader did not ask for and does not want to read what you sent. So you want to get the reader's eyes jumping back into the sales copy after he scans a column or a panel. Do it with tag lines.

11. Use ACTION VERBS to begin nearly every headline. I use a ton. Here are a few:

Get	*Find*	*Discover*
Capture	*Join*	*Select*
Save	*Sign Up*	*Uncover*
Tap	*Gain*	*Bring*

12. Use DIRECTIVE COMMANDS in your copy and graphics. Again I use a ton, like 12 arrows on one reply card in one self-mailer, and all these copy commands for a single self-mailer used to promote conference attendance:

Mail This Registration Form Today
Mail Now
Call Laura To Register
Bring Your Team

Illustration #53

Technique #737 lists 19 points to consider for your next self-mailer, and this piece uses them all. Note the arrow graphic on the lip, the tag line under the cities, the action verbs in the enumerated benefits, and — if you're in the mood — count the words in the headline, beginning with "Now" in the upper left corner and ending with the word "TODAY" just above the cities.

Sign Up At No Risk Today
Sign Up Now
Mail This Form With Check Today
Open Now
Reserve Your Seat Today
Pick Your Payment

13. Use some SMALL PHOTOS. They make readers peer at your piece. Peering is moving closer to what you promote.

14. Use ACTION PHOTOS. Something should happen in all of them. A portrait shot can show a smile. A product shot can have a person using the product. Ask your art director to help you on the shoot. I've found art directors are most imaginative in getting action into photos.

15. Use SMALL TYPE IN CAPTIONS to lead me into body copy.

16. Use TESTIMONIALS. Lots and lots of them.

17. Use GRAPHIC EMBELLISH-MENTS. Remember that I call them Doo-Dads and Doo-Daddies? Recognize that all the stars, arrows, asterisks, hands, numbers, and bullets you use are effective in guiding the eye.

18. Promise LOTS OF BENEFITS. Benefits can be promised either as a reward for reading the self-mailer or a reward for taking the action that the self-mailer promotes.

19. Make it QUICKLY UNDER-STANDABLE. Too many self-mailers are loaded with too much company background or history copy. Many self-mailers use flamboyant or psychedelic art treatments that cause readers to discard them. Present everything clearly. You do not need, and should not attempt, to be fancy when creat-ing a self-mailer. *Exception: using it to sell something super glorious, like a 9' x 15' mural. (Come see mine.)*

20. Shhhush, don't tell anyone you read this. Tell them there are only 19 techniques. This book gives you the bonus, the main technique...

One of the least known, and most effective techniques in creating successful direct mail is that you should not overly describe the product itself. This is especially true with self-mailers.

Oh, I know...you created the product, or manufactured it, or you're the leader of your entrepreneurial service company and you naturally want to glorify the wonders of your wonderful widget. It's your baby, so why shouldn't you be proud?

I'll tell you why, by *example*:

On my most successful seminar self-mailer, there were 450 square inches, but only 14-7/8 square inches described my product: the seminar topics. Just 3.3% was product. The rest sold the sale.

That's what you must do. SELL THE SALE.

Now, I'm not saying that 3.3% is magic. It's just an example of how much I'm willing to compromise myself. I invented the seminar. I promoted it. I taught it. In many cities. Publicly and for in-company presentations. Certainly I'm proud of it. It's my baby. But...

People aren't interested in what you sell. They're interested in why they should have it. Show me your new artificial intelligence screen or your new triple-layer bedspread and I say "that's nice." Tell me why it's wonderful for me and I just might write a check.

So the magic for you is: SELL THE SALE.

Illustration #54

There are two schools of direct mail thought with regard to self-mailer covers. One believes covers should be neat, simply-designed, and rather conservative, like this example from Administrative Health Management. Turn the page to see the same seminar self-mailer, redesigned by the author, using the points in technique #737.

ICD•9•CM
Diagnostic Coding
With an overview of CPT/HCPCS

MEDICARE MANDATED

1989

Vital - - One Day Seminar

REIMBURSEMENT
SOLUTIONS
FOR
PHYSICIANS ™

AHM SEMINARS
FOR THE
HEALTHCARE
PROFESSIONS
The Standard For Quality

Illustration #55

The author's treatment of self-mailer covers relies on split-test experience, which dictates that covers should present reader benefits and start selling immediately. Here is his rewrite/redesign work on the same 1989 seminar self-mailer, using the points in technique #737. If you were the target, which piece would get your attention?

How to Increase Insurance Reimbursement
and
How to Avoid a $2,000.00 Federal Fine
and

SPECIAL SEMINAR for your staff assistants who handle important claims paperwork

How to Satisfy Insurance Coding
and
How to Avoid "No Pay" Situations

all are explained for you with hundreds of instantly-useful tips, in plain English, without legal mumbo-jumbo, when you attend this highly-rated, one-day...

DIAGNOSTIC CODING
EVERYTHING YOU NEED TO KNOW FOR REIMBURSEMENT!

SEMINAR

ICD•9•CM
MEDICARE MANDATED

Yours Free!...at the seminar...

Comprehensive Coding Resource Workbook (CCRW)

1 Contains data you can to use immediately to speed reimbursement and achieve higher payments. $45.00 value, yours without charge at the seminar.

Diagnostic Coding Reimbursement Checklist (DCRC)

2 156 key do's and don'ts to guide you in preparing higher-paying claims, avoiding fee cuts, and getting paid faster. $15.00 value, yours free at the seminar.

INSIDE!...
Startling Facts about the relationship between diagnoses and payments!

"The greatest 'money-maker' for the physician. Well worth the investment."
Nelson J. Matos, staff assistant to Dr. John Katzenberg, Harvard, MA

"It's invaluable to have sources of information as provided by this seminar!"
Judith Ziemer, R.N., Long Beach Internal Medicine Group, Long Beach, CA

presented by
AHM SEMINARS for the Healthcare Professions

The Standard for Quality — Teaching by Experts

Now, Select the Day You Prefer at a Hotel You Prefer and
Immediately Increase Your Skills in Obtaining
The Highest Possible Fee Reimbursement

35,278 health care offices have benefited by the easily-learned techniques in this course...and now it's your turn. *SIGN UP TODAY!*

CHAPTER 16

CATALOGS

When it comes to writing catalog copy, your writer has the same backgrounding problem as with all other formats: understanding your list history.

As I mentioned in my column in *The Catalog Marketer*, your copywriter can do a better selling job for you if he knows a lot about the lists you have used and those you will use. Before writing, he should review and analyze mailing lists. He needs to know:

1. BAD PREVIOUS LISTS — so he can eliminate certain copy appeals he might otherwise use.

2. BREAKEVEN LISTS — so he can examine the copy that was used to see if it can be improved, and thus be successful in acquiring additional sales.

3. GOOD PREVIOUS LISTS — so he can determine like factors that influence his writing.

4. CUSTOMER LISTS — the longevity of your names and their buying history, similarity of names, amounts purchased, and percentages of payments via check, bill me, and credit card so he can structure his writing to your "hard core."

5. TEST LISTS — so he can determine appeals for each of them, or for clusters of similar lists.

6. GEO DISTRIBUTION — because he knows that names in certain areas need certain specific copy points.

7. LIST SOURCES — because he'll want to write copy that is targeted to the same appeals that worked to produce the names you already have or those you'll rent.

8. ORDER METHODS — because he knows that copy should stress phone convenience for those who like the phone, order form convenience for those who buy by mail, even telex for international companies. Do advise your writer of the percentages of orders by each method so he can determine the copy weight for each avenue.

9. TYPES OF NAMES — so he can write to individual clusters of names even though you mail to zillions. He'll weave specific points into his copy for business names, others for consumers, still others for those

people who buy at the company but take the product home.

10. EMPLOYMENT — with consumer lists, he wants to know typical occupations so he can consider copy points that enable the prospect to rationalize his purchase. With business lists, he needs to know job functions, titles, job longevity, types of firms, size of firms and what they market to whom so he can capitalize on this knowledge in his writing.

11. INCOME LEVELS — because he knows that copy written to all levels is less functional than copy that directs itself to specific levels. You do yourself a favor by acquainting your writer with the income ranges of the names on your lists.

12. INTEREST AREAS — so the shrewd writer can incorporate appeals to prospect interests, hobbies, or career advancement goals.

13. MARITAL STATUS — because your writer does not want to say that your stereo will be enjoyed by the entire family if you're using a list of newly divorced people.

14. COLLECTING PROCLIVITY — because writers know that people who collect will continue to do so. Mentioning this aspect of a product's value is a key point.

15. STATUS/ACHIEVEMENT ORIENTATION — perhaps the most important copy platform appeal considered by good writers is how to convince the reader that this product or service will give him greater status or enable him to achieve more. Authoring copy to hit this convin-

cer is exceptionally hard, and the copy is written differently for each group of different achievers.

Help your writer by giving him all this vital information, and more, and he will sell more.

> **Your writer will sell more if he recognizes that art attracts, enhances, and creates desire, but it's copy that sells.**
>
> **Far too many managers are mostly concerned with how their products look, what colors will be used, and how beautiful the catalog will be, often treating copy and the copywriter's role as secondary, sometimes providing unreasonable deadlines for writers who want to do a proper selling job.**
>
> **Copy is king.**

Management should learn, understand and accept the fact that the copywriter, like the manager, should be involved in every aspect of catalog creation, development and production, from initial product selection meetings to final blueprints and color keys. And that brings us to basic concepts of getting ready for catalog copywriting.

It is the copywriter's job to thoroughly study the audience and the product line before promoting the specific items in the catalog. That ideal study includes:

1. LIST EVALUATION AND ANALYSIS. Simply put, you cannot write selling copy unless you know who you're writing to.

2. OVERALL PRODUCT SELECTION. The writer must understand why each product or

service has been selected for this issue of this catalog, and he should have a voice in suggesting changes in product selection, especially if he feels that including certain products can destroy an overall "feel" of value and uniqueness for the catalog. He should also know why each product "fits" in the line being promoted. This often leads him to suggest additional items which can be profitable.

3. AUDIENCE HISTORY. A good writer approaches lists of customers differently than prospects, and he tackles different prospect lists differently. It is important to management to make all audience facts known to the writer at the outset. If he must write one version to both customers and prospects, he must be attuned to this.

4. INVESTIGATION. Give all products to the writer and let him play with them, and with all accessories. Also give him supportive literature and documentation on how each product was developed and manufactured. Allow time for your writer to "get the feel" of each item and to "feel good" about each item. He'll write better than if you simply give him a photo of your super fruit juicer.

5. FIELD TIME. Ideally, your writer should be able to test your products and see how they are used by the very people he approaches. The same applies to selling services in a catalog. Let your writer go with your service people to a few actual jobs. Let him examine your service contracts and policies. Let him go on sales calls, gauge customer and prospect reac-

tions, learn new benefits about what you promote.

6. QUESTION TIME. Before and during writing, the serious writer (and you wouldn't retain writers who aren't serious) must be able to question YOU, your engineers, producers, marketers, customers, and sales people. Deny this opportunity at your own peril.

7. THINKING TIME. The good copywriter doesn't just start writing. He thinks, sometimes for a long time before turning on his typewriter or word processor. His copy will flow beautifully and be more successful if he has had a chance to structure it in his mind.

EXAMPLE:

Liberty Life gave me six weeks to think about promoting an insurance policy. Everyone knows what an insurance policy is, but because I had six weeks, I was able to restructure the offer and create a more powerful promotion.

These seven points are ideals and many times deadlines and other business considerations do not allow a manager to exercise them all. But here's the proof:

I never had a computerized word processor until I was 45, and I was truly scared of getting one. I feared my writing would be structured, restricted, limited by the machine. Then I read what Isaac Asimov had to say about his machine. If he could use it, so could I. So I bought, not one, but two of the same computers he recommended in his articles and ads.

What was the convincer? Tandy gave Asimov many moons to play around, before writing. He tried it, invented on it, got frustrated with it, then discovered what it could do for him, and suddenly he was able to endorse it with the ultimate in compelling copy.

I didn't accept what he said because of who he is. Instead, I was motivated by the believability and frank statements that came from his thinking time, just as your prospects will be motivated by selling copy from a writer who has had ample time to get his feet wet with your sand clogs.

However, when catalog copy must fit in small space, writers have an exceptionally difficult job. But here's how to approach the task:

Before writing, review the major descriptive points and benefits. Then write the copy as long as it needs to be to cover everything. Tighten it. Rewrite it. And then:

1. SPEAK TO THE ARTIST to determine which typefaces will be used. What size? What width? For how many lines?
2. SPEAK TO THE TYPESETTER to determine the character count per line. If you're familiar with copy casting, you can do this yourself after your artist has indicated fonts, sizes, and widths.
3. SET TYPEWRITER OR WORD PROCESSOR MARGINS to the character count per line.
4. REWRITE THE COPY to fit the new margins.

In doing this, you will constantly be flustered by the narrow margins, but they will lead you to find shorter, crisper words, forcing you to edit your copy so it is truly lean.

Because your problem will be how to include all salient points, you may find it easier to write product description copy on a word processor that allows you to move words and phrases to different positions within each paragraph. You can do this several times, until the key sales messages fit the narrow margins.

The artist and writer should work together to achieve the desired "look" and selling messages.

This often means that after the writer has gone through the above editing steps, layout revisions will be required so that copy will not be short-changed. Each time there's a layout revision, the writer must re-edit and/or re-write, and that's another reason why a word processor will make the copy job go faster.

Arm your writers with the very best writing tools and background information. Then your catalog will produce sparkling results.

738 — CATALOG CHECK

If your catalog is valuable or if it offers products oriented toward a single interest area, consider putting a price on the cover: a small fee to cover postage and handling or catalog fulfillment, or perhaps a larger price as would be used for a book.

This technique started as a consumer audience stimulant, but has now spread to business-to-business marketing. The concept is this: if the catalog bears a cover price, it must be valuable. Maybe others pay that price. I got it free. How lucky I am.

René, what percentage of people will send a check for the catalog?

Very small. They'll see it as a lucky arrival. But, for those who do send payment, take the money and issue a refund certificate good on the first order from the catalog, or the next order, or whenever.

739 — POSTAGE AND HANDLING?

No matter how valuable your catalog is, if you want inquiries for it from businesses, associations, or institutions, do not try to collect a fee for catalog postage and handling.

740 — MAILING PACKAGE

If your products all fall into a similar category, put all of them together on a flyer, brochure, mini-catalog, or broadside and use it as an enclosure with an order form in every package you send out. Do this with solo mailing packages to get customers and with product fulfillment packages.

Especially test the solo routine. Automatically and immediately do the product fulfillment effort.

Usually, the new customer mailing insert is the first, prudent step toward determining whether you should, indeed, have a catalog. Tally the response to determine profitability. If it pays, do your catalog.

741 — ADDRESS CHANGE

If you produce a catalog, make certain that you include a form for recipients to use in changing their address.

Years later this will produce orders for you.

Years later, René?

Yes. You're not the only one to put catalogs on top of your water closet! Months later you look at them, maybe. But if you move, you thumb through them to decide if you should keep them. That's when you mail in the change of address card.

742 — SUBSCRIBER PITCH

If you include a change of address form in your catalog or publication, why not incorporate a small pitch to subscribe in the same coupon?

Frequently, just a couple of lines of type will produce additional revenue for you.

743 — PAID PROMOTION PIECE

Just because you mail your catalogs or bingo card booklets free to large rented lists is no reason to assume that people won't pay you to receive that promotion piece.

Next time around, include a bind-in asking for subscriptions, and you will be startled by the response and easy dollars.

Now this does open a can of worms. Who pays? Who doesn't? What about those people or companies that we definitely want to get our catalog but who haven't paid? Do we do a catalog subscription renewal series?

All these questions can be answered. Unfortunately, not in a book, because every situation is different. My point in mentioning this technique is that it can assist you to greater revenue and show you that your catalog may be valued by its recipients.

But there's a nice, little gesture you can make if you charge for a subscription:

Take the money. Then print a discount coupon for the amount that the catalog subscriber paid. Mail that coupon to the subscriber and tell him it's good on his next order. What rapport you'll build!

744 — NUMBER OF COUPONS

A number of coupons for subsidiary services, information booklets, or individual products — judiciously spaced within the pages of a catalog or publication — spur response to bind-in cards and other order forms, even though the coupons may not be returned in significant numbers.

745 — AT-HOME SHOPPING

As our society rapidly moves toward smaller families with greater numbers of working women, at-home shopping becomes an appealing aspect of direct mail marketing.

Take this as a tip to study whether your current product line can be converted into a catalog or booklet presentation inviting consumers to shop at home.

746 — HOW TO ORDER

In multi-product promotions such as catalogs or booklet self-mailers, your 800 number presentation and other directions on how to order should appear or, be referred to, on almost every page or spread, including your front and back covers.

Give the reader a way to order immediately when seeing a desired item.

747 — BEST BUYS

Slow-moving products in a multi-product presentation often will get a second or longer look by your direct mail prospects if you flag such products as "best buys" or "newly discounted" or with similar appropriate terminology.

Those little bursts or flags guide the eye, make the products more exciting, entice readership.

748 — JAZZING UP THE COVER

To avoid the deja vu feeling about your catalog covers, prominently display "143 new products" and/or "30% more pages" and/or "10% lower prices," or other appropriate wording in a slash, flag, or banner across the face of the cover. It can also be in a burst.

This easy technique lends excitement to the cover and invites the reader to go inside for wonderfulness.

749 — PRINTING AN INDEX

If your catalog exceeds 24 pages, print an index of product categories either on the front or back cover or far forward in the catalog to facilitate reader searching.

Ask 1,616 people in your company to double-check the index. Indexes are constant homes for typos.

750 — RAPID SHIPMENT

Catalog and merchandise promotions of any kind are more successful if you frequently stress your rapid shipment.

751 — ADDITIONAL ORDER FORM

If you produce a catalog, remember to enclose at least one bind-in envelope for orders, but also have an additional order form printed in the catalog to pick up additional orders after the envelope has been used.

752 — MULTIPLE ORDER FORMS

A catalog mailer discovers that it almost always pays — whether mailing to business and industry, or to a consumer audience — to use more than one order form.

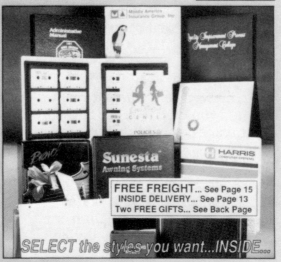
Illustration #56

This catalog cover, by the author for Vinyl Industrial Products, uses technique #746 in the display of 800 numbers and technique #749 in the use of an index. It also displays the products being promoted and presents user benefits and price savings.

You might consider binding in an order form, printing a couple on catalog pages, and blowing one in loosely so that it falls out when the catalog is skimmed by thumbing.

No, no, René. You can't do that with conservative businesspeople. You'll offend them, won't you, by asking for the order so many times?

I doubt it. And I doubt it based on testing, which is the only way to form a conclusion in direct mail marketing.

A few years ago, I recommended Technique No. 752 to Marti Campbell at American Productivity Center in Houston. She then split-tested one order form against two. When that worked, I asked her to split four against two. When that was successful, Marti split-tested eight against four. Her employer did very well because of this technique. So did Marti. She got promoted, and then sought new horizons.

Your horizon is unlimited, especially when you mail to those conservative businesspeople (who really aren't all that conservative!). Consider it this way:

At the office, I'm not the only one who can order from your catalog. Chances are good that more than one decision-maker in the company can order from you.

At home, well, of course, you'll accept an order from more than one member of a household.

And, there's another point about this technique:

Often, I can order from you today, and then need something else (or more of the same thing) from you next week. You must give me extra order forms so that I then have a chance to send you extra money.

753 — ONE-STEP OFFER

If you run space ads to generate catalog inquiries, try switching them to a one-step offer. Just revise your inquiry-generating ad to include a sales pitch that will promote sales of specific products as well as catalog inquiries.

Sometimes sales produced by such ads can pay the advertising cost, so your catalog inquiries are generated without an acquisition cost.

754 — BIND-IN REPLY CARD

If you have a major catalog of consumer products of interest to a wide variety of people, try binding in a reply card saying "Mail this card for our free catalog of men's items." You can use the same technique for women's items, plumber's supplies, sporting goods, mechanic's measures, household appliances, and so on. This applies to the business world, too.

The objectives are to give an impression of having several different catalogs and to identify specific interests of those prospects who really are interested in receiving more mail from you.

755 — BUYING CLUB

If you're a catalog marketer mailing to consumers, consider forming a buying club and offering a discount on all your merchandise if a small membership fee is paid up front.

The membership fee cuts your acquisition costs. And those who respond will be more likely to order from you in the future because they are members getting a special discount.

756 — EDITORIAL FEATURES

Orders from catalogs often can be increased significantly if space is judiciously used for editorial features promoting the use of specific items featured in the catalog.

Then, if you use editorial features in your catalog, run short cover blurbs calling attention to those articles. Often prospects who would not otherwise look at your catalog will be drawn into it by the promise of interesting, informative articles.

How long or short, René, can these features be?

They can be just a paragraph or two, but you're better off with a nice long story, perhaps several hundred words.

EXAMPLES:

If you sell shrubs to resort managers or consumers...your long story can tell me how to plant them, how to fertilize, how to water, when to plant.

If you sell office products to retailers...your long story can talk about product usefulness, saving employee time, reducing filing problems, profits, inventories, accounting procedures.

If you sell replacement displays to businesses...your long story can talk about preventing downtime, increasing production, the ease of replacement, rapid shipment, manufacturing quality.

Here's the most powerful way to use editorial features:

Do NOT simply write a wonderful editorial feature and put it on one page. Start it, perhaps on page 4. Have it continue on page 9. Then, the reader must turn to page 16. Then to page 21. The idea is to interest me in the article and then get me moving through the entire catalog so I see all your products throughout the catalog.

And, this leads us to the next technique, one of the most potent concepts for all catalog marketers as it gives the reader of your catalog a perception of newsworthiness:

757 — A MAGALOG: CATALOG FOR THEATRE-GOERS AND MANY OTHERS

In December of 1968, Armina Marshall and Philip Langner, at The Theatre Guild in New York, hired me to solve a difficult marketing problem: how to produce a catalog for theatre-goers. I had to sell them tickets to several different plays at the same time, but not on a subscription plan. We knew what the plays would be, and the locations, but not the actors or actresses. Can you imagine promoting *Hello Dolly* without Carol Channing?

Your normal catalog product presentation just wouldn't do for folks who love serious Broadway plays and high-priced musicals.

So I invented (or created) what I believe was the world's first MAGALOG: a catalog in magazine format. You may prefer saying a catamag, but I prefer MAGALOG.

Perhaps because I've spoken to well over 15,000 marketing executives, the term "magalog" has gradually crept into our marketing vocabulary. Several marketers have adopted it, including U.S. General Supply in selling tools and nuts and bolts to home workshop addicts and to commercial repair shops, and Warshawsky-Whitney in selling auto add-ons and repair kits to both consumers and retail establishments like service stations and auto body shops.

The concept is to let the reader believe he's getting a magazine, which is fun to read, and then he discovers that he can go to the theater, or buy tools, or fondle auto repair kits.

An interesting method of doing this comes from another client, Crutchfield Car Stereo in Charlottesville, VA. Bill Crutchfield — who moved his business and his residence from his

Illustration #57

That's Julie Harris on the left, in Forty Carats, *and Morris Carnovsky on the right, as King Lear, both gracing covers of Gnam's original magalogs — technique #757 — for The Theatre Guild, proving that even a hard-selling marketing man can design with class when the audience is appropriate. Note that these covers appear to be on magazines. The publications are catalogs in magazine formats, containing show descriptions, ticket prices, seating information for specified dates, and articles about the plays and musicals. Thousands of theatre-goers ordered their tickets by mail, eliminating the cost of commissions to brokers, and telling The Guild which of its shows were going to be well-attended in which of its seven cities across America. As issue after issue hit the mail, Gnam and Guild promotion manager Bill Dempsey sold ads in this magalog — to top-drawer advertisers like Diner's Club, TWA, and many restaurants. This magalog also used the technique #756 concept of including editorial features in its pages.*

bedroom to a huge multi-building estate with a private lake (by doing this technique with his catalog) — doesn't call his catalog a catalog. It's a magalog, but I recommended calling it a Car Stereo Buyer's Guide. That implies that you *should* buy, which implies that you *want* to buy. In other words, we're saying Bill's catalog is a helpful thing, not strictly a sales pitch.

Working with Bill's advertising manager, John Wade, we completely devoted the first 15 pages to articles

that help you determine the key facts about car stereos: speakers, antennas, boosters, woofers, and tweeters. Product pages followed the "editorial" pages.

And, in some instances, I have editorial and product pages interwoven. But now that you have the idea from Crutchfield and Gnam, think of your own product line...

Can you write articles that are HELPFUL to me...MEANINGFUL to me...EXPLAINING to me...treating me like someone who wants to be informed, enlightened, and given useful data before considering a buying decision?

If you can, you've got me hooked into reading, studying, and buying from your catalog. Here are three diverse *examples* of how you can use this technique:

You sell computer software? Use a magalog with articles to explain:

- the differences between different types of software, or language adaptability in ASCII, C, ASSEMBLY, COBOL or FORTRAN...
- the differences between machine and program languages...
- the suitability of cassette or disk programs, header cards, gratis utilities, complimentary patches...
- the possibility of updating and expanding.

You sell books? Use a magalog to teach the teachers you mail to:

- how each title or series of titles makes the teacher's work so much easier...
- how parents love having their children read these good books...
- how books are rated by professionals and selected for your catalog...
- types of books that are appropriate for each grade level...
- how to select books that are read versus those that are looked at.

You sell laboratory testing devices? Use a magalog with articles teaching lab technicians and managers:

- how different devices differ...
- how they work and how to use them...
- how easy they are to operate...
- the types of tests they perform...

- the supportive materials needed for various types of tests...
- the reliability factors of glyco-hemoglobin evaluations...
- the ratings and approvals of professional organizations.

Whatever your product line is, you can write articles about your products, their suitability, their usefulness, your very fair pricing — even about how carefully you pack and ship your products.

Any product line, René?

Yes. The craziest assignment I ever had in the catalog field was to write a magalog for U.S. Pencil & Stationery Company. My job was to write articles teaching businesspeople how to use ballpoint pens.

Don't laugh...I did it. My articles covered all these fascinating topics:

- pens as corporate gifts
- pens you can re-sell to make money
- pens to tie-in to other products you already sell
- pens as inserts in your company's mailings
- the care we take in manufacturing our pens
- how you can have your logo on your pens
- how to write a catchy slogan for your pens
- how to get other companies and organizations to give away your pens
- the history of modern writing instruments
- how we manufacture the ink for our pens
- why our pens write smoothly
- how long a good pen should last
- how to determine how many pens your company needs
- how to buy your pens at a discount

- the difference between every-day office pens and executive pens.

Now, if I could be that creative about ballpoint pens, how creative can you be about much more important products.

Another *example* of how to use the magalog concept comes from my friend Don Feltner, owner of Don Feltner Photography in Wheat Ridge, CO.

By attending my seminars in several cities, Don learned the magalog concept rather thoroughly. He kept asking me questions about it, too. Then, he invented his own form of magalog, on newsprint.

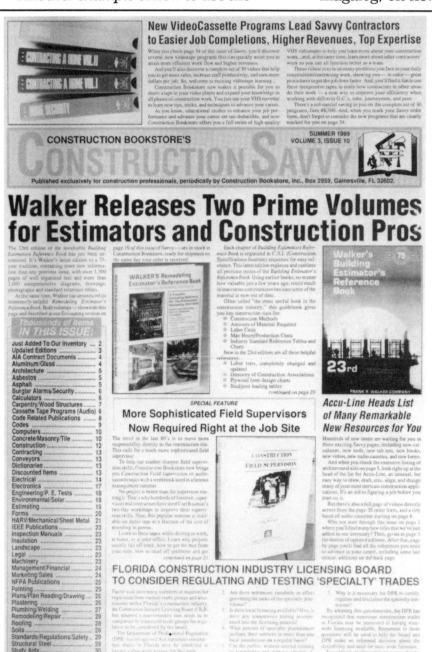

Illustration #58

Taking technique #757 to its maximum, the author produces both versions of Savvy shown on these pages for Construction Bookstore, Gainesville, FL, on IBM-compatible desktop 386 systems.

Each issue makes heavy use of product photos and stories about books, tapes, forms, and tools, plus important information about state licensing requirements.

Thus, each issue provides helpfulness to the reader, as well as a complete source for references in his specific trade.

He publishes books, runs seminars, sells postcards, promotes photography marketing kits, and somehow manages to take pictures (also for an income). He put all the items together in one magalog and wrote lead-in stories for each category of product. And he did it in just two colors instead of his previous full-color sample mailings!

Worked like a charm, he reported when he visited me for another day of consulting.

The key is that a MAGALOG gets people to read your catalog. Isn't that what you want them to do — read it — so they can order?

Maybe a magalog IS for you.

Illustration #59

When news of updated publications, licensing changes, or new state-required forms happens, it is reported in Savvy, which has become so popular that hundreds of calls are received each month requesting this unusual magalog.

Maybe it should be called a "newslog", since it is printed on newsprint. Newslog or magalog, it has eliminated hundreds of smaller mailings on individual products and produced top profits for Gnam's client. And, in case you have not guessed, it's far less costly than normal catalogs.

Special Edition!

Savvy Explodes with Early Announcements of More Than 60 Electrical References...and You Can Have Great Price Savings on Them!

CONSTRUCTION BOOKSTORE'S
ELECTRICAL SAVVY

SUMMER 1989
VOLUME 3, ISSUE 10

Published exclusively for construction professionals, periodically by Construction Bookstore, Inc., Box 2959, Gainesville, FL 32602

A Special Savings Opportunity from Construction Bookstore

BEAT PUBLISHERS' PRICE INCREASES ON 1990 NATIONAL ELECTRICAL CODE AND RELATED BOOKS COMING SOON

This special issue of *Savvy* presents a giant collection of current and soon-to-be-released electrical books, but the prices on the new 1990 National Electrical Code and related books will cost up to 30% more, according to the publishers.

Some publishers haven't even determined what they will be charging for their 1990 editions.

HOW YOU CAN USE INSIDER PRICING TO MAKE GREAT SAVINGS NOW

You should know that, historically, publishers have three sets of prices:

1. *Pre-publication prices*...available only to a few select insiders in the publishing world,
2. *Regular prices*...established as new and updated titles are released, and
3. *Increased prices*...forced on publishers by rising paper and printing costs, postal rates, and normal increased overhead costs.

YOU DON'T HAVE TO WAIT FOR PUBLISHERS' PRICE HIKES

Construction Bookstore now is able to offer you our special pre-publication pricing on dozens of top books.

Just thumb through this issue of Savvy right now and mark the books you'll be needing. Order before August 31 and you'll make significant savings.

You only have a short time to make these savings. Many of these books will have revised prices as soon as they are issued by the publishers. That's why it's important to you — now — to select all the electrical references you'll need, and order them at our special pricing.

CHECK OUT ALL THE UPDATED TITLES STARTING ON PAGE TWO

"Wow!" That's what you'll say when you see all the books we've lined up for you, way in advance of those "regular" and "increased" prices. You save on each book, and the savings mount up as you select your new electrical library.

Remember, too, you can order your new 1990 National Electrical Code in your choice of looseleaf, handbook, or paperback — along with many other NEC-related items — right now...before these books are released and are thus subject to increased pricing. At the same time, be sure to order your new Codetabs for your NECs. These exclusive tabs make it easy for you to find specific references in the mammoth NEC books.

All in all, you'll make some super savings by investing a few minutes with this issue of Savvy. It's your key to low prices. Hurry to beat the deadline and beat the price increases. Use your order form on page 15. Use it today.

SPECIAL PRICING IN THIS ISSUE

ENTIRE SAVVY FULL OF BARGAINS

CHECK THROUGH THIS COMPLETE ISSUE

Make Your 1989 Savings on the New 1990 National Electrical Code®

Right now, you can make substantial savings on the official 1990 prices for the looseleaf and paperback editions of the new 1990 National Electrical Code by using the order form on page 15 in this special electrical edition of Savvy.

And, all three versions — looseleaf, paperback, and handbook — along with many NEC-related items and special electrical references are listed for you in this issue.

FREE GIFT #1

Order before August 31, 1989, and you can have your 1990 NEC looseleaf personalized with your name on the cover at no extra charge.

FREE GIFT #2

Order before August 31, 1989, and you'll get a package of Construction Bookstore's Official '90 NEC notepaper — 50 sheets that fit right in your binder.

Get a big jump on your competitors — and enjoy our special savings for you — by being "first in line" for shipment of the new 1990 NECs. The sophisticated Construction Bookstore shipping system allows us to send all orders in the exact sequence that they are received. By placing your order

now, you'll be way ahead of the thousands of folks who wait until the last minute to act.

NOW, WE CAN SHOW IT TO YOU

You've waited to see what the new NEC cover will look like, and now Construction Bookstore is pleased to announce to its customers that NFPA has selected the official cover design for all three versions of the upcoming 1990 National Electrical Code.

After rejecting more than six cover designs, NFPA selected a granite-gray color with the artwork as shown here.

The looseleaf version of the 1990 NEC will feature a double-vinyl constructed 7-ring binder. This means the normal vinyl binder will have an additional clear vinyl overlay for increased durability and wear.

YOUR NAME ON IT!

Remember that we'll put your name, or your logo or symbol, right on the cover of the 1990 NEC looseleaf — at no charge!

Act today to beat the special August 31, 1989 deadline by using the order form on page 15.

HERE THEY ARE!

NATIONAL ELECTRICAL CODE·1990

NATIONAL ELECTRICAL CODE·1990 HANDBOOK

Hundreds of Items IN THIS ISSUE:

UPDATED TITLES START ON PAGE 2
ELECTRICAL SECTION BEGINS ON PAGE 10
SEE THE COMPLETE INDEX ON BACK PAGE

ALL PRICES in This Issue are good until AUGUST 31, 1989

CHAPTER 17

SALES LEADS

Your company does NOT have an international monopoly. Your company DOES have good competitors. And the competition poses problems for your sales force because...

1. The competition goes after the same potential customers, and
2. The competition wants to get your active customers away from your company, and
3. If your salesperson could spend all his time soliciting business from just one POTENTIAL customer, he probably would get that business, and
4. If your salesperson could spend all his time with just one CURRENT customer, he might never lose that customer.

But each salesperson must seek business from several prospective companies at the same time that he works to convince several current customers to remain with your company and to increase their purchases. He's just too busy to do everything, and that's the main reason why your salesperson needs direct mail.

Direct mail supports the salesperson. It is his "calling card" when he can not be there, and it continues his sales effort and reinforces his messages.

Your competitors know their biggest dollars come from their biggest prospects. Therefore they logically spend the most time on the biggest prospects. Thus, your salespeople need promotional support to go after those companies which can become large customers. And for those big companies which are now your active customers, your salespeople need promotional support to help prevent the competition from getting your business.

The competition does not spend much sales time on smaller companies which may not be worth several personal sales visits. For instance, 85% of American businesses employ fewer than 100 persons. Those companies are thus classified as small businesses, yet they offer tremendous and often-missed sales opportunities at better gross profits. The profits on such sales often are better since smaller customers may not buy at bulk sales discounts.

Your company can be smarter than the competition by using direct mail to support busy salespeople who can not spend all their time soliciting business from smaller companies.

This support can:

1. Familiarize executives at those smaller companies with your products and services,
2. Warm up those executives for future sales visits, and
3. Produce "qualified" leads from those companies so the salesperson does not waste his time on fruitless visits.

The competition also knows that some potential customers are located far away from a sales office or they may be in areas that are not usually visited. So the competition does not send its salespeople to call on those prospects.

Your company can be smarter by using direct mail to get the executives at those distant companies to request a visit by your company salesperson. Then, when the your salesperson arrives, he is responding to a request for a sales presentation. That beats a cold call.

Direct mail is NOT intended to replace a good salesperson. You may need salespeople to educate prospects, counsel them, explain products, point out the benefits of dealing with your company, and produce orders.

But demands on your salesman's time are growing and the personal sales call rate has been going down because your company salespeople are so busy, and because the executives they call on have many pressures on their time.

This is not a unique problem. The sales call rate in America has slipped from six per day to five per day and, as I keyboard this, is approaching four per day for many salesmen. Some international industrial firms count themselves lucky if top salesmen make just two sales visits a day. Instead, they use direct mail to keep their names in the minds of current customers and potential customers. Their mailings educate prospects about manufacturing care and details, product uses and benefits. That's what your new mailings must do for your salespeople.

The next problem you face is that orders are not always produced by a single executive at a prospect company. Often, several executives are involved.

But your salesperson usually can't see each decision-making executive, or each executive who influences the decision. And just one person in the target company can ruin the salesperson's entire pitch, especially if that person was not at the salesman's presentation. But your company direct mail can reach those important people to tell them the details that the salesman wants them to know.

Often, the target company does not inform your company about a new product for which your products or services would be perfect. Because your salesperson can not be at the target company every day of the year, he may miss a sale when those new products are being planned or produced.

But your company direct mail can support your salesperson when he is not there, reminding the target company's executives to call him, reinforcing an image of your company so that when your salesperson arrives, his job is easier.

Thus, we see that your salesman's rough job is to face these 10 constant problems:

1. COMPETITION wants your prospective customers.
2. COMPETITION wants your active customers.
3. Salespeople are OVERBUSY.
4. SMALL TARGET COMPANIES may not be worth cold calls.
5. Prospects may be too DISTANT for sales calls.
6. Prospects need FAMILIARIZATION.
7. Prospects need EDUCATION.
8. Non-qualified Leads WASTE TIME.
9. SEVERAL DECISION-MAKERS are involved.
10. PLANNING STAGES are difficult to determine.

But now to make your life easier, here is a summary of the 14 main reasons why your company can capitalize on direct mail to back up your sales force:

1. Direct mail REINFORCES your company's position with current customers.
2. Direct mail STIMULATES prospective customers to do business with your company.
3. Direct mail EDUCATES your prospects and customers.
4. Direct mail PERPETUATES YOUR IMAGE as a solid company.
5. Direct mail REMINDS prospects and customers when the salesperson cannot be there.
6. Direct mail REPEATS MES-SAGES from the salesman, giving added ordering incentive.
7. Direct mail REACHES SEVERAL INFLUENCERS and key decision-makers within each target company.
8. Direct mail EXTENDS YOUR REACH to large and small targets.
9. Direct mail TRAVELS DISTANCES, reaching executives at target companies far away from your sales office.
10. Direct mail PRODUCES QUALIFIED LEADS for your company's salespeople.
11. Direct mail REDUCES TIME your salespeople would waste on fruitless sales calls.
12. Direct mail MAKES MORE SALES CALLS for your busy salespeople.
13. Direct mail ALERTS PLANNERS to consider your company when they contemplate or design a new product.
14. Direct mail MAXIMIZES SALES EFFECTIVENESS by providing a constant stream of supportive, explanatory information.

And those 14 points are why direct mail marketing should be regarded as one of the best friends a salesperson has.

758 — PROMOTION PIECES

The larger the company you mail to, the more promotion pieces you must send to that company to be effective. Remember that several executives and other employees may be involved in the decision-making you want.

A good *example* of this is the meteoric rise of Fred Smith's Federal Express from six packages a day at the start in 1974 to 30,000 packages a day by 1980, and who knows how many today as Federal grows by 30% a year. This jump was caused by television exposure and by mailing more than three pieces to almost every target company on Federal Express' rented mailing lists. Frequently, Federal receives inquiries from 3, 4, or even 5 different employees at a single company.

When FedEx goes after a market, it really goes — by mail, by publication ads, by television. By 1986, a tiny upstart company had grown to 38,000 employees, a huge fleet of planes and trucks, and $2.5 billion in sales. Learn the lesson of targeting to more than one executive, and learn it well.

759 — QUICK FOLLOW-UP

The longer it takes you to respond to an inquiry, the less chance you have of making a sale.

760 — NEGATIVE RESPONSE?

Getting a response of any nature from a prospective customer is better than getting no response, even if the response you receive is negative.

The reader who volunteers a response is now subconsciously binding himself closer to you, creating a stronger relationship on which you can capitalize with future mailings.

That's why many mailers include an "I'm not interested" box on the lead cards...to get a response of some kind that can be used for future promotion mailings.

761 — PLAYING ONE OFF THE OTHER

When mailing to business audiences, remember that every business likes to think that it is the most informed and up-to-date in its arena.

Therefore, if you mention that competitive businesses are receiving information or using specific products that you promote, it makes it necessary for me to consider inquiring or ordering from you so I can stay abreast of my competitors.

762 — WARMING UP

Direct mail and sales literature are efficient methods of warming up a prospect for a salesman's visit.

If yours is a high-ticket item, consider splitting your mailing, having half the respondents get a pitch for a salesman's visit while inviting the other half to request literature.

763 — A FEW QUESTIONS

If your salesfolk are being flooded with leads you derive from direct mail, try qualifying the leads even more than you do now by asking respondents to answer a few — not many — questions on the reply forms.

How many questions, René?

Not more than three, possibly four.

This will only slightly reduce the number of leads, but will give the salesperson more ammunition in making a call. It will also tell you more about the nature of the lists you are using.

764 — CONFIRMATION MAILING

To qualify a sales lead prior to turning it over to salesmen, dispatch a confirmation mailing to the inquirer.

Promote your deal harder to the inquirer with this confirmation mailing and get him eager — or intentionally kill his eagerness — for the salesman's eventual call.

765 — SALES FORCE

Your direct mail is working fine. Your space advertising is producing the results you want. Isn't now the time to add a sales force or add to your existing sales staff?

Perhaps. While salespeople can't say the things you can in the vivid color and with the total presentation you can employ in your literature, frequently they can boost sales by friendly, spoken words.

766 — LOCALIZED PROMOTIONS

It is usually foolish to expect that your branch office, franchise or representative dealer, independent sales agent, or other arm's-length party will conduct its localized promotions according to your specifications.

Handle them yourself and imprint the local name and address data.

767 — REPORTING DATA

Don't rely on salespeople to bring you lists of their contacts and other prospects.

Most sales personnel are primarily oriented to actual sales in a one-to-one relationship and are grossly inaccurate and slow about reporting data.

768 — SIMPLE ANNOTATED FORM

When giving a new lead to a salesperson, also give him a simple form to annotate as to the results of the sales call and his impression of the quality of the lead — whether there's a sale or not!

This will enable you to better evaluate your lists for future lead-getting mailings. Penalize the salesperson who doesn't complete the forms and submit them in a timely manner.

You can make the annotating and filing of these forms extremely easy by supplying your sales force with portable computers. You do not need full-screen editors, spreadsheets, and other

marvels on them. A laptop computer will do fine. You set up the screens. The salesperson fills them in and transmits them by modem at the end of each day. The next morning, your sales manager can review all of them on his desktop computer or a printout.

Such fast actions can lead to additional sales, a more information-loaded database, and greater control over the efforts of the salespeople.

I've used laptop computers on airplanes, in taxis, in limos, in hotel rooms. And if I was able to learn how to use them and upload and download, it should be easy for any of your salespeople as well.

769 — SALES PITCH

If you intend to send a salesperson in response to an inquiry, say so when soliciting the inquiry!

Your respondents then automatically are qualifying themselves as receptive to a sales pitch.

770 — NO SALESMEN

When making free offers to businesses, institutions, consumers or associations, decide in advance whether it is necessary for a salesperson to visit following receipt of the inquiry.

If it is not necessary, dramatically state that "no salesman will call" and you will automatically receive higher response.

771 — PHONE NUMBER?

In requesting a phone number from a respondent, consider whether you simply want to say "phone" and leave a blank line, or whether you want to use wording along these lines: "phone, so we can acknowledge your order."..or..."phone, so we can alert you to fast-breaking developments."

Giving a reason for requesting phone numbers can produce more of them and overcome resistance by some respondents who otherwise might think they will be inundated with sales pitches.

772 — UNRELATED GIFT?

When using a free gift for an inquiry mailing program, make sure that the gift is a booklet or similar product-related offering.

Unrelated gift offerings will produce fewer qualified leads and unnecessarily add to your conversion costs.

773 — MORE MYSTERY

If you are attempting to receive an inquiry or use your promotion as the first step in a two-step mailing series, the less you disclose, the more mystery there is. And the mystery is more likely to achieve a response to the first step than stating all points.

Tell just enough to intrigue the recipient of your mailing piece. Then, the second mailing, which attempts the conversion to a sale, discloses the full pitch with several enclosures, usually at least a letter, reply card, and brochure.

774 — THE ENTIRE STORY?

In direct mail attempts to acquire leads for salespeople to follow up, it again is better to leave a mystery about certain details regarding your product or service, rather than to tell the entire story in the lead-acquisition mailing.

If you tell the entire story, you can convince me that I know enough to not need the salesperson for more information.

775 — BOTH SEXES

When creating campaigns directed to businesses, associations, professions, or institutional markets, do not assume all readers are males!

I have worked with female editors, female steel executives, females in top and middle level executive positions

This sales lead reply card, by the author for Miracle Span Steel Buildings, illustrates three techniques:

#770 — the stub indicates "no salesman will visit unless you request him,"

#771 — the phone number copy says "we must call to verify delivery of package, but no salesman will visit without your advance okay," and

#772 — all six premium items are directly related to the product (a grain storage building for large tract farmers) and service (installation) being promoted.

in a variety of industries, even government. The number of competent, skilled decision-making females is increasing rapidly. Carefully structure your promotion so it is acceptable and meaningful to both sexes.

776 — DISCARDED MAIL?

Remember that one of a secretary's prime duties is to filter and organize incoming mail for the boss.

Mail directed to a business or professional audience that is blatantly male-oriented may be discarded by a female secretary or receptionist and never be shown to the boss.

777 — SECRETARY AS YOUR ALLY

Your job in business-to-business direct mail is to get your mail to the right person and that may mean turning

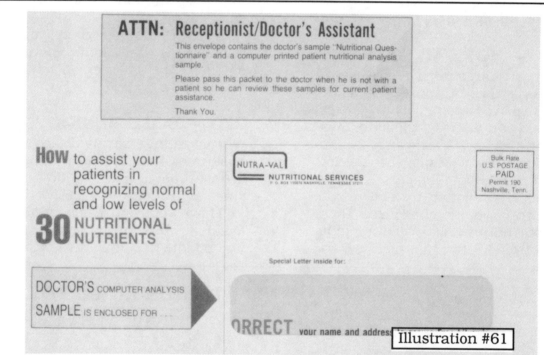

Two Gnam samples from the chiropractic world — a 6x9 envelope above for Nutra-Val Nutrition Services, and a #10 below for Clinic Management Associates — demonstrate using offset printed copy messages on envelopes to attract a secretary to being your ally, technique #777. In both instances, the doctor's name shows through the window.

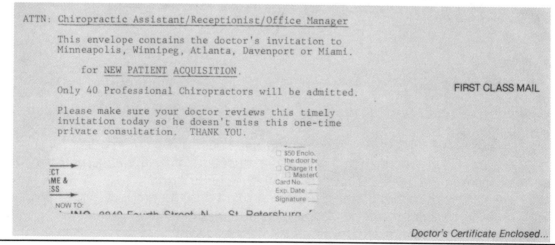

the secretary into your ally! You may be able to accomplish this by using copy messages directed to the secretary. At the very least, do not offend the secretary or other "pass-along" people.

Years ago, the concept was: "how can I get my mail past the secretary."

Today, she — if she is a she — is part of the decision process. If your mail properly addresses the seriousness of your communication in a totally businesslike fashion, she can be a valuable part of your sales effort. How? By flagging your mail for the attention of her superior.

Remember, too, that her superior may be either male or female.

778 — WAVE MAILING TECHNIQUE

If you have a limited budget and are trying to sell a big-ticket item or obtain a new customer who can be worth a lot of money in the future, have you considered using the wave mailing technique?

Simply spread your budget over a series of mailings dropped every other day (or on another similar schedule) so your recipient receives a number of promotions, each concentrating on a different product benefit with the final mailing giving a summary of all benefits...a final clincher toward a big-ticket sale.

779 — VARIED VISUAL IMPACT

When mailing continually to the same audience, try changing your visual impact so the recipient doesn't have that feeling of "deja vu."

If he thinks he has already seen your promotion and discarded it, he may not respond. So, at the very least, change color of ink and stock — but preferably also alter the format and the sales pitch.

780 — MAILING SERIES

The higher the price of a product or service, the more effective a series of mailings is likely to be, especially if dispatched 1-2-3.

The series builds up enthusiasm and interest, hopefully to a fever pitch.

781 — LOW-PRICED PRODUCTS

A series of mailings is less likely to be cost-effective — on a cost-per-order basis — than many single promotions when selling low-priced products or services.

782 — FOLLOW-UP PACKAGE

Against your standard follow-up package, test a simulated carbon copy of the original letter by printing the original on yellow bond with the word "copy" overprinted in a second color.

Use the same second color for a penscript memo angularly inscribed at the top. Your recipient will feel you believe it is urgent for him to get a second look at the letter, and he may be more inclined to respond to a second exposure.

783 — INTERNAL HOUSE ORGANS

Many companies find it efficient to enclose their internal house organs with promotional letters to their customer file.

Frequently, customers establish an on-going rapport with the selling company and are interested in its internal workings. Such communication provides a friendly backdrop for further selling.

784 — EDITORIAL?

Is your product suited for editorial coverage via publications, such as in a magazine's new product guide?

Such editorial descriptions appear to be publication endorsements, and the leads they produce often are among the best in producing additional sales.

785 — POSTCARD SELF-MAILER

Direct mail need not be expensive to be productive with sales leads.

Consider using a postcard self-mailer to announce price bulletins, new product launches, warehouse closeouts. The postcard can be an effective marketing tool. Remember to use key elements of successful direct response advertising on the card.

786 — COMPANY SLOGAN

Have you been using a company slogan that is meaningless today?

Can the slogan be reworded to tie in with a specific product or service you are now marketing?

Is the slogan necessary?

787 — SUPERSTARS

Are there any "superstars" in your organization, such as exceptionally-learned individuals, nationally-recognized figures, leading lights in your profession?

If so, a short biography (that specifies their relationship to the product

70 J Chestnut Ridge Rd.
Montvale, N.J. 07645

First Class Mail

In an unpressured atmosphere out in the sticks of New Jersey, a computer service bureau prints millions of list rental labels each week and delivers them in 72 hours . everywhere in the USA.

Illustration #62

Here are both sides of a lead-acquisition postcard self-mailer, technique #785, for Automated Resources Group by Gnam. Be certain to use at least one photo on such cards. More people in a company will see the card if it has photographic treatment.

And we enjoy our work.

Printing labels and providing tapes for mailing list rentals isn't very hard work, but it is exacting and the thinking behind it must be as accurately-conceived as the programming.

Away from the sirens and traffic jams, we concentrate on our work and it's even pleasant for us to put in extra hours to make sure that the right selections are made, the proper codes are inserted, the orders go out right on time.

That's why large list owners like GAF and Davis Publications, and small ones like Puzzle Lovers Club and Falcon Steel, rely on us for three essential mailing list assignments . . . all at our low rates!

• LIST RENTAL FULFILLMENT on labels or tape
• MERGE/PURGE   • LIST MAINTENANCE

Automated Resources Group, Inc.

70 J Chestnut Ridge Rd.
Montvale, N.J. 07645

TOM AMORIELLO
212-564-6410
201-391-1300

being offered) may increase your response by establishing credibility for your operation. It belongs on a brochure or insert in a promotion mailing, not in the letter.

788 — PROTECTION ORGANIZATIONS

If you are a member of the Better Business Bureau, a Chamber of Commerce, a major trade association having great respect, or a consumer protection organization, think about saying so on some — but not all — of your letterheads.

Though not always for promotional mail, but frequently for fulfillment letterheads, this proves to your prospects that you are customer-oriented and adhere to honorable practices.

789 — READING TIME

If you are mailing to busy people in business or industry, try printing (in small type) at the head of the letter, or even on the outgoing envelope, the reading time for the material enclosed.

Tell your prospect that your material is worth that much time.

790 — DECEMBER MAILING

While December historically is a poor month for mailing to consumers, it is not for mailings targeted to businesses.

Certain businesses, like catering, have more activity in December than in other months. But as long as your sales lead mail arrives prior to the last two weeks of December, it stands as good a chance to be read as mailings arriving in other months.

791 — AUTHORITATIVE LETTERHEADS

Authenticity in direct mail is difficult to achieve, but it can help establish a rapport so your sales message gets a warm welcome. One method of doing this is to strive for an authoritative letterhead

Perhaps enhance this effort by using a photograph of the writer in your mailing.

792 — MAIL DELIVERY TIME

There is nothing wrong with asking your current customers (not your prospects) to assist you in keeping tabs on mail delivery time.

Simply insert a business reply card in your next customer mailing and ask the recipient to note the date of arrival on the card along with his city and state and return it to you. Better yet, imprint his name and address on it so all he has to do is mark the date of arrival.

Then, use that information in planning sales lead mailings.

793 — ASSISTANCE APPRECIATION

If you ask your customers to keep track of mail delivery time, you should include some promotional copy indicating that you appreciate their assistance and that their replies will aid you in serving all customers better.

Then, when you have that response, be nice and send a thank you note, or a discount coupon, or a little gift.

794 — LISTING YOUR PHONE NUMBER

Listing your phone number, especially on sales lead mailings, nearly always reinforces the feeling that yours is a legitimate operation.

This may sound like "below the basics" to you, but if you check your incoming mail you'll frequently find sales lead letters that do not bear a phone number. You need the number to assist you in getting response, but you also need it to convince the prospect that your company is here to stay.

795 — FREE MEMO PAD

Want to discover if your sales promotion materials are read?

Include a response card offering a free memo pad or other item just for indicating the date on which the promotion was received.

Another method is to eliminate the response card and just mention the free gift in small type, hidden somewhere in a column of other information. Some folks call this a "buried offer." (Others say "buried offers" are offers made at the end of a long sales letter.)

If you bury your free gift offer and still get requests for the gifts, you'll surely know that your material is being read all the way through. When you send the gift, also dispatch a nice note of thanks.

796 — SUFFICIENT SALES PERSONNEL

If you are trying to secure leads for salespeople by mail, remember that you must have enough able bodies to follow the leads.

Nothing will turn a prospective purchaser off more quickly than not receiving what he requested, whether it's a product shipment or a sales call. Failure to have sufficient sales personnel to handle your new leads turns those leads into very cold sales calls.

797 — TELEPHONE SOLICITATIONS

If you currently use a sales force, remember that the cost of a sales call is constantly climbing.

It may pay you to serve marginal customers more efficiently and less expensively by direct mail or telephone solicitations.

798 — DATA REQUESTS

In lead-acquisition programs, do not ask the prospect for so much information (to arm your sales force) that the prospect is turned off from responding.

Know when to stop asking for data.

799 — COMPLETE READERSHIP

If your goal is to educate me in advance of a sales call, do not let me know that that is your goal.

Instead, ask me to decide whether I want your free booklet. Completely describe everything in the booklet so that I become "educated." You are more likely to achieve complete readership in this fashion.

800 — SALES LEAD MAILINGS

When sending a series of sales lead mailings to the same audience, frequently the follow-up mailings do not have to be as lavishly illustrated as earlier mailings in the series.

Often, if your first mailing or two is in full color, you can switch to two colors as the series progresses since those later mailings are reminders.

But then try to wind up with a colorful, convincing presentation.

801 — PASS-ALONG READERSHIP

There are three levels of pass-along readership that you may desire:

1. having the recipient pass the mailing up to a higher employment level,
2. having the recipient pass the mailing piece down to a lower employment level, or
3. having the recipient pass the mailing piece on to a peer.

In writing and designing your

promotion piece, think about the level of pass-along readership you desire.

802 — TITLES

Is your salesperson a salesperson, or can that person be called a "design consultant," a "remodeling consultant," a "real estate evaluator," an "investment counselor"?

Think about giving your salespeople titles that indicate they do more than sell: they advise. This technique can squeeze out a few more leads from your prospecting mail.

803 — FREE SURVEY

If your staff includes a qualified expert in your field, consider offering a "free survey" or "comparative cost study" geared to the needs of the business or institution you are approaching.

Frequently, this concept will get your salespeople in the door much quicker than asking for an actual order by mail, especially if the cost of your product or service is high.

804 — LEAD RESPONSE?

If you are mailing for sales leads, carefully consider whether you want high and unqualified response or low and qualified response.

If you are going the former route, make the offer as attractive as possible, and load it up with valuable free offers.

If going the latter route, tone down the offer, perhaps build in some negatives and make it less attractive for the recipient to respond.

Discuss these differences with your agency or consultant to produce the kind of response you truly desire.

805 — FREE ESTIMATES

Suppliers in a variety of service fields can achieve higher direct mail lead response if they offer free estimates rather than attempting to sell the actual service with a one-shot mailing or series of mailings.

Lead mailings can stress the free estimates, but should also mention "no obligation." There can also be a free gift for allowing your representative to visit.

The entire idea is to get "your foot in the door."

I used all three techniques successfully in a single mailing in acquiring sales leads for both an aluminum siding and a carpeting business that I once owned in the Carolinas. Prospects were given a free estimate, at no obligation, with a free set of tableware just for allowing the salesman to measure the house, either for siding or carpeting. The close rate was very high, but I'll never forget that often the first question the salesman was asked was: "Did you bring my silverware?"

René, did you really run siding and carpeting businesses?

Yes. I had made a killing in the stock market and put that profit in those businesses. Like the puzzle business mentioned earlier, these endeavors formed a viable laboratory for me to use in testing lots of different techniques.

What happened with the siding and carpeting businesses?

My partner and I built them to a desired level and then sold them both.

Okay, but aren't these strictly consumer lead-getting techniques?

No, no no! They work well with businesses, too.

An example, please, René?

I recommended a free seminar and a free manual with free estimates at no obligation to Coflexip in Texas. They sell huge contracts for building *undersea* pipes to and from oil rigs in the Gulf of Mexico. Then I made the same recommendations to Werner Pipe in Oklahoma. They sell *underground* oil well pipes. Both market to giant corporations. Both used the techniques with great success.

You probably don't need any help with the free estimate and no obligation portions of this recommendation. But, the key is to adapt your free gift to the nature of the audience.

Read my chapter on premiums to get some ideas. And remember that your gift to businesses, the professions, and institutions should be perceived as much more valuable than a set of flatware imported from Korea. The Korean flatware or something similar, however, may work very well for you in many consumer approaches. Or you may be able to find a gift that's more product related to reduce the number of gift seekers who aren't inclined to buy.

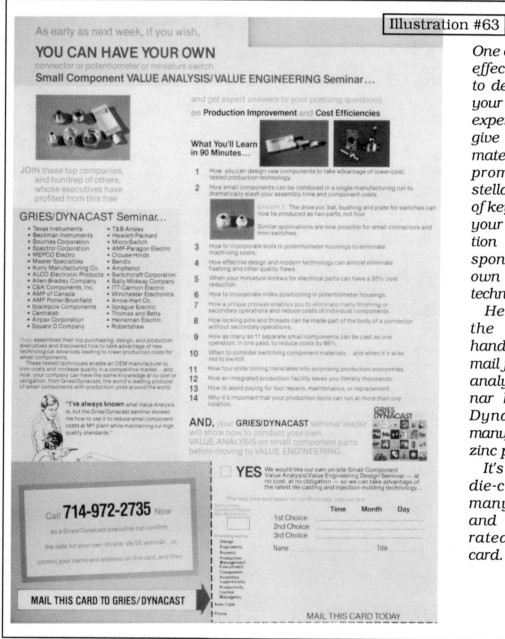

Illustration #63

One of the most effective ways to demonstrate your company's expertise and give free estimates — or to promote the stellar services of key people in your organization — is to sponsor your own seminar, technique #804.

Here's how the author handled direct mail for a value analysis seminar by Gries/ Dynacast, a manufacturer of zinc parts.

It's full-color, die-cut, with many photos and a perforated reply card.

CHAPTER 18

SWEEPSTAKES

Sometimes I get all wound up presenting what I hope proves to be helpful information — and thus here's your treatise of vital sweepstakes considerations for the direct response marketer, starting with the negative and positive aspects of these popular promotions.

A common myth is that customers obtained from sweepstakes promotions do not become repeat purchasers.

Not so. They do purchase from additional mailings, but the percentage of sweepstakes-obtained customers who become repeat purchasers is lower than when compared to the percentage of repeat purchasers obtained from promotions not based on sweepstakes.

Thus, whenever a marketer plans to launch a sweepstakes, he should cautiously test against that sweepstakes by dispatching a non-sweepstakes mailing to a split segment of his prospect lists.

If you use a sweepstakes, you probably will discover that it will increase your pull at least by three to four times the total number of purchases produced without a sweepstakes. Sweeps, however, do not necessarily produce long-term customer loyalty. You must test and analyze your back-end.

While a sweepstakes doubtless will increase the number of orders you receive, it may also tend to reduce the size of the average order because many of the extra sales are from those who are only interested in the sweepstakes and its prizes.

But if you're planning to do a sweepstakes, the first step is to consider lottery laws of the United States Postal Service. Lotteries have three elements:

1. Prize, or an item of value you offer to a winner,
2. Consideration, which is defined as something the customer must pay or do, and
3. Chance, defined as winning without any skill being involved.

Eliminate any one of those three elements — Prize, Consideration or Chance — and you are no longer viewed as running a lottery, which is strictly illegal. Include all three elements and your promotion is illegal.

Most marketers solve this problem by not restricting entries to those who purchase. This eliminates *Consideration*. Make it clear that prizes are part of the offer, but if I check the "no" box on the order form, my name will still be entered in your sweeps, because no purchase is needed. Those who check the "yes" box also are entered, and "yes" indicates a purchase.

Be careful not to hide behind religious cloth. It is true that churches and other nonprofit groups advertise bingo games and raffles by mail. Such events contain all three lottery elements. But the Postal Service regards them as "beneficial" lotteries and overlooks enforcement of the lottery laws for such good cause sponsors. However, the Postal Service does have the right to prosecute sponsors of "beneficial" lotteries, and the last chap who tried one — with a catalog for a famous Northwest hospital — escaped jail only by moving to Canada.

You can't eliminate *Prize* from the three elements, or you'll lose the attraction of this special promotion. Can you eliminate *Chance*? Yes, in some instances. Then you do not have a sweeps. You have a contest, which must be one of skill. I ran dozens of contests for 17 years, paying over $400,000 in cash awards, and receiving many millions in entry fees. But you have to do them legally, and that is quite involved.

Also, because contests require entrants to be skillful, they produce fewer respondents than sweepstakes. Eliminating luck, as you and I would call it, or *Chance*, as it's officially called, is not the best route for sales.

Stick with a sweepstakes, if you test it.

Many mailers who employ sweepstakes promotions forget that they can mail a second, third, or even tenth time to the "no" respondents. A differ-

ent offer to "no" respondents frequently pulls sufficiently high response to be cost effective.

Remember that "no" respondents to a sweepstakes offer can be rented to other marketers just as any direct mail respondent can be rented. This is a frequently-overlooked income source. And even though the "no" names can not be merged with the "yes" entries, and therefore are not worth the same rental price as those who ordered, rental income from "no" respondents still often offsets other costs.

However, don't test a sweeps with your current customer list. Test it first in acquiring new customers. If it boosts your average order level as well as your new customer generation, then expand it to your customer base.

And, don't use a sweeps unless you're prepared to invest a lot of executive time, thinking it through, analyzing and projecting a campaign, becoming an instant expert, and getting outside expert guidance. Recognize, too, that creative and art costs for sweepstakes are greater than for most other promotions.

One more NO-NO: Don't use syndicated sweepstakes that have not been used successfully by other marketers. Let someone else waste the money testing it. Syndicated sweeps have only a narrow chance of success. Their deadlines are too long. The prizes often aren't appropriate for your audience. And the syndicator gets your names!

Now, we'll discuss structuring prizes and rules.

Cash is the most appealing and popular prize, and it produces the greatest number of respondents. Tied for second in interest are new automobiles and new homes. Third is a trip. Fourth are high-ticket consumer electronic items. Fifth are personal-use items for the home. Other merchandise offerings have less appeal.

Sometimes it is more important for you to offer a different kind of prize as the main attraction. For instance, business marketers may want a product they manufacture to be the prize so all entrants have greater qualification for future sales leads.

In this instance, and in all others, because cash draws best, you should consider offering equivalent cash as an alternate prize. The winner then decides if he wants your monster machine or dollars. Do this and you'll have greater appeal while reinforcing the value of your product line.

But, in any case, don't run a sweepstakes without following these general guidelines:

1. A consumer sweeps with only four or five top prizes will do you absolutely no good. You need the top prizes to attract people to your event, and hundreds or thousands of additional smaller prizes to encourage response. People just don't think they have a chance to win the top prizes, so you must reinforce your original attraction by adding a number of prizes that realistically seem within reach.

2. If you offer cash as a prize, use a notarized statement that the cash is on deposit. Put the notarized statement in a fancy border and reproduce the notary's seal.

3. If you use merchandise as prizes, have a notary witness your contracts for merchandise fulfillment, and use that notarization in your promotion.

4. Remember that Uncle Sam requires you to state the odds that an individual entrant has for winning. If you can't predict

the odds, your attorney may permit this wording: "The odds of winning any prize will depend on the number of entries received."

5. If you don't state the probability of winning, and even if you do, it's a good idea to guarantee that certain prizes, preferably at least the top three, will be awarded even if the "lucky" numbers are not received. If you omit a guarantee on payoff, you lower response.

6. Remind your readers that most folks invited to participate do not, and therefore the odds of winning may be much greater than the official odds.

7. Be certain to state the final cutoff date for entries. That date spurs response. You can extend it with a second mailing bearing a new cutoff date.

8. Hire an independent judging agency to select the winners and state that organization's name in your rules. You can get extra mileage from the judging if a famous person does the drawing of the top prize. Of course you'll photograph the big event and use it for future promotion.

9. Be sure to state that your employees, those of your suppliers and ad agencies, and members of any of those families are not eligible to win. This is a law, and it works for you by letting the reader see his chances are better.

10. Make your winners sign an affidavit of eligibility, and put a "save harmless" clause in it.

11. Your rules should give you rights to promotional use of all winners' names, addresses, and photos.

12. Do get photos of the winners and use them with testimonial letters to reinforce the fact that you do pay off. You may wish to enhance your future sweepstakes promotions by having winners' photographs showing through large window envelopes for the best lists.

13. Provide a method for each entrant to receive a complete list of winners at no cost.

14. Stipulate that all federal, state, and local laws apply to your sweepstakes and that the event is void where prohibited by law. This is a must because local authorities change their laws without notifying your corporate counsel.

15. You may consider adding copy indicating that prizes returned as non-deliverable will be considered awarded. This is to prevent a future complaint after the event is over, so you can close your books.

16. Be sure to accrue the cost of all prizes and fulfillment on your books if your sweepstakes deadline is after the ending of your fiscal year. Your accountant may advise you that certain other costs, like promotion for the sweepstakes, also may be accrued.

Now, I'll discuss increasing attraction to your sweeps by using psychological prize structures. We know that cash is the most appealing and popular prize, producing the greatest number of respondents, with cars and new homes tied for second in interest.

But there are times when we do not want to make cash the first prize. For example, we may be mailing to very low income consumers who might believe that $100,000 or more is beyond their reach, even if part of a contest or sweepstakes. At the same time, we may want to minimize our prize cost.

This was the situation I faced when structuring prizes for the Canadian National Lottery.

Allowing your copywriter access to VisiCalc (or any other spreadsheet software) on a microcomputer can solve these vexing problems for you, because as he works with you on the prize structure, he develops copy points that are appropriate to the list audiences you'll attack.

As the accompanying Visi chart shows, I minimized the cash investment in prizes by using several home products that my client could purchase at significant discounts. But I also positioned the Eldorado as the top prize, since the audience could relate more to any kind of car than to great amounts of dollars.

Then, I developed three second prizes in cash, in amounts my client's audience could fathom, but appearing glorious.

By using the "what if?" function in VisiCalc, my favorite before Excel, I was able develop these additional copy points:

1. The name of the sweepstakes — Crazy 8's.

2. A total number of prizes conforming to the name, 8888.

3. Fourth, fifth, sixth and seventh amounts that doubled the prize number —44, 55, 66, 77 — thus hitting the always present "doubling" urge that entrants have.

4. Future value and the possibility of greater retained customers by offering tickets of phenomenal future worth, thus giving this sweepstakes a $42 million total promotion value at a cost of only $94,256.

5. Attraction for even the most

```
┌─────────────────────────────────────────────────────────────────────┐
│                        ┌──────────────────┐                          │
│                        │ Illustration #64 │                          │
│                        └──────────────────┘                          │
│                                                                      │
│                WWF CATALOG — SWEEPSTAKES AWARDS                       │
│         Prepared by René Gnam      SWEEPS1...Crazy 8's                │
│                                                                      │
│           QTY  ITEM              RETAIL OFFERING COST EA EXPENSE      │
│                                                                      │
│ 1st Prize    1  Cadillac Eldorado  24000   24000   22000   22000     │
│ 2nd Prize    3  American Dollars   10000   30000   10000   30000     │
│ 3rd Prize    5  US Savings Bonds    1000    5000     500    2500     │
│ 4th Prize   44  Pentax Camera Kits   525   23100     269   11836     │
│ 5th Prize   55  Earhart Luggage Sets 350   19250     198   10890     │
│ 6th Prize   66  Oster Kitchen Center 240   15840     126    8316     │
│ 7th Prize   77  Express Tickets        1      77       1      77     │
│ 8th Prize 8637  Mystery Gifts          1    8637       1    8637     │
│           ────                                                       │
│           8888                                     125904   94256    │
│                                                                      │
│ Perceived Value of Future Lottery Tickets at retail     550000       │
│ Perceived Value of Future Lottery Tickets as prizes   42350000       │
│           TOTAL Promotional Value of Prizes:          42475904       │
└─────────────────────────────────────────────────────────────────────┘
```

pessimistic prospects by having 8,637 mystery gifts, so each fence-sitter could see he had a good opportunity to win something.

6. Identifiable home-use prizes that are highly desirable but which lower-income folks rarely have a chance to purchase.

Study the chart. It's one of several "what if?" versions developed for just one sweepstakes. Develop your own prize structures, remembering to start with a careful study of your list universe, and allow your consultant to develop a different set of structures. Then compare them and run, perhaps with a split test on prize structure.

Because wonderful sweepstakes promotions have the power to boost your response sky-high, let us concentrate on proper positioning for copy extolling sweepstakes in your catalog.

Keep this checklist handy:

1. Promote the sweepstakes on the front of your mailing envelope or catalog, including the total number of prizes, the total dollar value of the prizes, the deadline, photos of the top prizes, and one or more copy lines advising the reader where in your mailing he can find the entry blank for the sweepstakes.

2. Promote the sweepstakes briefly on the back cover of your catalog or the back of a self-mailer or outgoing envelope with a mention of the total number of prizes, the total dollar value of the prizes, perhaps a photo of the top prize, and a brief copy line directing the reader to the sweepstakes entry form.

3. Use filler headlines, often called tag lines, at the bottom of several pages, referring the reader to the entry form.

4. Use small filler copy next to display art indicating the total dollar value of the prizes and location of the entry blank, but do NOT imply that purchase is necessary.

5. Use small filler stories with photos of previous winners and how they loved participating. Scatter these, ending each with

entry blank directional copy.

6. Include extensive references to the sweepstakes in a letter.

7. Do NOT refer to the sweeps next to 800 numbers unless you clearly specify that 800 numbers are for charge card ordering only. Otherwise, you'll have thousands of calls tying up your switchboard.

8. Try to restrict sweepstakes entries to written form.

9. Include a how-to-enter column, perhaps next to a full display of prizes, accompanied by all the rules.

10. Use "win" bursts throughout a catalog: "WIN," followed by a photo and words describing individual prizes, then followed by "see page XX."

11. Savvy marketers restrict sweepstakes entries to the order form (or a photocopy thereof) and use extra prize displays and promotional copy on the order form.

12. Entering should be as easy as possible, preferably with a checkbox choice:

☐ *YES, I'm ordering on this form. Please enter my name in your sweepstakes.*

☐ *No, I'm not ordering now, but please enter my name in your sweepstakes.*

13. "Don't Forget" boxes or bursts can be placed on various spreads, again accompanied by "see page XX."

14. Split test bind-in and blow-in postcards in catalogs, some used to get referral names, others for copy on the sweepstakes.

15. Try an extra bound-in ordering envelope with a tail. The envelope appears after 25% of the pages in a magazine or catalog.

The tail follows 75% and is strictly devoted to sweepstakes promotion.

16. Find space on the outside of your reply envelopes for the same two checkboxes as in No. 12. This saves you tons of hours of opening envelopes without orders.

17. Use the address section for one or two copy lines about the sweepstakes.

EXAMPLE:
"$100,000.00 Sweepstakes Entry Inside for René Gnam"

18. Using a carrier envelope? Use it for sweepstakes copy.

19. Add a sweepstakes reminder paragraph to your "how to order" column within a catalog or product self-mailer.

And why would you do all this? Because sweepstakes attract non-buyers and convert them to buyers!

But, you also have 27 major emphasis points for these attractive promotions:

1. Emphasize the total number of prizes more than the top prize(s) so everyone feels there's a good chance to win.

2. Be sure to use copy points that are appropriate to the list audiences you attack.

3. Stress the overall cash value, but also be sure to cite the cash value of each individual prize. An exception would be mystery prizes which may or may not carry an actual cash value.

4. Stress the joy of using your prize(s).

5. State or imply that certain prize(s) are what the entrant "always wanted."

6. Make a comparison between Mr. or Ms. Average American

versus Mr. or Ms. Money Bags, and relate prize(s) to that comparison.

EXAMPLE:

"Now you can win the kind of house that only movie stars can afford."

7. When citing retail value, consider a counter to the mental argument that certain prize(s) can be locally obtained at significant discounts.

EXAMPLE:

"Of course you might be able to buy these linens for less than the full retail value, but won't you be pleased if you win them — Free!"

8. Mention the status of ownership of fine items.
9. Position the top prize as possible, but stress that all prize(s) will be awarded.
10. Repeatedly state that you can't win unless you enter.
11. Restate the rules in an appealing fashion.
12. Emphasize that entry is free, but also stress that the reason for conducting the sweepstakes is to draw attention to your fine products.
13. Point out that since not everyone enters, chances of winning are better than one might think.
14. Invent a marvelous name for your sweepstakes and let it contain an element of wealth or attainable victory.
15. Concoct an unusual number of prizes — not a rounded number. Many folks play the numbers and 1,234 prizes is a far more appealing number than 1,000, or 1,200, or 1,250.
16. Even though your entrants may be enticed by great enthusiasm for a specific prize, like a car, you can increase your pull if you allow entrants to exchange the top prize(s) for great amounts of dollars.
17. Remember that so-called "lucky" numbers are 3, 7, 11, and numbers that add to those figures. Thus, 43 prizes in a certain category is viable as a puller, likewise 47.
18. Remembering that many players have a "doubling" urge, be sure to promote double-number prize(s), like 11, 22, 33, 44, and so on.
19. You want each fence-sitter to know he has a good opportunity to win something, so stress the number of previous winners you've had, the amounts they won, the total cash value of all prizes you've paid, and similar reinforcers.
20. Indicate, when true, that your prizes are items which most folks rarely have a chance to purchase, or which are not universally available, or which are exclusive.
21. After a careful study of your list universe, identify your audience in your headlines, especially when segmenting your markets.
22. Repeat the ease of entering.
23. Stress the need to enter immediately.
24. Describe exactly how winners are selected.
25. Communicate the excitement of how prize(s) are turned over to winners.

EXAMPLES:

"Imagine opening your mail and discovering your $25,000 prize check"

...or...

"How great you'll feel flying first class to Paris for your new wardrobe."

26. State that the invited contestant may never again get this opportunity.

27. Tell your entrants that top prize winners become very famous, are photographed, get their names in the papers, and attain a new status with their peers.

No, you'll not want to incorporate all 27 points in each sweepstakes event, but do review this checklist with your consultant and refer to it when you devise your next promotion.

And a final note before releasing you to the balance of this chapter.

> **Sweepstakes are powerful pullers. They dramatically increase the results you'd normally get. Trouble is, they tend to train your audience to expect more sweeps.**

Reader's Digest finds it nearly impossible to conduct non-sweepstakes mailings today because everyone expects a sweeps from Pleasantville. Think carefully.

But you know how sweeps hike response. Perhaps the risk is worth it for you, just as it has been for Publisher's Clearing House. How would you know?

Start a new company or division with sweepstakes as the main promotions. Compare results against your current company or division which doesn't use a sweeps. Which does better for you?

806 — BACK-END SWEEPSTAKES MAILINGS

The most effective back-end sweepstakes mailings have prizes oriented toward the interest areas of your consumer or business prospect's view of your product or service.

Respondents from sweepstakes carrying such prizes are more renewable than respondents from sweepstakes with non-affinity awards. But you'll have far fewer respondents than with prizes of cash, homes, or cars.

807 — SWEEPSTAKES

While a sweepstakes doubtless will increase the number of orders you receive, it also is very likely to reduce the size of the average order you receive.

Many of the extra sales are from those who are merely interested in the sweepstakes.

808 — HIGHER-PRICED ITEMS?

When using a sweepstakes with a catalog promotion, you can achieve 30% to 50% higher response due to the sweepstakes alone.

But remember that the sweepstakes may draw attention away from higher-priced items in the catalog.

809 — YES-NO APPROACH

A good sweepstakes mailing with a very attractive prize and an interest appeal allied to the list you are testing can produce 15% to 30% total response in yes's and no's — if a yes-no approach is used.

This can be a vital marketing tool for you if you want to repetitively approach the same list universe to get high product exposure.

810 — INCREASING YOUR PULL

If you test a sweepstakes, you probably will discover that it will increase your pull at least by three to four times the total number of purchases produced without a sweepstakes.

The sweepstakes, however, does not necessarily produce long-term brand or customer loyalty.

811 — LOOPHOLES?

Remember that in a sweepstakes in America, all prizes must be awarded and you must clearly state that fact, along with the percentage likelihood of an individual winning (the odds!).

This significantly increases your costs, but it also is the reason why sweepstakes are frequently effective.

Can you find some loopholes in this requirement, René?

I suppose so.

812 — THOUSANDS OF SMALLER PRIZES

A sweepstakes that has only four or five top prizes will do you absolutely no good.

You need the top prizes to attract people to your mailing. But thousands of additional smaller prizes are the way to encourage response. People just don't think they have much of a chance to win those top prizes, so you must reinforce your original attraction by adding a number of prizes that realistically seem within reach.

813 — CASH!

Regardless of the type of contest you use — and this includes sweepstakes — cash is the most appealing and popular prize, and it produces the greatest number of respondents.

Next in interest is an automobile or a home. Third is a trip. Other merchandise offerings have less appeal.

It helps to offer equivalent cash for many of your top prizes.

814 — PHOTOS OF WINNERS

When running contests or sweepstakes, try to get photos of the winners and use them with testimonial letters to reinforce the fact that you do have a legitimate offer.

This is one of the strongest promotional techniques you can use. Showing actual winners, quoting them, citing their cities and towns, and stating how much they won — all are powerhouses in getting response.

It has been one of my most successful techniques for the Canadian National Lotteries and it is employed by every savvy sweepstakes or contest promoter.

815 — GOOD ODDS

When running a contest or sweepstakes, remind your reader that most people invited to participate do not, and that's why the odds of winning may be so much greater.

816 — LARGE WINDOW ENVELOPES

Sweepstakes promotions can be enhanced by using large window envelopes and having winners' photographs showing through them.

817 — NO NEED TO ORDER

When using a sweepstakes, you must clearly state that your reader can enter and qualify for a prize whether he places an order or not.

That's the law. But it also tells him you are fair.

818 — "NO" RESPONDENTS

"No" respondents to a sweepstakes offer can be rented to other marketers, just as any respondent to your direct mail can be rented.

This is an income source frequently overlooked by mailers who are otherwise blinded by the large number of "No" respondents.

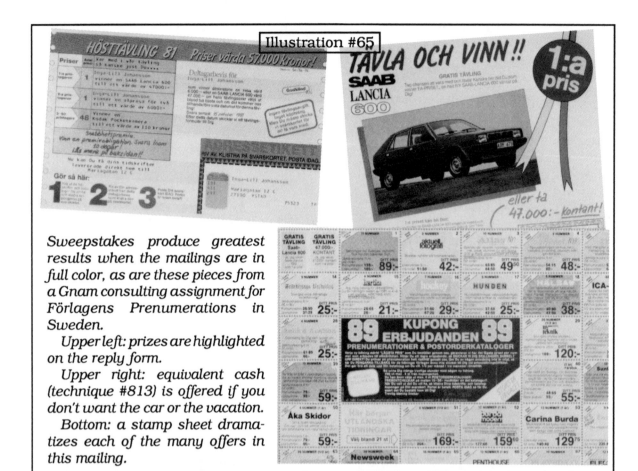

Illustration #65

Sweepstakes produce greatest results when the mailings are in full color, as are these pieces from a Gnam consulting assignment for Förlagens Prenumerations in Sweden.

Upper left: prizes are highlighted on the reply form.

Upper right: equivalent cash (technique #813) is offered if you don't want the car or the vacation.

Bottom: a stamp sheet dramatizes each of the many offers in this mailing.

819 — DIFFERENT OFFER

Many mailers who employ sweepstakes promotions forget that they can mail a second, third, or even tenth time to the "No" respondent.

A different offer to the "No" respondent frequently will pull a sufficiently high percentage of response to be cost effective.

820 — BAD DEBTS

You get more bad debts and cancellations when using sweepstakes and contests and premiums than when you do not use those incentives.

821 — LOWERING THE EXPENSE

Very large quantity mailers sometimes discover that a sweepstakes substantially lowers the expense normally incurred for premiums, cash discounts or free merchandise given with an order.

The total cost of all prizes often is significantly less than the cost of cash discounts or premiums.

822 — NOTARY WITNESS

If you use merchandise as a prize in a contest or sweepstakes, consider having a notary witness your contracts for merchandise fulfillment, and use that notarization in promotions.

823 — PRIZES ON DEPOSIT

If you offer cash prizes as part of a contest or sweepstakes or drawing, use a notarized statement that the prizes are on deposit.

Put the notarized statement in a fancy border and reproduce the notary's seal.

CHAPTER 19

FUND RAISING

When working with fund raisers, I frequently find that many of them are very shy about approaching their active donors for additional contributions. Thus, they produce less revenue than they could acquire for their good work.

Active donors already have decided that they like your cause, your institution, or your charity. When they first donated, they probably felt a little twinge about not giving more. You've often felt that twinge yourself. You gave $2 to the paper boy at Christmas, and when you went back in the house you wondered if you should have given $5. You sent $250 to a needy relative and wished you had sent more.

Since the twinge — a desire to help even more — is there, it is natural that your active donor will, indeed, give more if you tell him how important his added contribution will be. It will help you get out the vote. It will add the latest technology to your medical laboratory. It will feed another starving child.

Accepting my "twinge" concept, now please acknowledge that there are three key aspects of increasing donations from current donors:

1. Massaging your database for more frequent donations,
2. Upgrade mailings,
3. Splinter funds.

Let's talk briefly about each of these.

Aspect 1:
A database, as discussed previously in this book, is a repository of information on a person. In addition to the name and address record, it includes data on the amount of the last contribution, frequency of contributions, appeals responded to, source of name, and other facts and factors you can massage.

EXAMPLE:
Let's say I responded to your June appeal to help find housing for victims of a mountain disaster in Spain. I sent you $150.

You may now consider:
● Asking me for another $150 next June for the same victims,
● Approaching me about a mountain disaster in Chile,

- Switching me to a quarterly or monthly aid program for the stricken victims in Spain,
- Asking me to continue contributing to the Spanish victims while adding donations for those in Chile,
- Upgrading me to a higher dollar level with a word processor or computer letter.

Because all the information you need is on your computerized database, it should be easy to generate the mail that brings more revenue from me and from all other active donors meeting a matching set or similar range of criteria.

Aspect 2:

Now, as we consider upgrades, remember that twinge. I'd like to give you more money, but I just haven't been approached about it.

You should immediately thank me for the $150. And, why not use that thank you letter to ask me for another amount — perhaps small, perhaps even double — ..so you can give help to more victims? Point out what another $50 would do. Another $100. Another $150.

If I do respond to this approach, again acknowledge my fine action and then, a few weeks later, go to an ongoing contribution plan so I can truly help those homeless Spaniards.

If I do not respond to this approach, remember that I still have that twinge. Wait a short while. Send me a report on what my money has done. With it, request additional help at a slightly higher level than my $150. Make me feel good about what I've done. Tell me what my next $200 will do.

If I do not respond to this approach, leave me in your database, but be sure to include me in your next mass effort for the Spanish victims,

the homeless in Chile, and others you aid. Cite my $150. Mention a specific amount that I should give this time. Give me the opportunity to specify an even higher amount.

If I do not respond to this approach, you still mail to me again, this time asking that I repeat my previous donation.

Of course, I will still continue to receive your special appeals, emergency fund appeals, reports on your progress, perhaps newsletters showing how my money has been spent, and occasional word processor or computer letters soliciting added donations.

Aspect 3:

Splinter funds are a marvelous opportunity for you to boost your revenues. Let's explain it by switching now from aid to the homeless to a college seeking expansion funds.

Your database identifies me as a donor from your mass appeal. Did you remember to allow me to indicate how I wanted my funds spent? Good!

Now go through your database and get a breakdown of all donors by spending area. Examples include: construction, library, athletics, medical, music. How many names have given to each category? Enough for a mailing? Fine!

Establish a splinter fund: The University of Michigan Music Foundation, for example. All those who previously designated their money for the school of music, now get special appeals just for your musical marvels.

Again, ask your donors to specify areas that they love: classical, jazz, baroque, dixieland, composing, woodwinds, percussion...all are examples, not imbedded in a score!

Tally your response. These donations will be higher than your split

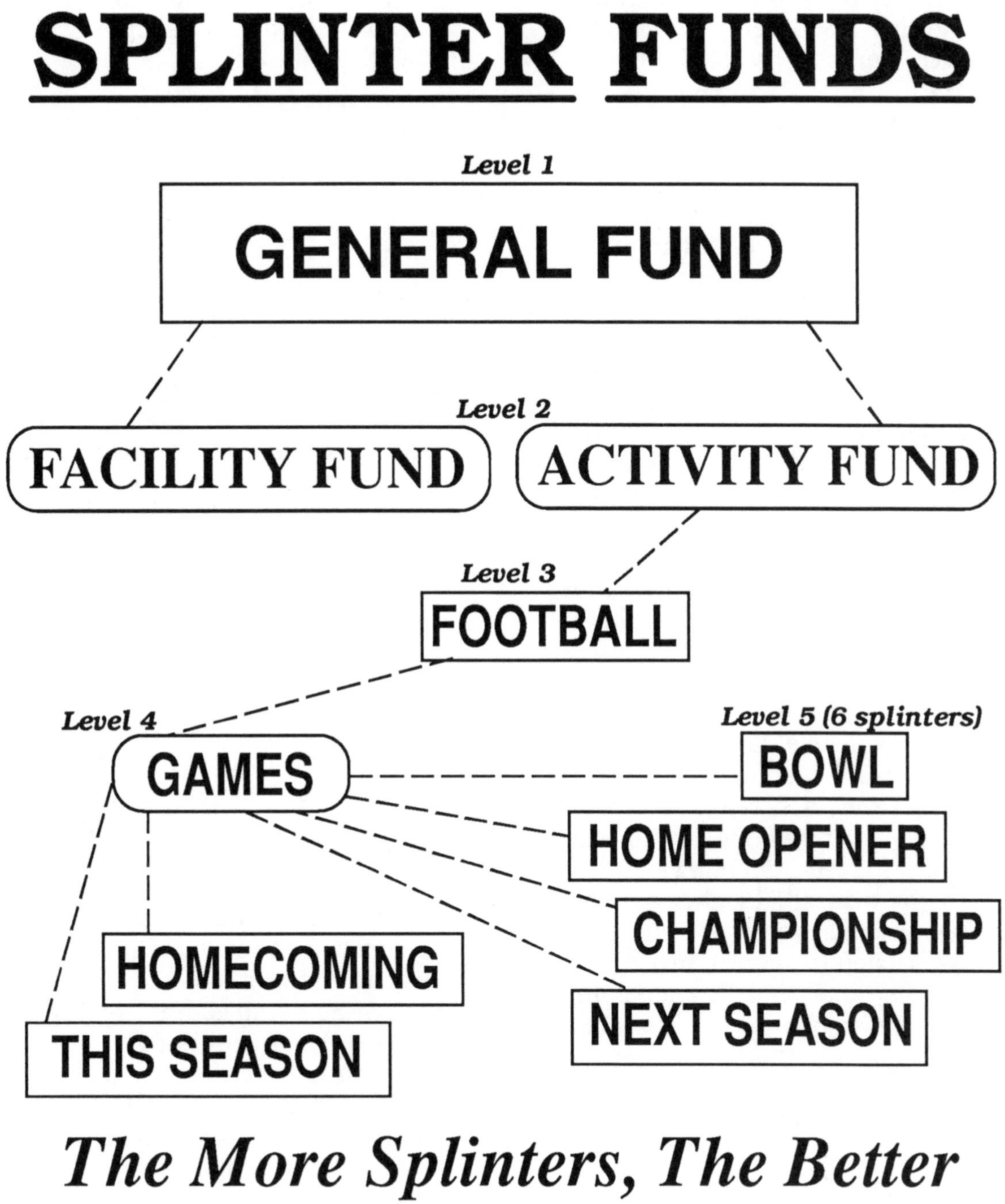

SPLINTER FUNDS

Level 1

GENERAL FUND

Level 2

(FACILITY FUND)   (ACTIVITY FUND)

Level 3

FOOTBALL

Level 4

GAMES

Level 5 (6 splinters)

BOWL

HOME OPENER

CHAMPIONSHIP

NEXT SEASON

HOMECOMING

THIS SEASON

The More Splinters, The Better

Illustration #66

Reproduced from the author's database seminar presentation on fund-raising techniques for The University of Michigan and Athletic Business Magazine is this overhead projection of a typical splinter campaign, showing five levels of donation interest with six splinters at the fifth level. Donors at each level are asked specifically how they'd like their contributions employed. Telling donors their contributions can be applied to selected items leads to more contributions and more dollars.

test against the general fund. And if you receive 1,600 donors for classical, there's another great splinter fund for you.

Again you ask for spending specifications, for example: performance, conducting, history, romantic, operatic, American, piano, classical harp, guitar, or symphonic. If symphonic pulls best, maybe you have new splinter funds for concerti, ensembles, or full orchestration.

Splinter funds, depending on the size of your donor universe, can go on seemingly forever. The concept is to isolate specific interests of your donors and then cater to those interests, rather than just promoting your general fund.

The same technique holds true for the homeless. Instead of only promoting the general fund, your splinters could include: food, clothing, shelter, education, job training, or relocation.

For any cause, any institution, any charity, the splinter fund is a marvelous way to increase your revenues because it identifies my special area of interest and allows me to satisfy my twinge! I'd rather support symphonic studies than operatic, even though I listen to several opera companies on the Public Broadcasting System. If symphonic is my special interest, give me the opportunity to help your symphony.

René, does this mean I should abandon my general fund appeals?

No, no...heavens, no!

The general fund is a great way to get and retain a lot of donors who do not want to classify their contributions. But it also enables you to isolate areas of specific interests so you can form high-pulling splinters.

Moreover, the dollars per donor will be higher in the splinters than in the general fund.

EXAMPLE:

Maybe I want to end nuclear threats to society. Your political party or candidate is against nuclear arms development. It or he is also against a lot of other things, as well as for a lot of other things — though perhaps they just don't interest me so much. So maybe I'd only give you a token donation for the general political campaign. But if I then receive an anti-nuke mailing, my enthusiasm for your party or your candidate could be higher, and thus the chances of your receiving a larger check also would be higher.

Really, René, this works in political mail, too?

Yes. I did it for John V. Lindsay and Hubert Humphrey. A republican and a democrat. Lindsay got elected and Humphrey got re-elected. Try it.

The problem you face, and I understand it, is that a fund-raising organization has so many pressures that it's difficult to sit down quietly and invent new marketing approaches to generate the cash that enables that organization to do additional good works. Sometimes, the ongoing pressures are so great that it's difficult to just maintain the current donor level.

Find the time, and perhaps the counsel, to develop database massaging, upgrades, and splinters that are in keeping with your overall mandate. These efforts will yield your greatest growth.

824 — TAX DEDUCTIBLE DONATIONS

If a donation to your organization is tax deductible, do not hesitate to say so...and do it forthrightly, proclaiming the fact that it will be a deduction.

This can lead to a larger contribution. A caution: check with your tax counselor before making this statement.

825 — DONATION AMOUNT

If your fund-raising mailing merely attempts to get pledges, always add a space on the order form for "donation amount enclosed."

That pledge form, so worded, may produce dollars and save you a follow-up mailing.

826 — HONOR ROLL NAME

If you are a fund raiser who publishes a roster of contributors, or a season program or annual directory of supporters, always ask prospects to "indicate precisely how your name should be listed in our honor roll."

Even if they have not yet decided to donate, they can become so intrigued with the idea of listing their names that they become more likely to respond.

827 — PLEDGE CARDS

Too many fund raisers are content to simply request even dollar amounts in their solicitations.

If your classification breaks are, for example, $100 for a sustaining member and $200 for a sponsor, try saying $100 to $199 for a sustaining member, and so on. Frequently, that will get you a higher donation per contributor.

Note that I said "frequently." That doesn't mean "always." It worked fine when I tested it for the American Leukemia Association, but Margrith Troller at the American Foundation for the Blind reported that it didn't work for her.

So, what do I do about this, René?

Test it with a split run of your pledge or donation cards. It will work better in going after actual donations instead of pledges, but in either instance it must be tested.

Why, René?

It's possible that a contributor ready to make out a $200 check will decide to send a little less when seeing the $100 to $199 range. Your overall dollar receipts might be less.

Another way around this is to change the levels slightly.

EXAMPLE:

$101 to $200. Then, $201 to $300. Again, you must test because a higher level donor may suddenly decide to lower the amount he or she sends.

Okay, René, but why did you say this works better for actual donations than pledges?

When you send the follow-up, pay-up request to the donor who pledged, remember that he pledged in a range. When he sent the pledge, perhaps he checked $201 to $300, thinking he'd write his check for $300 when your follow-up arrives. But some time has elapsed between the moment of his pledge and the arrival of your follow-up. Maybe he spent a lot of money in that time. Perhaps the time lapse allows him to rethink about a lower payment. And when the follow-up arrives, maybe he'll have forgotten that he meant to send $300. So, since he's in a range, he only sends $201 to your organization.

Ranges do work to increase your revenue, in some instances. But ranges don't do that, in other instances. So you're well advised to test this concept.

Who do I test it with, René, my current donors or prospects?

Prospects, for five reasons:

1. You have more prospects than

donors, so if it works on the test you'll have many more names to reach when you roll out.

2. You may not have enough donors to split test.
3. Most importantly, you know how much your donors contribute and that information is in your database. Your job with donors is to categorize them so you can move each category up with specific amounts in word processor or computer letters, or your job is treat each donor as an individual and move him up with totally personalized letters.
4. Your donors probably react very well to specific amounts and are used to that approach. Giving them a range may complicate their gift giving.
5. You've already tested several techniques to acquire higher pledges or donations from prospects and you're slowly running out of new lists. This technique may enable you to use marginally successful lists or re-use lists that previously showed a record of fall-off in dollar response. Not percentage of response. Dollar response!

828 — DIRECT MAIL COMMUNICATIONS

Instead of, or in addition to, requesting funds from your prospective business donor, why not ask that corporation to insert your mailing piece with its next direct mail communications, membership bulletins, or salesmen's notices.

Frequently, corporations like to do this to support a worthy cause and the added distribution is yours just for the cost of printing the piece.

829 — PURPOSES FOR FUNDS

When soliciting funds for a charitable organization or purpose, always clearly state the purposes for which the money will be used.

You are not raising funds for your organization, but for the individuals you serve! Your reader wants to know how his money will be used, and you do not want him to think his money goes for your salary.

830 — EMOTION TAPPING

When doing fund-raising mailings, remember that a photograph often taps peoples' emotions better than words.

But that photograph must be accompanied by a caption or other hard-hitting copy to immediately transfer the interest in the photo to interest in the appeal.

831 — BEGGARS' CLOTHES

For some offers, it is essential that your mailing piece look like it is wearing "beggars' clothes."

For example, most fund-raising appeals that are too slick or glossy do not work.

832 — DESIGNATED AMOUNTS

You will discover that you will receive higher dollar volume in contributions if you clearly specify designated amounts on the response form instead of asking the prospect to fill in the amount he is willing to donate.

833 — ELIMINATING DUPES

If your mailings are large and there is a possibility of duplication, do not hesitate to use an explanation of your

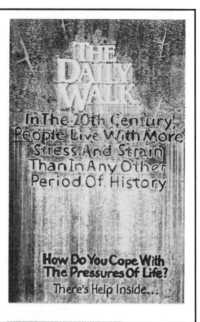

Illustration #67

Gnam's fund-raising clients — Walk Thru The Bible and the Bob Hope Heart Research Institute — do not overlook revenues possible from publications like these.

Technique #834 suggests that you use a BRE for sales of books and subscriptions, but also be advised to use a standard mailing package: envelope, letter, order form, and a brochure or fact sheet.

Other inserts, like the quote René wrote for Bob, can be tested against packages without such inserts.

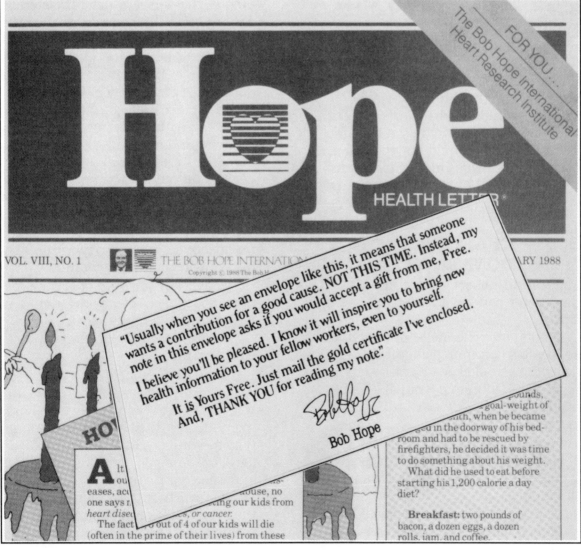

FOR YOU . . .
The Bob Hope International
Heart Research Institute

VOL. VIII, NO. 1   THE BOB HOPE INTERNATIONAL   ARY 1988

Copyright © 1988 The Bob H...

"Usually when you see an envelope like this, it means that someone wants a contribution for a good cause. NOT THIS TIME. Instead, my note in this envelope asks if you would accept a gift from me, Free.

I believe you'll be pleased. I know it will inspire you to bring new health information to your fellow workers, even to yourself.

It is Yours Free. Just mail the gold certificate I've enclosed. And, THANK YOU for reading my note."

Bob Hope

attempt to identify and eliminate dupes.

Mention that occasional errors occur. Show your readers that you care and you do not like to waste money on duplicate mailings. The duplication errors, of course, are because the prospects have achieved such status — in their business, profession, or community — that their names are found on many lists of noteworthy people. And that is what you should say in your mailing.

Flattering them will remove their dislike for repeated mail delivery from you. More importantly, it may lead them to consider another donation.

834 — REPLY ENVELOPES

Fund raisers who test reply envelopes versus business reply envelopes can make the former more palatable and understandable to the donor by placing copy like this on the envelope:

"We would normally prepay the postage, but by placing your stamp here you help us hold down costs so your donation does more good work."

But do use business reply when seeking subscriptions or book orders.

835 — CHARGED DONATIONS

Many fund raisers do not know that donations can be charged to credit cards!

Folks may be more inclined to send you a donation pledge if they can delay the actual expenditure by charging it. This technique is super by mail, but be careful with it at fund-raising events.

Why, René?

Because you're wise not to go after pledges at certain events. Instead, get the money.

Can you give me an example, René?

Yes. In late 1986, I donated myself and various goodies as "an eligible bachelor" in the "Bachelor Bid" fundraising event for the March of Dimes. Women were there to bid on prize and date arrangements offered by the 22 bachelors. Bill Walker, the March of Dimes coordinator, told me that pledges at these events often backfired because the winning bidders frequently got cold feet after meeting the men they "won."

Bill and his committee members announced that winning bidders had to make out a check or sign a charge card slip before the next bachelor was being auctioned. (Bill was right. My "winner" backed out of the date but paid her credit card charge.) About 80% of the winners used their credit cards. Only a few had brought checks.

René, is this typical with events?

No. Many events produce cash instead of checks and credit card donations. But nearly all of them have found that a great many pledges at these activities are of momentary motivation, and thus go unfulfilled if there's a time lapse.

It's different by mail. When a mailing arrives, the prospective donor sees the credit card as a payment delaying device. It also enables the prospective donor to pay portions of his contribution each month.

Okay, René, should I tell the prospect about spreading out donation payments on a credit card?

Yes. Here's an *example* of copy you could adapt:

"Even if you're limited in the amount of money that you can contribute today, you can help save more starving children by charging your donation to your credit card. Your credit card bill doesn't come for a month, and then you can pay portions of it over several months. Then you'll know that you're sending the gift of life to a needy child every month."

CHAPTER 20

<u>TESTIMONIALS</u>

Besides being totally believable, you must *convince* me to respond. That means you must prove you're okay to deal with. There are several methods of doing this.

First...You can cite FIELD DATA.

EXAMPLE:
"200,000 of our Mushroom Incubators have been working for the last 26 years and not one has been returned."

Even if that sentence is true, it sounds unbelievable. So, if you use field data, cite a believable margin of error.

EXAMPLE:
"200,000 of our Mushroom Incubators have been in rigorous use for 26 years by 23,708 commercial greenhouses, and we either repaired or replaced the 13 that malfunctioned."

This copy states the field data and reinforces the feeling that your company is okay because you fix all malfunctions.

Second...You can cite TEST DATA.

EXAMPLE:
"We plugged it in the wall and it worked."

Test data is vital with any kind of mechanical, electrical or component item. You must tell me it works, but I may not believe you. WE performed the test is NOT as good as *Good Housekeeping*, U. S. Testing Laboratories, Underwriters Laboratories, or other testing organizations that I may respect. Still, I might wonder if the test was fixed. So show me a photo of the test in progress and perhaps a notarized statement about the validity of the test results.

Third...You can cite ATTITUDE DATA.

"We're IBM, so, of course we're good."

Attitude or reputation copy may help you if you're the proven leader in your field, but minimize its presentation because I may or may not have a favorable impression of your firm.

Fourth...You can cite MARKET DATA.

"We're Savin and we're outselling Xerox."

If it's true, use it. It's powerful. But don't say Xerox is bad. Just cite the market facts. And don't do as Savin does and say "we're the fastest-growing copier company." Some people think "fastest-growing" means you're really a small firm, or maybe you're growing so fast that you have growing pains and can't service my machine. Of course, you may not say you're the "largest" because that could mean you're stodgy and complacent, perhaps not providing good service.

Fifth...You can cite TESTIMONIALS, and these really do sell.

Testimonials prove you're okay because other people are backing up your advertising. The four different types of testimonials are:

1. CUSTOMER TESTIMONIALS

In consumer mailings, customer testimonials sometimes increase response by as much as 30%.

Customer testimonials in mailing to businesses, institutions, and the professions have an enormous effect on response, sometimes doubling your results.

In consumer mail, recipients may think you paid for the quote. In business mail, if your testimonials have attribution, no one will think you bribed a company. For example, my seminar announcement mailings use testimonials to validate the worth of my course. If you can quote a customer in my field, maybe my competitor, you'll truly motivate me to respond.

2. CELEBRITY TESTIMONIALS

The negative factors with testimonials from celebrated people are: (a) I know he's paid, and (b) I may not like that particular celebrity.

Celebrity testimonials work best for fund-raisers, publishers, associations, and insurance. But in using celebrity testimonials, ask the famous person to endorse your company, not its products. Art Linkletter and Arthur Godfrey said they knew the insurance company and it wasn't a rip-off. They didn't say they bought the insurance.

3. EXPERT TESTIMONIALS

Endorsers should be selected for their prominence in specific fields. Thus, Fran Tarkenton is fine for sports equipment. Mario Andretti is super for auto products. Dr. Denton A. Cooley is a perfect endorser for artificial arteries being marketed to cardiovascular surgeons (and I had the happy occasion to design his logo and product packaging).

Recognize that your audience knows your experts have been paid. But if they are acknowledged, well-known experts in your field, that's still okay because the reader assumes that Ella Fitzgerald and Chuck Mangione wouldn't endorse Memorex unless it was good tape.

But the best testimonials are in the fourth category.

4. A GROUP OF EXPERTS

No matter who you mail to — businesses, industrial firms, banks, consumers, association lovers, or contributors — a testimonial from a group of experts is best because almost no one thinks that a group can be bribed.

EXAMPLES:
The American Dental Association endorsing Crest.

A magazine in your field endorsing your product.

A trade association endorsing your company.

A newsletter endorsing your expertise.

And if you can't get a formal group of experts, then use many individual experts and lump them all together. Make it truly impressive if you can.

If you have the space, list 348 individual experts. I've used as many as 91 in my seminar announcement brochures. Addco Industries in Fort Lauderdale uses 14 to sell anti-sway bars to car repair shops. America's Best uses 90 to sell Sylvania Light Bulbs, many on a separate testimonial insert in their mailings.

> **Use testimonials properly and your response goes up!...always!**
>
> **The reason is simple: When you say you're good, people discount your back patting. But when others say you're good, ah!**

836 — BIG NAMES

When using big names as testimonials, try to have names that are well known in your specific field.

Jimmy Connors could be fine if you sell tennis rackets, tennis shoes, or tennis balls. But he wouldn't be so superb for needlepoint patterns.

837 — CUSTOMER-WRITTEN TESTIMONIALS

Whenever possible, use customer-written testimonials rather than writing them yourself.

Often you've seen testimonials like this:

"Loved your 14-function strobe light," A.J., Missouri.

Immediately you react by saying to yourself that no one would use "14-function" in a testimonial. Your second reaction is to question who A.J. is. Third, you ask where in Missouri.

So, when you use testimonials, use the words of the writer and give full attribution.

"What if you don't have any quotes, René? Can you make them up?" That was a query I had from a Christian bookseller at a seminar in Atlanta.

I responded: "Would God lie?"

And then I explained that a better procedure would be to write a draft and ask a customer if he'd like to rewrite it. Another technique is to take notes of favorable comments folks make on the phone, and send those comments to them asking for permission to quote.

838 — FAMOUS FOLKS

Famous folks can be important if you have a consumer product, service, or publication.

There's nothing wrong with saying that Robert Redford eats your cheese, sleeps between your sheets, uses your dust cloths, wears your underwear, or subscribes to your publication if, in fact, he does and if you do have orders from him. But don't say he really relishes your product or service unless you have his signature and authorization to say so.

Check with your attorney as to how far you can go with this technique.

839 — HOUSEHOLD NAMES

Does your company have a long list of satisfied customers who are household names, such as, Xerox, Kodak, or Pepsi?

If so, why not cite them in your advertising? Check with your attorney and you doubtless will discover that it is okay to cite them, provided that you only say that they are your customers.

Over that listing, use a heading that indicates "among the users of this automatic elevator shaft greasing agent are." The heading entices the reader while the listing convinces him you have decent customers.

Then, follow the listing with a directive statement, like "join these successful elevator operators by ordering your supply of Goo Grease today." That directive statement steers the reader toward your order form.

You can expand on this concept with geographic considerations...

1. Consider examining your total customer database. Select the well-known and not-so-well-known customers in each geographic region you attack. Or arbitrarily divide your customers into sections of the country, or states.
2. Print your testimonial insert or brochure in split runs. So many for the Southwest. So many for the Northeast. Each split contains the customer names in its region.

This technique lets prospects see that you have many customers in the prospect's home area. "If all these folks have bought from your company, I guess I'd be making a safe decision," he says to himself.

840 — READING THE MAIL

If you are the president of your corporation or the advertising manager — and, especially if you are the person

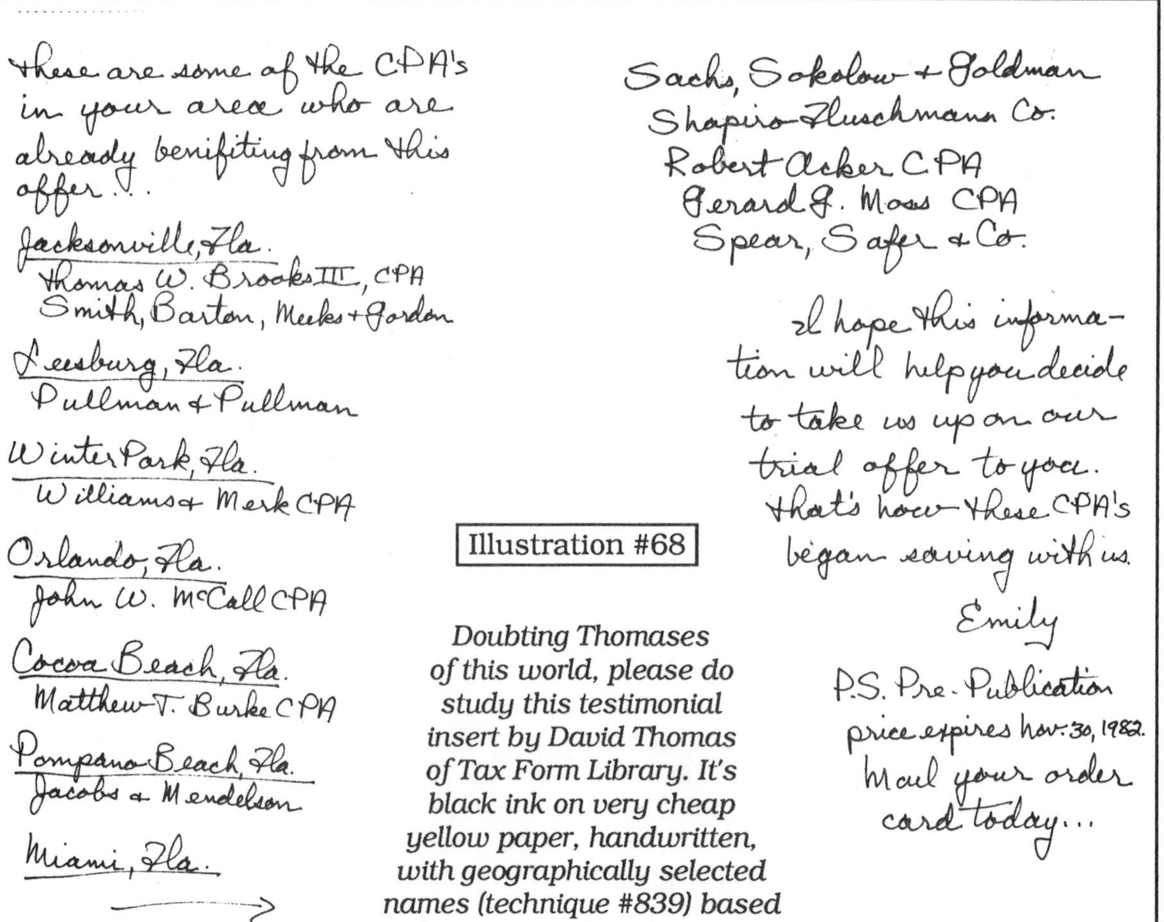
these are some of the CPA's in your area who are already benifiting from this offer...

Jacksonville, Fla.
Thomas W. Brooks III, CPA
Smith, Barton, Meeks + Gordon

Leesburg, Fla.
Pullman + Pullman

Winter Park, Fla.
Williams + Merk CPA

Orlando, Fla.
John W. McCall CPA

Cocoa Beach, Fla.
Matthew T. Burke CPA

Pompano Beach, Fla.
Jacobs + Mendelson

Miami, Fla.
→

Sachs, Sokolow + Goldman
Shapiro-Fluschmann Co.
Robert Acker CPA
Gerard G. Moss CPA
Spear, Safer + Co.

I hope this information will help you decide to take us up on our trial offer to you. that's how these CPA's began saving with us.

Emily

P.S. Pre-Publication price expires Nov. 30, 1982. Mail your order card today...

Illustration #68

Doubting Thomases of this world, please do study this testimonial insert by David Thomas of Tax Form Library. It's black ink on very cheap yellow paper, handwritten, with geographically selected names (technique #839) based on a target list. David combined #839 with #691 after a consultation meeting with René Gnam, and then reported a 50% response boost on packages with this insert compared with packages not containing this insert. And he mails to conservative tax accountants in every state. Outrageous? Yes, but it works well!

in charge of direct response promotions — go into your mail room and read the mail periodically...at least once a month.

You will get a better view of the nature of your customers, what they are saying to your company in their responses to your promotion efforts, and how they are reacting. You'll even see some testimonial letters you didn't believe existed.

841 — TESTIMONIAL LETTERS

Instruct your mail room that all testimonial letters should be referred to you.

Maintain a file of them, or photocopies thereof, and refer to them when creating the next promotion piece. Often your current customers or subscribers or donors become a fertile source of ideas that can be incorporated in your future campaigns.

842 — "TESTIFYING" WRITER PHOTOS

Testimonials have far more power if they are accompanied by photographs of the "testifying" writers, especially if those photographs appear to be of folks one normally would associate with your kind of endeavor, rather than models posing for a fee.

843 — USING CASE HISTORIES

Citing actual case histories or user reports on how your product or service benefited purchasers is a potent way to reinforce your sales claims.

But be certain that such case reports are not overly lengthy or the reader will fascinate himself with the stories and forget your message.

Using photos with case histories gains readership, and the photos help explain your message.

844 — ACTUAL CUSTOMERS

Try telling your prospective customers how many actual customers you have, so your prospects are assured that they are jumping on the bandwagon.

845 — CURRENT CUSTOMERS

While getting new customers or subscribers is probably your most important job, it is also important to consider the value of your current customers or subscribers.

Why not select 20 or 30 of your oldest customers at random and write them a nice "thank you" (that doesn't try to sell anything) for their having been with you so long? Sign the letter yourself by hand. Insist that your mail room forward the responses to you.

You may discover that not only have you endeared your customers to you, but you have now produced some unsolicited testimonial letters that will go a long way toward increasing future response.

846 — EDITORIAL REVIEWS

Published editorial reviews of your product or service frequently can be reprinted, almost as testimonials, to give credence to your offer and enhance your promotions.

If you are just going to quote the news report, try to at least reprint the logo of the newspaper or magazine. Get permission from the publication to quote the review. That gives you the chance to say: "reprinted with permission from *Rock & Dirt*," which implies that *Rock & Dirt* is endorsing you. When *Rock & Dirt* endorses you, *Pit & Quarry* may be quick to follow. Then you may get *Brick & Clay Record*, and on and on.

Most publications will be very happy to give you permission because they get the publicity, and their logos fly all over the country on your direct mail.

Don't forget to do the same thing with reviews from newsletters. They're terrific because most people regard newsletters as having authoritative reportage.

Illustration #69

All attendee comments in this brochure are quoted with written permission

YOU CAN VERIFY THE VALUE of this top program...

Here are just a few 1983 attendees who invite you to call them about the benefits of René Gnam seminars:

"I received so many ideas from Rene's seminar 3 years ago, I had to come again just to get updates. Rene has fast delivery with 100s of ideas in a short time."
Vern Schultz, V & S ENTERPRISES, INC., Mundelein, IL...312-949-1015

"Well worth coming back. Beyond improvement. Thrilled by profitable wave mailing concept, list experimentation. Best liked opportunity to meet with Rene. Outstanding lecturer. Keeps your attention."
Dr. David G. Brown, AMERICAN UNIVERSITY, Washington, DC...202-686-2368

"Very impressed. I've done a great deal of research, but I am astounded at all I've learned in this short time compared to months of reading. Everything was profitable for me, but probably most profitable: copy & test results with ideas for immediate use on mailing lists & split testing. Rene is dynamic, almost charismatic, in ability to use his voice to get points across. Those who haven't attended should know how much they are missing."
Sheila M. Brumfield, YOURS TRULY, Baton Rouge, LA...504-292-4005

"Vast degree of information usefully presented. Profitable immediate ideas for multiple product lines, long range development of an advertising program. Excellent presenter. Well worth the time."
William H. Martin, HUSKER SYSTEMS, Omaha, NE...402-558-5702

"Great seminar. Very good."
Janet C. Hoyle, HOYLE & HOYLE, Greensboro, NC...919-378-1050

"Super pointers on layouts and what to say. Very informative."
Lennox Wilson, ACCESS, Norristown, PA...215-272-4807

"A-1. Those who haven't attended should know the advantages of having a great speaker."
Kim Klopping, HAMPTON BUSINESS MACHINES, Chicago, IL...312-774-2556

"Beyond improvement. Gained confidence to create effectively."
Rick Kerbel, SUNFLOWER SOFTWARE, Shawnee, KS...913-631-1333

"Super. I am excited by profitable wave mailing concept for IRA's and split testing. Those who haven't attended should know these ideas can be used immediately. Excellent presenter. More than worth time and money."
Jim Wallace, FIRST NATIONAL BANK OF COMMERCE, New Orleans, LA...504-561-2100

"Much more than I expected! Organized, profitable ideas on tests, response. Rene is vibrant, colorful, in control. If you haven't attended yet, you should know this seminar is results-oriented." Glen B. Moody, PROMOTION CONCEPT SERVICE, Charlotte, NC...704-535-7527

"Good seminar. Satisfied. Immediate list information. Future wave mailing ideas. Like just about everything. Good information. Rene keeps interest up. Very helpful in all areas."
Opal Smith, 74 RANCH BEEF, INC., Houston, TX...713-667-7440

"There must be some improvements needed, but I don't know what. Overall OUTSTANDING. Learned how to get my products across to the reader."
Ron Rocheleau, NEWLINE SOFTWARE, Littleton, MA...617-486-8535

"Learned what not to do & how to advertise to professionals. Super."
Gary S. Rasmussen, GCOMP, San Bernardino, CA...714-888-2422

"Terrific. Second time attended and well worth it. Liked fast pace. Practical. No ivory-tower theory. Most profitable ideas for immediate use on color, paper, ink, copy. If you want to make your direct mail program work, you need to attend. Rene Gnam is terrific!!" Dian Comerford, ASSOCIATION FOR RETARDED CITIZENS, Austin, TX...512-454-6694

"Terrific. Very pleased. Profitable ideas about color use, design, splits & waves. Liked entire seminar. Have lots of ideas to take back to my company."
Rubye Samilton, TAFF INSURANCE AGENCY, Oklahoma City, OK...405-843-7911

"Seminar is great, super, terrific, beyond improvement. I am satisfied, excited, thrilled, most educated now. Can't wait to get back to the office. All knowledge gained will be most profitable on mailers, flyers, brochures. Time flew too quickly. Gnam is motivating, interesting, entertaining, most enjoyable. Definitely an idea a minute. I am very impressed with the amount of material I obtained, will remember and will implement."
Sher Broussard, TOUPS SPECIALTY ADVERTISING, Thibodaux, LA...504-447-5114

"TERRIFIC! What I liked best was details of how to improve advertising. Excellent program. Extremely helpful presentation."
Harry R. Miller, MICRO INNOVATIONS, Toledo, OH...419-471-1245

"I am excited. A-1 seminar. Profitable ideas on contrasting colors, order forms, list selections. Exciting, entertaining, valuable seminar. I received lots of PRACTICAL ideas!" Vicki Christian, MEREDITH CORPORATION, Des Moines, IA...515-283-2303

"Super seminar. Dynamic, very good speaker."
Pat Diehl, KRES ENGINEERING, Irvine, CA...213-957-6322

A popular question at René Gnam's direct mail marketing seminars concerns techniques for displaying testimonials. Review this section of one of his seminar promotion mailings as a guide to his comments:

1. Don't use a bland heading, like "our customers say." Instead use a headline that leads readers into the quotes.

2. Use one typeface for the quote and another for the attribution line. Some readers only want to read the quotes while others want to know who gave them. Two type styles or weights lets them read as they choose.

3. Use a full attribution line, including full names, cities and states.

4. When you have permission, use area codes and phone numbers. Many people will call quotation givers.

5. Position your quotes on a section of the mailing that will be retained by the recipient so he can show these marvelous words to others.

6. Trim quotations. More shorter quotes work better than fewer long quotations.

CHAPTER 21

REPEAT & RENEWAL SALES

This chapter presents well over 40 specific techniques you can use to increase your repeat orders and renewals. But, before I begin, let me say that even though you keep accurate records of these responses to your entire repeat effort series, there's something that can puzzle you.

For simplicity, let's say you do all your repeat efforts on a calendar year basis. Your historical track record indicates that Mailing #1 yields 28% response, #2 garners 22%, #3 captures 14%, #4 produces 9%, #5 achieves 4%, and #6 gets 2%. That totals 79%. Not bad.

But this year, #2 only pulled 3%, reducing your overall response to 60%. Horrors!

Hold on a minute. Maybe it's not the fault of the mailing.

Sometimes, our overbusyness, haste, and finely-critical examinations of mailing results tend to isolate us from the world. We sit at our powerful micros and run oodles of spreadsheets and compare them with oodles of others and come up with few noodles for our noodle!

For example, consider this:
Did the overall nature of your database change in the last year? Did the nature of your industry change? Did people in your database grow up — in age, money, or achievement levels — or fall down...monetarily, as a result of industry-wide calamities, or perhaps because typewriters are being replaced by computers and word processors? Did you use unusual sources to build your customer, subscriber, member, or donor base? Did you acquire a competitor's file because it matched your profiles, or so you thought?

Those are a few of the reasons why year-by-year analyses of repeat and renewal efforts may vary. And there's still another reason.

When Ronald Reagan was shot in Washington, direct mail results fell sharply. For all efforts. By all marketers.

When Fidel Castro plucked a chicken at the United Nations and talked about rocket rattling, all direct mail response in the United States fell.

So, the next time you do your analytical review, examine your results just the way you do now — with a calendar of key events beside your spreadsheets.

And, recognize that sometimes those huge events can be great opportunities for you.

EXAMPLE:

Nikita Khrushchev waddled to the podium at the United Nations and proclaimed "we will bury you." Well, that's not what he said. A translator goofed. Nikita said "we will outpace you." The point of the message was lost in the translation and, as a result, many good people had heart quivers.

My client at the time was Translation Company of America. You can imagine how quickly I prepared a mailing, showing Nikita's puss, proclaiming that "the point of your message may be lost in the translation." It was a repeat business mailing, sent to all TCA's customers, just as fast as we could humanly get it in the mail. It pulled like gang busters!

You have these repeat sales opportunities too. You don't have to limit yourself to your regular renewal series.

When a big event occurs, think about it as you view your TV screen or scan your newspaper. Ask yourself: is this event an opportunity for my organization to do a special repeat sales or renewal mailing?

In most instances, the big event won't be appropriate for a new effort. Or the publicity and recognition factor will be lost before your mailing arrives at your customer's home or office. But for those few occasions when you can tie into a big event, you may pull a landslide in response!

But, don't stop your thinking there! Maybe you can pre-plan a special renewal effort to tie in to a known future event. Why not? I knew that a new tax law would be passed in the fall of 1986. Everyone knew that. So, in the months before Congress finally acted, I created mailings for several clients, urging their customers to sign up before '86 became '87 so they'd get a tax break. Worked wonderfully.

What am I saying here? Brainstorm freely!

847 — REPEAT SALES

Renewed or repeat sales slash the most expensive portion of any overall promotion program: the acquisition of new customers, new members, new donors, or new subscribers.

Thus, the first place to look for the easiest increase in profitability in a direct mail program is at efforts to increase the renewability of the existing customer base.

848 — GOOD PULSE

The amount of renewal or repeat business from your current subscribers or customers is an accurate reflection, a good pulse, of how your product or service is being received by your customer base.

A fall-off in renewal or repeat business could indicate that your product or service is falling off in interest, or appeal, or utilitarian nature to your buyers. Thus, it pays to keep an accurate tally of every renewal order received to determine whether you need to revitalize your product or service — and perhaps your marketing, too.

849 — PRICE RAISE

A healthy renewal rate of steady repeat business from your present customer base often indicates you can raise your price.

850 — SPENDING LESS

The remarkably high amount of renewal or repeat business that can be produced fairly easily by direct mail also reduces the amount of new business that must be obtained from prospects and inquirers at a higher cost.

The greater the volume of business from renewal or repeat customers, the less you need to spend on more expensive prospecting and inquirer promotions.

851 — COST PER ORDER

The cost per order on renewal or repeat business from existing customers or subscribers or donors is far lower than the cost per order when going after prospects or inquirers.

For this reason, you should focus attention on renewal or repeat business efforts and increase your budget for these promotions.

852 — REPEAT BUSINESS PROMOTION

Revenues produced per order from current customers, members, donors, or renewal subscribers are greater than revenues received per order from prospects or inquirers.

So, consider an additional repeat business promotion, or improving the quality of a current renewal mailing to further increase this revenue from your existing customers.

Step on it. Do it now. It's one of the best ways to make money.

853 — COMPARING COSTS OF ACQUIRING SALES

The magazine industry offers us a good chance to compare costs and results of increased response percentages on renewals (repeat sales) versus new customer acquisition.

Usually a publisher can anticipate a cost per subscriber of approximately 10% of the subscription rate in acquiring a renewal. Thus, a $15.00 renewal would cost approximately $1.50 to acquire. Acquiring a new subscriber, however, frequently can run two or three times the price of an annual subscription — in our example, $30 to $45.

Thus, mathematics clearly dictate that an increase of just one percentage point in response on renewals would have to be matched by an increase of 10 or more percentage points on new subscriber acquisitions, proving that it is more desirable — almost without exception — to devote concentrated effort to improve renewability and repeat sales than to focus most of our attention on new customer acquisition.

854 — CONSIDERING MAILING PROGRAM IMPROVEMENTS

The most important thing for efforts in improving a mailing is to get a repeat or renewed sale. This is because repeat or renewed sales:

1. are less expensive to get,
2. frequently yield significantly higher response percentages, and
3. prepare your receptive audience for still another renewed or repeat sale.

855 — FORMER CUSTOMERS

Someone who has bought from you in the past, but is not currently a customer, is a better prospect for buying from you in the future than someone who has never purchased from you.

Use your expired subscription list, your former customer file, your previous donor list, your ex-member roster constantly.

856 — EFFECTIVE LIST

Even though your former customers may be five or six years past their last purchase, they still constitute an effective list that can produce orders at a lower acquisition cost than rented lists.

How long can you continue using those old names, René?

I've gone back 14 years on some lists, profitably.

857 — SPECIAL MAILING

Are you a publisher anticipating a postage increase, or are you a product merchandiser anticipating a boost in the cost of materials and/or components?

Try a special mailing.

Specifically cite the anticipated increase. Indicate that a renewal subscription or additional purchase at this time protects your customers from future rate increases.

You can also consider offering a saving in this special mailing. Or you can show a comparison of what the customer or subscriber would pay at the future rate versus the current rate and allow him to sign on again at today's rate.

858 — REPEAT SALES PROMOTIONS

If your customer, subscriber, or donor base isn't terribly tiny, you can test your renewal or repeat sales promotions.

Aim at the entire audience with two good test promotion packages and spend more money on them — or on two series of packages — than you would on your new customer acquisition programs.

859 — RATES GOING UP

"Rates going up" combined with an urgency pitch becomes the strongest copy message possible in soliciting a renewal or repeat sale.

Never hesitate to use that approach if you can support it.

860 — PRESENT CUSTOMERS

Keep on mailing to your present customers (as frequently as you can) until such time as those efforts to get repeat business become less profitable than mailing to acquire new customers or new business.

861 — CUT-OFF RATE

Special renewal or repeat business mailings are quite effective. These include renewal up-sells upon acquiring a new customer, mass renewal efforts aimed at an entire customer base at one time, and specific seasonal approaches.

All such efforts, however, should contain a precisely-stated urgency with respect to a cut-off date for acceptance of the renewal or up-sell order.

862 — FIRST TWO PROMOTIONS

The greatest response to renewal or repeat sales efforts comes as a result of the first two such promotions in a longer series.

Concentrate your creative efforts and perhaps increase your expenditures on those two promotions.

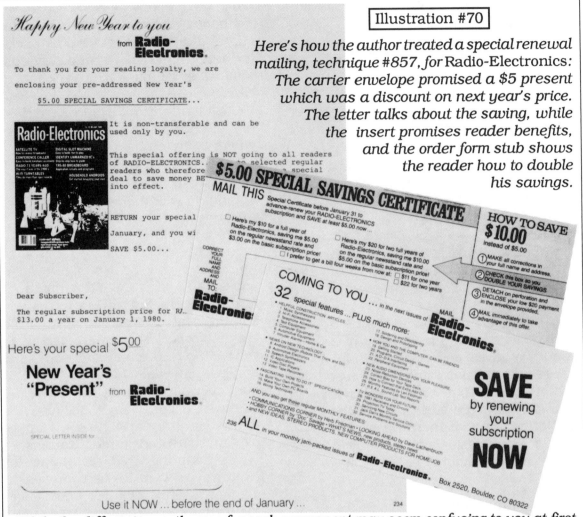

Here's how the author treated a special renewal mailing, technique #857, for Radio-Electronics: The carrier envelope promised a $5 present which was a discount on next year's price. The letter talks about the saving, while the insert promises reader benefits, and the order form stub shows the reader how to double his savings.

While the different copy themes for each component may seem confusing to you at first glance, the publisher reported that this mailing produced more instant cash flow than any other promotion in the 50-year history of the magazine. There are two reasons: (1) it went only to active subscribers who obviously have a relationship, even if distant, with the magazine, and (2) it offered them a special deal that was not available to everyone else. Mailings like this create a bandwagon effect. Everyone wants to jump to action.

863 — LOYAL CUSTOMERS

The key copy messages in acquiring renewal or repeat sales are urgency, product improvement, termination if there is inaction, and a little razzamataz about being a loyal, valued and revered customer, subscriber, member, or donor — highlighted by special offers not available to anyone else.

Reselling the product is the least important copy message since the recipient already has full knowledge of your product or service.

864 — RESELLING YOUR PRODUCT

Reselling your product in renewal or repeat sale efforts becomes increasingly important only as the sales series continues.

Thus, renewal package #6 would contain far more product sales pitching than renewal package #1 or #2.

865 — TRACKING YOUR RESPONSE

In testing renewal or repeat sales packages against the previously-winning control series, do not accept a package versus package result as the conclusive figure to analyze!

Your new single-package winner may have an adverse effect on the remaining packages in the series. The total sales produced over the length of the series is more vital to you than the results of any one package in the series.

I understand your last sentence, René, but how could a single effort have an adverse effect on the other packages?

A copy phrase, or a discounted offering, or a premium, or any of a number of other aspects may influence reactions to later mailings. Most marketers feel that Mailing #1, for instance, has little effect on Mailing #2. Not so. Even if there's a month between mailings, there can be a connection in the mind of the recipient.

Here's an *example*:

Mailing #1 looks terrific. It's fascinating to hold and examine. I stare at it for several minutes. Something interrupts me, so I set it aside and never get back to it. Mailing #2 comes in next month. I glance at it, recognize that it's from you, see that it has a similar message. Because I stared at Mailing #1 so long, I may believe I already answered #1 and therefore don't need to respond to #2. So, I discard #2.

#1 may have pulled wonderful response. But, because it subliminally affected my view of #2 — and perhaps other mailings in the series — I never respond to any of the mailings. That's why you must track your response over the entire course of the full series.

866 — REPEAT CONCEPT

To boost response to repeat sales efforts directed to former customers, try adapting your winning new customer mailing package to the repeat concept.

But hold this off until you're close to the end of the series of mailings you're dispatching.

Why hold off, René?

Because less expensive efforts should do well in the early stages of the series.

You might even hold this technique until the complete renewal or repeat series has been concluded and you're approaching old expires or former buyers. You do know that you should treat expires differently from current folks who you're trying to renew. So the expanded copy and display material that's in the new customer package may do well for the expire package. Why? Because it's more expository and gives the target explanations and rationalizations.

In adapting this technique for expires, you want to start your package approach with an acknowledgement that your recipients used to be active buyers. But with renewal or repeat people, you'll be acknowledging that they're current. Treat them as separate groups of wonderful people and you'll garner greater response.

867 — COST ECONOMY

Early mailings in a repeat sales series may go at bulk rate for cost economy.

Stamps, or metered first class mail, are more vital with later packages in the series because they increase the feeling of urgency.

868 — INCREASING CRESCENDO

Deadline or urgency copy is the single most important message in renewal and repeat sales efforts, and should

be presented in an increasing crescendo as follows:

MAILING #1
a simple statement of approaching termination,
MAILING #2
protect against administrative
processing problems by reordering now to avoid missing an
issue or shipment,
MAILING #3
you've had it, that's it. Your

subscription or service is being
terminated unless we receive
the enclosed card by the precise deadline. Renewing or
reordering after that deadline
will be taking a risk of missing
more than one issue or shipment.

So, now, René, you're saying three
mailings are sufficient in my series?
No, no! These three examples are
just to illustrate the concept of an

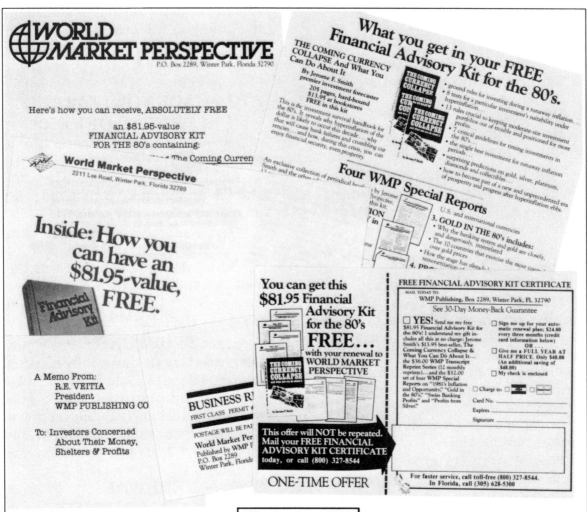

Illustration #71

*Technique #866 suggests that a new customer mailing can be adapted as a repeat or
renewal promotion to former customers. Here's a case, for World Market Perspective,
when the author did it the other way around. He created this mailing, complete with a
premium offer, for former subscribers and the client revised it for prospective subscribers. It worked fine for both groups, but pulled best with names that previously had
received the publication. Note the use of headlines on all pieces in this mailing.*

increasing crescendo. You can have a dozen or more mailings in this series.

869 — FORMER CUSTOMER MAILINGS

Expired or former customer mailings — a continuation of a renewal or repeat sales series — should stress urgency in the following fashion:

MAILING #1
We've knocked you off the list, but if you hurry you can get back on right away,

MAILING #2
We know you don't want to miss too many more, so respond now,

MAILING #3
Hey, haven't you missed getting your whoopie juice?

And how many mailings, René, can there be in an expire or former customer repeat business series?

As many as prove profitable.

870 — GIFT GIVING?

Is your product likely as a gift?

Many marketers overlook the fact that the very product they sell on a one-to-one basis could be used by their regular customers as gifts on holiday occasions. A fine time to request gift orders is when doing regular repeat sales mailings — but not when going after renewal subscriptions or memberships.

Whoa! René, why not?

Because you must make sure that I get back on board before you try to sell me on giving gifts. The cardinal guideline for subscription and membership promotions is to get the subscriber or member signed up before selling anything else.

However, there's nothing wrong with asking for a renewal or repeat order when soliciting gift business.

871 — REBATE CERTIFICATE

A refund or rebate certificate is a dramatic way to spur additional sales from your product line.

Enclose it with your repeat sales effort, and it should greatly boost response.

872 — SPECIAL PRICE CERTIFICATE

Try incorporating a special price certificate in your first fulfillment mailing, and you will create a strong desire to use the value proclaimed on the certificate.

873 — ACKNOWLEDGING REPEAT ORDERS

All repeat or renewal orders should be acknowledged.

Along with such acknowledgement should be another pitch to further increase the quantity ordered.

Say, René, can I do that with subscriptions, too?

Sure. I do it all the time. Even *The Wall Street Journal* does it.

874 — REPEAT SALE STUFFERS

Never overlook the possibility of using renewal or repeat sale stuffers in all other communication packages, whether of a selling or public relations variety, to your active customer, donor, or subscriber base.

875 — RENEWAL SUBSCRIPTION PROMOTIONS

Some publications use as many as a dozen different renewal subscription promotions to the same active subscriber and find that each of those mailings pays off — proof that a direct marketer's key job is to look for as

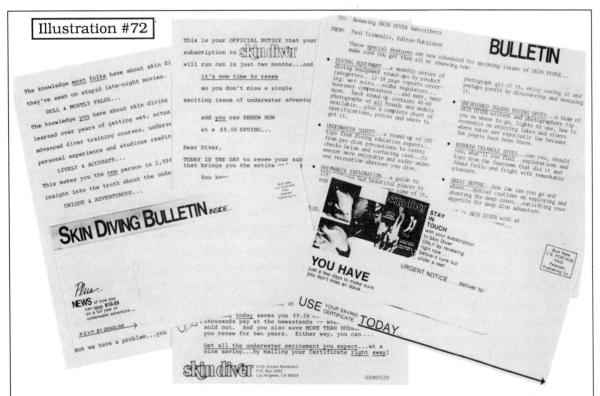

Just three of René Gnam's renewal letters and two envelopes for SkinDiver Magazine are shown here to illustrate techniques #875 and #877. Note that while the envelopes are the same size, they have totally different design. And these three letters, like the others in the complete series of seven mailings, are all different sizes: 14x8-1/2 folded to 7x8-1/2 on the left, 7x10-1/4 in the center, and 8-1/2x7 on the right. Be certain your renewal and repeat efforts present a variety in sizes, colors, and design — so your recipients don't think they've received the same mailings before.

many renewal or repeat sale possibilities as he can find.

Marketers in fields other than publishing either are shy or lax in soliciting repeat business. Take a tip from publishers: mail more repeat business promotions, and you'll have more repeat trips to the bank!

But be sure to vary the look, size, and perhaps even the colors.

876 — RECOMMENDING A FRIEND

Use inserts in your product fulfillment shipments to get a customer to recommend a friend or colleague to purchase from you.

On those inserts, add a pitch for the current customer to buy a second product, renew in advance, or enroll for a longer period.

This is a frequently-overlooked technique for getting earlier renewals and more repeat orders. After all, you have lots of mail going to your current customer base. So always find a way to have it get you more sales.

877 — VARYING YOUR STYLE

If you mail regularly to your proven customer list, try not to maintain too much of an identity, typestyle, and paper "feel" in repeat sales efforts.

Your readers will immediately identify the mailing as being yours, and if you have not established satisfaction or a proper "fulfillment rapport," you are likely to get lower response than by varying your typestyles, copy styles, and design elements.

878 — REDUCING RATES

Regularly reducing rates for renewal or repeat sale promotions is a good way to convince the subscriber or customer to wait around for a further reduction.

But, René, what about all those subscription and membership mailings that continually lower the price as their mailing series goes on?

Not so many publishers, are doing that these days and I don't know a single association that still does it. There may be a special offer now and then, but gone is the era of reducing the price a bit from mailing to mailing. It never truly paid off in the old days, and it doesn't now.

The exception, of course, is that certain huge-circulation magazines, which must meet promises to advertisers on the numbers of recipients, still continue to drop rates. But they're doing it less in the 80s than they did in the 60s and 70s.

879 — CONTINUITY SALES

If you are engaged in continuity sales such as subscriptions, education courses, or clubs, a special price or bonus gift now and then will help convince your members or subscribers that you care about them.

This may go a long way toward producing multiple product purchases from one mailing, or multiple-year subscriptions.

Then, when you deliver the item, enclose a request for an additional order or another renewal.

But, René, how many times can I ask these good customers to send me more money?

As often as you'd like. Dan Sullivan, at Frost & Sullivan in New York,

mails 50 weeks of the year, to his customers, each mailing with a new opportunity to send Dan money. And he produces a lot of money for his business reports.

If Dan's businesspeople aren't upset by all that mail, consumers won't be either.

880 — PRODUCT STUFFER

Always consider using a "bounce-back" or product stuffer with a fulfillment shipment or invoice.

Additional inserting cost usually is minimal, and frequently you can use your existing promotion pieces to pick up additional sales. However, when you use it with an invoice, remember to add a few lines to the invoice suggesting that I upgrade my purchase, extend my subscription, increase my donation, or otherwise be good to you with my checkbook.

René, are you always after money?

Usually. It helps my clients stay in business!

881 — OVERUSING CUSTOMER FILE?

I have not seen a single case of overuse of a customer file by the owner of the file! And, I've been creating direct mail for 30 years.

882 — RENEWAL AT BIRTH

When your package arrives, you are reaching your new customer at his hottest moment, his most appreciative moment. He's opening a package of goodies.

What a delightful time to reach him with a renewal or repeat sales offer. Put it in that package. Or mail it to him even before he gets your great big box.

Wait a minute, René. Didn't he just buy? Wouldn't you offend him?

No. Read this material all the way through, very slowly, and in step-by-step fashion, I'll show you how to make money with this concept without offending your new customer.

In the publishing world, this promotion is called a "Renewal At Birth" mailing. To know how to do it successfully, you have to know what it is.

Years ago when postage was cheap, many publishers used to send an acknowledgement mailing to their new subscribers. That practice is almost non-existent today, thanks to Uncle Sammy's soaring rates. But that old-fashioned idea of thanking someone for an order has given rise to the Renewal At Birth concept — and it's working. The concept is to sell a renewal to a new subscriber immediately on receiving the new subscription order.

It is adaptable to many fields, and here's how to make it work for you:

1. Record all new subscriptions on a mini-reel once a week.
2. Use that mini-reel to address your Renewal At Birth and send it out weekly.
3. In the last week of your publishing cycle, merge the mini-reels with your master file so you can fulfill subscriptions.

The minor problems you face are: (1) careful lettershop planning, and (2) the new subscription order that really is a renewal.

YOU can handle the careful lettershop planning, while your computer people should be able to assist you in checking to make sure that all new subs really are new subs. Perhaps a quick zip-check from a hard-copy printout of your active file can identify those new subs that really are renewals, and then you can delete them from your Renewal At Birth pitch.

This dramatic sales attempt works because you are hitting the new subscriber right after he or she has accepted your initial offer, the moment when he believes you're right for him. It works because you are showing instant service to your new sub. This is the time when your new subscriber loves you more than at any other time during his or her subscription.

However, there are some small dangers in doing this unusual subscription promotion, and in adapting it to other marketing arenas:

1. You can have computer snafus and mail to the wrong people.
2. Unhappy subscribers, displeased with your editorial contents on receipt of the first issue, may immediately cancel.
3. You incur the possibility of refund requests on the original new subscription.
4. You may give the reader a feeling that you're out for every buck.
5. You may wind up with subscriptions that last too long for publishing economics in volatile inflationary days.

But there are many good reasons to do a Renewal At Birth, which my client, Terry Miller at *National Hardwood Magazine*, laughingly called a "rebirth" mailing until he started to make money with it:

1. You cream the best, most dedicated subscribers.
2. You hit them when they're most likely to love you and respond again.
3. You renew them for a longer period, and thus cut your renewal costs over the long haul. In fact, you dramatically cut those costs.
4. You get additional and immediate cash flow.

5. You prove subscriber renewability immediately so your prospective advertisers are happy.

6. You prove satisfaction with your editorial product...and again your prospective advertisers love you.

7. You are thanking your subscriber and establishing a feeling of caring for him or her.

8. If you offer a Renewal At Birth at the exact same rate as the original subscription, or at an additional saving, you really surprise and delight the new subscriber.

René, this seems like a tricky mailing to do for any field?

Yes, it is. Especially when you adapt it to fields other than publishing.

Okay, René, any special guidelines?

Yes. Here are the vital copy points to express:

1. Your copy tone MUST be warm and friendly, written in a welcoming spirit.

2. Your copy MUST congratulate the subscriber on his or her wise decision to subscribe.

3. Your copy should take that wise decision as a transition point...and then go into the up-sell attempt.

4. Your copy must clearly state that the subscriber does NOT have to renew or extend at this time.

5. BUT...Your copy must point out why it would be wise for the subscriber to renew or extend right now.

6. Your copy must leave the up-sell commitment up to the subscriber. No urgency or force can be in the up-sell message.

7. Your copy should tell the subscriber that he or she is a special person, specially entitled to this special deal.

8. You can employ a businesslike tone to a business publication subscriber, but you still must have a warm approach, just as you would do with a subscriber to a consumer book.

9. You must come across as a concerned, caring publication, not as a gobble-up-every-buck company.

10. Your postscript and the close of your letter should reinforce direction to the name and address of the subscriber pre-printed or labeled on the order form, to remind him to check his address for accuracy so he doesn't miss an issue.

11. Your postscript can gently remind the subscriber of his great chance to send you more money.

The reason why I've gone to such lengths to present this concept is that most direct marketers hesitate greatly about trying it. More often than not, they study the idea and say "it's not for me."

It can be adapted to just about any kind of product or service. Fund raisers, for example, have been making hay with this technique for decades. At the moment that I make my first donation, out goes another mailing asking for more money. That's smart!

How would I do it with a service business, René?

Here's a quick *example*:

Dear Mr. Gnam,

Your decision to accept our discounted service contract on your new Minolta EP-450-Z office copier was very wise. You will save $328.85 this year.

And you can save another $328.85 by extending that contract now, before we return to our regular rates. The enclosed gold certificate enables you to double your savings. Use it today.

In my work for Minolta, the copy isn't quite that stark. But those two paragraphs should sum it all up for you. Try a Renewal At Birth. It makes money for you. Easily. The new-fashioned way!

883 — ADVANCE RENEWAL EFFORTS

In repeat sales or renewal selling approaches, do not hesitate to test postcard self-mailers or double-postcard self-mailers as advance renewal efforts early in the life of your subscriber, customer, or donor.

These inexpensive mailings serve to skim the most-likely-to-respond people from your active customer base, provide you with rapid sales, and curtail the number of successive pieces that must be mailed to the same names.

884 — EXTENDING CREDIT

Extending credit to a repeat or renewal customer whether via a credit card or a billing series is a pretty safe bet because of the customer-seller rapport.

It also produces more immediate response to the first renewal or repeat sales effort, and thus reduces the necessity of mailing a long and costly series.

885 — EXPIRED AUDIENCE

One inexpensive way to reactivate former customers, donors, or subscribers, is to create a co-op mailing to your "expired" audience and allow non-competitive inserts in that co-op.

The inserts frequently pay the entire cost of the mailing so your reactivation promotion gets a free ride.

886 — CUSTOMER SERVICE DEPARTMENT

Do not forget to keep on selling with your customer service department.

Place a photo and/or copy line regarding your products on your letterheads that are used to respond to customer inquiries regarding product performance, durability, and delivery. Every piece of mail going to a customer, prospect or inquiry — even form letters — should contain a reason why future use of your product will pay off.

Give your customer service people brochures and order forms that they can insert with their outgoing mail. You'll get a high payoff on this, and those inserts don't cost extra postage!

CHAPTER 22

AFTER THE ORDER

When an order is received, many business and consumer marketers say to themselves "okay, we got it," and then they rest.

"Rest" is a kind word.

Doesn't it gripe you that an airline spends thousands of dollars in advertising to get you to fly from Memphis to Naples? You adhere to all the airline's requirements and buy your ticket in August for a flight in December. You reconfirm the day before the flight. You get up early, gulp your coffee, and rush to the airport, getting there an hour early. Then, moments before the plane leaves, you're told you've been bumped because of overbooking. All other flights are full. You'll have to stay overnight at the airport. Maybe there will be a seat for you tomorrow, maybe not. Don't you just love that?

That's what this chapter is all about. Being nice to your customers who cost you a fortune to obtain. Being nice, so you retain them. Being nice, so they buy from you again.

The Memphis to Naples scenario is true. It was December of 1986. Northwest Airlines. "We made a mistake," the airline rep was quoted by United Press. "Our people lied to the passengers." Imagine that!

I wasn't booked for that flight. I just read about it. But I fumed in sympathy, then remembered what happened when Pan Am made a mistake on one of my tickets from St. Croix to San Juan. They marked it as an 11:30 p.m. departure. The plane left at 11:30 a.m.

Believe it or not, I got Pan Am to charter a plane to get me to San Juan and then put me on the overnight cattle car to Kennedy so I could make my next day's business appointment. Pan Am was nice on that occasion, so I continued flying Pan Am for quite a while. And, there was the time that Pan Am sent me a $25 check because an aircraft supplier in New Orleans forgot to load Jack Daniels for those of us in first class.

I remember these nice things. I don't fly Pan Am, for many reasons, these days, but I still remember and tell others.

Your customers remember. They tell others.

How much money do you spend at hotels? How many hotels have sent you thank you letters, encouraging you to return? Until modern marketing courtesies, resulting from frequent guest programs, hit the hotel scene, only Sheraton Fisherman's Wharf and The Plaza sent me thank you letters.

Now, more hotels are recognizing the value of customer communications.

> **To build your business, it's essential to: (1) stay in contact with your customers, (2) thank them for their purchases, and (3) alert them to your new products and services.**
>
> **Ongoing communications do these things for you. So does exceptional care by your customer support staff. Both efforts should be encouraged by senior management.**
>
> **But since ongoing printed communications — like newsletters and bulletins — often can speak for your company when a customer representative is not on the line, concentrate your initial concern "after the order" on these valuable efforts.**

Recognize that value for your business. It builds business!

887 — SECOND SHIPMENT

Just because I have already purchased your product does not mean that I have no use for a second shipment of the same product from you.

Enclose a pitch to buy again when you ship the original product.

888 — DUPLICATE BROCHURE

Ask your readers to pass a duplicate brochure on to an interested friend or colleague.

889 — GET-A-FRIEND OFFER

If yours is a club operation, repeat your get-a-friend (GAF) offer on a brochure in addition to the separate GAF slip.

890 — GAF SLIP OR CARD

If the GAF referral technique works for you, try doing it at the time when your reader is hottest for you.

When sending him his premium, for example, or even before shipping his first order, enclose a GAF slip or postcard with an acknowledgement letter.

891 — WORD PROCESSOR LETTER

On GAF promotions, consider using a word processor letter to the list of names derived from the promotions.

Illustration #73

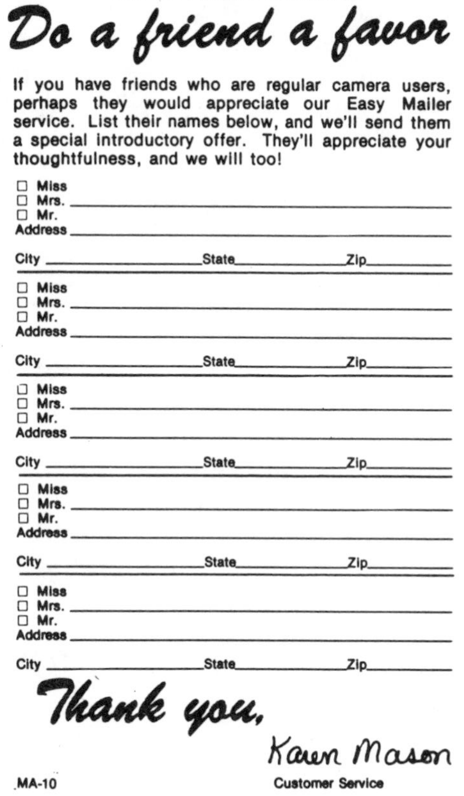

Do a friend a favor

If you have friends who are regular camera users, perhaps they would appreciate our Easy Mailer service. List their names below, and we'll send them a special introductory offer. They'll appreciate your thoughtfulness, and we will too!

☐ Miss
☐ Mrs. _____
☐ Mr.
Address _____

City _____ State _____ Zip _____

☐ Miss
☐ Mrs. _____
☐ Mr.
Address _____

City _____ State _____ Zip _____

☐ Miss
☐ Mrs. _____
☐ Mr.
Address _____

City _____ State _____ Zip _____

☐ Miss
☐ Mrs. _____
☐ Mr.
Address _____

City _____ State _____ Zip _____

☐ Miss
☐ Mrs. _____
☐ Mr.
Address _____

City _____ State _____ Zip _____

Thank you,

Karen Mason

MA-10   Customer Service

In 1970, the author created this GAF slip, technique #890, for Artz Photo Supply in Aberdeen, SD, and the headline has since been copied by dozens of marketers in many different fields. Go ahead. Use it. It works.

Then your first sentence could say, "John Jones recommended that I write to you because he believes you're the kind of person who will be interested in..."

If you don't think this is effective, you're missing a good bet. It works like a charm.

892 — REFERRAL SALES SYSTEM

If the GAF technique works well for you, can you consider using a referral sales system?

Those customers who frequently get friends for you might become good salespeople if offered a commission or discount rate on their own purchases. Test this only with a small sampling.

And there's an even easier system you can try. Create a referral letter and enclose a reply card or two. Mail this package to regular customers and watch new orders come in from total strangers.

893 — SPECIAL RATE

Is it possible for you to have a special rate for those customers who have been with you a very long time?

That will keep them happier longer.

894 — CUSTOMER SUGGESTIONS

If you have an ongoing or continuity sales program such as a club, or monthly purchase plan or subscription, ask your customers for their suggestions on improving your product or service.

You won't receive a large response, but one valuable idea gleaned from your response can repay the effort many times over.

895 — BRANCHING OUT

If you have built a solid customer base selling a product with which you have become identified, is it possible to branch out and sell other products to the same list?

Frequently, the answer is YES, because your customers are loyal and know you live up to your word. Try a special offer on a different product, provided the numbers make sense.

896 — ISSUING REFUNDS

When issuing refunds, enclose an "I'm sorry, but we still love you and want you back at some time in the future" letter to show your customer (who, after all, will remain on one of your prospect lists) that you still care about him.

897 — REFUND AND REORDER

When sending a refund, enclose an order form for the customer to order again, and be sure to also enclose a letter suggesting a new order.

Many times your customer may have temporarily run short of cash. When he gets his refund check from you, he has money in hand...for you?

Oh, come on, René. That's crazy, isn't it?

Yes, it is, but it works. Earlier in this volume I mentioned my Puzzle Lovers Club. For 17 years, it was my testing laboratory for hundreds of techniques. I'd try them on my club members with my own money. Then, if they paid off, I'd recommend them to my clients.

I'm recommending this to you because I personally saw my own checks coming back with handwritten letters apologizing for the refund requests. It cost us next to nothing to insert the letter and order form with the refund check. The letters were printed by my favorite moonlighting printer. The order forms were left over from my mass mailings.

You have leftover order forms, too.

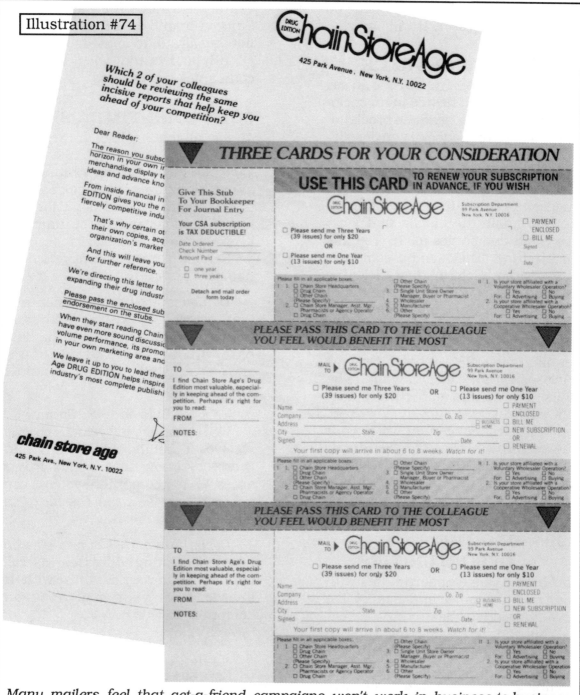

Many mailers feel that get-a-friend campaigns won't work in business-to-business marketing, but this one did when René Gnam created it for Chain Store Age. It was mailed to subscribing pharmacists, technique #892, with three reply cards: one for the subscriber to renew his subscription, and two for his associates to take their own subscriptions — either at home or business address.

Note that the headline on the letter will show through the window of the #10 envelope giving this package double use: once as a mailing using a right-window #10, and again as a package insert using this left-window #10. Thus, for instance, conference attendees open their packages of tapes and find this promotion packet, hopefully passing it along to their fellow druggists who could benefit by ordering.

Use them with a short letter done on your word processor. It will pay off.

898 — REFUND CHECK

If you are sending a refund check, say so with the check nested in an enclosure bearing a big headline proclaiming "Your refund check is enclosed!"

Make sure the enclosure clearly presents your company logo, name, and mailing address and contains a suggestion for a future purchase.

Don't make the mistake that package goods companies make. You ask for a refund. They send a computer check without a letter, just tucked in an envelope. They don't care about their image or the impression they're making for possible future sales. Taylor's Champagne did that when sending my 1985 rebate. Nothing enclosed with the check. What a glorious promotional opportunity they missed.

You ARE concerned with your impression for future sales. Send your refunds and rebates properly. Gain the good will that a check should bring you.

899 — INCOME OPPORTUNITIES

You have income opportunities with your own customer and inquiry list beyond product sales.

You can rent your names, run seminars, do your own package insert programs, sponsor your own co-op mailings, and create dozens of ways to boost your revenues.

900 — RENTING NAMES

While you may own a mailing list, you do not own the names on the list.

You have the right to use them, but several other mailers in several other fields, as well as competitors of yours, also have the same names. Since everyone uses those names, do not be afraid to mail to them frequently and to rent them to outside companies for income.

901 — ONE-TIME USE

Almost all mailing lists are rented for one-time use only.

Make sure anyone renting your names recognizes that fact by a statement in writing. And don't forget to insert dummy and decoy names to keep the world honest.

René, what are dummy and decoy names?

Dummies are names of non-existent people at existing addresses, inserted permanently in your database without the knowledge of anyone on your staff or at your computer service bureau.

EXAMPLE: Brandy R. Gnam

When Brandy, my golden retriever, receives a mailing that I did not authorize, I know that someone with access to my computer systems copied or otherwise used the file. That person can go to jail.

Decoys are names of non-existent people at existing addresses, inserted temporarily in your database with the knowledge of your staff and your computer service bureau.

EXAMPLE: Jack A. Gnam and Jenny A. Gnam.

Let's say I rent my file to the *Encyclopedia of Flora & Fauna.* Jack A. Gnam goes into the label or tape run as a decoy for just that renter.

I also rent to General Eclectic. Jenny A. Gnam is inserted for just that rental.

If Jack gets more than one Encyclopedia mailing, or if Jenny gets more than one from the Eclectic people, then I know who has copied my list without authorization. They, too, can go to jail without collecting $200.

Dummies are to keep your staff and computer people honest.

Decoys are to keep renters honest. Change your decoys each time you rent your file.

You can sue, and you will win, if your list is abducted. And I'm happy to say that a few folks have gone to jail and/or paid stiff fines for violating their list rental agreements.

Okay, René, I've read enough in this book to realize that you're up to something with Jack A. and Jenny A. Who are they?

My asses.

Your what?

My asses. If you'd like to know more about Jack Ass 3523 and Jenny Ass 3518, you can check their documents with the Bureau of Land Management division of the United States Department of the Interior. They are truly "official" asses, certificated by the federal government, listed as "adopted by René Gnam," rescued from the great Cottonwood Mountains in the northwest section of Death Valley Monument Park, where two-legged asses shot at them with rifles and shotguns from helicopters and called it "sport."

They were written up in the March-April 1986 issue of *Countryside & Small Stock Journal*. If you can't find it, send me a note and I'll be happy to send you a dot matrix reprint.

Oh, René, you're talking about burros, aren't you?

No. Burros are born in domesticity, asses in the wild. But my caretaker, Erma Huffman, is doing a great job at taming Jack and Jenny. And at Christmas in 1987, a little lassie was born to Jenny. She's Jessie. We love her too. She's a burro.

902 — AVAILABLE NAMES?

The size of your list is not the determining factor in whether you rent it or how you price it.

The determining factor is whether the names on your list are or are not available with the same history and selection via another source. If so, you still could set a more favorable price.

903 — SELLING EDGE

If the names you are offering for rental are available through another source, consider your demographic selections, acquisition dates, and updates very carefully prior to announcing the rentals.

You may have a selling edge hidden in your superior procedures.

904 — CONSULTING LIST MANAGER

If your customer list, or any other list you own, is available for rental use by others, consult your list manager, be he internal or external, before scheduling your mailings.

Block out periods when you don't want rental promotions to reach your customers.

905 — CLEANING YOUR LIST

Determine whether your list manager can suggest mailings by his renters to clean your list for your future use.

906 — PROMOTING RENTALS

When planning to clean your list, advise your list manager of your cleaning schedules so he can properly promote rentals with that information.

This is especially important if your list has been on the market for a long time. Folks who rented from you before want to know that the list is newly updated so they will consider renting from you again.

907 — INCREASING BOTTOM LINE

To increase your annual bottom line on mail marketing, increase the frequency of your mailings to your customers.

Too often, mailers shy away from additional promotions to their customer files, feeling that they will be offensive to their regular customers. The opposite is true. Those customers respect your promotion efforts and frequently look forward to them.

Look forward to them, René?

Yes. In many fields, promotion mailings are reviewed by executives as an information source. A prime example is in manufacturing. Users of products from many manufacturers want to receive updates via the mail. You may regard your mailing as a promotion, but your recipients may be looking at them to see if you have new models, new add-ons, new usage techniques.

Is this true, René, for service businesses?

Sometimes. An example is my own consulting, creative and seminar business. For many years, executives on certain of my in-house databases received at least one mailing a month on certain aspects of my business. Most of those mailings were strictly promotional.

Then, in the fall of 1986, I renewed retainer clients who increased their work assignments at the same time as starting construction on my Client Guest House and writing this book under contract with Prentice-Hall. Being overloaded, I decided not to solicit or accept any new work. Thus, I stopped mailing.

The phone rang. Several times. People whom I had not heard from in years asked what happened to my mailings. They were studying my mailings to see how I did them, what concepts were expressed that they could adapt, what was new in direct marketing. They missed getting my promotional mail.

The good news today is: this book obviously has been completed, the Client Guest House is in beautiful shape, I'll take a vacation very soon...and we'll start our mailings again.

908 — VALUE OF INQUIRY NAME

How valuable is an inquiry name on your mailing list? Only you can answer that question after testing mailings over a long period of time.

But, consider this:

When I was 12 years old, I inquired about a subscription to *Writers Digest*. Although I never subscribed, I am still receiving their direct mail at my parent's home...39 years later! I told that to the folks at *Writer's Digest* when they hired me to create a new mailing for them a few years ago, and they told me that those old names were still pulling very well.

Funny thing about those old names:

The Newspaper Institute of America has been renting them from *Writer's Digest* ever since I was 12. My parents still receive the NIA mailings, with the same misspelling *Writer's Digest* has for my name. Yet, NIA has found them profitable for the same 39 years.

This concept won't always be successful for you. The crime is deleting inquiry names too soon.

909 — FORMER CUSTOMER NAMES

How long should you keep former customer names on your promotion lists?

As long as they continue producing a cost per order that is acceptable to you.

910 — ADDITIONAL MAILINGS

Business from your current consumer customers usually constitutes at least 50% of your total revenues, perhaps 70%.

If you're a business-to-business mailer, your current customers give you 70% - 80% of your total revenues.

That's why it's vital to consider additional mailings to present customers. They are your most likely source of added profits.

911 — PRIDE IN PRODUCT AND COMPANY

Be proud of your product, and perhaps implant a proud image in the mind of your customer by sending an address confirmation letter before you ship his order.

Tell him he should confirm the address to assure that he gets the order you're acknowledging. In the same mailing, perhaps you'll enclose an offer to step up the order to a larger quantity or longer-term commitment. And of course you'll be acknowledging and thanking this wonderful customer for his order.

You'll also be showing your pride in your company, convincing him that your organization is quite okay to deal with.

912 — LETTER OF ACKNOWLEDGEMENT

When someone buys by mail, he deserves the same courteous "thank you" that you would expect when buying at a retail store.

You spent a lot to get his order. Send him a friendly acknowledgement letter, and your next promotion will be more favorably received.

913 — PRE-RELEASE TESTING

Are you keeping track of how often I buy from you, how much I spend each time, how much my total expenditures with you have been?

If you're not, you're losing an opportunity for marvelous pre-release testing.

It goes like this:

You're thinking about launching AWE, a new product, but you're not exactly sure that it's a worthwhile effort. Scan your database and select only those customers who have bought often and whose expenditures rank "way up there."

Mail them a special offer asking for an advance deposit on this wonderful new Automatic Word Eater. If you get enough deposits, launch AWE. If you don't, return the deposits with a thank you letter and a small certificate good for a discount on a future purchase of any other product you promote.

It's your dedicated, hard-core buyers who will let you know if your Automatic Word Eater will be a fine success.

Don't forget your tracking! You'll need records on sources for all names.

914 — REINFORCING SALE

Always reinforce your sale in your warm welcoming or acknowledgement letter.

Do not be content to merely acknowledge or confirm the order, subscription, or donation. Tell the purchaser why he was wise to make the decision he did.

This reduces the number of refund requests.

915 — KEEPING CUSTOMER HAPPY

If you don't ship 1-2-3, is it possible for you to send an acknowledgement of payment notice, and a warm letter, to avoid irritating a customer?

916 — DELAYING SHIPMENT

If you must delay shipment of your product, delivery of the first copy of your publication, or the beginning of your service to a new customer, be sure to acknowledge the order promptly and advise the customer when he can expect fulfillment.

That advisory note should contain copy reinforcing his wise decision to purchase from you.

917 — DELIVERY TIME

If you delay shipment to process a check or verify credit, notify the prospective client of delivery time in the solicitation promotion, but refer only to the time that it takes for the product, or merchandise, or subscription to arrive.

This will cut down on your correspondence, and keep your customers much happier. It shows them you care and want to be of service to them.

918 — START-UP MATERIALS

If you delay shipment and do send a notice of its delay, can you refer to such notice in your promotion literature as "start-up" materials?

Then, your prospective customer feels he will be served not only with the fulfillment shipment, but also with additional special packets of materials. You will send them, won't you?

919 — 30-DAY SHIPMENT

If you're not going to ship within 30 days of order receipt, the FTC says you must notify your customer and ask if he still wants your product or now desires a full refund.

920 — CUSTOMER ACQUISITIONS

Always maintain your source codes on customer acquisitions right on through several mailing periods.

Then, when examining your repeat or renewal orders, tabulate them by original acquisition source, and you will have a fine guide to which sources (lists or publications) might give you long-term payouts on future new business acquisition programs.

921 — COMPLETE FULL NAME

Always instruct your list maintenance service to maintain the complete full name of every customer on your file, including his or her title (Mr., Miss, Mrs., Ms., Dr., Rev., Sgt., etc.).

A customer who specified how his name should appear when he first ordered from you likes to see it that way. If your future mailings use the title the way he gave it to you along with the spelling of his name the way he supplied it, he will be more favorably disposed toward opening and reading your mail.

922 — DELETING RECORDS

Too many of us are too quick to delete records from out database files. True, you should delete those that can't be reached, after you've done your double-checking, because of incorrect addresses.

But should you delete them forever, René? No.

I'm sure you've discovered, as I have, that perhaps a year or two after deleting a record, suddenly you get another transaction for that same person or company. Once deleted, you can't find the previous history. Horrors.

Yes, I have a solution for you.

When we delete a record, it doesn't vanish. We've programmed our systems to delete the record from DATABASE, the name we lovingly call our database, and move it to ARCHIVE, a separate file of deleted records.

That way, we don't waste outgoing mail and we still can retrieve information if the party we deleted suddenly becomes active again.

923 — FOLLOW-UP LETTERS

One of my favorite pastimes on airplanes is to use one of my laptop computers to draft follow-up letters to customers, inquirers, even selected segments of my database.

This is a good excuse for you to fly first class! After all, you must use your flight time for productive company work.

Way above the clouds, it's peaceful and quiet, and there are no interrupting phone calls...yet! It's a super place to think creatively. Try it. You'll pay for many more flights.

924 — DOUBLE-CHECKING

Throughout this book, I've stressed double-checking. Errors can happen to anyone.

Wouldn't you have been unhappy if the 1,001 promised techniques in this book had been only 998?

Without double-checking, that's what you would have received. I made an error in numbering items on an early draft. Items 922, 923 and 924 were missing. The same error passed through several stages of proofing, by me, by my publisher, by various wonderful people who caught other things but missed the three missing items.

But just before sending the revised draft to Prentice-Hall in July 1988, I gave the disk to my secretary for a final going-over. She found that three items were missing. We all need to double-check. And then do it again.

925 — SUPERVISION

Supervise your fulfillment operation and billing department assiduously. Too often, the wrong fulfillment packages are shipped, and customers who have paid get billed unnecessarily.

These problems are vexing for the consumer to resolve, and they create ill will which frequently cannot be repaired — losing you customers who have cost you a great deal to obtain.

926 — GIFT RECIPIENT NAME

When a customer uses your product as a gift and instructs you where to mail it, be sure to retain the name of the gift recipient.

Computerize that list and use it for your future promotions. Tailor letters to the gift givers and the gift recipients. Suggest to the recipients that they can repeat their purchases for themselves and give gifts to those they adore.

I recommended this to Tom Broyles at Eilenberger's Butter Nut Bakery in Palestine, TX. He's using it. He repeats using it. He's selling a lot of fruit cakes, apple cakes, apricot cakes, and pecan cakes. I just bought another batch myself. Everyone does.

927 — NOT AT THIS ADDRESS

When the postal service returns third class mailing pieces you sent to customers on your own house list marked "undeliverable as addressed" or "not at this address," you should:

Remail to those names by first class mail, and you'll then discover that more than 20% of them really are deliverable and a significant number are forwardable. If your selling price is high, this is a vital technique to adopt immediately.

928 — ADDRESSING LEGEND

When you have nixie returns on customer names, mail the same piece in a larger envelope via first class, using the exact same address legend.

Enclose a memo requesting the correct addressing information, and you will discover that a sizable percentage of those "nixies" were, in fact, deliverable. Another sizable percentage will respond to that information request and give you an addressing legend you should use in the future.

929 — ZIP CODE ACCURACY

When converting your lists to computer, you can logically expect approximately 5% errors on zip coding. If you mail via third class postage, this means that at least 5% of your customers no longer will receive your mail.

Thus, it is vital that on customer file conversions you double check the accuracy of zip codes.

930 — BILL-ME-LATER ORDER

Whenever you have a "bill-me-later" order, be sure to enclose your bill with the product when you ship it to encourage rapid payment.

Your invoice reaches the buyer at the moment when he's overjoyed at receiving the product, and thus is more likely to pay promptly.

However, if at this stage you discover that you are getting an abnormal amount of slow-pays or no-pays, switch your billing and shipping procedure, as follows:

1. Send a bill for the postage and handling charge. Indicate on it the total price of the item ordered and that the invoice for that amount will be included in the package you'll ship after receipt of the postage and handling charge.
2. Ship the product and product invoice immediately to all those who pay the postage and handling invoice.
3. Don't ship it to those who don't pay that first invoice promptly. Instead...
4. Send them an acknowledgement letter, thanking them for

their order and asking them for their credit card authorization number so you can ship after billing the total amount to their credit card.

5. Ship the product immediately to all those who give you their credit card information.

6. Forget the others. Put them on your prospect list as code J. Oh, you can use any code you wish. J is my code for "jerks I never want to deal with."

Well, René, why spend the money to put them on your list?

Two reasons:

1. When I run my list, I can suppress (not address) all those coded as J.

2. When I run my list against someone else's file in a merge/purge, that J is assumed to be my customer in the merge. So if the deadbeat's name appears on the rented file, it won't be used to address my mail.

931 — VERIFYING ACCURACY

Remember that thousands of postal workers find it easier to return something to you than to check or correct the address to which you have mailed that item.

This means you should not accept a customer or inquirer designation of a zip code as being 100% correct. When you convert such names to computer, run them against the official zip code tape or look them up to verify accuracy.

In 1979, some estimates said 20 to 30% of USA adults did not know their zip codes. In 1985, George Gallup reported that 64,000,000 Ameri-

can adults could not properly address an envelope.

Horrors, René. Will these figures improve?

Not quickly. Unfortunately, our educational techniques and standards are decreasing, despite recent attempts to improve them. Boston University reports that candidates for English teaching degrees score lower in English than candidates for any other degree. In Atlanta in 1984, 26% of English teachers flunked college requirements for English teaching degrees.

If the teachers can't teach, and if the techniques and standards are far lower than when you went to school, chances are pretty good that those who are in school now will be less adept than you are. So you must check the address information that your customer sends to you. It's another reason why you want to imprint all your order forms with that same information...so it gets to him.

Now, René, aren't you being a bit unduly harsh about our country's educational system?

No. I wish you were right, but no, I'm not at all unduly harsh. In December of 1986, The National Assessment of Educational Progress, founded by Congress and often called "The Nation's Report Card," disclosed these distressing figures:

● Over 75% of 11th graders do not perform adequately on tasks involving skills for success in academic studies, business or the professions.

● 75% of 11th graders, 82% of

8th graders, and 98% of 4th graders do not perform adequately when asked to compare and contrast "the easiest analytical task assigned."

- 50% of 11th graders, 66% of 8th graders, and 91% of 4th graders do not write at "adequate" levels.

These conclusions, based on testing 55,000 public and private school students by the Educational Testing Service of Princeton, NJ, are especially worrisome because you'll note that inadequacy percentages are higher with the very young. Couple those statistics with the fact that 29% of American high school students are promoted to the next grade when they don't qualify, and you begin to cry inside about how our country will fare in a competitive global economy.

In 1987, two Stanford University professors, Judith Langer and Arthur Applebee, said "students at all grade levels are deficient in thinking skills." If they won't be able to think, don't know and can't write, it becomes essential that:

1. We all do something to correct this educational depression with the utmost speed, and
2. Your order forms be absolutely clear, easy to fill in, and perhaps use graphics to guide the eye, and
3. Your staff be instructed to double and triple check the accuracy of all names and addresses.

932 — EXTENDING TIME PERIOD

If you have received decent (but not terrific) response from your promotion effort, try mailing to the rest of the names on the list with a follow-up offer indicating that the time period has been extended due to additional inventory or late mailing.

933 — CORPORATE EXECUTIVES

If you attempt to build your prospect list of corporate executives by offering free samples to associates, be certain that the form you use for the initial recipient to indicate additional names has a clearly designated space for the title or job function for each name.

If you forget this simple step, the respondent may simply give your form to a secretary to fill out with all names in a department, and you may be reaching an inappropriate audience with the additional names.

934 — LIST OF ADDITIONAL NAMES

One good way to build lists of executives at business addresses is to write to the one name you have and request a list of additional names, all of whom will receive a free booklet, free sample, or free trial subscription.

The recipient of your mailing piece feels good in "awarding" your free offer to his associates, and you succeed in building your prospect list.

Oh, nonsense, René. Professional people won't do that?

Well, I suggest that you call Elsie Showalter at S.N. Publications in Chicago. She's being doing it successfully for years. She asks hospital administrators and supervisory nurses to fill out a form with the names and responsibilities of other supervisory nurses in the hospital and other health care facilities. They do it. Elsie gets her forms back, some handwritten, some beautifully typed.

Then she sends copies of her magazine to the new names. After a

Make one small decision today
and you'll ORIGINATE MORE LOANS
for years to come...

Illustration #75

It's easier than mc
need is the advance
those "rate shopper

Dear Mortgage Profession

If you had $100 for ever
with you, you'd be singi

The problem isn't f
converting those "n
loan buyers. And,

You'll probably agr
experience of those
loan business than

You need the advanced re
making the sales you wan

*Now, You
can hike* The nation's leadin
realtors, and other
easier for you.

*your
bottom
line!* She's Debra Jones,
Corp., and a freque
probably heard peop

Between extensive consul
and published several ex

AudioCassette Train
Newsletters...all h

Now You Can **Originate
Many More
Loans!...**

*faster, easier, and more often
by using the savvy advice of*
Debra Jones
*the expert who has trained
thousands of high producers!*

Creating A
Sales
Team

For Fastest Service, call Toll-Free, Today...
or use this courtesy, postage-paid envelope to make sure
You get all your **Debra Jones** Reference Resources.

Mail promptly.

NO POSTAGE
NECESSARY
IF MAILED
IN THE
UNITED STATES

BUSINESS REPLY MAIL
FIRST CLASS   PERMIT NO. 6080   Denver, CO

POSTAGE WILL BE PAID BY:

Bulk Rate
U.S. POSTAGE
PAID
Permit No. 947
Denver, CO

Now Yours, from the expert who has trained thousands of
loan officers, mortgage brokers, realtors,
and other leaders in financial services...

boost income.
erful techniques.

**SUCCESS SECRETS THAT EASILY, QUICKLY
LEAD YOU and YOUR TEAM TO
ORIGINATE MORE LOANS**
AND CONSISTENTLY BUILD SOLID SALES
WITHOUT EVER TAKING ADVANTAGE OF ANYONE

*our skills
e in sales*

*OPEN NOW... and start achieving more success with the WINNING METHODS
that are paying off handsomely for America's most productive professionals...*

*Here is the author's creation, for Hark & Associates, that solved a perplexing marketing
problem on a low budget: a single mailing for prospects, customers, and inquirers,
technique #939, but to different groups at different times as names are acquired.*

*This package — letter, brochure with order form, reply envelope and carrier envelope
— is used successfully to sell books and tapes to names on rented prospect lists, to
customers who have bought one product or service but not all, and to inquirers from
Debra Jones' seminars to the mortgage banking profession. It is also used as a follow-
up mailing, and the brochure is now included in Debra's seminar handouts.*

while, she stops sending free copies and starts selling paid subscriptions to all those new names that she acquired because she had the courage to try this technique.

People like to help each other. Please give them that opportunity. At the same time, they're helping you.

935 — REDUCING FALSE CLAIMS

If you receive excessive complaints about non-delivery, try using a different address on the package containing your product shipment.

You may discover that some people love your product so much that they want a second one. If they write to the separate address used on the shipment, you automatically know this is the case.

This is a dandy way to reduce false claims.

936 — CURRENT FULFILLMENT PROCEDURES

Be especially careful to review shipping material, cartons, packing methods, and carriers.

Frequently, you can reduce costs if you make a careful analysis of your current fulfillment procedures.

937 — MEMBERSHIP PLAN

If you sell your products, services, newsletters, or magazines as part of a membership plan, remember that members consider themselves more a part of your group or family than do customers or subscribers.

Therefore, it is vital to follow up with a list of membership benefits, a welcome-to-our-club folder and other reasons why the respondent has been wise to become a member. Otherwise,

you will lose many repeat orders from your members.

938 — COLLECTION EFFORTS

If you have large collections to make on high-ticket items, consider using the telephone for collection efforts before getting into a dunning series.

Then your word processor dunning series can make mention of a telephone promise to pay.

939 — ANSWERING QUERIES

Answer all mail from your readers, whether they are customers, inquirers, or prospects.

All these wonderful people should receive at least one mailing from you, and any who write individual letters should receive personalized responses.

The inquirers about your products or services can be upgraded to purchasers. The inquirers about how you have fulfilled their orders can receive letters that, once again, make them happy to do business with you.

Even those who have been offended by your mail or do not have legitimate complaints can become more favorably disposed toward your future promotions if their queries are answered.

Of course, you'll occasionally run across a code J who keeps on writing forever. Sooner or later, you'll have to stop answering him.

940 — RETURN CARDS

If you sell retail products or merchandise and your customers return warranty cards, service guarantees, and other registration cards to you, do not overlook mailing to the list of those who have returned such cards!

They are, we hope, satisfied customers who will buy from you again.

CHAPTER 23

INTERNAL HANDLING

I have a wonderful team here at my little Response Ranch in Florida. Leslie is my secretary and Marie is her part-time assistant. Erma takes care of my animal menagerie. Robert is our chauffeur and Vince is our foreman. Craig fixes fences and does what Vince calls "grunt work." Carol does the cleaning.

But Erma has stuffed envelopes for Leslie. Marie has nursed a sick animal for Erma. Robert has helped serve seminar luncheons. Carol has done odd jobs. Vince has cleaned the pool when Craig has been helping whomever. Even wives and husbands pitch in when we need an extra hand.

Do you have that good-natured, friendly, cooperative spirit at your organization? I hope so. It pays off. Your customers will recognize it on the phone. Here's how:

A family named Miller in Chicago owns a company named Quill. Those wonderful people sell office supplies by mail. We buy a lot from the Miller brothers. We've never met them or spoken with them. We used to buy from a variety of sources that used United Parcel Service to make it convenient for us. But we don't save the competition's catalogs any more. Now we buy, almost exclusively, from Quill.

Every time we've had a question, a bright and sparkling person has answered the phone. When the question couldn't be answered instantly, she'd call us back. If she didn't get back to us the same day, the supervisor would call to apologize and promise a call the next day.

When we ordered 12 conference tables and Quill's supplier delivered 4 broken and 2 of the wrong model, my secretary called Quill. The telephone rep actually thanked her for the call! The same day, we had cheerful information on how Quill was handling the correction. Two days later, a confirmation arrived. Next, Quill called us and told us not to pay for the 6 good tables until the entire order was correct. Finally, a truckman arrived to pick up the bad tables. Everything was cheerfully resolved.

How can you forget the smiles and understanding in the voices of the Miller employees? You can't. They make you feel good.

In contrast, I booked a table and rooms for New Year's 1986 at the local Holiday Inn where I previously had run seminars and been responsible for functions of up to 350 people. All of that previous business had been on credit. Just my word, or my secretary's, by phone.

But for New Year's, a grating voice told me I'd have to drive there personally and present my check in advance. Wouldn't even take a credit card number. Didn't bother to check the file when I asked. Wouldn't connect me with the sales manager.

I took my New Year's party to a resort instead. Holiday Inn lost. Quill keeps winning. And, I guess you know what I'm going to say next.

Work to make your people happy. If they're happy working for you, they'll be happy on the phone and by mail with your customers. You can hear smiles on the phone. You can see them in letters. Smiles make customers want to come back.

Strengthen your internal situation so everyone is a sparkling, not rehearsed, public relations agent. Then, examine your bottom line. Better, isn't it?

---

941 — COPY READING, PROOFREADING

Copy reading and proofreading are two different facets of promotion production — and you must do both!

Copy reading is ascertaining that all facts are correctly and accurately stated, that you can support them, and that they dovetail with your overall objectives.

Proofreading is double checking the accuracy of spelling, typesetting, and punctuation, and also determining whether there is a desired consistency in punctuation style. Don't be pedantic about consistency in your proofing. Your goal is smooth flowing copy.

There may be times when budget considerations or rapid deadlines prevent you from doing your best to make a direct mail promotion as readable as you'd like it to be. I understand. In fact, I often tell my seminar audiences that it's more important to get the mail in the mail than it is to create a perfect mailing.

But you don't sell if you don't communicate. And you don't communicate if your promotion can't be easily read and quickly understood.

That's why I'm so ardent about taking creative liberties with punctuation. I allow textbook violations. I'm after smooth reading flow.

EXAMPLE:
Semicolons DO NOT EXIST. They have no earthly purpose. If you think you need a semicolon, you really need a new sentence.

Here's why:
Semicolons are sore thumbs that block the eye from reading on. Worse yet, they remind people of legal documents. That's where we see the most semis.

To read the legal contracts they write, attorneys often have to place one finger on the first semicolon and another on the next semicolon, and then try to understand what's between the two fingers. Similarly, in insurance policies, the semicolons obfuscate the disclaimers. You only get paid if you lose nine fingers and your left leg on a rainy Thursday when a crescent moon is perpendicular to Saturn's middle ring.

People don't know how to write with semicolons and they find it difficult to understand writing that contains them. Use semicolons, and you

---

PROOFreading and COPYreading

Proofread to find spelling and punctuation errors.

You can't afford to proofread 17,000 times, but if your name was J. W. Marriott, you'd wish you had caught Marriot in the headline of an ad urging meeting planners to recommend your hotel.

Copy read to check all facts in your presentation. For instance:

If your copy refers to "red tide sweeping over the ocean" as a communist horde about to attack, your copy reader should question whether you really meant a springtime algae bloom that kills salt-water fish.

A good procedure is to:

A. Elect the fussiest person on your staff as copy reader. Charge that individual with checking dates, rates, claims, guarantees, offers, premiums, and all facts.

B. Pick a team of two clear-eyed, erudite nit-pickers as proofreaders. Let them first read every-thing individually. Judy then reads everything aloud, including punctuation, to Jeff. Then, Jeff reads it all aloud to Judy. The reader reads. The listener marks errors.

C. Now, let copy readers proofread and proofreaders copy read.

D. Proofreaders and copy readers must work in a sound-free area with no interruptions. Let them take a day off and work at home.

Remember that *Sports Illustrated* once sent out a price hike mailing containing the wrong new price. Remember that Chevrolet Nova, to Hispanics, means Chevrolet No Go. You wouldn't make those errors, would you?

Do COPYread and PROOFread every-thing, again and again, and then after you have sent all reproduction materials to those who must receive them, take extra photocopies home and check them over again on a weekend — yourself!

Illustration #76

Reprinted from René Gnam's RESPONSE REVIEW *Newsletter...see technique #941*

---

lose your audience. You remind them of the horrors of litigiousness and uninsured fingers. You don't want negatives in your direct mail promotions. Semicolons are 100% negative.

Similarly, a hyphen is a hyphen. A dash is two hyphens. Use a space before and after a dash so type isn't piled up. Use few dashes because they sit in the middle of a line, breaking the reader's thought chain. It's perfectly okay, according to René Gnam, to let an ellipsis substitute for a dash. An ellipsis? That's three dots.

Your proofreaders and copy readers must understand these points if your mail marketing is intended to be effective.

More now, about hyphens:

I agree with Winston Churchill, who once said: "One must regard the hyphen as a blemish." But I also agree with William Safire, who says: "Hyphens should be used mainly when not using them would cause confusion."

Here's an *example*...

A small-businessman (incorrect according to Webster) is a man who runs a small company. He could be tall or short.

A small businessman (correct according to Webster) is a tiny fellow. Do you mail only to tiny people?

Or, back to Safire again:

Webster says no hyphen is needed in the word "belllike." But those three L's together are awkward. Was "belllike" easy for you to fathom at first glance? Try it in helvetica where it will appear as four capital I's. How many more electronic door ringers would you sell if they had "bell-like" chimes?

So, use some common sense. Hyphenate when it improves comprehension. Otherwise, drop those blemishes.

Yes, René Gnam is bold. He says go ahead and violate textbook idiocies on punctuation, hyphenation, even spelling, if doing so will make your message easier to understand. But don't violate common sense just to be clever.

You see, if I could write an entire book with few dashes, few hyphens and NO semicolons, you can make your copy just as readable for your readers.

Go ahead. I challenge you. Try to find one semicolon in this book. (If you're successful, my publisher didn't read this.)

942 — INSPECTING PRINTOUTS

It's a good idea to carefully inspect printouts of each list you rent before sending the list to a mailing service.

Why? So you can determine whether the computer service has furnished the specifications you requested.

Let your list supplier deliver the labels to your office for you to check before they get dispatched to the lettershop. You will have a small re-dispatch expense to the lettershop, but you will be able to double-check such vital items as:

- state selection,
- sex selection,
- three-line versus four-line addresses,
- title selection,
- count accuracy,
- zip sequencing,
- and the all-important factor of coding.

Okay, René, but I have confidence in my suppliers. Do I still have to do this?

You should because there's one more checking point that almost every mail marketer forgets. Here it is:

You have studied many available lists and then selected the one or ones that you feel appropriate for your proposition. If you are correct that these lists are appropriate for you, they should contain the names of some of your current customers. Even if you've used the world's most super-stellar merge/purge program, some of those names will still be on the labels you rent because no merge/purge program is 100% infallible.

Now, when you examine the labels, if you can't find any of your current customers, something is drastically wrong!

All the selections and coding might be right, but the wrong list may have been inadvertently used by a night operator whose unintentional sleepiness led him to hang the wrong tape. Imagine what that would do to your results.

If you can't recognize any of the names on the labels you are renting, call your list supplier instantly. That's too slow. Call him this very second! Now! Pronto!

943 — IN-HOUSE PRODUCTION

Even if you have a large and well-skilled in-house printing and mailing facility, you may wish to give those aspects of your promotion production to an external source so you can guarantee meeting your deadlines.

Experience proves that hundreds of other jobs are "more important and more urgent" to the in-house production facility, thus delaying your efforts and frequently reducing their effectiveness.

944 — PROGRESS REPORTS?

You need not worry about your creative person's willingness to do the best possible job with your direct mail. His job or next assignment depends on it.

Do not constantly ask him for progress reports, or you will preclude his best efforts.

Sales promotion writing? Ah, that's a different ball game because the writer probably knows that you can't always measure results as well as you can with direct mail created to produce responses.

945 — PROMOTION WRITER

Don't tell your promotion writer everything there is to know about your business.

Do tell him or her almost everything there is to know about your audience, your product, and the realities of the current marketplace.

946 — CREATIVE PROJECT DEADLINE

Do set a workable deadline for your creative project. Make it realistic and not a falsely urgent rush.

That's the best way to get the creative individual's best effort.

947 — BONUS CHECKS

Once the creative and production aspects of your campaign are over, your supervision does not cease.

Instruct your mail room staff about the importance of keeping accurate tallies by key code. Tell them why and what the effect can be on their future if they submit inaccurate reports. Get them involved!

One dandy way to do this is to give a small bonus for every order or inquiry correctly coded by your tallying staff. Perhaps it's a dime, perhaps more. At the end of each month, each employee doing the tallying receives a bonus check.

Yes, I've worked with organizations that have deducted incorrect coding from paychecks. Now that's an incentive!

948 — PURCHASING AGENTS

If yours is a large corporation with a centralized purchasing department, rarely let a purchasing agent purchase any printed item related to your direct response advertising.

Not having a direct marketing education, most purchasing agents do not recognize the importance of:

1. paying a bit more for the proper quality to enhance your sales message, or
2. paying a bit less in certain circumstances where it will not adversely affect your response, or
3. ganging more than one promotion piece on a single printed sheet to effect cost-per-order economies.

949 — DOUBLE CHECKING SPECIFICATIONS

Be certain to double-check your purchasing department's specifications to your printers and lettershops.

Because of a minor economy, a

well-meaning purchasing agent may change your original creative specifications, and as a result you may not achieve the impact your layout was designed to produce.

950 — EDITING

After your complete promotion package has been created and approved, but before you set type, reread every word to make sure that not a one is offensive to any segment of your audience.

If you find an offensive word or two, or a phrase or a sentence, edit it.

951 — STREET ADDRESS

If you sell consumer merchandise by mail, recognize that people will have more confidence in dealing with you if you use a street address rather than a post office box for ordering.

This guideline does not necessarily apply to promotions aimed at business audiences because many very large and well-known corporations use post office boxes for mail delivery in order to get the mail faster each day. That fact is well recognized by other businesses.

And in my case, the mailman ar-

BORDERLINES You Can & Should Avoid

If your mail is offensive to a female secretary, the boss will never get it. If a female executive participates in decision making, or is the decider, you won't get the order. If you promote services and your mail reaches a male boss, he may think your sexist copy means you won't work well with his female associates.

But sexist copy isn't the only offender in the direct mail world. So is copy that, perhaps unintentionally, offends single executives, gays, the elderly, newly-divorced people, intentionally childless couples, or people of a particular race or religion.

When you're editing your final direct mail copy, have a variety of people on your staff review it for offensiveness. If any word or phrase is borderline, edit it. If you're not sure whether your copy is or is not sexist or otherwise offensive, cut out the questionable wording and rewrite that sentence.

Here's a horrid example, written (I kid you not) by a woman executive, promoting membership for the Florida Direct Marketing Association:

Until now, all of us who have anything to do with Direct Mail Marketing here in Florida... had to fly by the seat of our pants or panties.

That headline could have been rewritten as...

Until now, all of us who have anything to do with Direct Mail Marketing here in Florida... had to struggle to find sources of information and share ideas with successful executives.

That would NOT have *run the risk* of turning off anyone — and since it provides more meaningful promises, it just might get the reader to read a lot

further without wondering why pants or panties...or pants and panties...crept into the copy.

If it's borderline, *eliminate it!*

What we must all realize when mailing to business addresses is that a woman frequently sees the mail before it gets to the proper executive...and that executive may be a female with enormous purchasing power.

Here are some other examples of offensiveness in recent direct mail copy. Review them to decide how you might change the copy so the mailings would have a greater chance for success:

How to become a $100,000-a-year executive and delight both your wife and secretary — by Steffen Steffen Associates, Westport, CT
Your wife will love the fringe benefits — by American Yacht Charter Conferences, St. Thomas, USVI
Spouses are welcome. They always have time for sightseeing — by American Management Associations, New York, NY
While you're in Riviera Beach, your wife will find lots of activities to keep her busy — by Fiscal Policy Council, Miami, FL
Are you handling your job just like a woman — by Business Week, New York City, NY
A natural kind of love — by Columbia Pictures, Los Angeles, CA
Closets fit for a queen — by Gulf American Land Corp., Miami, FL

Eliminating borderline copy hikes your likelihood for success. It allows your targets to read and respond.

| Illustration #77 |

Reprinted from René Gnam's RESPONSE REVIEW *Newsletter...see technique #950* rives at our office at 1:30 p.m., sometimes. But because we use a post office box, we get your mail at 9:00 a.m., always.

952 — FIELD TESTING

Going out into the field and interviewing prospective purchasers about your newly-created direct mail piece before you print is a good way to get some feedback before incurring major budget expense.

But do not rely on everything you hear in those interviews, because most of your prospects will be telling you what they think you want to hear.

953 — IN-HOUSE COMPUTER FACILITY

If you have an in-house computer facility — or do your own database work on a micro or mini — you must double check the maintenance and handling of your mailing lists!

Be certain you select professional input people, because errors and lack of expertise will cost you more than going to an external source.

However, you can often find bright youngsters for input work and train them to be extremely accurate. I've had success doing this with work-study students from local high schools. But, if you go this route, be certain that a skilled person on your staff, or a consultant, does the training and double-checking.

You not only seek to avoid errors in input, but you want to be certain that the computer system gives you what you need. Thus, the entire database setup needs a careful review on a periodic basis, just as the staff work requires similar supervision.

954 — PROMOTION MATERIALS

In launching a new product or service or publication by mail, have your promotion materials reviewed by a consultant before you print.

Doing it yourself because "I know my audience" is a good way to get lower response.

955 — DIRECT RESPONSE CONSULTANT

If your list currently is on your in-house computer, call in a direct response consultant or a computer consultant skilled in the mailing list field to analyze how your list is being handled.

You may find:

1. there will be additional income applications for list usage that you currently cannot explore because of an inadequate system, or
2. additional information may be added to the file to increase income opportunities, or
3. you may be able to extract data not now being used and thereby increase income, or
4. you may be able to make additional selections or combinations of selections to increase income, or
5. you may be able to devise new reports giving you more pertinent analysis for future income, or
6. working together, you may spot new merge possibilities between files, or
7. crossover sales possibilities may spring up, or
8. all of the above and much more!

Okay, René, what other cautions should I have on external handling? Read this chapter!

956 — OUTSIDE SUPPLIER

Whenever you give a job to an outside supplier, the trickiest aspect is determining a proper deadline for correct performance on that job.

One good way is to ask the supplier how long he thinks the job should take him. Then, double his time estimate so he can do the entire job over if he has neglected to follow your instructions or has otherwise goofed.

957 — COMPUTER HOUSE

When using a computer house for any form of mailing list processing or converting or maintenance, make absolutely certain that it has the programs you need and has worked for several other list owners in the past.

Check its customer roster and do not hesitate to call some of those clients to determine their satisfaction with the computer service. Do not try to train the computer service facility and do not accept a statement that the programs you require will be "up" shortly.

You must have professionals handling your lists, or you may lose a fortune in lost sales opportunity and also wind up with an inaccurate list or lost data.

958 — WRITTEN UNDERSTANDING

Any time you give a computer facility a list or source documents to create a list, make certain you have a written understanding that the names on that list belong to your company and cannot be attached, misappropriated, or otherwise used by computer folks.

This is true with large or small lists. Each name and address record may be vital to your future revenue.

Recognize, too, that the size of your list is not the determining factor in deciding whether to computerize it. The determining factors are frequency of that list's use and access to its data.

959 — UPDATING MAILING LIST

Every time you update a mailing list, make sure you require your computer source to give you an activity report showing every transaction on the file accomplished by that update.

Without such a transaction summary, it is impossible to trace what happened to the names you added, deleted or otherwise adjusted.

960 — COMPUTER SERVICE BUREAU

Remember to instruct your computer service bureau or your list broker to print your key codes on mailing labels.

Often this can be done at no cost, and it is a far more efficient manner of coding direct mail than imprinting codes on order cards.

961 — INDIVIDUAL SPECIALISTS

Usually avoid using the external source that proudly proclaims that it can do "everything" for your promotion campaign.

Use individual, competent specialists for each vital area and you should have a lower-cost promotion that likely will be more effective.

More effective, René? That doesn't make sense?

It does. If you have a timed mailing — and you nearly always will if you adopt my profitable technique of using a deadline in just about every

This René Gnam mailing for The Christian Writer *has many inserts. Your natural inclination might be to give it to a single printing supplier so as to have less hassle for yourself. Please don't. If that supplier doesn't have enough of the right size presses, or enough press time, you can run into delays. Instead, follow technique #961 and let a variety of specialists handle each aspect of timely production.*

promotion — getting it out on time makes it more effective than sitting around and waiting for your single supplier to get it done.

Believe it or not, you usually have fewer delays when an envelope house makes the envelopes, one or more lithographers do the printing, and a lettershop does the inserting and mailing than when you put the entire job in one shop.

962 — INCOMING AND OUTGOING MAIL

It is not a good idea to have your incoming mail and fulfillment handled by the same shop that dispatches your outgoing mail.

There's too much of an opportunity for falsifying reports so mailings which are most profitably handled by the lettershop are those receiving the most favorable key code reports.

963 — ADVERTISING AGENCY?

If you're considering using an advertising agency to create and produce your direct response, how many agencies should you interview?

The answer is no more than seven, selected as follows:

- two one-man bands where the principals are likely to give you their own best ideas,
- two big agencies with complete media set-ups which can introduce you to new ways to market your product,
- two or three medium-sized agencies which may be able to give you everything you need on your budget.

964 — CRISIS RESCUE ASSIGNMENTS

Many corporations, associations, and institutions believe that any advertising agency can create successful direct mail or sales promotions. I get a lot of "crisis" rescue assignments because of that thinking error.

Use a general advertising agency for its specific areas of previously-demonstrated expertise. Use a direct response pro or agency for direct response advertising.

Pitfalls stumbled into by those unskilled in direct mail promotion can be extensively expensive.

965 — SPECIALIZED PRINTERS

Don't believe that one printer can print every promotion you create. We have reached an age of sophisticated specialization in printing services.

Shop around and you will discover that certain printers are more appropriate for brochures, others for reply cards, others for stamps and tokens, and so on.

966 — KNOWING YOUR PRINTER

Do not deal with your printer strictly by mail or telephone.

Visit his shop and make sure he has the proper, modern equipment, an efficient and productive staff, and a client roster that includes deadline-conscious direct marketers.

967 — SLOW SEASONS

Ask your printer what his normally slow seasons are.

Then attempt to make a deal with him whereby he will give you a lower price — just to keep his press running — on certain standard forms, reply envelopes and other pieces you can print in advance and store for later use.

968 — THE ONLY CRITERIA?

Did you accept a printer's bid because his price and quality and previous history of delivery were what you required? Well, those are not the only criteria.

Consider whether he has the proper press blanket sizes for your next job. Otherwise:

1. You may have additional expenses because he may have to farm your work out,
2. You may have additional bindery costs resulting from the farming,
3. Your deadline might be missed.

969 — FAVORITE PRINTER?

You say you've been using a favorite printer for a long time?

How about checking occasionally with the competition to determine whether your printer has slowly increased his prices above current levels you can obtain elsewhere.

970 — QUALITY AND RELIABILITY

It is especially easy to make a mistake in ordering printing on a cost-per-thousand basis. For instance, Supplier A's quotation at 10¢ or 15¢ less per thousand than Supplier B is not sufficient reason to select Supplier A.

Low quote notwithstanding, will Supplier A deliver on time and will his printing make the impression you want for the prospects who receive your mail? The better quality and/or reliability of a slightly higher-priced supplier may do the trick for you far more effectively.

971 — SUPPLIER SALES PEOPLE

Don't neglect good supplier salespeople as a source of ideas. True, they can break up your work day and divert your attention from more productive and scheduled projects.

So schedule them, perhaps with a one-day-a-month salesmen's day. They get around and view lots of operations, and thus frequently can pass winning ideas to you.

972 — SOURCE ASSISTANCE

If you are new to direct mail and sales promotion, remember that every consultant, agency, broker, manager, compiler, envelope house, and letter-shop can recommend you to several sources for assistance.

If the individuals you have contacted cannot recommend you to those sources, they do not have the experience you need for your programs.

973 — GIMMICK SALESMAN

Beware the gimmick or format salesman who tries to convince you to use his particular product.

Chances are it's the one on which he makes the most profit. Examine it with a view toward how it would work for you, of course, but also consider competitive formats.

While his gimmick or format may be a good method of involving your reader and attracting attention, the best way to increase response, after finding good lists, is to change your offer and use copy that immediately relates your product or service to the reader's self-interest.

And did you ever consider that you might be able to print a similar format at lower expense? You might. Usually not, but...

Whenever you fall in love with a particular format that's patented by a particular supplier, ask yourself whether the quantity you'll be mailing would enable you to produce a very similar format less expensively yourself!

974 — LIST COMPILER

A list compiler is only as good as his sources.

Make sure you ask about the specific sources — directories, rosters, attendees lists — that were used in the compilation of each specific list you request from a compiler.

975 — LIST BROKER SPECIALISTS

Do not deal with just one list broker or compiler. Compare the recommendations from each and then determine who you are using for each specific order.

Each broker or compiler can bring you different experience, and each will have a different view of the value of your business for his or her company.

When you'd like to compare list recommendations from your current source, or get new ideas, you might call Sue Polan at Response Mailing Lists, 305-652-4610. Yes, that's one of my companies.

976 — FREELANCE COPYWRITER

René, if you're hunting for a free-lance copywriter for your promotion pieces, must he or she — in addition to having direct response copy experience — have specific experience in your field?

The answer is preferably, but not necessarily. If he has successfully sold a wide variety of direct response items, especially including subscriptions and insurance (the toughest propositions to sell), chances are he can do a good job for you.

977 — LIMITED CREATIVE COPYWRITERS

For critical projects, rarely use a creative copywriter or consultant who has worked for only one or two organizations all his life, unless he's worked for your competitor.

He brings you the knowledge and experience thresholds of only those one or two companies.

978 — THE BEST COPYWRITERS

Use the best writers you can find and pay them a bit more than they ask to give their best product!

What, René? You'd spend my money like that!

Yes, here's why:

If a writer quotes you $3,000, tell him you'll give him $3,300. He'll be so startled that he may put everyone else's work aside and concentrate fully on your promotion. If that extra 10% results in 1/10th of a percentage point

in increased response you may be far ahead of the game.

P.S. I learned that from a client who once surprised me with extra money on a writing assignment. You can imagine my positive reaction.

979 — CREATIVE PERSON

Working with the modern creative person is not a difficult undertaking.

Give him or her adequate backgrounding, a full description of your goals, adequate history of your customers' purchasing habits, an indication of what worked and what didn't...and then go away and let your creative person work unencumbered by a daily flow of questions and phone calls from you.

980 — RESEARCH MANAGER

Unless your company has an experienced survey research manager, you are better advised to hire an outside research consultant when you want to survey your customer or prospect audience.

Survey research is so complicated and question phrasing so vital that you must have expert assistance or you will not get back the true information you require.

981 — OBJECTIVE OBSERVER

Remember that an early impression of your product or service from a previously-established relationship or from a first view of your promotion piece is extremely difficult to change.

That's why it's a good practice to find an intelligent, objective person, far removed from your organization's environment, to view your entire creative effort before you rush it to print. Often such an outsider can offer valuable tips on making your presentation more palatable.

982 — GUARANTEED PERCENTAGE

Any consultant, agency, creative individual, or mailing list source guaranteeing a certain percentage of response to your continuing direct mail efforts is a logical candidate for you to avoid.

983 — CONSULTANTS

Do not be afraid to use consultants for specific aspects of your direct response and sales promotion campaigns. You already use financial consultants in the form of accountants, controllers, and tax advisors. And you're not hesitant to hire legal consultants.

Similarly, there are specialists for almost every field of marketing. Interview a few. Work with one on a short trial basis. Then determine whether the input from a fresh mind can be valuable to your operation.

984 — FRESH IDEAS

In retaining a consultant, you are mainly looking for fresh ideas and evaluations of your operation.

Probe his mind and encourage him to get back to you with memo lists of his ideas.

| Illustration #79 |

Reprinted from René Gnam's RESPONSE REVIEW *Newsletter ... see technique #983 (also #953 in Chapter 23).*

New Computer Woes from Oklahoma...

On a consulting visit to a new direct marketing operation in Oklahoma, consultant René Gnam discovered and corrected woeful database programming fields. You might review these errors to be certain your mailings are effective:

◆ First name, middle initial, and last name all were in one field. It would be impossible to address a letter to Mr. Jones or Ms. Smith or to search by last name.

◆ No fields existed for effort keys or list codes. Analysis would be impossible.

◆ No addition was possible for dollar value of multiple orders, so the client couldn't compute customer value levels.

◆ No distinction was made between home and work addresses or ship to and bill to addresses, meaning follow-up mailings could go to the wrong address.

The client had installed an expensive mini and used a programmer recommended by the hardware manufacturer. You know better. Use direct response specialists.

CHAPTER 25

POSTAL QUESTIONS

Don't you get angry when your telephone company suddenly tells you that you have a new area code? Usually that notice comes with little advance warning and you're stuck with a last-minute job of notifying all your customers and reprinting all your stationery, promotional materials, and office forms.

Well, please don't think that the phone company has an exclusive on such shennanigans, frequently called "progress."

Your beloved postal service acts similarly with notices about changes it suddenly makes in zip codes. You get very little advance warning, and, as with the phone company, you have no voice in the matter.

That's why you rarely should have inventories that will last over a year or two. Sooner or later, the phone company and/or the post office will make your inventories obsolete.

At least the telephone company will allow you to pay for its referral number service after an interim changeover period. The post office, on the other hand, just sends your incoming mail back to the sender after expiration of the changeover period.

I can understand doing that with personal, residential mail. Certainly Aunt Clara and Uncle Abe can notify their comparatively few relatives, friends, and charge facilities of their new address within the one-year changeover period.

But businesses with thousands, or even millions, of customers have a more difficult and far more expensive job. It takes several notices to those customers to get them to jot down a new address. Sometimes it takes several notices to directory publishers to get them to do it right. And how many people, companies, and libraries continue using old directories with our old listings?

> Since businesses keep the post office in business, don't you agree that the post office should help us defray our cost of notifying customers when it arbitrarily changes our addresses? I think so. It's to the post office's advantage to have us send those costly notices. It means less work for the mailmen and more money for the postal service.

Here's a lulu of an example of what we all put up with:

When you read this, my zip codes will be changed from 33589 to 34689 and from 33590 to 34690.

As you know from reading this book, the 34689 zip applies to my street address and 34690 is for my post office box. Okay, so far? But we were not notified of any impending change by this writing.

It seems that many Northern migrants are moving to Florida, and the post office believes that too many people here have the same zip code. Of course, ZIP+4 was supposed to solve that problem.

But it's not good enough, apparently, because now our regional postal executives are asking Washington to change our zips so fewer people and companies will be in each of the new zips they'll assign. Washington will make whatever decision it wants. That decision will be made by people in a different office from the ZIP+4 staff.

How do I know about 34689 and 34690? An enterprising newspaper reporter interviewed a postal bigwig about the 1986 Christmas Card season and printed a few paragraphs about the impending zip changes in her story tucked away deep inside the Saturday paper. She reported that 34689 and 34690 are what our local postal people want.

What did I do in the meantime? Exactly the same as you would do. Exactly the same as you're doing now. We sit and wait until a newspaper reporter gives us the final word. If we miss the story in the paper, don't worry. The post office will stick a slip in our incoming mail about a month before the change.

Wonderful, isn't it? We pay the taxes that enable the loafers to loaf, and to earn higher salaries than school teachers, and to complain because our mailboxes are more than so many inches from the curb, and to misdirect our mail, and to tell us we've addressed our customers incorrectly when the postal service supplied the wrong change of address information.

Now you know why I've entitled this chapter "postal questions."

I got a kick reading the 1985-1986 United States Postal Service ads that touted ZIP+4 by quoting Robert Turley of AT&T's American Transtech: "The changeover process was surprisingly easy and economical." Sure, if you have AT&T mainframes and a staff of programmers. Pity the poor folks with minis. Greater pity to those of us who use micros.

Do you know why the zip code was invented in the first place? Postal workers can't read. So ZIP, which means "Zoning Improvement Plan", was designed to let machines read. That was way back in 1965. As I proof this just as summer 1989 begins, the post office still hasn't bought enough machines to do the reading. They keep saying so each time they file their annual budget. They've said it for 24 years.

I remember the postal people testifying in Congress in 1965. Zip code, they promised, would mean speedier delivery of all classes of mail. Maybe that's why so many businesses today choose independent couriers or fax when the mail has to get where it's going on time. Now, USPS is saying exactly the same thing about better service with ZIP+4. Oh, by the way, ZIP+4 sounds like it means 9 digits. Do that with fixed fields and see how fouled up you'll be. It's 10 digits due to Washington's insertion of a hyphen between the ZIP and the 4.

Washington? I was there in 1965, testifying before the House Post Office and Civil Service Committee several times, and also before the House Subcommittee on Postal Facilities and Modernization. You'll find some of my testimony on pages 145-149 of H.R. 5180, relating to mechanization and zip code implementation.

At that time, my office was on 57th Street in New York City, while my fulfillment company was exactly 71 blocks away. First class mail took 3 - 4 days between those two points. It still does. So domestically, things haven't gotten worse...or better.

Today, I have a business partner who owns an advertising agency in Denmark. It takes my airmail letters 8 - 14 days to get to him. His get here in 4 - 7 days. Why? I asked my sectional center representative about this. "Outbound mail gets held up at Kennedy," I was told. "Not inbound?" I asked. "No."

"Why?" I asked again. "Who knows," the gentleman shrugged.

Who knows, indeed.

Who knows why standard delivery time for third class mail from one point within a city to another point in the same city is 3 - 7 days? Why should it take so long when we sort it? Do you believe you can count on 3 - 7 days? Don't be silly.

Who knows how long it takes for your first or third class mail to get delivered across the country? No one. You no longer can accurately predict delivery. That's because we now have the "speedier" zip code program and the "even speedier" ZIP+4.

I was in London a while back. Pretty big city. At a morning meeting with my solicitor in one postal code area, he decided he needed a newly written document from another solicitor in another postal area. My attorney's secretary typed a letter requesting the new document and mailed it at about 10:15. I sat there astonished as my solicitor told me to come back "before 4" to collect the reply. I was astounded. You can't do that in St. Louis, or Louisville, or any city in Louisiana, all smaller than London. I came back at 3:30. The secretary handed me the reply. It had a cancelled stamp on it. The request and the reply to it had been delivered across town in a single day.

Do you know what's wrong with our post office? I do.

Our postal executives like to compare our service with other countries in the world. That inflates their egos and makes them complacent because we rank pretty high. Naturally. Many third world countries can't pay their postal workers very much. But they can't send men to walk on the moon either. We do. They don't have the technology. We do. But we mis-manage the advanced technology that we have. We constantly tell ourselves we're pretty good, and the truth is that we're not so bad. It's just that merry old England treats business like business. We don't.

Imagine that! Postal workers in Britain get paid less per hour, but they work harder and faster and more accurately in a country that we often say is behind the times!

Now, I make a good living because we do have a functioning post office. Most of the mail does get delivered somehow, sometime. That helps me employ lots of other people at lots of supplier companies. I'd make a better living and employ a lot more people if we had more than a post office that just functions.

Would someone with greater clout than me please tell that to the head honchos at the United States Postal Service? I did, before Congressmen. Few people reacted.

But there's hope...

> **Some day, some how, some way, we'll get a postmaster general who once ran a successful direct mail business.**
>
> **Wow! Wouldn't that be just terrific? It would. For every business in this land!**

985 — POSTAL SERVICE

The postal service moves the mail that is easiest for it to handle first.

Thus, if you use carrier-sequenced bulk rate mail, it frequently is delivered before first class mail, even though you pay less.

986 — SPEED OF DELIVERY

As your quantity of third class mail increases, the speed of delivery of that mail increases.

Post offices would sooner get rid of a complete sack than individual pieces, and they would sooner get rid of a full trailer load of mail than an individual sack.

987 — DIRECT MAIL CREATIONS

If you are curious as to whether your direct mail creations are mailable according to postal statutes, consult with the Mailing Requirements Officer in the nearest big city.

This postal official is supposed to be able to respond to any question regarding layouts. Photocopies of proposed layouts should be sufficient to secure a ruling. If your regional Mailing Requirements Officer cannot answer your inquiry, he will obtain a ruling from Washington...someday.

988 — POST OFFICE SCALE

Can you use your office scale to weigh your mailing piece to determine postal rates?

No! Use the scale at the post office of dispatch!

989 — SATURDAY MAILING

If you are using first class mail to businesses, try not to mail on Thursday or Friday as your promotions would be arriving on Monday — the heaviest day for receipt of mail at business addresses.

If your mail arrives on Tuesday, Wednesday, or Thursday, there is a better chance of the executive having time to give your promotion piece thorough consideration.

So, mail on Saturday. It pays off.

990 — ADDRESS CORRECTION REQUESTED

Ask the post office for "Address Correction Requested" service only on your house list mailings. It's too expensive on mailings to rented lists, prospect lists, and other external files.

However, you may wish to test the "nixie" factor on outside lists by asking for address correction service on a small test quantity. In that event, make sure the owner of the outside list will reimburse you for nixies.

Do you do that, René?

Yes, but rarely. I recognize that it's valid for marketers who have rather low selling prices. Most of my clients, if their products have teeny-weeny prices, sell them in quantity. The others usually sell the high-priced spread. In both of those situations, it doesn't pay to test the nixie factor. Your bottom line is what's important. You're making enough money on those who do reply, so why worry excessively about those who don't get the mailing. If the list is good enough to reach payout, that's it!

Of course, you need to use your return address on the outgoing envelope if you intend to have the postal service send back address corrections.

René, are you saying that there are occasions when I might not use my return address?

Sure! Frequently! You don't always need a return address. Why start a mailing with an address? Think about it. When you place that address in the upper left corner, it's the first thing that your recipient sees. Maybe, in some instances, it will prevent you from being as creative as you might otherwise be in using that space to start selling.

The only time you're required to use a return address is when you mail at discounted non-profit rates. And, fairly soon I predict, those discounts will disappear anyway. So then all of us will be free to eliminate our return addresses if we so desire.

991 — COUNTRY'S STAMP
If you have a general consumer product, you may want to try mailing from Canada or Mexico into the United States using a stamp of the country from which you are mailing to increase interest and provoke readership.

992 — CREATING GOODWILL
Sometimes a postage meter imprint denoting a worthy cause on the envelope that you use to pitch a product or service to a prospect can create goodwill for you as a mailer who cares about the world, the environment or social issues.

However, it won't increase your response unless your promotion ties in with that worthy cause, and then the increase will be very small.

993 — METERED MAIL
If you use metered mail, don't forget that you can design a special advertising message to go with the meter imprint. The only instances in which I've seen response go up by this technique have been in political or cause fund-raising.

Most mailers who use these special, and very low cost, imprints, never bother to split-test them. Probably because the imprints are so inexpensive, the mailers figure they're not worth a split-test expense. But did you ever stop to think that the meter imprint might depress response? It could.

994 — BULK RATE
When mailing bulk rate, remember that precancelled stamps slightly outpull meter impressions, which slightly outpull printed indicias.

995 — SURCHARGES
Ask the regional director of your post office for a template that shows standardized envelope sizes which are not subject to surcharges for first class and single-piece third class mail.

996 — SERVICE RATE
Remember that the United States Postal Service recently changed its regulations to say that any letter or other mailing piece affixed to the outside of another mailing piece now travels at the service rate appropriate for the "principal mailing piece, regardless of the class of the mail enclosed."

Thus, the old technique of affixing a first class letter to a fourth class

Illustration #80

Examine the outgoing #12 envelope below. Notice how this René Gnam creation for The Practice Builder *starts selling immediately, technique #990. If, on the other hand, it had started with the client's return address, it would have slowed the reader from getting to the sales message. Yes, there are times when it helps your image to have a more conservative envelope bearing more acceptable display material.*

But when an envelope containing such powerful inserts starts selling instantly, it warms up the recipient to the sales message inside. It starts him in your direction!

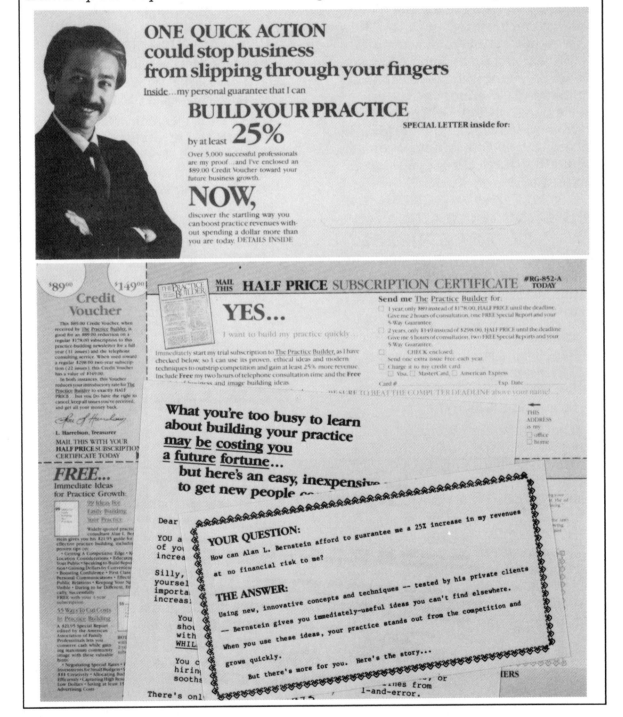

parcel will no longer do as a method of achieving first class delivery for fourth class matter.

997 — MONTH AND YEAR

If you cannot put a date on your direct mail letter — because it is going by third class and you are worried about delivery — you can achieve the effect of a date by simply using the month and year or a phrase such as "July 1999 — our 16th year of service."

Or, you can do as Ronnie Reagan did when running for re-election to Pennsylvania Avenue.

He dated his letters "Thursday."

If you received them on Friday or Saturday, you were happy. If you got them after the weekend, you figured the post office was tardy.

998 — P.O. BOX AND STREET ADDRESS

If you use a post office box for your mail delivery point, also include your actual street address on a line just above the post office box.

EXAMPLE:
René Gnam Consultation Corporation
1 Response Road
Box 3877
Holiday, FL 34690-3877

That's how my letterhead reads. Mail goes to the post office box, while I reassure hesitant prospects that I'm not hiding behind a post office box number because I do have a street address.

But recognize that any citizen can go to the post office and ask for the correct name and address of a box-holder. By federal postal regulation, the local postmaster must give this information to an inquirer. Thus, if you really do have a fly-by-night, rip-off operation and want to hide behind

a post office box number, you're out of luck. Thankfully!

René, is this a good time to ask how you happen to have a Response Road in two states?

Sure. Technique No. 196 describes how I got it in Massachusetts. But in Florida, I really do live and work on a street named Response Road. I named it. Why not? I own it. And, it's on the official county map as of November 3, 1986. The correct street address is:

René Gnam Consultation Corporation
1 Response Road
Tarpon Springs, FL 34689-9484

Note the different city and zip code. We use the street address only for United Parcel, Federal Express, Emery, Purolator, and other couriers. All U.S. Mail goes to the post office box in Holiday.

Okay, René, why a post office box in a different city from your home and office setting?

It's another one of those postal follies, like Bethesda, MD, being in the sectional center for Washington, DC. In my case, the post office in Holiday (Pasco County) supervises the post office in Tarpon Springs (Pinellas County). Holiday gets the mail faster.

Now, René, why is all this important to me?

Because you want to establish a unique address somewhere so you can trace what other mailers are doing. Here's an outline:

I use 1 Response Road for all my normal business endeavors. But if I want to learn how often ABC Company mails to its prospects, I may use 2 Response Road. Then, I might use 3 Response Road for XYZ Company.

If I get XYZ mail at 2 Response Road, I know that XYZ has rented a list from ABC. If I'm XYZ's competitor, then by seeing how often XYZ rents from ABC, I'll have a good inkling that perhaps I should test the ABC list.

You're cagey, René. Is that legal?

Yes it is, and it's fun. Place your name on various lists that you suspect are used by your competitors. Use a slightly different address for each list. Keep a log book of how the incoming mail is flowing. You'll learn more than you ever expected.

But, what if I don't own a road?

You own a house? Use different apartment numbers.

You live in an apartment? Use different first names.

You live with a wonderful person who is the only "entitled" name at your address? Invent different company names or change his or her name.

It can be done. The information you'll derive is enormous.

But, René, you never said how you got the money to buy Response Road and Response Ranch?

I worked hard. Still do.

999 — CORRECTED ADDRESSES

Whenever you receive a post office correction on your mailing list, immediately mail the same promotion piece to the new "corrected" address.

A number of the "corrected" addresses will, in fact, be incorrect and you will receive a second "correction" which is likely to be more accurate than the first. You also will receive some orders from the re-mailing, frequently sufficient orders to pay the cost of re-mailing to verify the "correction" that wasn't in error.

Well, René, could I run my list against the NCOA file?

You could, if you want to spend a lot of money for next to nothing. NCOA (the United States Postal Service's

attempt to maintain a National Change of Address file) is loaded with goofs by the Post Office.

For instance?

Okay, two *examples:*

1. For business-to-business mailers...the NCOA list doesn't make any attempt to identify different business names at the same address. Thus, if one business moves out of a building that's about to be torn down, the post office doesn't change the addresses for all the other companies that are about to move. It has no way to get all those addresses easily. And if you have two companies in that building and notify the post office of your new address for one of the companies, but not the other, the NCOA file won't have both.

2. For consumer mailers...NCOA doesn't recognize apartment numbers. This may seem daffy to you. What's the big deal about the difference between Apartment 10J and Apartment 10K? A very big deal. You see, the post office has a regulation which says "mail will be delivered to the address to which it is addressed." So, if your prospect's apartment isn't recognized by NCOA, and if you don't have the correct apartment number, the 238,000 proven carriers of the mail have the right to not deliver your mail. And they won't! If you address to Martin Miranda at Apartment 10J and he lives in Apartment 10K, he may not get your wonderful mailing.

Yikes, René! What's the solution?

Maintain your file with all the due

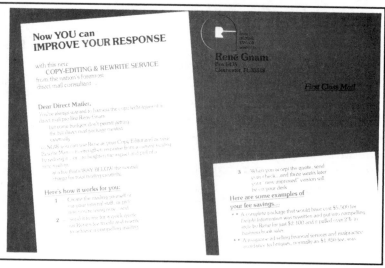

Illustration #81

Technique #1,001 asks you to consider an unusual size for your mailing, like this post-card for the author's copy-writing service. It's 9-1/2 x 6-1/8, way over standard size.

But it's also done in full color and presents a letter on a slant.

Unusual? Yes! And that's what your mail must be to stand out and get attention.

diligence you and your staff can muster. Pray a lot. Mail a letter to customers who the post office says have incorrect addresses. Ask them to supply every detail of their address for you.

EXAMPLE:

As I was editing the final version of this book on the microcomputers at my desk, my secretary mailed two letters on the same day to a client whose office is just 22 miles from mine. He owns the building. There is no other denizen of that building.

Both envelopes were addressed exactly the same, using the same block of address text on my secretary's computer. One came back marked "NSN." NSN means "no such number." My secretary called the client. His secretary acknowledged that we had the right address and that her boss had, indeed, received the other letter.

So a hint for you here is to call customers when you get NSN mail.

1,000 — DIMENSIONAL STANDARDS

As a final checking point before setting type, review the size of your final piece against the Dimensional Standards template issued by the postal

service. This applies to both First Class and Single-Piece Third Class (not bulk). Also, be sure to check your reply envelope size against the template.

If either the outgoing piece or the incoming piece is over the "standards," you will be spending more on postage than you might anticipate.

1,001 — AN UNUSUAL SIZE

When planning and designing your mailing for first class or single-piece third class, consider the Dimensional Standards, but also consider the impact that a larger or "unusual" size piece would have.

I have sometimes been willing to pay the extra postage cost because of the greater attention commanded by an unusual size. Not always. Sometimes.

Remember that I usually want my outgoing mail to look, or feel, or seem a little different from all the other mail that reaches my targets. Sameness is dull and boring. Being different can attract attention.

You want to attract attention. Getting noticed in a pile of mail is the very first step in getting your mail opened.

Go for it!

CHAPTER 26

BONUS IDEAS

This is the "surprise" section of this book, and thus, I'm free to chat about anything that strikes my fancy. My fancy wants to talk about jargon. Use jargon carefully, please.

Many beginning copywriters don't realize the importance of using jargon carefully. Pros in every field will know if you've used their "slanguage" properly, and one error kills response.

Jargon's fine, if you know how to use it. Often it tells your reader that your company really does know its business in his field. That's supportive. That's wonderful. But overuse jargon and you convince me you're scheming.

A typical example of bad jargon is probably on or near your desk right now. It pervades software documentation. Manuals seem unable to escape jargon, perhaps because people who write about computers are in love with computer machinations and the jargon that goes with them. They also seem to speak a language beyond the comprehension of R2D2.

Eliminating jargon from software manuals becomes more important as more people use computers. (Microsoft Corporation agrees, and some of the comments in this chapter introduction are based on "typos.doc" in MS Word V 4.0.) The same is true in direct mail creativity as we explore wider markets.

My example for this dissertation is that the new breed of computer owner is an expert in particular business, scholarly, or industrial tasks, but uninterested in computers except as tools for getting the job done faster, easier, and more thoroughly. For these people, jargon is a hindrance, a stumbling block, an irritation. Sales of particular software or "bundled" computer systems will be limited if jargon confronts prospective purchasers.

EXAMPLE:
The word "replicate" constantly crops up in many spreadsheet programs. It usually is a verb command meaning "copy exactly" in those programs. No such dictionary meaning exists.

The dictionary says a "replication" can be a copy, but "replicate" and "replicated" are adjectives referring to items folded back over themselves. Thus, "replicated paper" would be folded paper. Then, the computer "replicate" isn't defined similarly in all spreadsheet software. Some replicate exactly, while others allow you to make changes during replication.

This illustration indicates that jargon in any field can be an effective shorthand among those who understand it, but it is a barrier to the uninitiated. I doubt that those who spray jargon around the landscape really intend to offend or cut off others who don't know the lingo, but the effect is the same regardless of the motives.

> **To replace jargon in your direct mail, try supporting the illustrations with callouts to important features. Then, even if you cannot avoid the jargon, at least the user has a clearer image of how some of the ideas fit together.**

Back to the computer industry.

Until now, manuals have tried five solutions, with varying success:

1. Give definitions with examples in a "help" file that can be accessed and read on the screen as well as in the manual.
2. Provide glossaries of technical terms in parentheses in the text.
3. Provide a glossary of terms, usually as part of the manual addenda.
4. Express the ideas in other words.
5. Provide templates as samples of how to process certain applications.

Each of these solutions helps the new reader, but each also has drawbacks. The best solution will come from a new generation of software that is free of jargon, because a new generation of computers will provide significant built-in resource chips and expanded mother boards to support advanced software applications.

Similar thinking is required in direct mail copywriting.

You may know everything there is to know about trochanters and haversian canals. But are all the doctors and nurses you write to familiar with them? Perhaps it would be better to say "bumps on bones" and "channels in bones." Perhaps not. Perhaps there are better words.

The point of this illustration is that even though I had to learn about those wonderful bone attributes before I could write about them — and I did — I had to recognize that the jargon might not be understood by all who read it.

Yes, you certainly do need to know about some of the technicalities of a product or service or market. But be cautious not to weave too much of your new knowledge into your copy.

And be extremely careful with that "new" word: *enhancement.*

You and I know that an enhancement is an improvement.

In the computer world, many people today say that enhancements really are corrections to enable the software to do what it was supposed to do when it was first released. So, if your product has "enhanced" features, it may signal some folks that the product never worked right before!

Does all this tell you that direct mail marketing is hard work? It is.

When you started reading this book, I didn't say your marketing endeavors would be easy. But I certainly hope that this book has made them easier!

And, with that in mind, here are some more techniques for you...

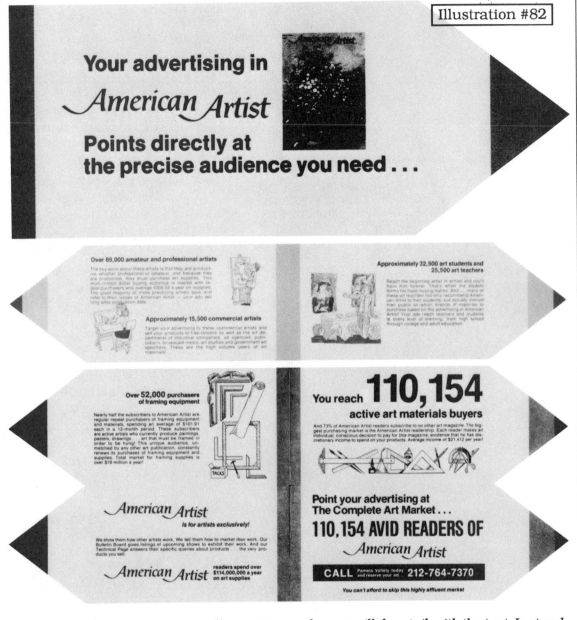

Since this is a bonus section, my illustrations no longer will dovetail with the text. Instead, I'll present some of my favorite mailings and give you some added recommendations for your own mailings. We'll start with a very low budget (they're not bad, if you do some extra thinking) that I had on this mailing for American Artist.

It's all one color — black — on yellow stock. The entire mailing is just this folder, a short one-color letter, and an old envelope from inventory.

But note the drama of the simulated pencil points. With just two extra cuts, I've made the folder look like a cluster of artist's drawing pencils. From top to bottom, you're looking at the front cover, the first unfolded spread, and then the inner spread. Nifty.

My recommendation to you: when you're on a very tight budget, sit under your favorite palm tree and fold some paper. You'd be surprised at the new ideas you'll get.

And now we move on with a high budget (aren't they grand, when you can get them) that I had on this mailing for Penthouse.

Almost everything is full color, including both sides of the outgoing envelope. But there's a hidden technique that applies to all mailers, not just those who are after subscriptions.

Notice that you can't read the left edge of the letter copy? That's because all those magazine covers are on a flap, folded over the letter. It forces the reader to peek underneath. When he opens the flap, he sees more pretty pictures on the left, and gets the full letter on the right. Got the concept? Involve your reader with the letter — physically! Once he opens the flap, he almost has to read your letter copy. Well, at least the headlines. Neat idea? Even if you're a cave-dweller without a palm tree, you can still get marvelous ideas by folding paper. Go ahead. Try it on your favorite rooftop garden.

1,002 — SOMETHING EXTRA

Scratch your head. Can you give your customer something extra without charging him or her? Something the customer doesn't expect when ordering, but which is very pleasing on receipt of the order?

For instance, you purchased this book anticipating 1,001 techniques. Here we are with No. 1,002 and a few more follow for you and others on your staff to review. You have a "bonus" you didn't expect from the promotional copy.

Doing this creates good will with your customers and can make future sales easier. Your mail will be looked at as coming from "good guys." Think about it and try to do it whenever possible.

It is called "lagniappe," giving something extra without charge. Ask a New Orleans eatery for a dozen shrimp or clams and you'll get 13. The thirteenth is "lagniappe."

1,003 — ONLY ONE ADDRESS

Use only one address for your company in each mailing, or you will confuse the recipient of your mailing piece.

Decide — before you write copy — whether you are going to use your headquarters address or an individual branch office address, whether you are going to use the editorial publishing office address or the subscription fulfillment address.

One...or the other...not both!

1,004 — CONTINUED MAILING

Continue mailing to inquirers who have not purchased for as long as the mailings prove profitable.

Some mailers can send 10 or 12 different packages to inquirers before the cost of converting that inquirer to a purchaser becomes prohibitive.

1,005 — A FRIENDLY GREETING

Instead of using occupant mail or rural route mail or boxholder mail with "householder" or other innocuous designations, try to add some warmth and friendliness on the line usually reserved for "boxholder."

A local retailer, for instance, could say "Hello neighbor."

Remember that most people look at their names and addresses because a name is one of an individual's most prized possessions. If you can't use the name, a friendly greeting may open the door for you.

1,006 — METRIC SYSTEM?

If you like the metric system in referring to sizes or capacities, by all means use metric measurements — but in North America be sure to accompany the metric measurements with the equivalents in inches or pounds.

1,007 — MATCHBOOK ADVERTISING

Often totally ignored by direct mail marketers to consumer audiences is the vast potential of matchbook advertising. Matchbooks are printed in the billions. You can control distribution areas to meet your specifications.

Do not expect high response rates. And test this medium only for inquiries with a small, but statistically random spread throughout your geographical area. If you start with a relatively small quantity and tally up-front responses with a spreadsheet evaluation that includes back-end

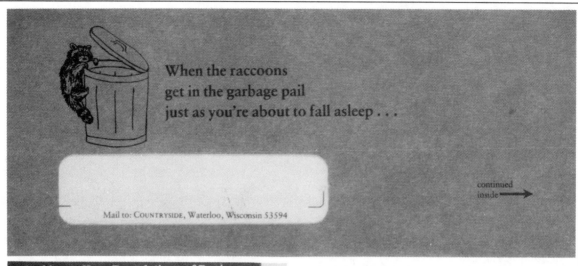

When the raccoons
get in the garbage pail
just as you're about to fall asleep . . .

Mail to: COUNTRYSIDE, Waterloo, Wisconsin 53594

continued
inside →

Inside . . . Your Foundations of Business Excellence on Audio-Cassettes!

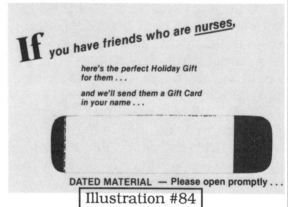

If you have friends who are **nurses**,

here's the perfect Holiday Gift
for them . . .

and we'll send them a Gift Card
in your name . . .

DATED MATERIAL — Please open promptly . . .

Illustration #84

To illustrate how a direct mail designer's thinking and execution must change as his target audience changes, here's a variety of first impressions these Gnam readers get:
  TOP: Just black ink is used on orange paper to attract homestead owners to this renewal mailing for Countryside. MIDDLE LEFT: Full color on semi-gloss stock is used to convey quality to business executive audiences for Newstrack Executive Classics. MIDDLE RIGHT: Two ink colors are used on white to ask nurses to give gift subscriptions to Nurses' Drug Alert. BOTTOM: Three colors plus a slanted black-on-yellow sticker invites exhibit booth managers to a DisplayMasters educational seminar.

YOU ARE INVITED to learn 200 new ways to . . .

★ DISCOVER Newest Trends in Exhibiting with Trade Shows,
★ GET Pre-Screened, Pre-Qualified Leads and Convert Them,
★ CAPTURE More Sales with Trade Shows,

on Tuesday, December 11, 1984 at the new Minneapolis Amfac Hotel

where you'll hear three of America's most successful consultants
Allen Konopacki   Rene Gnam   Dick Swandby
give you an exciting treasury of sales and marketing concepts
you'll be quick to adopt . . . all yours for just $95 at:

YOU CAN SEND UP TO 3 EXECS. ONLY

Exhibit Excellence & Effectiveness

OPEN THIS INVITATION & DISCOVER HOW HELPFUL ONE DAY CAN BE . . .

conversions, you may open a new, cost-effective source of customers.

1,008 — ENTICING SCENTS

Did you know that your direct mail can smell? Companies like 3M and Creative Perfumers can provide a fragrance for your direct mail promotion.

Scents entice recipients to open the mailing, fondle it, smell it, respond to it.

1,009 — SCRATCH AND SNIFF

Now you can have "scratch and sniff" with more than one odor on the same promotion page. A recent promotion used three different scents on the same page.

While this is extremely costly, it can be appealing, especially when used for food and beverage offers.

1,010 — WARMING TO A NAME

Does your signature have to be William or Constance or James or Rebecca?

Would Bill or Connie or Jim or Becky be warmer and more appropriate for your specific audience?

1,011 — BUSINESS REPLY SHIPPING LABEL

If you have always used reply envelopes or business reply envelopes, consider testing a business reply shipping label, printed exactly as you would a business reply envelope.

Just enclose it instead of an envelope. It's far less costly to you, permits the recipient to use his own envelope, and may not cut down on your response. Test it in a small quantity before rolling out.

In testing a business reply shipping label rather than a business reply envelope, be sure to identify the sticker with copy such as the following: "No stamp needed if you use our postage paid sticker on any envelope you have!"

What, René, a business reply shipping label?

Sure, it dramatizes the value of the offer you are testing. It's also great to enclose if you guarantee product returns. And you can use it effectively with review panels that must evaluate your product and then return it with comments. Or use it to get materials back from your sales force.

1,012 — RENE GNAM'S TESTED TECHNIQUES

While the techniques I have presented in this book have been based on extensive testing with my United States clients over the past 30 years, prepublication conferences with mail marketers in other countries have indicated that nearly all of the concepts and specific recommendations in this volume work just as effectively on other continents.

My personal direct mail marketing experience in Canada, Australia, the Bahamas, Brazil, Bermuda, New Zealand, West Germany, Japan, Switzerland, Korea, the United Kingdom, Singapore, and all the Scandinavian countries indicates that this is, indeed, true.

So you may wish to consider adapting your current winning promotions to markets in other countries, recognizing, of course, that what you translate from American English doesn't always mean the same thing in another language. (It doesn't always mean the same thing in other English speaking countries, either.)

Illustration #85

Two different copy and design orientations are used in these two mailings seeking the same goal: registration at a vacation island.

The top piece, for the International Association of Medical Specialists, presents many benefits and uses full color.

The bottom piece, for the author's St. Thomas seminar, is printed in green ink only on blue stock, and presents a few selected benefits for direct mailers.

There is more than one way to make a dollar.

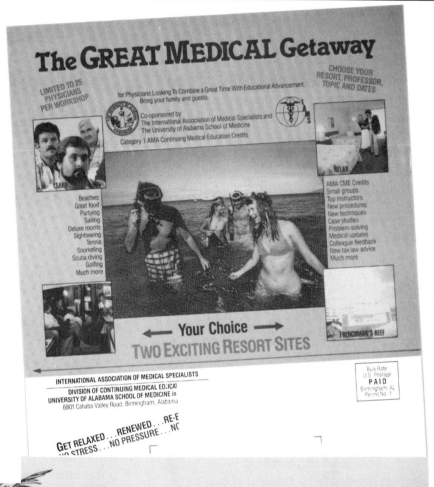

1,013 — A COMMENTARY ON OVERCOMING ADVERSITY

When I finished the first 25 chapters of this book, I set my lifetime project aside. And then, I woke early one day, strolled with my animals, plucked tangerines and lounged in my gazebo, clarifying editing that could be of value to you as you use my book to assist you in your direct mail marketing.

I took a short swim, then returned to Wendy and Wilma, my twin side-by-side word processors. As I wrote this chapter, I thought of the unusual way this book was produced, tight deadlines we all face, and production snafus that suddenly confront us. So allow me to indulge myself, please, with these few personal notes on what you can do — if your determination is there — when faced with the adversity of something you can't control.

I had written my rough draft of this manuscript with dictating machines over the course of many years. My secretaries transcribed, typed, retyped, and retyped again. Then, thinking I was going to self-publish the book, off it went to Jim Bryan at Jim's Quality Typesetting in Dunedin, Florida. He set the original version.

But business boomed and I just didn't have time to handle all the production details. It was more important to me to consult and create for clients, build my new Client Guest House, expand the ranch, and run my enjoyable seminars. So my good friend Anver Suleiman, the superior brain behind The Marketing Federation, rescued me with an introduction to Tom Power, a senior editor at Prentice-Hall, which became my publisher. Tom asked me to expand the manuscript by 30-35% so it would be usable as a college text in addition to being a reference for our prime audience of direct mail marketers.

Shortly after that introduction, lightning hit Response Ranch. No people or animals were hurt. But our complete phone system, all stereos and TVs, the satellite and VCRs, seven of our nine computer systems, and all eleven hard drives were wiped out — despite three universal power supply systems. The manuscript now existed only on Compugraphics disks. All my keyboarding was gone!

But Jim Bryan lent me his disks. Bunny Rauch, her brother Harry, and Jon Johnson converted all that keyboarding into ASCII so I could use MS-DOS to upload to Microsoft Word on new computer systems speedily obtained through Donna Gicking and Gary Emerson of Kemper Insurance. Of course, I then had to learn new software to strip out the imbedded Compugraphics codes. The next step was downloading to ASCII again, and transferring via RS232 to an older TRSDOS-based system so I could do my manuscript expansion editing in Scripsit, a faster word processor for me (at the time) since it was the first one I used.

When the manuscript for this book came back from Prentice-Hall, I had mastered the techology that you've probably mastered too. Now, I have lasers and other wonderfulnesses for word processing. Wendy and Wilma are gone. My lovely computer word processors now are Prudence and Patience.

You guessed it! I moved everything back to DOS — PC-DOS 3.3 — and with MS-Word V-4.0 produced this newly revised version on a souped-up PGI 386 with an Apple NTX laser printer. Then, up it all went into Page-Maker 3.0 for typesetting, copyfitting, and pagination by yours truly.

The benefit to you? I had to go through every thought twice more, updating some more...so you are holding the very latest output. Use it well!

And so, with thanks to Anver and Tom, Bunny and Harry and Jon, Donna and Gary, and especially to Jim, voilà...here's the book.

When sudden adversity hits you, your campaigns, or your projects, take a break. Then ask your friends for advice, for help. It will work for your dilemma as it did for mine.

One more personal note...

My Mom taught me how to type when I was 11. I received my first writing paycheck when I was 12. But when she saw the 105,164 words (Wendy and Wilma counted them) in my original 25 chapters — excluding captions, front and back matter — her smiles and voice lit up the landscape. Some mothers teach their children how to play a piano. Mine taught the literary piano. I think she did a good job, and I wanted you to know that.

1,014 — A FINAL WORD ON WINNING WITH DIRECT MAIL

To make the purchase of this book really pay off handsomely for you, remember that these techniques are to be carefully selected for each new promotion.

You should not attempt to incorporate every technique in each mailing. Rather, you should be searching for the breakthrough techniques that lead to winning direct mail.

While recognizing that all direct mail must be appropriately created to suit its target audience, I always attempt to be a bit daring in my quest for a breakthrough, perhaps a bit larger in size, bolder in tone, more graphic in design, more enticing with offers, more venturesome in testing new and different concepts. That's why my mail stands out from most other pieces that accompany it to a businessperson at a desk or a consumer at home.

Your readers will read only what appeals to them. Stretch your imagination so you create appeal, and use the appropriate techniques you need as a springboard to success.

I wish you Many Happy Returns

Epilogue

ABOUT DIRECT MAIL

It was New Year's Day in 1982. Many good friends gathered with Maxwell Sackheim, one of response advertising's all-time greats, at his son Sherman's house in Clearwater. We partied.

Max had reviewed and commented on early work on this volume and, in the shaky hand of a man well in his ninth decade, he wrote these words: "René Gnam's new book belongs in every direct marketer's library." Then he said, "I'll think of something else for the book, but if I don't get around to it, you tell 'em my Seven Deadly Mistakes."

He didn't get a chance to do "something else for the book." As he would probably say, he's in "that great response market in the sky." So, as Max instructed — and to both honor the man usually credited with launching the direct response profession and present a fitting windup to my tome — here are...

Seven Deadly Direct Mail Mistakes

by Maxwell Sackheim, 1890-1982

Most Direct Mail advertising calls for some sort of response. To be effective, therefore, it must be opened, read, believed and acted upon. But even if a direct reply is not desired, direct mail advertising should attract, interest and convince or it is wasted.

By eliminating one or several of the Seven Deadly Direct Mail Mistakes described here, your efforts will surely improve, whether you are selling goods, services or ideas, by mail, through stores, or through other channels.

DEADLY DIRECT MAIL MISTAKE #1 — Give the Prospect a Good Reason for Not Opening Your Mailing. The surest way to ruin a mailing is to give the prospect a good reason for not even opening the envelope! This can be done in a number of ways.

One is to tell so much on the envelope that the reader "knows" he doesn't want what you're offering inside.

Still another is to be so smart, so clever, or so unbelievable as a result of whatever you print on the envelope that the recipient subconsciously says "Nuts," "Baloney" or worse, "More Junk Mail."

Rather than risk the danger of printing anything on the envelope which might give anyone a good excuse for throwing it away unopened, use a blank envelope.

Even this might be a dead give-away to some sophisticated prospects. It is better by far to use the envelope as a vehicle for carrying a message in words or pictures which might be strong enough to be used as the headline of an advertisement.

Such a headline should convey news — a promise of information — a promise of an advantage to the reader, a promise of such importance that the reader cannot afford to deny the mailing at least an opening.

If you can't say anything on the outside of the envelope that will be of genuine interest to the reader, say nothing.

DEADLY DIRECT MAIL MISTAKE #2 — Give the Reader a Reason for Not Reading Your Mailing. Having induced the reader to open your mail, even if only by giving him no reason for not doing so, you are faced with the possibility of his discarding it unless his interest is held.

It is not enough to give him no reason for throwing your mailing away — you must definitely give him a reason for holding onto it and reading it!

You can accomplish this only by promising an adequate reward for his time and attention.

He must be promised NEWS of interest to him. He must be offered a CURE for whatever SYMPTOM he "suffers" from or can be "made" to suffer from!

Examine any mailing carefully. Take it out of the envelope just as any recipient would. What's the first thing you see? What's your quick impression? Is someone trying to sell you something? Is it likely to cost you money or will it do something for you? Are you being "sold" or invited to "buy"? What are all the enclosures about? Do they clutter the mailing up or make it look more interesting? Is the letterhead too revealing? Uninteresting? Too dull to invite a reading of your letter? Does the salutation promise you an adequate reward? Does the processing defeat the purpose intended? Is the offer attractive enough to deserve "top billing" or should it be "buried"?

Beware of the "so what" reaction. Indifference is normal. Only by shocking the reader, startling him, waking him up, can you gain the attention that will induce a reading of your mailing.

You know the fundamental urges which motivate people — the desire for love, beauty, wealth, leisure, approbation, health and so on. Among these you must find or create the symptom which your product or service cures. The more common the symptom, the wider your market.

If your mailing does not offer a "cure," you have given the recipient an excellent reason for not reading it.

DEADLY DIRECT MAIL MISTAKE #3 — *Make Trivial Tests.* Too many direct mail people are addicted to the insidious habit of over-testing. So serious is this disease that, where it exists in its most pernicious form, the unsuspecting victim loses his ability to think for himself, to judge, to make decisions, to act. His muscles of courage become atrophied and his power of discrimination calcifies. He believes the easy way out of any selling problem is to test. Why think when it is so easy to get the correct answer by mailing a couple of thousand?

But — is testing the key to personal success, or may it not, like fire, be a good thing only if there isn't too much of it?

If every test could safely be projected, much of the fallacy of testing would be eliminated. But we know how much difference there can be between the result of a test and the result of mailing.

Too many things can happen in these fast-moving times to destroy the logical or mathematical projection of a test. Within the span of a season, a month, or even a week, marked economic, competitive, or psychological changes can take place, and when they do, "blooie" go your expectations. And the element of elapsed time is only one of the dangers.

I have known of campaigns based on the result of a 200 test mailing — of weighty decisions arrived at by virtue of an infinitesimal difference in results between the use of stamps instead of metered mail, between colored envelopes and white, between No. 10 envelopes and No. 6.

One would think, after so many years of recorded experience, we would have learned that tests do not always tell the whole truth — that we will never completely formularize direct mail as long as there are changes in the weather, in world conditions, in domestic affairs, and even in local conditions from month to month and from week to week — that we will never be able to project a test with absolute assurance that the final result will be true to our original projection as long as an interval of time elapses between tests and mailings.

I am not arguing against testing, but against trivial testing. I object to tests which try to determine the best day of the week on which to mail, to tests which are intended to prove whether a price of $1.98 is better than $1.99, to tests of half a dozen or more slightly different letters, and to tests of 500, or even 1,000 to determine whether a proposition or a list is worth going ahead with on a large scale.

Tests that tell you nothing or actually mislead you are worse than none.

DEADLY DIRECT MAIL MISTAKE #4 — *Make Sales, Not Customers.* The difference between profit and loss in almost any business is the difference between creating a customer and merely making a sale. The one-time buyer can be a liability instead of an asset because of the selling and other costs involved in putting him on your books. A customer is someone you can afford to lose money to get. How much you can afford to lose depends on how many repeat sales you expect to make, how soon you make them, and your margin of profit on each. If you want to go broke selling direct by mail, make sales, not customers.

The best way to get new customers is to make offers your prospects can't resist. Bring them into your "store" with special sales, special bargains, special deals. Once in, they'll buy more than enough to offset the cost of getting them in. Cleverness, smart talk, wonderful logic, can only go so far. No matter how you juggle words, the order blanks spells out what you are offering.

Another way to get a new customer is to spend more time and thought on ex-customers. They dealt with you before and know you. If you mistreated them, confess your "crime," and beg forgiveness. If your values weren't as good as they are now, tell them why. Don't give up too easily on those names. You rent them to others — how come they can make them pay? What have you done to have driven them away from you? Find out, if you can, and bring them back on your active list.

Finally, establish your acceptable percentage of returns on the basis of making customers, not sales. It's the sound way, the only way to build a successful business.

DEADLY DIRECT MAIL MISTAKE #5 — *People Won't Read Long Letters.* The whole question is, what is a long letter? Any letter that is uninteresting is a long letter! Even a short letter can seem long! Indeed, a short paragraph can seem long, and a short first sentence can make the rest of the letter unnecessary if it doesn't say and mean something worthwhile to the reader.

Revising the old cliché — it isn't how you say it but what you say that makes the difference between a successful letter and a failure. The slickest writing, the finest paper, printing and art work, can't make a good idea out of a bad one or an attractive offer out of a poor one.

Give me the right merchandise, the right price, and the right audience and if I have enough to say I will make ten pages of typewritten copy pay better than one, two or three. On the contrary, with nothing much to work on, and nothing much to say, a single page might seem longer than ten pages of interesting material.

Don't be afraid to use many paragraphs, many pages, if you need lots of space in which to tell your story. It's far better to do a complete selling job on 2% than a half-selling job on 10%. If anything, most letters are too short because of the fear of making them too long.

Don't believe "people won't read long letters." People read long books, take long trips, watch long movies and plays, and read long letters provided they justify the time. They must be interesting. They must promise a profit, in entertainment, in money, in enlightenment.

Letters are long only when they seem long, when they are deadly dull, obviously selfish, when they are written to sell, not to serve.

DEADLY DIRECT MAIL MISTAKE #6 — *Let the Lists Go to the Last.* Direct Mail is a bull's-eye medium. Its very reason for existence rests on its ability to select the prospect or customer and aim a silver bullet with your story.

The reason many mailings fail is that they are directed to too many wrong people. Wrong people can be people who have moved, died, or who never in the world could afford or want your product.

The "right people" start with your own list — and it behooves you to keep that list clean. Whether active customers, inactives or old prospects, there is no waste quite comparable to waste on your own list. Next come the lists of mail-order buyers of related products. After that, mail-order buyers of unrelated products who have purchased through a plan similar to yours, i.e.: open account, C.O.D., cash in advance, time payment, etc. Finally, compiled lists, preferably by logical occupations or classifications: doctors, lawyers, engineers, clergymen, automobile owners.

If you can't spend the necessary time to find the right kind of lists for you, or if you just don't trust yourself, consult a reliable list broker as you would a doctor or an attorney.

The selection of lists is so vital a part of Direct Mail that to give it less than the most serious thought and analysis is to commit one of the biggest Direct Mail Mistakes possible! For nothing can take the place of the right marketplace!

DEADLY DIRECT MAIL MISTAKE #7 — *Forget That Your Letters Are You.* Every letter you write is YOU. Every letter you send is your personality on paper. Whether you mail one or a million, each letter tells what YOU are.

When writing to a prospect, transform yourself into a prospect. Write yourself a letter. Begin where your thoughts are — on yourself, your home, your loved ones, your symptoms. Find a point of contact. Despite the many times you have been warned to think of your prospect and his problems first, and yours second, too many mailings still ooze with selfishness. Let your credo be "I want to serve you" — not "I want to sell you." Take your customers and prospects into your confidence. Make them your friends. They'll listen to you, will read your literature, if you make it inviting, interesting, entertaining. The moment your letters get draggy or braggy, stop. But no matter how many pages you write, if they're interesting, keep writing. You know the difference between service and self-interest. Put that into words.

If every letter you mail is YOU, it should have its face washed, hair combed, shoes shined, trousers pressed. It should command respect, earn a hearing, and deserve consideration.

You wouldn't call on a prospect dressed like a Bowery Bum. Nor should you come dressed in white tie and tails. Just be yourself!

Originally published as a direct mail sales booklet by SACKHEIM ADVERTISING.
Republished in *My First Sixty Years in Advertising*
by Maxwell Sackheim, © 1970, **PRENTICE HALL, INC.**

Maxwell Sackheim	Co-founder:	The Book of the Month Club
	Advisor to:	Columbia Record Club
		The American Express Credit Card
		The Literary Guild

GOOD BOOKS

With this volume in hand, you will naturally want to know which other books are most helpful to beginning and professional direct marketers. Visit your library. Find these:

Start with Bob Stone's epic *Successful Direct Marketing Methods*, then Jim Kobs' very fine *Profitable Direct Marketing*. Move on to Ed Nash's *Direct Marketing Strategy/Planning/Execution*. Then take a nice, long vacation to study Dick Hodgson's *Direct Mail and Mail Order Handbook*.

You will also want to review writing strategy in Gene Schwartz' *Breakthrough Advertising* and the basics of mail response in Julian Simon's *How to Start and Operate a Mail Order Business*.

But above all, buy these two books and read them annually: *Tested Advertising Methods* and *How to Make Your Advertising Make Money*. Both are by John Caples, whose guidelines often have inspired me to greater bottom-line creativity. If you can't afford to test your direct mail efforts, do what John recommends. I do. I've been fortunate to count him as a personal friend. And I must say that the teachings of this 80+ genius will still be legend when you and I are no longer at a keyboard.

But when a man is such an omnipotent wordsmith, you must also find out more about him. So read *John Caples: ADMAN* by Gordon White and perhaps you'll react as I did:

Dear John,

A very rare thing happened yesterday.

The latest John Caples book arrived and, as with every new book arrival, I briefly thumbed it...then it grabbed me, so I took it out by the pool and started reading it. Moments later I ran inside for a pen.

Back to poolside, making marginal notes here and there.

Dusk arrived, so I switched to the indoor patio and continued reading. Damned if I didn't read it all the way through and let life's pursuits just wait! John, you not only write good copy, you ARE good copy!

I think I'll keep John Caples: ADMAN off my bookshelves. I'll want to read it again, maybe each time I start a new assignment. Just knowing you as a friend has been a delight, but your books will continue teaching me for years to come. This book breathes!

Nine days later, I received this note:

Dear René,

I have worked on book advertising many times over the years. I have seen many testimonial ads for books.

But I've never seen a testimonial with such enthusiasm, sincerity and sales power as your wonderful letter.

I'm going to carry your letter in my pocket so I can reread and enjoy it at frequent intervals. René, thanks so much.

The book you're holding gives you techniques. John's books give you concepts. Please use Caples and Gnam, side by side.

Books open minds. Good books on advertising open creative minds.

ABOUT THE AUTHOR

René Gnam
mail address: Box 3877, Holiday, Florida 34690-3877
courier address: 1 Response Road, Tarpon Springs, Florida 34689-9484
telephone: **813-938-1555**
facsimile: **813-934-0416**

Direct Response Consultant...

Serves an average of 100 organizations annually (on location and in Florida). Typical clients: General Motors, Norelco, PMA Industries, Kundbiblioteket AB, California Polytechnic State University, Practice Management Associates, *Radio-Electronics*, Positiv Fritid Handel, Dealers A-V Supply Co., American Productivity Center, Crutchfield Car Stereo, The Drawing Board, *American Journal of Ophthalmology*, TJM, Metpath Laboratories, Construction Bookstore, TWA, Gries/Dynacast, *Mustang Monthly*, Baldwin United Corporation, National Retail Merchants Association, Liberty Life Insurance.

Direct Mail Creator...

Creates dozens of individual mailings and campaigns annually, for small firms and major corporations. Typical clients: McGraw-Hill, *Saturday Evening Post*, Gurney Seed & Nursery, KCI Communications, Hark & Associates, *American Artist*, Horizon Sportswear, American Diabetes Association, Cincinnati Chamber of Commerce, Diner's Club, *Athletic Business*, *Armed Forces Journal*, U.S. Pencil & Stationery Co., Dee Cee Laboratories, U.S. Department of Commerce, Masport America, Petersen Publications, *Christian Herald*, Media Inc., Administrative Health Management Group.

Author...

Kentucky Educational Television affiliate of the Public Broadcasting System produced René Gnam's first book, *The Business of Direct Mail*, to accompany his 12-program PBS videotape series on direct mail. His numerous articles on direct mail marketing techniques have been published in: *Direct Mail Bulletin* by Standard Rate & Data Service, *Target Marketing* by North American Publishing Co., *The Catalog Marketer* by Maxwell Sroge Publications, *Direct Marketing* by Hoke Communications, *The Direct Response Specialist* by Stilson & Stilson, *Folio* by Folio Magazine Publishing Corporation, *Personal Communications* by FutureComm, Inc., *Educational Dealer* by Fahy-Williams Publishing, *Special Events* by Miramar Publishing, *DM News* by Mill Hollow Corporation, *Hotline* by The Newsletter Association.

In-Company Training Leader...

These leading corporations are among many which have retained René Gnam to conduct staff workshops: Prenumerations Forlagens AS, The Bell System, Wonder Steel Manufacturing, TWA, General Motors, Gries/Dynacast, EBSCO & Vulcan Industries, American Health Consultants, Baldwin-United Corporation, Blue Cross/Blue Shield, Clairol, Novo Enzyme Industri AB, Hot Line Marketing, University Associates, Meredith Corporation.

Seminar Leader and Keynote Speaker....

In addition to private seminars at his Response Ranch, René Gnam has conducted many industry events for a variety of sponsors, including many regional advertising and marketing organizations, and: COMDEX, Insurance Marketing Services, A/S Forlaget Borsen, Ski Industries of America, Agricultural Publishers Association, Mail Advertising Service Association, Magazine Publishing Week, AS Hjemmet Fagpresseforlaget, Marketing Week, Greater Independent Association of National Travel Services, Educational Paperback Book Association, ASCOT Tire Services, Society of National Association Publications, Newsletter Association, DisplayMasters, Dorn Communications, American Association of Conservation Information, Western Publishing Association, Folio's Face-to-Face, Executive Marketing Services, Conference Management Corp., *Sextant*, Georgia Industrial Developers Association, *Athletic Business*, National Association of Advertising Publications, Marketing Federation, National Center for Database Marketing, The Professional Seminar Association, and the National Speakers Association.

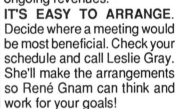